Environmental Law in Bangladesh

Environmental Law in Bangladesh

Mohammad Ershadul Karim

This book was originally published as a monograph in the International Encyclopaedia of Laws/Environmental Law.

Founding Editor: Roger Blanpain
General Editor: Frank Hendrickx
Volume Editors: Kurt Deketelaere

Wolters Kluwer

Published by:
Kluwer Law International B.V.
PO Box 316
2400 AH Alphen aan den Rijn
The Netherlands
E-mail: lrs-sales@wolterskluwer.com
Website: www.wolterskluwer.com/en/solutions/kluwerlawinternational

Sold and distributed by:
Wolters Kluwer Legal & Regulatory U.S.
7201 McKinney Circle
Frederick, MD 21704
United States of America
E-mail: customer.service@wolterskluwer.com

ISBN 978-94-035-1546-5

e-Book: ISBN 978-94-035-1216-7
web-PDF: ISBN 978-94-035-1226-6

The Author

Mohammad Ershadul Karim, LLB (Hons.), LLM (University of Dhaka), PhD in Nanotechnology Law and Policy (Universiti Malaya), is a senior lecturer at the Faculty of Law, Universiti Malaya, Malaysia and was awarded the PhD for a thesis titled 'Human Health and Environmental Implications of Nanotechnology in Malaysia: A Legal Study'. He has been teaching Research Methodology, ICT Law, and Privacy and Personal Data Protection Law and has widely published in peer-reviewed journals and presented papers in a number of national and international conferences in his areas of interest, i.e., 'legal and regulatory aspects of nanotechnology', 'emerging technological applications and relevant legal issues', 'privacy and data protection law', 'human right to health', 'legal research' and 'renewable energy law', etc.

The second edition of his monograph titled *Cyber Law in Bangladesh* was published by Wolters Kluwer in 2022, and his co-authored book titled *Personal Data Protection Law in Asia* was published by Thomson and Reuters, Hong Kong in December 2017. Dr Karim has covered chapters on the legal system of Afghanistan, Bangladesh, Bhutan, Iran, Nepal, Maldives and Myanmar in GlobaLex, New York University, United States (US), and developed the Research Guide on Nanotechnology Law and Policy and South Asian Association for Regional Cooperation (SAARC) for the same database. His contribution on 'Nanotechnology and International Environmental Law' was included in a book as a chapter published by the Royal Society of Chemistry, the United Kingdom (UK) in November 2016. His contributions on 'Legal Issues in Polymer Nanocomposite', 'Functionalised Nanomaterials: Selected Legal and Regulatory Issues' and 'Functionalised Nanomaterials: Selected Occupational Health and Safety Concerns' were published as book chapters by Elsevier Inc; 'Biosensors: Ethical, Regulatory, and Legal Issues' was published as a part of Springer Nature's Handbook of Cell Biosensors; and 'Nanoproducts and Legal Aspects of Consumer Protections: An Evaluation' was included in the Springer Nature's Handbook of Consumer Nanoproducts.

Dr Karim has been managing the National Chapter on Bangladesh for the Yearbook of International Environmental Law published by Oxford University, UK, since 2013. As an enlisted lawyer with Bangladesh Bar Council, having the qualifications to practise before Bangladesh Supreme Court, Dr Karim was instrumental in developing the Bangladesh Code, a collection of thirty-eight volumes containing all existing Acts of Parliament, Ordinances and President's Orders in force in Bangladesh between

1836 and 2006. He was also a member of the translation team of the Bangladesh Code. Besides, Dr Karim served as the Web Administrator and Editor of the first-ever online case law database of Bangladesh, Chancery Law Chronicles (www.clcbd.org) for six years.

Dr Karim has been consulted by different national and international organizations including Japan Government's Patent Office through Kyoto Comparative Law Center, United Nations Development Program, United Nations Women, World Intellectual Property Organization, World Bank Group, European Union, Canadian International Development Agency, Japan International Cooperative Agency, Consumer International, Prime Minister's Office of the Government of Malaysia and Ministry of Justice, Abu Dhabi.

Table of Contents

Table of Contents

List of Abbreviations

3G	Global Growth Generation
AD	Appellate Division of the Supreme Court of Bangladesh
ADP	Annual Development Programme
AFOLU	Agriculture, Forestry and Other Land Use
AOAC	Association of Officials of Analytical Chemist
BAPA	Bangladesh Poribesh Andolon
BARC	Bangladesh Agricultural Research Council
BAU	Business as Usual
BCCT	Bangladesh Climate Change Trust
BCSIR	Bangladesh Council of Scientific and Industrial Research
BECA, 1995	The Environment Conservation Act, 1995 (Act No. 1 of 1995)
BEEC	Bangladesh Energy and Electricity Council
BELA	Bangladesh Environmental Lawyers' Association Limited
BFD	Bangladesh Forest Department
BFIDC	Bangladesh Forest Industries Development Corporation
BFRI	Bangladesh Forest Research Institute
BJRI	Bangladesh Jute Research Institute
BLAST	Bangladesh Legal Aid and Services Trust
BNWLA	Bangladesh National Women Lawyers Association
BRICM	Bangladesh Reference Institute for Chemical Measurements
BUET	Bangladesh University of Engineering and Technology
CASE	The Clean Air and Sustainable Environment Project
CBD	The Convention on Biodiversity, 1992
CFC	Chlorofluorocarbons
CFT	Contained Field Trial
CITES	Convention on International Trade in Endangered Species of Wild Fauna and Flora, 1975
CLC	Chancery Law Chronicles
CO	Carbon Monoxide
CTC	Carbon Tetrachloride

List of Abbreviations

DG	Director General
DLR	Dhaka Law Report
DMDP	Dhaka Metropolitan Development Plan 1995–2015
DoE	Department of Environment
EAGLE	Emerging and Growth Leading Economies
ECA	Ecologically Critical Areas
ECC	Environmental Clearance Certificate
EEE	Electrical and Electronic Equipment
EEZ	Exclusive Economic Zone
EFCC CIP	Country Investment Plan for Environment, Forestry and Climate Change (2016–2021)
EIA	Environmental Impact Assessment
ERA	Environmental Risk Assessment
FAO	Food and Agriculture Organization of the United Nations
FCK	Fixed Chimney Kiln
FPSP	Fundamental Principles of State Policy
FY	Financial Year
GDP	Gross Domestic Product
GED	General Economic Division
GMOs	Genetically Modified Organisms
GNI	Gross National Income
HBFCs	Hydro Bromofluorocarbons
HCD	High Court Division of the Supreme Court of Bangladesh
HPNSDP	Health, Population and Nutrition Sector Development Program
HRPB	Human Rights and Peace for Bangladesh
ICCWC	The International Consortium on Combating Wildlife Crime
IEL	International Environmental Law
INDC	Intended National Determined Contribution
IPC	Infection Prevention and Control
IPPU	Industrial Processes & Product Use
ISO	International Organization for Standardization
ITPS	Intergovernmental Technical Panel on Soil
IUPAC	International Union of Pure and Applied Chemistry
LDC	Least Developed Country
LRGD	Ministry of Local Government, Rural Development and Corporations
MEAs	Multilateral Environmental Agreements
MoEF	Ministry of Environment and Forests
MoEFCC	Ministry of Environment, Forest and Climate Change

MPO	Master Plan Organisation
MSP	Marine Spatial Planning
NBSAP	National Biodiversity Strategy and Action Plan for Bangladesh
NDC	Nationally Determined Contribution
NO_2	Nitrogen Dioxide
NSDS	National Sustainable Development Strategy
NWP	National Water Plan
O3	Ozone
OECD	Organisation for Economic Co-operation and Development
PA	Protected Areas
Pb	Lead
POBA	Poribesh Andalon Bangladesh
PPP	Public-Private Partnership
RES	Renewable Energy Sources
RMG	Readymade Garments
SACEP	South Asia Co-operative Environment Programme
SBSRB	Ship Building and Ship Recycling Board
SCOB	Supreme Court Online Bulletin
SDGs	United Nations Sustainable Development Goals
SO_2	Sulphur Dioxide
SPARSO	Bangladesh Space Research and Remote Sensing Agency
SVRS	Sample Vital Registration System
UN	United Nations
UNCLOS	United Nations Convention on the Law of the Sea, 1982
UNDP	United Nations Development Program
UNEP	United Nations Environment Programme
UNESCO	United Nations Educational, Scientific and Cultural Organization
UNFCCC	United Nations Framework Convention for Climate Change
US EPA	United States Environmental Protection Agency
VNR	Voluntary National Review
WARPO	Water Resources Planning Organisation
WEEE	Waste Generated from Electrical and Electronic Equipment
WEF	World Economic Forum
WHC	The World Cultural and Natural Heritage, 1972
WHO	World Health Organisation
WIPO	World Intellectual Property Organization
WMO	World Meteorological Organization

List of Abbreviations

General Introduction

§1. GENERAL BACKGROUND OF THE COUNTRY

I. Geography and Population

1. Bangladesh, literally the land of Bangla language-speaking people and officially the People's Republic of Bangladesh,[1] is situated in the north-eastern part of South Asia and covers an area of 147,570 sq km or 56,977 sq miles. The country is located between 20° 34' and 26° 38' north latitudes and between 88° 01' and 92° 41' east longitudes. The Bengal Delta on the Ganges-Bramhaputra-Meghna river system, consisting of two Himalayan rivers, i.e., the Ganges and the Brahmaputra, and one non-Himalayan river, i.e., the Meghna, is one of the largest deltas in the world. About 80% of the country is a floodplain, 12% is hills and 8% is a terrace. Besides, the country has 118,813 sq km of marine area.

2. Being the youngest nation-state of South Asia, Bangladesh is almost entirely surrounded by India, except for a short south-eastern frontier with Myanmar and a southern coastline on the Bay of Bengal. Even before 2015, Bangladesh used to have some of the most perplexing territories on the planet due to the presence of first-order as well as even second-order enclaves and exclaves with India in the northern region. Bangladesh and India used to share the most enclaves in the entire world, and Dahala Khagrabari was the only third-order enclave in the world. However, on 31 July 2015, the governments of these two countries, on the basis of the Land Boundary Agreement, 1974 and Protocol of 2011, physically exchanged 51 former Bangladeshi enclaves in India and 111 former Indian enclaves in Bangladesh.[2] The country is a plain land except for some hilly areas in the Myanmar border area, and some highlands can also be identified in the Sylhet region. Only around 13% area of land is covered by forest.

3. Bangladesh is a riverine country with 310 rivers, including tributaries crisscrossing, and these rivers have been playing an influential and decisive role in the economic development and progress of the country. The country shares fifty-seven transboundary rivers with the neighbours, where fifty-four rivers enter the country

1. Article 1, the Constitution of the People's Republic of Bangladesh, 1972.
2. Ministry of External Affairs, Government of India, Exchange of enclaves between India and Bangladesh, 20 November 2015, https://www.mea.gov.in/press-releases.htm?dtl/26048/Exchange_of_enclaves_between_India_and_Bangladesh.

from India and three from Myanmar. Natural disasters, e.g., floods and cyclones, etc., are very common in the context of Bangladesh, though there are some positive sides to the floods since they carry forward silt to make the soil of the country very fertile. The Padma is the longest river of the country, whereas the Meghna is the widest river where at one point the river is 12 km wide. Other principal rivers are the Jamuna, the Brahmaputra, the Surma, and the Karnaphuli.

4. With only 1,052 metres (3,451 feet) in height, Saka Haphong in the south-easter Mowdok Range is the highest peak in the country. On a sunny day with a clear sky just before the winter season (in November), people can enjoy the splendour of the world's third-highest mountain peak of Himalaya, Kanchenjunga, from the northern district of Thakurgaon and Panchagarh. The second longest and the longest unbroken sea beach in the World is situated in Cox's Bazar, in the south of the country. Another 18 km long and 3 km wide beach at Kuakata, Patuakhali, is famous for enjoying an unobstructed view of both the sunrise and the sunset every day over the Bay of Bengal.

5. Bangladesh is the seventh most populous country in the world and more than 1,000 persons live per square kilometre in this densely populated Bangladesh. Dhaka (formally spelt as 'Dacca' till 1982) is the capital of the country, and with a glorious history of more than four centuries, Dhaka is one of the most densely populated megacities in the world. Whereas, Chattogram (previously 'Chittagong') is dubbed as the commercial capital of the country.

6. Islam is the state religion of the Republic; nevertheless, it is the constitutional responsibility of the state to ensure equal status and right in the practice of religious rituals of other religions such as Hindu, Buddhist, and Christian.[3] According to the latest Bangladesh Demographic and Health Survey, 2014, Bangladesh is primarily an Islamic country where almost 90% of people are Muslims, whereas 9% are Hindus and other religions constitute the remaining 1%.[4]

7. Bangladesh has the highest number of youths, and in the recent report published by the World Economic Forum (WEF), based on key areas, i.e., education, economic participation, health, and political empowerment, Bangladesh ranked the second most gender equal country in Asia and the top country among the South

3. Article 2A, the Constitution of the People's Republic of Bangladesh, 1972. Article 2A was substituted by s. 4 of the Constitution (Fifteenth Amendment) Act, 2011 (Act XIV of 2011).
   It may be relevant to share here that the issue of state religion was first inserted in the Constitution through the Eighth Amendment in 1988. The Eighth Amendment to the Constitution introduced Islam as the state religion of the country. It is claimed that this 'has caused substantial damage to the secular character of the Constitution of Bangladesh putting the members of the minority communities i.e., Hindus, Christians and Buddhists, in an unequal position in relation to the Muslim' and has tampered the basic structure of the Constitution. *See*, Shah Alam, 'The State-Religion Amendment to the Constitution of Bangladesh: A Critique', *Verfassung und Recht in Übersee/Law and Politics in Africa, Asia and Latin America* 24, no. 2 (1991): 209–225.
4. Bangladesh Demographic and Health Survey, 2014, March 2016, p. 1.

Asian nations. The demography of the country is diversified with the presence of a good number of indigenous communities.

8. As of January 2018, a total of 104.1 million voters were listed in the electoral roll. Of them, 50.42% were male, and 49.58% were female voters. With an area of 147,570 sq. km and a population of about 166,280,712 (July 2014 est., The World Fact Book, CIA), the country has a very high population density at 1,033 persons per sq. km. The population data as per Sample Vital Registration System (SVRS), 2015 Report and the project population of the country are shared in the Tables 1 and 2.

Table 1 Population Data as per SVRS, 2015 Report (in Million)

	1 July 2013	*1 July 2014*	*1 July 2015*
Total	154.7	156.8	158.9
Male	78.3	78.6	79.6
Female	76.4	78.2	79.3
Urban	42.6	44.1	–
Rural	112.1	112.7	–
Annual Growth Rate	1.37	1.37	1.37
Sex ratio (males per 100 females)	102.6	100.5	100.3
Density (per sq. km)	1,049	1,063	1,077
Life expectancy at birth: both sex	70.4	70.7	70.9
Male	68.8	69.1	69.4
Female	71.2	71.6	72.0

Source: Statistical Pocket Book, Bangladesh, 2016.[5]

Table 2 Projected Population (Million)

	July 2011	*July 2015*	*July 2019*
Total	151.41	158.96	167.37
Male	77.85	81.63	85.86
Female	73.56	77.33	81.51
Sex ratio: (males per 100 females)	106.00	106.00	105.34

Source: Statistical Pocket Book, Bangladesh, 2016.[6]

5. Bangladesh Bureau of Statistics, SID, Ministry of Planning.
6. *Ibid.*

9. Bangladesh has come a long way by making remarkable strides in reducing poverty. This is due to its diversified and strong economic growth, which helps to alleviate poverty in a slow but sustainable manner. According to the Household Income Expenditure Survey (2016–2017), the poverty reduction pace has slowed down and still almost 25% of the population lives below the poverty line.

10. The overall national poverty rate has fallen for both the urban and rural areas, although the pace is different. In urban areas, the rate is slower than that of rural areas. It is important to share here that 90% of poverty reduction transpires in rural areas, and most of this reduction in poverty is contributed by the employment in manufacturing industries or services sectors. The manufacturing sector, to be specific, the RMG industry itself, caters to reducing 85% of the poverty in the urban areas. It is obvious that in urban areas, poverty reduction is led by welfare gains from employment opportunities in different industries. The demographic and social indicators of the country are projected in Table 3.

Table 3 Demographic and Social Indicators

Indicators	*Data*
Total Population	158.9 million
Male	79.6 million
Female	74.5 million
Growth rate	1.37
Total fertility rate (15–49 years)	2.10
Life expectancy at birth	70.9 years
Male	69.4 years
Female	72.0 years
Literacy rate of population (7+ years)	63.6

Source: Bangladesh Bureau of Statistics, 2017.[7]

11. Successive governments have invested heavily in education, especially for women and girls. Primary education is free and compulsory for everyone where the government provides free textbooks, both online and offline. The government also provides stipends and scholarships to the girls until the twelfth grade. Some relevant statistics relating to education sector and literacy rates are shared in Tables 4 and 5.

7. *Ibid.*

Table 4 Number of Institutions, Teachers and Students by type of Education, 2018

Type of Institution	*Institutions*	*Teachers*	*Student*
Primary	133,901	623,964	17,251,350
Secondary	20,467	243,880	10,330,695
College	4,419	120,934	3,872,960
Madrasah	9,303	113,761	2,453,364
Professional	877	10,816	168,469
Teacher Education	216	2,700	35,071
Technical and Vocational Education	5,897	34,716	891,964
University	135	28,568	856,726

Source: Bangladesh Bureau of Statistics, Ministry of Planning, Bangladesh Statistics, 2019.

Table 5 Literacy Rate of Population

		2015	*2016*	*2017*	*2018*
7 Years+					
National	Both Sex	63.6	71.0	72.3	73.2
	Male	65.6	73.0	74.3	75.2
	Female	61.6	68.9	70.2	71.2
Rural	Both Sex	57.2	65.5	66.5	67.6
	Male	59.2	67.7	68.6	69.7
	Female	55.1	63.3	64.4	65.5
Urban	Both Sex	73.3	77.7	79.5	80.1
	Male	75.3	79.6	81.5	82.0
	Female	71.2	75.8	77.5	78.2
7 Years+					
National	Both Sex	64.6	72.3	72.9	73.9
	Male	67.6	75.2	75.7	76.7
	Female	61.6	69.5	70.1	71.2
Rural	Both Sex	57.6	65.4	66.1	67.3
	Male	60.6	68.4	69.0	70.3
	Female	54.6	62.4	63.2	64.4

		2015	*2016*	*2017*	*2018*
Urban	Both Sex	74.7	80.7	81.1	81.7
	Male	77.7	83.3	83.8	84.3
	Female	71.8	77.9	78.4	79.2

Source: Bangladesh Bureau of Statistics, Ministry of Planning, Bangladesh Statistics, 2019.

II. Social and Cultural Characteristics

12. Under the Constitution of Bangladesh, 1972, the adoption of measures to conserve the cultural traditions and heritage of the people, so as to foster and improve the national language, literature and the arts that all sections of the people are offered the opportunity to contribute towards and to participate in the enrichment of the national culture, is an obligation of the state.[8]

13. The official language of the country is Bangla, [9] and with a significant number of speakers from the Indian state of West Bengal and Assam, this is the sixth most-spoken language in the world. It is the only language in the world for which some students sacrificed their lives in 1952 when this part of the world was known as East Bengal and was part of united Pakistan and when the then Pakistan leaders wanted to declare and impose Urdu as the only state language of the country. In 1999, the United Nations Educational, Scientific and Cultural Organization (UNESCO) realizing the importance of this tragic event and to commemorate the 'language martyr' declared 21 February as the 'International Mother Language Day' to be observed every year globally.

14. Baul songs, the traditional art of *Jamdani* (cloth) and *Shital Pati* (cool mat) weaving, *Mangal Shobhajatra*, a festival to celebrate Pahela Baishakh (the first Day of Baishakh, the first month of Bangla new year) on 14 April every year, organized by the students and teachers of Dhaka University's Faculty of Fine Art since 1989 are listed on the UNESCO Representative List of the Intangible Cultural Heritage of Humanity. Historic Sixty Dome Mosque of Bagerhat, ruins of the Buddhist Vihara at Paharpur, and the Sundarbans, one of the largest mangrove forests in the world, are on the list of UNESCO World Heritage. Mahasthangarh and its Environs, the Lalmai-Mainamati Group of monuments, Lalbagh Fort, Holud Vihara, and Jaggadala Vihara are the sites on the tentative list of UNESCO World Heritage.[10]

8. Article 23, the Constitution of the People's Republic of Bangladesh, 1972.
9. Article 3, the Constitution of the People's Republic of Bangladesh, 1972.
10. Bangladesh, Properties inscribed on the World Heritage List, http://whc.unesco.org/en/statesparties/BD.

III. Political History and Structure

15. The written history of present Bangladesh can be traced back to AD 400 when the then Bengal came under the control of the Gupta Empire.[11] The Moguls ruled this part of the world between the thirteenth to the eighteenth century. After the first industrial revolution and as a process of expansion of colonialization, the British East India Company came here and established a factory in 1633 at Hariharpur based on a Farman received from Mughal emperor Shahjahan.[12] Gradually, the East India Company started to develop interest in areas beyond their initial business plan. Ultimately, this East India Company, by means of conspiracy with their local aide, took the controlling power by defeating the then Nawab Sirajuddaulah in the battle of Palashi in AD 1757. With this incident and capitalizing on the ignorance and simplicity of the mass people of this area, the dark history of British oppression and brutal torture of the locals started, and the Company received the sovereign power to rule this part of the world on behalf of the British Crown. During that time, the present Indian states of Bihar and Orissa were also a part of the Bengal Presidency, established in 1765 and were governed from Kolkata.

16. In 1773, the permanent settlement system, the greatest landmark in the history of Bengal, was introduced, and through this system, the property rights were granted to the local *zamindars* or landlords. Thus, the Zamindari system was introduced, and the Bengal middle-class group was emerged as a bridge to connect the elites and the root level masses.[13] From the 1800s, the Company concentrated on developing the legal system for the smooth functioning of their activities and started to replace the existing custom-based legal system with a codified one, following similar development in Britain. Subsequently, the East India Company started to become weak economically, the locals started protests, and the first war of independence in the form of a Sepoy Rebellion took place between 1857 and 1859. Consequently, the British Government established the British Raj to govern and administer the Indian subcontinent, including the then Bengal.

17. Due to the geographic location, the territory comprising present-day Bangladesh and the Indian state of Assam was known as East Bengal between 1905 and 1912, and the area comprising the present Indian states of West Bengal, Bihar and Orissa was known as West Bengal. It was difficult for the British administrators to govern such a huge territory properly. Moreover, East Bengal was dominated by the Muslims, whereas the Hindus were a majority in West Bengal. Due to continuous and systematic repression and injustice of various nature by the British administrators, people of this region started to protest and stage demonstrations resulting in independence and nationalist movement. The British administrators realized this, and in response applied the tricky 'divide and rule' policy. Consequently, the then Viceroy of India, Lord Curzon, announced the decision of the partition of Bengal in

11. History, Banglapedia, http://en.banglapedia.org/index.php?title=History.
12. East India Company, Banglapedia, https://en.banglapedia.org/index.php/East_India_Company,_The.
13. *See generally*, Sirajul Islam, *The Permanent Settlement in Bengal: A Study of Its Operation 1790–1819*, First Edition (Dacca: Bangla Academy, May 1979).

July 1905. Mass people, irrespective of class and religion, protested this decision of partition and started movements to motivate the general mass to use locally produced products boycotting British goods. Even with such protests, mostly isolated and unorganized, the British rulers administered the Indo-Pak subcontinent until AD 1947.

18. In AD 1947, the independent states of Pakistan and India were created based on religion – Muslim majority people decided to form their country as Pakistan, while Hindu majority people formed their country as India. The present territory of Bangladesh then became a part of Pakistan and was known as 'East Pakistan'. The capital of the newly emerged independent Pakistan was in the western part, while the eastern part remain satellite. During this time, people of this part had also suffered mercilessly as the Pakistani rulers used to collect the revenues from agricultural products to preserve and decorate the western part of Pakistan. This part remained neglected, and no meaningful development could be noticed though Pakistan started to become an economically strong country. As a result, the leaders of East Pakistan, present-day Bangladesh, started to organize the locals and raise their voices against all sorts of political and economic oppressions.

19. After the Declaration on the Granting of Independence to Colonial Countries and Peoples, adopted by the United Nations (UN) General Assembly in 1960, as a reflection of international law concept of people's right to self-determination, Bangladesh emerged on 26 March 1971 as an independent country on the world's map following a war of liberation for nine months and achieved victory on 16 December 1971.[14] Thus, the birth of Bangladesh presented a new perspective in the relevant international legal regime as the country did not get independence fighting colonial rulers.[15] Since during the British rule, present Bangladesh was a part of then India till 1947, and subsequently, it was part of Pakistan till 1971; therefore, many events of historical importance which are covered under this monograph, e.g., law and regulation of environmental components and their protection, etc., will be identical with that of the history of the then India and Pakistan.

20. Bangladesh is a member of most of the leading international and regional, political and economic organizations and has signed most of the relevant international human rights instruments. The country's commitment to international peace and peaceful settlement of international disputes is reflected in the Constitution of the country.[16] Bangladesh is a leading troop-contributing country for the UN peacekeeping mission. The Permanent Mission of Bangladesh in the UN has been leading the Group of Least Developed Countries since October 2015.

---

14. For authoritative discussions on the history of the country, *see*, A. Riaz, *Bangladesh: A Political History since Independence* (London: I.B. Tauris & Co. Ltd, 2016); R. Srinath, *A Global History of the Creation of Bangladesh* (Cambridge, MA: Harvard University Press, 2013).
15. *See*, for more, M. Rafiqul Islam. *The Bangladesh Liberation Movement: International Legal Implications* (Dhaka: University Press, 1987).
16. *See*, Preamble and Art. 25, the Constitution of the People's Republic of Bangladesh, 1972.

21. An elected single-chamber Parliament in Bangladesh, known as Bangladesh *Jatiya Sangsad* (House of the Nation), is primarily responsible for making laws.[17] Though Westminster Parliamentary form of government is now followed, after the independence of the country in 1971, in the various junctures of history, the country had a Presidential form of government as well. The country introduced the concept of a non-party caretaker government to run the national election through the Thirteen Amendment to the Constitution and used this system in the national elections held between 1990 and 2008. In 2011, this system of non-party caretaker government was overturned following the decision of the Bangladesh Supreme Court.[18] Since 1991, when the country has restored democratic rule, the President as the head of the state holds a mere ornamental position, whereas the Prime Minister as the head of the government has been exercising the real power in running the day-to-day activities in the state functioning of the country.[19]

22. For this monograph, it is very significant to know the administrative structure of the country as environment-related various initiatives are taken locally, and domestic laws of the country empower the local government administration to implement these legal provisions. The country is divided into eight administrative divisions in Dhaka, Chattogram, Rajshahi, Khulna, Rangpur, Cumilla (previously 'Comilla'), Barishal, and Sylhet. These Divisions are again divided into 64 Districts, 492 Upazilas, 4,571 Unions, 19 City Corporations, 330 Pourashavas.[20]

IV. Economic Characteristics

23. Even though the share of manufacturing and service industries has been growing in recent years in the economy of the country, Bangladesh is mainly known as an agricultural country. During the Pakistan period, in present-day Bangladesh, which was known as East Pakistan, 64% of lands of the province could be cultivated, and about 82% of the workforce was employed in the agriculture sector. This part used to produce 76% of the raw jute of the world and being a fish-producing area due to the presence of a huge number of water bodies, this part used to export fish to India also. Dacca, as it was spelt then, was the home of famous Dacca muslins[21] and a land of cottage industries, e.g., handloom, conch shell, brass, and bell-metal industries, mat making, and bamboo and cane work. In 1962, in the province

17. Article 65, the Constitution of the People's Republic of Bangladesh, 1972. In *Mofizur Rahman Khan v. Govt. of Bangladesh* (1982) 34 DLR (AD) 321, it was held that the legislature has power of retrospective legislation and retrospective validation of invalid law. Parliament is the supreme legislative authority subject to the constitutional limitations – one of the attributes of legislative supremacy is its power to pass any law on any subject, not prohibited by the Constitution, both prospectively and retrospectively. It can equally validate, subject to Constitution, any earlier law found invalid either prospectively or retrospectively.
18. *Abdul Mannan Khan v. Bangladesh* (2012) 64 DLR (AD) 169.
19. Article 48(2), the Constitution of the People's Republic of Bangladesh, 1972.
20. Bangladesh Bureau of Statistics, Ministry of Planning, Bangladesh Statistics, 2019.
21. For a concise history of Muslin of Dhaka, *see*, Mohammad Ataul Karim & Mohammad Ershadul Karim. 'Protection of "Handicraft" as Geographical Indications under Municipal Law, TRIPS and

of East Pakistan, there were twenty-two textile mills, seven sugar factories, eighteen match factories, seven glassworks, 178 hosiery factories, a paper mill, fourteen jute-mills, twenty-eight aluminium works, a cement factory, a newsprint factory, a fertilizer factory, a shipyard and a dockyard.[22]

24. At the time of independence in 1971, the country was portrayed as the 'bottomless basket' or 'international basket case' by some group of people who were sceptical about the consequences of independence of the country. After a mere five decades, the country can be seen as a 'basket full of achievements, success stories and opportunities'. The country has attained tremendous progress and success in various socio-economic sectors. Since the 1990s, with the functioning of the country through the democratically elected government, the country has started to witness economic progress, which in the long run assisted the country in achieving four targets of the Millennium Development Goals well ahead of time.[23] The country has set global examples in reducing early deaths of infants and child mortality, and women empowerment. Being a moderate Muslim country, Bangladesh has done much work to improve the status of women.

25. It is a matter of fact that even a few months ago, the country was considered as the largest least developed country (LDC) in the world in terms of skilled human resources, economic size and a high share of manufactures in total export, which reached 90.5% in 2013 when it was about only 26.2% for LDCs.[24] Even after being an LDC, the country reduced the extreme poverty level from 31.5% in 2010 to 24.3% in 2017. Nevertheless, due to the continuous economic progress, it is likely to be the first LDC ever to graduate to lower-middle-income country based on all three criteria, i.e., per capita Gross National Income (GNI), Human Assets Index and Economic Vulnerability Index.[25]

26. From an agro-based and densely populated country having suffered the severe effects and consequences of the Liberation War in 1971, the economic

---

BTAs vis-à-vis CETA: "Bangladeshi Jamdani" as Case Study', 7 *Queen Mary Journal of Intellectual Property* 7, no. 1 (2017), 49–73. It is a matter of great pride that in 2016, Jamdani, a modern deviated version of Dhaka Muslin, received the recognition by WIPO as the first-ever Geographic Indication product of Bangladesh.

22. S.H. Steinberg. *The Statesman's Year-Book: Statistical and Historical Annual of the States of the World for the Year 1962* (London: Macmillan & Co., 1962), 487.
23. In September 2000, the global leaders signed the United Nations Millennium Development Declaration at the United Nations Millennium Summit. The Declaration set eight ambitious but clear goals and measurable targets to combat poverty, hunger, disease, illiteracy, environmental degradation and discrimination against women by 2015.
24. S. Kathuria & M.M. Malouche. *Toward New Sources of Competitiveness in Bangladesh: Key Findings of the Diagnostic Trade Integration Study, Directions in Development* (Washington, DC: World Bank Publications, 2015), xix.
25. Md. Jahurul Haque, Chairman of BTRC, Speech delivered at the ITU-BTRC Asia-Pacific Regulators' Roundtable 2018, 6–7 Aug. 2018, Dhaka, Bangladesh, https://www.itu.int/en/ITU-D/Regional-Presence/AsiaPacific/Pages/Events/2018/rr2018/home.aspx.

progress of the country in recent times has made it a success story globally. Bangladesh joined the lower-middle-income country category on 1 July 2015 and expects to receive the status in 2024.[26] Already, the country has successfully fulfilled all the criteria.

27. Bangladesh has one of the fastest economic growth rates in the world in recent years, maintaining an economic growth rate of more than 6% for the previous seven consecutive years and more than 7% in 2018. The World Bank Group, in its latest report published in April 2019, predicted that Bangladesh would be one of the top five fastest-growing economies in the world with a 7.3% Gross Domestic Product (GDP) growth projection.

28. The recent economic success of Bangladesh has been recognized by various international bodies. Bangladesh was highlighted as the 'Next Eleven',[27] as a prospective country to join the Emerging and Growth Leading Economies (EAGLE)[28] and one of the Global Growth Generation (3G) countries.[29] Recently, in the platform of the World Economic Forum (WEF), the words 'aspiring 'tiger' economy' and 'one of Asia's most remarkable and unexpected success stories in recent years' were used to highlight the economic success of the country.[30] HSBC Global Research predicted that the country would be the twenty-sixth largest economy in the world in 2030.[31]

---

26. Based on per capita GNI, the World Bank classifies the world's economies into four income groups: (1) Low Income, (2) Lower-Middle Income, (3) Upper-Middle Income and (4) High Income. Accordingly, the countries with less than USD 1,025 GNI is placed in the group of low income countries, the countries between USD 1,026 and 3,995 GNI is placed in the category of lower-middle income countries, the countries between USD 3,996 and 12,375 GNI is placed in the category of upper-middle income countries and countries with above USD 12,375 are known as high income countries.
27. Jim O'Neil, the Chairman of Goldman Sachs Asset Management, listed Bangladesh as one of the 'Next 11' with Egypt, Indonesia, Iran, South Korea, Mexico, Nigeria, Pakistan, the Philippines, Turkey, and Vietnam. These countries could potentially have a BRIC-like impact in rivalling the G7. *See*, Sachs, Goldman, 2007. Brazil, Russia, India, China and South Africa (BRICs) and beyond. The Goldman Sachs Group/Global Economics Department, London; Sachs, Goldman, 2007. Global Economics Paper No: 153. The N-11m: More Than an Acronym, 28 Mar. 2007.
28. Spanish bank Banco Bilbao Vizcaya Argentaria (BBVA) introduced this idea in 2010 to describe the ten (EAGLE) countries that can generate 50% of the global economic growth between 2010 and 2020. Bangladesh was listed as one of the Nest countries with eleven other countries, i.e., Thailand, Nigeria, Poland, Colombia, South Africa, Malaysia, Vietnam, Pakistan, Argentina, Peru and the Philippines who were expected to deliver 8% for world's incremental GDP in same time.
29. Citi Investment Research and Analysis in their Policy Insight published in 2011 has listed Bangladesh as one of the global growth generators, i.e., 3Gs. with China, Egypt, India, Indonesia, Iraq, Mongolia, Nigeria, the Philippines, Sri Lanka and Vietnam due to their average real per capita GDP growth over the period 2010–2050 – 5% or higher at Purchasing Power Parity (PPP) exchange rates. *See*, Willem H. Buiter & Ebrahim Rahbari. *Global Growth Generators: Moving Beyond Emerging Markets and BRICs, Centre for Economic Policy Research, Policy Insight* No. 55 (April 2011).
30. K. Basu. *This Is What You Need to Know about Bangladesh's Remarkable Economic Rise* (24 Apr. 2018), https://www.weforum.org/agenda/2018/04/why-is-bangladesh-booming.
31. J. Henry. *The World in 2030* (28 Sep. 2018), https://www.hsbc.com/news-and-insight/2018/the-world-in-2030.

29. In the recent Human Development Index of the United Nations Development Program (UNDP), Bangladesh ranked 133rd out of 189 countries. The position of Bangladesh in the competitiveness ranking has recently shown improvement too. Bangladesh's ranking in the WEF Global Competitiveness Index for 2017–2018 has improved by seven places to 99th among 137 countries. However, there are challenges too. The country has the second most pro-capitalist population, and as a result, it was placed at the bottom in the list of innovative countries in the Global Innovation Index, 2018 developed by the World Intellectual Property Organization (WIPO). As the country is being governed by democratic governments since 1990, it can be anticipated that the success of economic developments will be reflected positively in the future indexes.

30. It has already been shared that Bangladesh was primary and historically an agricultural country blessed with very fertile land. Utilization of the fertile land coupled with the dedication of the peasants enables the country to take pride in being the fourth largest rice producer, second largest jute producer, fourth largest inland freshwater fish producer, second largest jackfruit producer, seventh largest mango producer, eighth largest guava producer and tenth largest tropical fruit producer in the world.

31. It is evident that the economy is gradually transforming from an agrarian to a strong industrial or resource-based economy, and the economy has been changing with the introduction of industries, manufacturing and service sectors. After Financial Year (FY) 2010, the industrial growth became faster; meanwhile, the growth in agriculture started to slow down. From 2011 to 2016, industry and agriculture output correspondingly increased annually by 9.5 and 3.4%. Because of this shift, both the economic growth from agriculture and the impact on reducing poverty from agriculture have lessened. At the same time, the service sector has shown a steady 6% growth from FY 2000 to 2016. This again exhibits that even the economy is no more sticking to agriculture, rather shifting towards a more resource and knowledge-based economy, bit by bit.

32. According to the Quantum Index of Industrial Production data in FY17, a substantial growth contribution came from several large-scale industries which include the manufacture of other non-metallic mineral products (32.3%), pharmaceuticals (32.1%), textiles (21.2%) and leather, and related products (53.4%). The overall growth cracked double-digit (10.2%) in FY17, which shows impressive sustainable growth in the industrial sector.[32]

33. The country exports RMG, textiles, chemical fertilizers, pharmaceuticals, processed tea, cement, sugar and leather goods, software, etc. It was also stipulated that FY18 and onwards the pharmaceuticals, leather products and textiles sector will lead the economy forward. Another two key factors to the robust economic growth of Bangladesh are export and remittance. Bangladesh is the fifty-fourth largest export economy, second largest exporter of RMG since 2009, and eighth largest

32. The World Bank, Bangladesh Development Update: Building on Resilience, April 2018.

remittance earning country in the world. The RMG sector has rebounded (raised by 7.4%), and the remittance is on an impressive recovery stage (16.5% growth) in FY18. During the first two-quarters of FY18, the readymade garments (RMG) contributed to export growth by 8.7%, and 56% of remittance income came from the Gulf region.[33]

34. Even though there are concerns regarding the flawed democracy of the country, the apparent political stability of the country, which started with the resuming of democracy in 1990, has played an obvious instrumental role in the recent development of the country. Some of the economic indicators of Bangladesh are shared in Table 6.

Table 6 Economic Indicators

Indicators	*Data*
GDP at current market price (in Tk)	17,329 billion
GDP at constant market price (in Tk)	8,835 billion
Per capita GDP in current market prices (in USD)	1,385
Per capita GNI at current market prices (in USD)	1,465
Growth rate at constant prices	7.11
Investment at current prices (in Tk)	51.39 billion
Inflation rate (%), General	5.92
Poverty rate for April-June, 2016	23.2
Extreme poverty rate for April-June, 2016	12.9
Total number of establishments	7,818,565
Total persons engaged	24,500,850
Total export (Million in TK)	3,003,837
Total import (Million in TK)	4,712,495
Share of RMG in national export	89.10
Economically active population (15+)	62.1 million
Employed population (15+)	59.5 million
Unemployed population	2.6 million

Source: Bangladesh Bureau of Statistics, 2017.[34]

33. *Ibid.*
34. Bangladesh Bureau of Statistics (BBS), Statistics and Informatics Division (SID), Ministry of Planning, Government of Bangladesh.

V. Main Environmental Problems

35. The findings of various literature, including reports published by the authoritative bodies, though developed using different methodologies and parameters, have been frequently reiterating that Bangladesh is one of the worst victims of climate change. In the recent World Risk Index, 2020, which measures exposure towards natural hazards, Bangladesh ranked 13th and one of the five in Asia.[35] In the Environmental Performance Index, 2020, the country ranked 162 out of 180 countries, though in the previous Index of 2018, the country was ranked 179th out of 180 countries.[36] The country ranked 116th out of 162 countries in the Sustainable Development Report 2019, which presents the sustainable development Index and Dashboards for all UN Member States and frames the implementation of Sustainable Development Goals in six board transformations.[37] Bangladesh ranked 115th in the Global Sustainable Competitiveness Index which is developed based on 127 measurable, quantitative indicators suggested by reliable sources such as the World Bank, the IMF and other UN agencies.[38] The country ranked 112th in the Global Sustainability Index which is developed based on the environment-related policies and actions taken by the countries in the area of pollution, climate change, policy, energy, oceans and biodiversity.[39]

36. Bangladesh, the newest independent country of South Asia and the largest delta in the world, has been facing various environmental challenges. Historically, this part of the world experienced some of the devastating and deadliest tropical cyclones. The Cyclone of 12 November 1970, known as Bhola Cyclone, killed 300,000 people marking it as one of the greatest natural disasters. The country has been facing all the three types of natural hazards, i.e., *atmospheric hazards caused by atmospheric processes*, e.g., various types of storms, *exogenic hazards caused by the earth surface processes*, e.g., flood and various forms of soil erosion, and *endogenic hazards caused by internal earth processes*, e.g., earthquake.[40]

37. Some of the most pressing environmental problems that Bangladesh has been facing, e.g., *inter alia*, are climate change, geophysical setting, ecosystem changes, overgrazing, import of hazardous wastes, deforestation, desertification, water and air pollution, population pressure, collapse and pollution of land resources, contamination of surface water and groundwater sources through toxic metals, water resources and lack of potable water, biodiversity loss, food security

35. World Risk Report 2020, Focus: Forced Displacement and Migration, https://reliefweb.int/sites/reliefweb.int/files/resources/WorldRiskReport-2020.pdf.
36. Environmental Performance Index, https://epi.yale.edu/epi-results/2020/country/bgd.
37. J. Sachs et al. *Sustainable Development Report 2019* (New York: Bertelsmann Stiftung and Sustainable Development Solutions Network (SDSN), 2019), https://sdgindex.org/reports/sustainable-development-report-2019/.
38. Global Sustainability Competitiveness Index, https://solability.com/the-global-sustainable-competitiveness-index/the-index.
39. Bangladesh – Ranked 211th in the Global Sustainability Index, https://earth.org/global_sustain/bangladesh-ranked-211th-in-the-global-sustainability-index/.
40. Natural Hazard, https://en.banglapedia.org/index.php/Natural_Hazard.

risks, depletion of energy resources, loss of biodiversity, illegal trade in wildlife, degradation of river and marine resources, etc.[41]

38. Bangladesh is one of the worst victims of global warming, primarily caused due to the emissions of Greenhouse Gases (GHGs) which are like blankets in the atmosphere which cause the trapping of the heat and warm the planet. Global warming is responsible for climate change which in turn contributes to an increase in the number of natural disasters such as floods, cyclones, and droughts. Though the export of RMGs and remittance earned and sent back to the country by the human resources employed all over the world help in fattening the national foreign reserve in recent times, the economy of the country which is dependent largely on agriculture is badly affected due to these natural calamities, and as a result, a significant number of the people are frequently displaced.

39. Some of these environmental problems are very unique and caused due to some isolated reason often triggered as a result of improper implementation of the existing laws and government policies. From the above list of these environmental problems, it is further evident that the problems that the country has been facing are originated either locally or regionally or as a consequence of global problems where Bangladesh is a helpless victim of general environmental problems caused due to factors where the country has very little contribution, e.g., global warming and climate change, etc. Besides, being a developing country, she has to face the consequences of improper development activities and geopolitical issues. Moreover, other contributing factors that add to the misfortune include the geographic location of the country where a huge number of populations live within a small area of land. On top of these contributing factors, it cannot be ignored that the country has very limited resources to fight the existing environment-related challenges which have been ever-growing.

§2. Basic Principles of Environmental Law

40. Environmental problems are physically, technically, and socially complex and at times, controversial as some environmental problems are local, while some are regional and some of these are the concerns of the global community. Thus, addressing environmental problems creates a lot of tensions among the different stakeholders. Environmental problems are physically complex due to the involvement of various components of the ecosystem; they are socially complex due to the presence of various actors where the human being does not intentionally cause harm to the environmental components though the way human beings live in the society

41. G.N. TanjinaHasnat, Md Alamgir Kabir & Md Akhter Hossain. 'Major Environmental Issues and Problems of South Asia, Particularly Bangladesh'. *Handbook of Environmental Materials Management* (2018): 1–40; Department of Environment, Facts about DoE, p. 3, Dhaka, July 2015; M.K. Hasan, A Shahriar & K.U. Jim. 'Water Pollution in Bangladesh and Its Impact on Public Health'. *Heliyon* 5, no. 8 (2019): e02145. Published 2019 Aug 2. doi:10.1016/j.heliyon.2019.e02145.

has some consequence and effect on the different components of the environment. Again, these problems are technically complex in the absence of available, reliable and adequate tools and mechanisms.

41. The desire to protect the environment from different kinds of degradation is at the very heart of environmental law. It is not only valuing the environment but also protecting its various components so that we the human being and all other creatures can live within the carrying capacity of the earth. The states have been playing a leading role in protecting the environmental components as they have the collective authority and responsibility in this regard. The protection of environmental components and management of environmental problems in a fair and just way require a legal and institutional framework coupled with financial and technological capabilities.

42. Though many legal instruments can be identified and referred to that have been dealing with individual components of the environment or species, general legal frameworks were not made initially keeping the protection of the environment in mind. Therefore, while the ongoing development activities should be going on, we need to consider the protection of the environment for the betterment of the present and future generations. Environmental law deals with environmental justice, i.e., justice between the nations, local community, or cross-generation or the justice that considers the right of the earth.[42]

43. International environmental law provisions, aiming at the protection of the environmental components, are predominantly principle based. Though this is understandable that principles set some high-level broadly stated rules aiming to achieve some targets or goal, a universally accepted and precise definition of the term 'principle' is difficult to share. According to *Black's Law Dictionary* Ninth Edition, 'principles' mean 'a basic rule, law or doctrine'. Principles are general rules, which 'are implicitly higher in the implicit or explicit hierarchy or norms than more rules: they express the fundamental obligations that all should observe'.[43] Nevertheless, the absence of such definition does not hinder the advancement and popularity of such regulation and therefore is found to be a preferred choice in various sectors involving diversified stakeholders in a complex situation such as environmental management, regulation of financial markets, and emerging technologies.

44. Legal and regulatory principles have some distinctive characteristics:

- 'They are drafted at a high level of generality, with the intention that they should be overarching requirements that can be applied flexibly to a rapidly changing industry.

---

42. For a general discussion on the basic principles of international environmental law, please *see*, Philippe Sands, et al., *Principles of International Environmental Law*. 4th edn (Cambridge, UK: Cambridge University Press, 2018); Erika Techera et al. (eds). *Routledge Handbook of International Environmental Law* 2nd edn (London: Routledge, 2021).
43. Julia Black, Martyn Hopper & Christa Band. 'Making a Success of Principles-Based Regulation.' *Law and Financial Markets Review* 1, no. 3 (2007): 191–206.

- They contain terms that are qualitative not quantitative; i.e., they use terms that are general and usually evaluative, e.g., "fair", "reasonable", "suitable", etc. as opposed to "bright line" rules (e.g. "within two business days", "turnover of £20m", etc.)
- They are purposive, expressing the reason behind the rule.
- They have a very broad application to a diverse range of circumstances.
- The Principles are largely behavioural standards – they are concerned with, for example, the "integrity", "skill care and diligence" and "reasonable care" with which authorised firms or approved persons conduct and organise their businesses and the fairness with which they treat customers and manage conflicts of interest.
- It follows that breach of a Principle must involve an element of fault.
- Breach of the Principles can be sanctioned through public (but not private) enforcement action.'[44]

45. The principle-based regulation is innovation-friendly and preferred in dealing with emerging matters due to some clear advantages. While it is believed that the detailed and specific rules or legal provisions provide certainty, they may not be suitable or adequate in constantly changing contexts which invite the scope of 'creative compliance'. Whereas, principles, since are flexible, are easy to comply with, at least theoretically in developed jurisdictions and thus, assist to fulfil regulatory objectives.[45] However, considering the practices and instances relating to the non-implementation of detailed and specific legal provisions in the context of a developing economy like Bangladesh, additional legal instruments should be considered to achieve the regulatory goals.

46. How each principle applies to a particular activity or incident typically must be considered with the facts and circumstances of each case, considering various factors, including its sources and textual context, its language, the particular activity at issue, and the particular circumstances in which it occurs, including the actors and the geographical region since the judicial effect of principles and concepts may change from one legal system to another.

47. The legal principles of International Environmental Law (IEL), being a sub-domain of public international law, are derived from two main sources: (i) the general principles of public international law which are also applicable in environmental matters, and (ii) the exclusive principles of IEL. Some of the principles of the first category, *inter alia*, include: (i) state sovereignty and territorial integrity; (ii) state sovereignty over natural resources; (iii) the do not harm principle; (iv) principles for the management of 'shared natural resources' following the principle of 'equitable utilisation' and 'transboundary cooperation'; (v) principle of management of 'common property' such as high seas and the living resources there;

---

44. *Ibid.*
45. *Ibid.*

(vi) principle of 'common heritage of mankind'; (vii) the obligation of the state to cooperate, inform and consult; and (viii) the principle of 'prior informed consent', etc.

48. Relevant international law instruments such as the 1972 United Nations Conference on the Human Environment held in Stockholm in 1972 (a Declaration was adopted after the end of the Conference which is popularly known as the 'Stockholm Declaration on the Human Environment, 1972') and the Rio Declaration on the Environment and Development, 1992 (a short document produced at the 1992 United Nations 'Conference on Environment and Development' and popularly known as the 'Rio Declaration, 1992') contain a list of principles of IEL. The list of some exclusive principles of the IEL includes, *inter alia*: (a) sustainable development, (b) common but differentiated responsibilities, (c) precautionary principle, (d) polluter pays principle, (e) prevention principle, (f) access and benefit sharing regarding natural resources, (g) common heritage and common concern of human kind, (h) good governance, and (i) principle of progressive realization and non-regression, etc.

49. The Brundtland Commission Report defines 'sustainable development' as 'development which meets the needs of the present without compromising the ability of the future generations to meet their own needs'.[46] The word –'needs' in the definition should be evaluated seriously. There are three dimensions of sustainable development: economic, social and environmental.[47] Though the Brundtland Commission is frequently given the credit to coining the concept of 'sustainable development', it is believed that Thomas Malthus, the founder of demography, has shared the idea of sustainable development and conservation first, though he did not understand the idea as the idea emerged long after his death.[48] After the USA, the English philosopher Bertrand Russel has defined the term 'conservation' as the preservation of ancient monuments and beauty spots, the upkeep of roads and public utilities and '. . .the preservation of the world's natural resources'.[49]

50. Equity is central to the attainment of sustainable development. The issues of intergenerational (between two generations) and intra-generational (the right of all people within the current generation) right to fair access to the earth's natural resources are reflected in article 3(1) of the United Nations Framework Convention for Climate Change (UNFCCC), 1992, the Convention on Biodiversity, 1992 and United Nations Economic Commission for Europe, Convention on the Protection

46. The Brundtland Commission, formerly the World Commission on Environment and Development, was founded in 1983 and named after the Chairperson of the Commission, Gro Harlem Brundtland. The Commission was dissolved after releasing the first report titled 'Our Common Future' in 1987.
47. General Assembly Resolution on 'Transforming our world: the 2030 Agenda for Sustainable Development', 25 Sep. 2015, A/RES/70/1.
48. Justice Mensah & Sandra Ricart Casadevall. 'Sustainable Development: Meaning, History, Principles, Pillars, and Implications for Human Action: Literature Review'. *Cogent Social Sciences* 5, no. 1 (2019): 1653531.
49. Brian William Clapp. *An Environmental History of Britain since the Industrial Revolution* (London: Routledge, 2014), at p. 1.

and Use of Transboundary Watercourse and International Lakes, 1992, the Desertification Convention, 1994, and the Stockholm Convention on Persistent Organic Pollutants, 2001.

51. In the case of *Metro Makers and Developers Limited and others v. Bangladesh Environmental Lawyers' Association Limited (BELA) and others*, 2012, 41 CLC (AD) [8366] = 65 DLR (AD) (2013) 181, in the landmark judgment relating to a case involving the development of a housing project filling the wetlands illegally, Justice SK Sinha, sharing the background of 'sustainable and environmentally sound development' linking this with the Rio Declaration on the Environment and Development, 1992 and Agenda 21, stated:

> The Brundtland . . .Commission's report defines sustainable development as 'development which meets the needs of the present without compromising the ability of the future generations to meet their own needs'. The principle envisages, firstly, that each generation should be required to conserve the diversity of the natural and cultural resource base, so that it does not unduly restrict the options available to future generations in solving their problems and satisfying their own values, and should also be entitled to diversify comparable to that enjoyed by previous generations. This principle is called 'conservation and options'. Secondly, generation should be required to maintain the quality of the planet so that it is passed on in no worse condition than that in which it was received, and should also been titled to planetary quality comparable to that enjoyed by previous generations. Thirdly, each generation should provide its members with equitable rights of access to the legacy of past generations and should conserve this access for future generations. This is principle of 'conservation of access.

52. It is widely accepted that modern IEL started to gain popularity after the Stockholm Declaration on the Human Environment, 1972. Thus, the formal emergence of IEL and Bangladesh as an independent state is contemporary. The legal discussion on the environment generally includes: biodiversity, chemicals and waste, climate and atmosphere, environmental governance, maritime and freshwater, land and agriculture. Therefore, this monograph will focus mostly all these sectors. Based on the nature of the environmental problems, different provisions of the environmental laws have local, regional, and international dimensions.

53. In the context of Bangladesh, though it is difficult to define 'principle', the Constitution (Fifteenth Amendment) Act, 2011 (Act XIV of 2011), while amending the Preamble to the Constitution, provides that 'the high ideals of nationalism, socialism, democracy and secularism, which inspired our heroic people to dedicate themselves to, and our brave martyrs to sacrifice their lives in, the national liberation struggle, shall be the fundamental principles of the Constitution'. Part II (Articles 8–25) of the Constitution of Bangladesh, 1972 contains the term 'principle' in its title, i.e., 'Fundamental Principles of State Policy'. Even though a legal definition of the term 'principle' is difficult to find out in the context of Bangladesh, this part of the Constitution, 1972 has included a few things as the fundamental principles of state policy.

54. Article 8(1) of the Constitution, 1972 provides that: 'The principles of nationalism, socialism, democracy and secularism, together with the principles derived from those as set out in this Part, shall constitute the fundamental principles of state policy.' Article 8(2) of the Constitution, 1972 provides for the applications of these principles and stipulates that: '(2) The principles set out in this Part shall be fundamental to the governance of Bangladesh, shall be applied by the State in the making of laws, shall be a guide to the interpretation of the Constitution and of the other laws of Bangladesh, and shall form the basis of the work of the State and of its citizens, but shall not be judicially enforceable.' Therefore, it can be seen that the state will use these principles in its daily activities. Thus, the principles are a way to make softer provisions initially to make these hard or binding ones gradually.

55. The first comprehensive and single environment Policy in Bangladesh was adopted in 1992 and the Environment Conservation Act, 1995 (Act No. 1 of 1995) (hereinafter 'BECA, 1995') was enacted as a significant contribution to that Policy of 1992. The BECA, 1995, as subsequently amended in 2000, 2002, and 2010, was enacted to provide for environment conservation, improvement of environmental standards, and control and mitigation of environmental pollution.[50] The law is special, and through the amendment of 2002, the provisions of the law were given overriding effects on the provisions of any other law or rules in force in the country; i.e., it was provided that the provisions of this law and the Rules framed thereunder shall prevail over the provisions of any other laws in force.[51] Subsequently, the Environment Conservation Rules, 1997 were formulated and the Environment Court Act, 2000 (Act No. 11 of 2000) was enacted for the proper implementation of these laws. This Environment Court Act, 2000 was subsequently amended in 2002 and 2003 and was finally repealed and replaced by the Environment Court Act, 2010 (Act No. 56 of 2010).

56. A statutory definition of the phrase 'environmental law' was included in section 2 of the Environment Court Act, 2000 when the law was amended in 2002. Accordingly, 'environmental law', for the purposes of this Act of 2000, means the BECA, 1995 and any other law specified by the government in the Official Gazette and the rules formulated under these laws, e.g., the Environment Conservation Rules, 1997 were formulated under BECA, 1995. When the Act of 2000 was subsequently updated, repealed, and replaced by the Environment Court Act, 2010 (Act No. 56 of 2010), the same definition of 'environmental law' was incorporated there as well. Thus, statutorily the BECA, 1995 and the Rules, 1997 will be treated as environmental law for the purpose of the Environment Court Act, 2010 (Act No. 56 of 2010) and for the rest, the government needs to issue additional Official Gazette.

---

50. Long title, the Bangladesh Environment Conservation Act, 1995 (Act no. 1 of 1995).
51. Section 2A, the Bangladesh Environment Conservation Act, 1995 (Act no. 1 of 1995).

Subsequently, the Brick Manufacturing and Brick Kiln Establishment (Control) Act, 2013 (Act No. 59 of 2013) was enacted, and it is provided that the environment courts established under the Environment Court Act, 2010 (Act No. 56 of 2010) shall try the various offences committed violating the provisions of the law of 2013.[52] Though it has been frequently shared in various forum that there are more than two hundred laws relating to the environment and environmental components, the government, for the purpose of this definition, has not declared any other law to be included within the definition of 'environmental law'. Yet, various laws have been enacted, and the Department of Environment (DoE) has been given extensive power and authority to implement the provisions of those laws.

57. The Ministry of Environment, Forest and Climate Change (MoEFCC) formulated the National Environment Policy, 2018 in line with article 18A of the Constitution of the People's Republic of Bangladesh for the protection and promotion of the environment. The Policy stipulated various objectives and set activities coupled with detailed implementation strategies aiming at the protection of various environmental components that can be considered by various ministries of the government, and Directorate, Department and Agency, etc., established under these ministries as guidelines. In particular, the Policy includes provisions on: land resources management; water resources management; air pollution control; safe food and water; agriculture; public health and health services; accommodation; housing and urbanization; education and mass awareness; forest and wildlife; biodiversity; ecosystem conservation and biosafety; hill ecosystems; fisheries and livestock; coastal and marine ecosystem; ecotourism; industrial development; energy and mineral resources; communication and transportation; human resources management; climate change preparedness; disaster management; science research; information and communication technologies; management of chemical substances; other pollution control; environment-friendly economic development; sustainable production and consumption; legal frame; organizational set-up; national environment policy compliance, etc.

58. Bangladesh has adopted the 2030 United Nations Sustainable Development Goals (SDGs) Agenda, and the SDGs were emphasized in the Seventh Five Year Plan 2016–2020 (7FYP) of the Government of Bangladesh through which about 82 percent of the SDGs have been incorporated into the 7FYP. The 7FYP, while putting emphasis on the goals of the SDGs and setting up priority areas, has set national environmental targets and goals to move the country towards a more sustainable economy and society. The 7FYP proposes a significant increase in the Annual Development Programme (ADP) allocations against the sectors dealing with sustainable environmental management. Through this 7FYP, the government has formulated economic growth strategies keeping climate change adaptation and mitigation issues into consideration. Besides, the Plan demonstrates a strong commitment towards harnessing a strong environmental and disaster management capacity enhancement process and adherence to green growth modalities.

52. Section 19, the Brick Making and Kiln Establishment (Control) Act, 2013 (Act No. 59 of 2013).

59. To monitor and assess the attainments of the targets of the SDGs, the General Economic Division (GED) of the Planning Commission in Bangladesh has conducted a data gap analysis for each of the 230 indicators suggested for SDGs monitoring, including 4 goals closely related to climate change and environment. The GED has also completed the mapping of Ministries/Divisions by SDGs targets (who to do what in terms of targets) which includes directly linked Ministries/ Divisions. Responsibilities of the different Ministries/Divisions as lead, co-lead, and associate agency of the government in realizing those goals and targets are set. Based on this mapping, the respective ministries/divisions have prepared their action plans which have already been approved.

60. A 'National Monitoring and Evaluation Framework' has also been published by the government, and a high-level National Committee for the monitoring and implementation of UN SDGs was established. Moreover, the government has also formulated the SDG financing strategy which contains, *inter alia*, an estimation of funds needed by 2030 to realize SDGs, financing strategies, and potential sources of funds. The GED has developed the Voluntary National Review (VNR) 2017 SDG tracker in June 2017 to present in the High-Level Political Forum held in July 2017.

61. The activities to develop the draft of the National Sustainable Development Strategy (NSDS) were started by the GED in 2009, and after updating and finalizing, the National Sustainable Development Strategy (2010–2021) was published in 2013 to balance the economic, social and environmental requirements of development and to track the formidable environmental challenges that Bangladesh faces on the way to development. The NSDS (2010–21) has identified five strategic priority areas, along with three cross-cutting areas, intending to achieve its stated vision and address long-term sustainability issues of productive resources. The strategic priority areas include sustained economic growth, development of priority sectors, social security and protection, environment, natural resources, and disaster management. The three cross-cutting issues that will support the sustainable development of priority areas include disaster risk reduction and climate, good governance, and gender.[53]

I. Definitions and Notions

62. Environment-related various relevant definitions can be found in different laws. Besides, the Supreme Court of Bangladesh, having the authority to interpret the statutes, can also define and interpret these terms. As many of the terms will be relevant to discuss in different parts of this monograph, this part will share only general definitions necessary for general understanding. The BECA, 1995, in section 2 has defined 'environment' as the interrelationship existing between water, air, soil, and physical property and their relationship with human beings, other animals,

53. Planning Commission, Government of Bangladesh, National Sustainable Development Strategy (2010–2021), http://www.plancomm.gov.bd/wp-content/uploads/2013/09/National-Sustainable-Development-Strategy.pdf.

plants, and microorganisms,[54] and 'environment conservation' is defined as the improvement of the qualitative and quantitative characteristics of different components of environment as well as prevention of degradation of those components, and 'environment pollutant' as any solid, liquid or gaseous substance which causes a harmful effect to the environment and also includes heat, sound, and radiation. Besides, the same provision of the Law has defined 'ecosystem' as the interdependence and balanced complex association of all the components of the environment, which aids and influences the conservation and development of plants and animals.

63. The BECA, 1995 has defined 'pollution' as the contamination or alteration of the physical, chemical or biological properties of air, water, or soil, including change in their temperature, taste, odour, density, or any other characteristics, or such other activity which, by way of discharging any liquid, gaseous, solid, radioactive or other substances into the air, water or soil or any component of the environment, destroys or causes injury or harm to public health or to domestic, commercial, industrial, agricultural, recreational or other useful activity, or which by such discharge destroys or causes injury or harm to air, water, soil, livestock, wild animal, bird, fish, plant or other forms of life. It may be relevant to share here that the exact definition of 'pollution' was included in the East Pakistan Water Pollution Control Ordinance, 1970 (East Pakistan Ordinance No. V of 1970) and the Environment Pollution Control Ordinance, 1977 (Ordinance No. XIII of 1977). Besides, the said law has further defined 'environmental pollutant' as any solid, liquid, or gaseous substance, including heat, sound, and radiation, which are or may be harmful to the environment.[55]

64. Under the BECA, 1995, 'wetland' means any land identified as a river, canal, beel, haor, baor, dighi, pond, spring or reservoir listed in the government record, or any wetland, floodplain area, any land containing fresh water and rain water as declared by notification in the Official Gazette by the government, Local Government or any government agency.[56]

65. These various definitions may give a general idea about the coverage or issues covered in the discussion of environmental law in the context of Bangladesh. The National Environment Policy, 2018, however, may provide a better idea on this as this Policy contains provisions relating to: (a) land; (b) water; (c) air pollution; (d) safe food and water; (e) agriculture; (f) public health and health services; (g) accommodation, housing, and urbanization; (h) education and mass awareness; (i) forest and wildlife; (j) biodiversity, ecosystem conservation and biosafety; (k) hill

---

54. Section 2, the Bangladesh Environment Conservation Act, 1995 (Act no. 1 of 1995). While defining the term 'environment', the BECA, 1995 has slightly changed the previous definition of the term included in the Environment Pollution Control Ordinance, 1977 (Ordinance no. XIII of 1977), which was repealed and replaced by the BECA, 1995. The Ordinance of 1977 defined the term 'environment' as the surroundings consisting of air, waters, soil, food, and shelter which can support or influence the growth of life of an individual or group of individuals, including all kinds of flora and fauna.
55. Section 2, the Bangladesh Environment Conservation Act, 1995 (Act no. 1 of 1995).
56. Section 2, the Bangladesh Environment Conservation Act, 1995 (Act no. 1 of 1995).

ecosystems; (l) fisheries and livestock; (m) coastal and marine ecosystem; (n) ecotourism; (o) industrial development; (p) energy and mineral resources; (q) communication and transportation; (r) human resources management; (s) climate change preparedness and adaptation; (t) disaster management; (u) science, research, information and communication technologies; (v) management of chemical substances; (w) other pollution control; (x) environment-friendly economic development, sustainable production, and consumption; (y) legal frame; (z) national environment policy compliance, etc.

66. It will be pertinent to share here that in many of these sectors mentioned above, there are additional specific policies, e.g., the Agriculture Policy, 2018, the Forest Policy, 1994 [the Forest Policy (Draft), 2016], the Water Policy, 1999, etc., which will be discussed in details in relevant places in the monograph.

II. Constitutional Provisions

67. The inclusion of provisions on the healthy environment in the Constitution of any country having written Constitutions, being the supreme law of the land, plays a significant role in terms of positive environmental outcomes aiming at the protection of environmental components.[57] It has been discussed already that globally, the environmental law matters were considered as a municipal issue and therefore, the discipline of IEL is of a recent origin, started in the 1960s. Noticeably, starting from the 1970s, more than a hundred countries in the world have amended their national constitutions to include the provisions relating to a healthy environment, and some countries have even recognized this as a right, i.e., right to a healthy environment.[58] In other instances, the apex courts of various countries having the authority to interpret the Constitution and nationals law, while interpreting various constitutional rights, e.g., fundamental right to life, held that the expression 'life' in the said constitutional right to life includes the right to live in a reasonably healthy and pollution-free environment.[59]

68. The emergence of IEL as a standalone discipline and the history of Bangladesh as an independent state is quite contemporary. Originally, there was no provision on the protection of the environment or environmental components in the Constitution of the People's Republic of Bangladesh, 1972, the supreme law of the

57. Chris Jeffords and Lanse Minkler. 'Do constitutions matter? The effects of constitutional environmental rights provisions on environmental outcomes.' Kyklos: International Review of Social Sciences, 69 (2) 294–335 (2016).

58. *See generally*, David R. Boyd. *The Environmental Rights Revolution: A Global Study of Constitutions, Human Rights, and the Environment* (UBC Press, 2011); David R. Boyd. *Constitutions, Human Rights, and the Environment: National Approaches*. In *Research Handbook on Human Rights and the Environment* (Edward Elgar Publishing, 2015).

59. Md. Ershadul Karim et al. 'Noise Pollution in Dhaka and the Constitutional Right to Life (29 June 2021)'. *Australian Journal of Asian Law* 21, no. 2 (2021): Article 5: 67–84, available at SSRN: https://ssrn.com/abstract=3875921; *Tan Tek Seng v. Suruhanjaya Perkhidmatan Pendidikan & Anor* [1996] 1 MLJ 261 [Malaysia].

land. Until 2011, though the Constitution was amended fourteen times, such a separate specific provision on environment or the protection of environmental components was not included there. Some provisions of the Constitution of Bangladesh, 1972, e.g., article 31 dealing with the right to protection of law and article 32 dealing with the protection of the right to life and personal liberty, were interpreted by the Apex court linking them with environment-related matters.[60]

69. In relation to a dispute relating to the advertisement of tobacco products, the AD held: 'that right to life [as guaranteed under articles 31 and 32 of the Constitution of Bangladesh, 1972] is not only limited to the protection of life and limbs but also extends to the protection of health, enjoyment of pollution free water and air, bare necessaries of life, facilities for education, maternity benefit, maintenance and improvement of public health by creating and sustaining conditions congenial to good health and ensuring the quality of life consistent to human dignity'.[61] It was further held that:

> Article 18(1) of the Constitution says that the State shall regard the rising of level of nutrition and the improvement of public health as among its primary duties, and in particular shall adopt effective measures to prevent the consumption, except for medical purposes or for such other purposes as may be prescribed by law, of alcohol and other intoxicating drinks and of drugs which are injurious to health. Though the aforesaid provision cannot be enforced by the Court it can be seen for interpreting the meaning of right of life under Articles 31 and 32 of the Constitution. A man has natural right to enjoyment of healthy life and longevity up to normal expectation of life of an ordinary human being. Enjoyment of healthy life and normal expectation of longevity is threatened by diseases, natural calamities and human actions. When a person is grievously hurt or injured by another his life and longevity are threatened. Similarly, when a man smokes which is injurious to his health he suffers ailments and his life and normal expectation of longevity are threatened. It is the natural right of a man to live free from all man-made hazards of life and such right has been guaranteed under the aforesaid Articles 31 and 32 of the Constitution subject to law of the land. No one has any right to endanger the life of the people which includes their health and normal longevity of an ordinary healthy person. Articles 31 and 32 of the Constitution not only means protection of life and limbs necessary for full enjoyment of life but also includes amongst others protection of health and normal longevity of an ordinary human being. It is the obligation of the State to discourage smoking and consumption of tobacco materials and the improvement of public health by preventing the advertisement of tobacco made products. Though the obligation under Article 18(1) of the Constitution cannot be enforced, State is bound to protect the health and longevity of the people living in the country as the right to life guaranteed

60. *Dr Mohiuddin Farooque and other v. Bangladesh and others* (Writ Petition No 891 of 1994); *Bangladesh v. Bangladesh Legal Aid and Services Trust (BLAST) and others* (2016) 8 SCOB (AD); *Government of Bangladesh and others v. Professor Nurul Islam & another* (2017) 9 SCOB (AD) 46.
61. *Bangladesh & ors v. Professor Nurul Islam & anr*, 9 SCOB [2017] AD 46, at para 52.

> under Articles 31 and 32 of the Constitution includes protection of health and longevity of a man free from threats of man-made hazards. Right to life under the aforesaid Articles of the Constitution being fundamental right it can be enforced by this Court to remove any unjustified threat to health and longevity of the people as the same are included in the right to life.[62]

70. The Supreme Court has thus been at the forefront and has been playing a leading role in shaping the environmental law legal regime of the country through judicial activism. As a result, the absence of environment protection-related provisions in the Constitution was not felt very seriously. Besides, looking at the socio-economic and political history of the war-ravaged Bangladesh till the 1990s, it can also be inferred that the policymakers of the country were not in a position to consider the environmental issues seriously in a true sense. Such a conclusion can be drawn looking at the legal and policy initiatives taken during the first two decades of the Independence, comparing these with that of the initiatives taken after the 1990s when the parliamentary democracy was resumed. Simultaneously, the paradigm shift of the global political scenario and the end of cold war in the 1990s also played an instrumental role. A number of leading and groundbreaking IEL instruments were adopted, and the policymakers of Bangladesh were encouraged to take initiatives to shape the environment-related legal framework.

71. Even with so many developments in the domestic legal framework, the provision relating to environmental protection was not included in the Constitution. Finally, the Constitution was amended through the Constitution (Fifteenth Amendment) Act, 2011 (Act XIV of 2011) to incorporate provision on the protection of the environment in article 18A, which provides that '[t]he State shall endeavour to protect and improve the environment and to preserve and safeguard the natural resources, bio-diversity, wetlands, forests and wild life for the present and future citizens'. This provision, being placed in Part II dealing with the Fundamental Principles of State Policy, is not judicially enforceable as discussed earlier.[63] Nevertheless, realizing the interrelated dynamics of the environment and sustainable development, the inclusion of this provision to protect and improve the environment along with the idea of sustainable use of natural resources, biodiversity, wetlands, forests, and wildlife, etc., is undoubtedly a welcoming development and a remarkable achievement in the context of a country that aspires to be a developed nation by 2041. The impact of the inclusion of such a provision in the Constitution can already be noticed since relevant laws enacted and policies formulated after this constitutional amendment have been referring to this provision in their Preambles to guide their implementation in line with the spirit of the Constitution.[64]

---

62. *Ibid.*, at para 54.
63. *Sheikh Abdus Sabur v. Returning Officer, District Education Officer-in-charge, Gopalganj and others* (1989) 41 DLR (AD) 30; *Kudrat-E-Elahi Panir and Others v. Bangladesh* (1992) 44 DLR (AD) 319.
64. *See*, for example, Preamble, the Bangladesh Biodiversity Act, 2017 (Act no. 2 of 2017); Preamble, the National Environment Policy, 2018.

72. Recently, in a dispute relating to chopping down of trees from Jhemai Punjee or Jhemai Tea Estate, Kulaura, Moulvibazar, Justice Hasan Foez Siddique of the Appellate Division of the Supreme Court (AD) has evaluated the provisions of article 18A of the Constitution and extended the provisions by stating that not only the state shall take initiatives in this regard but it is also the 'constitutional duty to safeguard the forests and wildlife of the country', 'fundamental duty of every citizen of Bangladesh to protect and improve the natural environment including forests' and 'sacred duty of everyone to protect forests, trees, flora and fauna'.[65] According to Justice Hasan Foez Siddique:

> The preservation of ecology and environment, based on the principle of sustainable development to reconcile the conflicting interest of development with the preservation of healthy environment has been recognized as a facet of right of life. The principle adopted is that ecology and environment are not objects of ownership but are nature's gift intended to be preserved in trust for future generation. The main motto of social life is to live in harmony with nature. Ongoing environmental degradation that is going must now come to a stop.[66]

73. Even though until 2011, there was no such provision in the Constitution of Bangladesh, 1972, this absence was not felt very seriously the higher judiciary of the country, i.e., both the Divisions of the Supreme Court were at the forefront and played instrumental roles in the development of environmental jurisprudence and legal regime in the country.[67] The Supreme Court, being the last place of citizens' hopes and aspirations and as the guardian having the mandate to interpret the Constitution of Bangladesh, 1972, has been guiding the nation by playing a crucial role in this regard and has, time to time, expanded the scope of various rights aiming to ensure the right to a healthy environment for the people of the land. The High Court Division of the Supreme Court (HCD), after the 1990s, influenced by the legal developments at the global level and in the neighbouring countries especially in India, started to interpret liberally the constitutional right to life to include the right to health, environment and shelter within the broader meaning of this right. In *Dr Mohiuddin Farooque and other v. Bangladesh and others* (Writ Petition No 891 of 1994), Justice ABM Khairul Haque, held at paragraph 42, that life means a '[quality] life among others, free from environmental hazards'. In the case of *Dr Mohiuddin Farooque v. Bangladesh & others*,[68] the petitioner, Dr Farooque, raised several issues, including the emission of hazardous smoke from motor vehicles and the use of audible signalling devices, which emit unduly harsh, shrill, loud or alarming noises. The petitioner submitted that, although it has not been explicitly included as a fundamental right in art 32 of the Constitution, the right to a safe and healthy environment is inherent and integrated into the 'right to life', and art. 31 prohibits the taking of any action detrimental to life, body and property. Therefore, the right

65. *Rana Surong v. Government of Bangladesh and others*, 2020(1) LNJ (AD).
66. *Ibid.*, at para 14.
67. For example, the Ministry of Industries framed the Ship Breaking and Recycling Rules, 2011 following the Directives issued by the HCD in *Bangladesh Environmental Lawyers Association (BELA) v. Bangladesh*, 2009, 38 CLC (HCD) [8173] = 7 LG (HCD) (2010) 118.
68. Writ Petition No 300 of 1995 (Vehicular Pollution Case).

to a sound environment should be considered a fundamental right under art. 32. In response, the HCD, after citing instances of improper implementation of relevant municipal laws, issued several directions including stricter implementation of laws to restrict noise generated from motor vehicles.[69]

74. The HCD further stated that: '[n]o one has any right to endanger the life of the people which includes their health and normal longevity of an ordinary healthy person by producing noise which is injurious to human health'. Moreover, it was held that 'the right to life under Articles 31 and 32 of the Constitution not only means protection of life and limbs necessary for full enjoyment of life but also includes, amongst others, protection of health and normal longevity of an ordinary human being'.[70] Through various subsequent decisions of the Supreme Court, this is now established that the constitutional right to life includes the right to environment and right to enjoy quality life free from environmental hazards, and some of these decisions will be shared in relevant sections throughout this monograph.

75. Very recently, the AD, concerning the law on smoking and tobacco product control, summed up the status and overall position on the rights enshrined in articles 31 and 32 of the Constitution in the context of Bangladesh in the following manner:

> '[the r]ight to life is not only limited to protection of life and limbs but also extends to the protection of health, enjoyment of pollution-free water and air, bare necessaries of life, facilities for education, maternity benefit, maintenance and improvement of public health by creating and sustaining conditions congenial to good health and ensuring quality of life consistent to human dignity.'[71]

76. The court further emphasized that:

> [n]o one has any right to endanger the life of the people which includes their health and normal longevity of an ordinary healthy person. Articles 31 and 32 of the Constitution not only means protection of life and limbs necessary for full enjoyment of life but also includes amongst others protection of health and normal longevity of an ordinary human being. . . [the] State is bound to protect the health and longevity of the people living in the country as the right to life guaranteed under Articles 31 and 32 of the Constitution includes protection of health and longevity of a man free from threats of man-made hazards. Right to life . . . being [a] fundamental right it can be enforced by this Court to remove any unjustified threat to health and longevity of the people as the same are included in the right to life.[72]

---

69. Writ Petition No 300 of 1995 (Vehicular Pollution Case).
70. *Dr Mohiuddin Farooque v. Bangladesh and others* (1996) 48 DLR 438, 441.
71. *Government of Bangladesh and others v. Professor Nurul Islam & another* (2017) 9 SCOB (AD) 46.
72. *Ibid.*

§3. Historical Development of Environmental Law

77. To trace the historical root of environmental matters in the Bangladesh context from the legal and regulatory point of view, a discussion on this area of law at the global level demands special attention. It may be relevant to share here that there are some disagreements or non-consensus among the scholars as to the precise origin of IEL. To some, the IEL is of a relatively recent origin since neither the Charter of the United Nations, 1945 nor the Statute of the International Court of Justice contains even a single mention of the words such as 'environment' or 'natural resource'.

78. The modern and formal development of this area of legal scholarship gains momentum with the foundation of the United Nations Environment Programme (UNEP) in 1972.[73] During that time, there were only a very few multilateral or bilateral agreements containing environment-related provisions, and only a very few countries had environment-related provisions in their domestic legal system.[74] This is perhaps due to the fact that traditionally under the rules of public international law, environment-related problems and concerns are seen as issues of national concern where every state enjoys the exclusive sovereign authority to deal with matters relating to the protection and preservation of the environmental components within their national jurisdictions.

79. Though this is agreed that this area of law started to emerge with the adoption of agreements relating to the protection of birds, fur seals, fish and wild animals, etc., at the beginning of the nineteenth century,[75] it is evident that an agreement was even signed by Austria, Baden, Bavaria, Switzerland and Wurtember regarding the regulation of the flow of water from Lake Constance in 1857 and after that, at least twenty-four multilateral environmental agreements were signed till 1900.[76]

80. Moreover, though environmental issues and concerns are seen as domestic matters and every country deals with these domestically based on their socio-economic, political, and legal preferences, this can be seen through the lenses of religious views also since major religions of the world in the respective scripts contain provisions relating to the protection of environmental components for the betterment of the present and future generations. The regions which have been being

73. Djamchid Momtaz, 'The United Nations and the Protection of the Environment: From Stockholm to Rio de Janeiro'. *Political Geography* 15, nos 3–4 (1996): 261–271.
74. Edith Brown Weiss, 'The Evolution of International Environmental Law'. *Japanese Year Book of International Law* 54 (2011): 1.
75. The multilateral environmental agreements that are shared in the popular literature in this regard are: the Convention Designed to Ensure the Conservation of Various Species of Wild Animals in Africa, which are Useful to Man or Inoffensive, 1900; the Convention for the Protection of Birds Useful to Agriculture, 1902; and the Convention respecting Measures for the Preservation and Protection of the Fur Seals in the North Pacific Ocean, 1911, etc.
76. *See*, University of Oregon, International Environmental Agreements (IEA) Database Project, available at https://iea.uoregon.edu/environmental-agreements-date.

practised in this part of the world, i.e., Buddhism, Hinduism, and Islam, similarly contain important provisions relating to the protection of environmental components.[77]

81. In one of the landmark judgments in the history of environment judicial activisms in Bangladesh, i.e., *Dr. Mohiuddin Farooque v. Bangladesh*, 1997, 26 CLC (AD) [505] = 49 DLR (AD) (1997) 1, 17 BLD (AD) 1997 1; 1 BLC (AD) (1996) 189 dealing with flood action plans taken after the severe floods of 1987 and 1988, it was claimed by the petitioner that one of such action plan, i.e., Flood Action Plan-20, would adversely affect and uproot about three hundred thousand people within the project area in Tangail and Sirajgonj and 'the extent of adverse impact outside the project area may encompass more than a million human lives, natural resources and the natural habitat of man and other flora and fauna'. When the petitioner moved to the HCD with a public interest litigation, it was an issue whether the petitioner has a right to petition as the petitioner was not directly affected and thus cannot be aggrieved. While referring to article 8 of the Constitution of Bangladesh, 1972, which dealt with 'absolute trust and faith in the Almighty Allah' as one of the fundamental principles of state policy, Justice Mustafa Kamal interpreted this in this way that: '[a]bsolute trust and faith in the Almighty Allah necessarily mean the duty to protect His creation and environment. The appellant is aggrieved, because Allah's creations and environment are in mortal danger of extinction and degradation'. It will be pertinent to mention here that this provision on 'absolute trust and faith in the Almighty Allah' was subsequently amended.

82. Environmental issues, in general and modern senses, have a close connection with various development activities of human beings extensively exemplified since the industrial revolution. However, if the discussions on natural resources and architectural heritage are considered, then the history should arguably be even older.

83. In the context of Bangladesh, the historical development of laws and policies relating to various components of the environment will be shared in relevant chapters of this monograph. Nevertheless, it is pertinent to mention here that undoubtedly, the rule of the East India Company and British Raj spanning for almost two centuries during colonial India is historically very significant in all sectors, including the legal arena. Since the present Bangladesh was part of India till 1947 and of Pakistan till 1971, the country already had some legal instruments and

77. *See generally*, Yale University School of the Environment, https://fore.yale.edu/Climate-Emergency/Climate-Change-Statements-from-World-Religions; UNEP, Religions and environmental protection, https://www.unep.org/about-un-environment/faith-earth-initiative/religions-and-environmental-protection; Shah Haneef, 'Principles of Environmental Law in Islam'. *Arab Law Quarterly* 17, no. 3 (2002): 241–254; Christopher G. Framarin, *Hinduism and Environmental Ethics: Law, Literature, and Philosophy* (New York, Routledge, 2014); Sandra Richter, 'Environmental Law: Wisdom from the Ancients'. *Bulletin for Biblical Research* (2014): 307–329; Padmasiri De Silva, *Environmental Philosophy and Ethics in Buddhism* First Edition (London, Macmillan Press Ltd., 1998).

has inherited some of the government institutions established even before the independence of the country, and these have been entrusted to continue their roles and functions including those responsible in the governance of environment-related issues.

84. Immediately after the Independence and after Bangladesh delegations led by A. Razzak, Ambassador Extraordinary and Plenipotentiary to Sweden, attended the historic Stockholm Conference on the Human Environment, 1972, some initiatives were taken in a war-ravaged country, and these reflect the commitments of the founding fathers of the country towards the protection of environmental components from various sources of pollution, primarily water.

85. The government promulgated two Ordinances to control water pollution and environmental pollution in 1973 and 1977, respectively. The Environment Pollution Control Ordinance, 1977 (Ordinance No. XIII of 1977) was basically the revised and updated version of the East Pakistan Water Pollution Control Board Ordinance, 1970 (East Pakistan Ord. No. V of 1970). This Ordinance of 1977, which was promulgated to achieve similar objectives as encapsulated in the 1970 Ordinance, provided for the establishment of the Environment Pollution Control Board. Accordingly, a sixteen-member Environment Pollution Control Board and another Environmental Pollution Control Cell were established in 1977. Subsequently, in 1985, the Department of Pollution Control was established, and this Department was subsequently renamed and restructured as the Department of Environment (DoE) in 1989.

86. Similarly, after the independence of Bangladesh in 1971, a Bangladesh Forest Department (BFD) was established under the Ministry of Agriculture to manage the reserved and proposed reserved forests, and this BFD remained as a Department under the Ministry of Agriculture till 1989. Later on, a Ministry, i.e., the Ministry of Environment and Forest, was established in 1989, merging the DoE and BFD to address the relevant issue. In 1992, the first National Environment Policy was formulated, and with this, the management and protection of environmental components started to take formal and institutional inception. The BECA, 1995 was enacted as a consequence of the Environment Policy of 1992, the Environment Conservation Rules, 1997 were framed to elaborate the provisions of the BECA, 1995 and the Environment Court Act, 2000 was enacted to set up environmental courts to implement and judicially interpret domestic environmental law provisions.

87. These BFD and DoE were then brought under the newly created ministry, i.e., Ministry of Environment and Forests (MoEF) in 1989. Recently, on 14 May 2018, the Cabinet changed the name of the MoEF to the Ministry of Environment, Forest and Climate Change (MoEFCC). This MoEFCC, previously the MoEF, as the main government body, has been functioning and discharging their mandated responsibilities through the Head Office, six regional or Divisional offices located in Dhaka, Chottogram, Khulna, Bogra, Barishal and Sylhet, two Divisional Environmental Labs and two Metropolitan Officers in Dhaka and Chottogram. Besides, there are some district-level offices as well.[78]

§4. Role of Government Institutions in the Shaping and Administration of Environmental Law and Policy

I. Governmental Institutions and Their Competence

88. At present, there are a total of 58 Ministries and Divisions, and 353 Departments under these Ministries having mandates to run various activities of the government of Bangladesh. These Ministries and Departments play decisive roles in implementing their responsibilities within their mandated areas. 'Rules of Business',[79] 'Allocation of Business'[80] and 'Bangladesh Secretariat Instructions' formulated under the 'Rules of business' [81] are important government policy documents that specify precisely the functions and responsibilities of different Ministries, Divisions and Departments. The 'Warrant of Precedence'[82] sets out the relative precedence or priority in terms of ranks of important officeholders belonging to the three organs of the state, i.e., executive, legislative and judiciary. This warrant or the order is generally used for the invitation of officeholders in important official functions including their seating arrangements, waiting in time to receive and see off, e.g., Very Important Persons such as the President and the Prime Minister when they go abroad and also receive their counterparts within the country.[83]

89. The concept 'environment' encompasses various diversified things and thus may involve many different government bodies at different levels of their involvements in their daily activities, which may neither possible nor desirable to cover precisely here. Nevertheless, in order to understand the government Institutions and their competence in the protection and preservation of environmental components, the National Environment Policy, 2018 may guide us in this regard as this Policy of 2018 contains provisions relating to: (a) land, (b) water, (c) air pollution, (d) safe food and water, (e) agriculture, (f) public health and health services, (g) accommodation, housing and urbanization, (h) education and mass awareness, (i) forest and wildlife, (j) biodiversity, ecosystem conservation and biosafety, (k) hill ecosystems, (l) fisheries and livestock, (m) coastal and marine ecosystem, (n) ecotourism, (o)

78. Department of Environment, Facts about DoE, p. 5, Dhaka, July 2015.
79. Cabinet Division, The Rules of Business, 1996 (revised up to April 2017), Government of the People's Republic of Bangladesh.
80. The Allocation of Business among the Different Ministries and Divisions, 1996 (Schedule I of the Rules of Business, 1996).
81. The first Secretariat Instructions was issued in 1976 under the Rules of Business, 1975 and was translated in Bangla in 1978. It was subsequently updated in 2008 and the existing one was updated in 2014.
82. The Warrant of Precedence, 1986. The AD of the Supreme Court addressed various aspects of the Warrant of Precedence. *See*, *Bangladesh v. Md. Ataur Rahman & ors.* 9 SCOB [2017] AD 1.
83. Warrant of Precedence, Banglapedia, http://en.banglapedia.org/index.php?title=Warrant_of_Precedence.

industrial development, (p) energy and mineral resources, (q) communication and transportation, (r) climate change preparedness and adaptation, (s) disaster management, (t) science, research, information and communication technologies, (u) management of chemical substances, (v) other pollution control, and (w) environment-friendly economic development, sustainable production and consumption, etc. In this segment, government bodies that are responsible to manage, govern and regulate these above-mentioned matters will be considered.

90. The National Environment Policy, 2018 has assigned various ministries and agencies to implement the Policy. An inexhaustive list of such ministries and agencies include: Ministry of Agriculture; Ministry of Chittagong Hill Tracts Affairs; Ministry of Commerce; Ministry of Environment, Forests and Climate Change; Ministry of Fisheries and Livestock; Ministry of Food; Ministry of Housing and Public Works; Ministry of Industry; Ministry of Power, Energy and Mineral Resources; Ministry of Land; Ministry of Law, Justice and Parliamentary Affairs; Ministry of Road Transport and Bridges; Ministry of Textiles and Jute; Ministry of Water Resources, Water Supply and Sewerage Authority; Bangladesh Agriculture Development Corporation; Bangladesh Atomic Energy Commission; Bangladesh Bureau of Statistics; Bangladesh Chemical Industries Corporation; Bangladesh Council of Science and Industry (BCSIR); Bangladesh Department of Consumer Protection; Bangladesh Haor and Wetland Development Department; Bangladesh Investment Development Authority; Bangladesh Safe Food Authority; Bangladesh Small and Cottage Industries Corporation; Bangladesh Space Research and Remote Sensing Agency (SPARSO); Barrendra Multipurpose Development Authority; Department of Agricultural Extension; Department of Environment; Department of Fisheries; Department of Fisheries Livestock; Department of Food; Department of Forests; Department of Local Government; Department of Maritime Transport; Department of Meteorology; Department of Public Security; District Administration of Bangladesh; Energy Regulatory Commission; Institute of Water Modeling; Police Administration; Metropolitan Police; Planning Commission; and Soil Resources Development Institute, etc.

91. The government has also established the ‘Executive Committee of the National Environment Committee’ with the ex officio members from different relevant government offices through a gazette notification issued on 11 January 2015 to review and assess activities on implementation of National Environment Policy by different ministries or departments and to provide suggestions, etc.

92. The government has also taken various initiatives. For example, the ‘Bangladesh Environmental Statistics Framework 2016–2030’ was prepared for the first time to be used as a guideline, strategic action plan and integrated platform for collection, analysis and dissemination of environmental data to support the UN SDGs, Sendai Framework for Disaster Risk Reduction, the Paris Agreement on Climate Change, Bangladesh Climate Change Strategy and Action Plan and 7th Five Year Plan.

93. The Country Investment Plan for Environment, Forestry and Climate Change (2016–2021) (EFCC CIP) was launched in December 2017 both as a tool to translate government policies into investment programmes and projects and to respond to the urgent need to address environmental degradation in Bangladesh and to improve the country's ability to meet the climate change threats. This Investment Plan is a multisectoral and inclusive government investment framework for mobilizing and delivering effective, coordinated, sustainable and country-driven investment programmes in environmental protection, sustainable forest management, climate change adaptation and mitigation and environmental governance. EFCC CIP has identified fourteen coherent and coordinated investment programmes under four thematic areas. There is a total of forty-three sub-programmes under these programmes. Moreover, CIP provides an estimate on the investment requirement, during the plan period, for addressing environment, forest and climate change issues confronted by the country, existing investment as well as investment gap. The total investment requirement is estimated at about USD 11.7 billion, of which 40 percent is already financed through the government's own budget allocations and by contributions from development partners. Financing gap is about 60 percent of the total investment requirement.

94. Bangladesh, as the largest deltaic floodplain in the world, released the Bangladesh Delta Plan, 2100, an integrated and holistic plan, developed with the vision to ensure long-term water management and food security, economic growth and environmental sustainability, while taking climate change into account. Besides, the plan includes strategies on various issues and proposes for the establishment of an institutional framework to coordinate the implementation of various investment plans and Master Plans consisting of projects/programmes to be implemented step by step in short to medium term.

95. As the name of the main ministry responsible in this regard in Bangladesh includes environment, forest and climate change, after the discussion on environment, it will be relevant to discuss about forest. In 1955, the then government of Pakistan established Forest Products Research Laboratory to research forest products. This Laboratory was renamed the East Pakistan Forest Research Laboratory in 1965 realizing that the tree stocks in the forest areas were declining. After the independence of the country, the Bangladesh Forest Research Institute (BFRI) was established under the Bangladesh Forest Department. The BFRI was placed under the Ministry of Agriculture in 1985 and under the Ministry of Environment and Forest in 1988. The BFRI has been functioning through two research branches: Forest Management Branch and Forest Products Branch.[84]

96. The Bangladesh Forest Industries Development Corporation (BFIDC), as the East Pakistan Forest Industries Development Corporation, was established in 1959 through the promulgation of the East Pakistan Forest Industries Development Corporation Ordinance, 1959 (East Pakistan Ordinance No. LXVII of 1959), which was

84. Background, Bangladesh Forest Research Institute (BFRI), http://www.bfri.gov.bd/site/page/99844564-c182-4d4c-961d-f47e161369ee/-.

subsequently adapted after the independence of the country in 1971 through the Bangladesh (Adaptation of Existing Laws) Order, 1972 (President's Order No. 48 of 1972). The BFIDC, while discharging both agricultural and industrial functions, is responsible to treat, season and extract forest products, such as timber, rubber and other forest products from the forest and rubber garden, to establish industries from the commercial use of these products, and to promote rubber cultivation in the country.[85]

97. The journey of Bangladesh National Herbarium was started in 1970 as a development project entitled 'Botanical Survey of East Pakistan' under the Department of Botany, University of Dhaka. Now, this Herbarium conducts a botanical survey, identify, collect and preserve all plant species, medicinal plants, economically important plants, etc. This office maintains herbarium database, preserves the plant specimens and relevant information, conducts research on and publishes plant taxonomy.

98. Finally, the issue that remains in the name of the ministry is climate change. With the aim to address the impact of climate change and vision to build a climate-resilient Bangladesh capable of dealing with the impact of climate change, Bangladesh Climate Change Trust (BCCT) was set up following the Bangladesh Climate Change Strategy and Action Plan, 2009 (BCCSAP, 2009) and the Climate Change Trust Act, 2010 (Act No. 57 of 2010). Following the enactment of this law of 2010, the BCCT was established in 2013 to implement forty-four programmes included in the BCCSAP, 2009.

99. Section 5 of the Climate Change Trust Act, 2010 (Act No. 57 of 2010), while dealing with the aims of the BCCT, provides that: '[t]he Trust shall have the following aims, namely –

(a) to make a necessary action plan for capacity building for adjustment of the people or groups of people of the affected and risky areas resulting from climate change, upgrading their life and livelihood and facing the long term risk, and to take measures for implementation thereof;
(b) to take measures for adaptation, mitigation, technology development and transfer, capacity building and funds for facing adverse effect of climate change on man, biodiversity and the nature.'

100. Whereas, section 6 of the Climate Change Trust Act, 2010 (Act No. 57 of 2010), while dealing with the objectives of the BCCT, provides that: '[t]he objectives of the Trust shall be as follows, namely –

(a) to use the fund of the Trust in facing the risk arising from climate change as a special case out of the development or non-development budget of the Government;

85. For more about Bangladesh Forest Industries Development Corporation, *see*, http://www.bfidc.gov.bd/.

(b) to initiate and implement suitable action plan for implementation of special programme regarding climate change and ensuring sustainable development;
(c) to initiate project or programme regarding institutional and social capacity building of the local people and development of human resources in the grass root level for facing climate change;
(d) to undertake necessary action research in the field of adaptation, mitigation, technology transfer and finance and investment for facing climate change and in the light of the research result, to initiate and implement pilot programmes with dissemination of such result;
(e) to make necessary action plans of different terms for adjustment with climate change and facing damages and to initiate and implement programmes or projects on the basis of them;
(f) to assist the climate change cells or focal points formed in different Ministries and the DoE in respect of climate change including the Climate Change Unit established in the Ministry of Environment and Forest for playing their effective role;
(g) to assist in initiating suitable programmes and implementation thereof to eradicate poverty by building up the institutional, social or local people's capacity for creating public awareness on possible environmental disaster arising out of climate change and for facing the disaster; and
(h) to assist any emergency activities following any natural disaster arising out of climate change.'

101. Section 15 (1) of the Climate Change Trust Act, 2010 (Act No. 57 of 2010) provides for the establishment of Climate Change Trust Fund to be developed through: (a) money granted by the government from the National Budget; (b) money received from the donor countries, organizations and institutions approved by the government; (c) money received from the local and foreign sources approved by the government; (d) income accrued from the investment of the fund; (e) money received from any other sources approved by the government. It is further provided that a maximum of 66% money from the government grants may be spent every year on the projects of programmes relating to the aims and objectives of the Trust, and the minimum 34% money and the unspent money shall be credited to the Fund.[86] The Economic Relations Division under the Ministry of Finance functions as the National Designated Authority of Green Climate Fund, the global fund created under the UNFCCC, 1992 to assist the developing countries in addressing climate change challenges.

102. Various other policymakers have been taking different relevant initiatives also. For example, Bangladesh Bank, the central Bank of the country, has introduced the Green Banking Refinance Scheme in August 2009 to provide soft loans to the industries to consider using environment-friendly technologies, e.g., solar

86. Section 15(3), the Climate Change Trust Act, 2010 (Act No. 57 of 2010).

panels, biogas plants and industrial effluent treatment plants to reduce industrial pollution and increase energy supply. Besides, in cases of development projects, the government needs to follow the guidelines relating to environmental protection. For example, to get the funding of the World Bank, the government needs to conduct environmental assessment following the World Bank's Operational Policy on Environmental Assessment.

II. The Actual Role of Government Institutions

103. The previous section has already shared the list of various ministries, departments, government agencies and institutions responsible for governing and regulating different aspects of the environment. The main ministry or lead agency responsible for the management and administration of environment-related matters is the MoEFCC, which was known as MoEF till 2018, and two main departments, i.e., DoE and BFD established to fulfil the mandates of the Ministry. Besides, some other organizations have also been established under this Ministry. These are: BFRI, BFIDC, Bangladesh National Herbarium, BCCT and Bangladesh Rubber Board.

104. According to the Schedule I to the Rules of Business, 1996, i.e., Allocation of Business among the Different Ministries and Divisions (as revised up to April 2017), the MoEFCC, formerly the MoEF, is responsible for monitoring the following matters:

1. Environment and Ecology
2. Matters relating to environmental pollution control.
3. Conservation of Forests and development of Forest Resources (Government and Private), forest inventory, grading and quality control of forest products.
4. Afforestation and regeneration of forest extraction of forest produce.
5. Plantation of exotic cinchona and rubber.
6. Botanical Gardens and Botanical Surveys.
7. Tree plantation.
8. Planning Cell—Preparation of schemes and co-ordination in respect of forest.
9. Research and Training in forestry.
10. Mechanised forestry operations.
11. Protection of wild birds and animals and establishment of sanctuaries.
12. Matters relating to the marketing of forest produce.
13. Administration of B. C. S (Forest).
14. Liaison with International Organisations and matters relating to treaties and agreements with other countries and world bodies relating to subjects allotted to this Ministry.
15. All laws on subjects allotted to this Ministry.
16. Inquiries and statistics on any of the subjects allotted to this Ministry.
17. Fees in respect of any of the subjects allotted to this Ministry except fees taken in courts.

105. The DoE, the main body under the MoEFCC responsible for governing environment-related matters, is mandated under various laws and policy documents to perform the following duties:

- survey of pollution by industries, identifying the polluting industrial establishments and encourage/compel them to adopt pollution control measures, and in case of necessity, take legal actions through the operations of mobile courts and by filing legal cases in the environment court following the provisions of the Environmental Protection Act and the rules and regulations formulated under these;
- fixation and collection of damages from the polluters of the environment;
- inspection of newly established or existing industrial plant/project after application and issuance of environmental clearance certification to these after necessary inspection and investigation;
- review and approval of the report on environmental impact assessment (EIA) of development activities taken by Government and non-governmental organizations and individuals and provision of suggestions in the completion of EIA;
- acceptance of complaints on environmental pollution and the settlement of these after investigation, take actions against indiscriminate hill cutting, the survey of vehicles, and running of mobile court operations against polluting vehicles;
- monitoring of the quality standards of air and water, and analysis of samples of air, water and liquid waste in laboratory;
- regular analysis of samples of water collected from different ponds, wells and drinking water from different parts of the country to ensure the quality of these, preservation of data, and submission of reports;
- taking of necessary actions to fulfil the domestic, regional and international level obligations derived from various regional and international conventions, agreements and protocols on the environment;
- adoption and implementation of activities at national and international level to address the effects of climate change;
- adoption of actions to conserve the biodiversity and protection of biosafety;
- to take actions to control the import, transport, use, etc., of toxic and hazardous chemical substances;
- to control ozone layer depleting materials;
- taking effective initiatives aiming at sustainable biodiversity management with the participation of people in environmentally critical areas;
- running of awareness campaign on environment protection and taking of actions to avail environmental affairs related information to all, and to duly celebrate the environment-related internationally important days;
- formulation and distribution of State of the Environment Report;
- to run activities in partnership with different social/cultural/economic groups to encourage public participation in environmental conservation and management;
- adoption and implementation of various projects and research on environmentally important issues;
- taking of legal actions on the production and marketing of banned polythene shopping bags;

- provide environmental feedback by reviewing and evaluating various projects/ initiatives taken at government and private levels;
- arrangement of training, workshops, exchange meetings, etc., aiming at the capacity building of the public and private sector regarding environmental conservation and management;
- to play an active role as committee members of almost all the ministries and its subordinate departments, district and upazila level.

106. The DoE is responsible for implementing the provisions of several policies and laws, both primary and subsidiary. The list of such laws, *inter alia*, includes: (a) the Environment Policy, 2018; (b) the BECA, 1995; (c) the Environment Conservation Rules, 1997; (d) the Environment Court Act, 2010; (e) the Ozone Layer Depleting Substances (Control) Rules, 2004; (f) the National Biodiversity Strategy and Action Plan, 2016–2021; (g) the National Biosafety Framework, 2006; (h) the Noise Pollution (Control) Rules, 2006; (i) the Medical Waste (Management and Processing) Rules, 2008; (j) the Bangladesh Climate Change Strategy and Action Plan, 2009; (k) the National 3R Strategy for Waste Management, 2010; (l) the Hazardous Waste and Ship Breaking Waste Management Rules, 2011; (m) Biosafety Rules, 2012; and (n) the Brick Manufacturing and Brick Kiln Establishment (Control) Act, 2013, and so on.

107. The Director General of the DoE, the main authority responsible for implementing the provisions of the BECA, 1995, may, subject to the provisions of the BECA, 1995, take such action as he deems fit and necessary for the protection of the environment, development of environmental standards, and control and mitigation of environmental pollution, and may give necessary written instructions to any person for discharge of his duties under this Act.[87] In particular, and without compromising the totality of the aforementioned powers, such activities shall include all or any of the following functions, namely:

(a) coordinate with the functions of any authority or body concerned with the purposes of this Act;
(b) prevent potential accidents that may cause environmental degradation and pollution, take safety measures, and prescribe and provide instructions for the remedial action of similar accidents;
(c) advise or instruct the person concerned on matters relating to the environmental use, storage, transportation, import and export of hazardous substances or their components;
(d) search and research on information related to environmental protection, development and pollution and cooperate with any other authority or organization in similar activities;
(e) give orders or instructions to the appropriate authority or person for testing, controlling and mitigating any place, premises, plant, machinery, manufacturing or other processes, material or substance for environmental development and pollution control and mitigation purposes;

87. Section 4(1), the Bangladesh Environment Conservation Act, 1995 (Act No. 1 of 1995).

(f) collection, publication and dissemination of information on environmental pollution;
(g) advise the government to refrain from all manufacturing processes, products and materials which may cause environmental pollution;
(h) conduct drinking water quality monitoring programmes, prepare reports, and give advice or, as the case may be, instructions to all concerned to follow the drinking water standards.[88]

108. Besides, the BECA, 1995 has also empowered the Director General (DG) to give directions to stop the production, import, marketing, sale, display for sale, storage, distribution, transportation for commercial purpose or commercial use of anything, including polythene shopping bag, etc., that is harmful to the environment.[89] Any instructions given by the DG may contain matters relating to the closure, prohibition, or control of any industry, enterprise, or process, and shall be bound to comply with the instructions. However, before closing or prohibiting any industrial factory, enterprise, or process, the DG shall send a written notice to the owner or occupier of that concerned industrial factory, enterprise, or process to give a reasonable opportunity to make its activities environmentally friendly. The DG may also mention in the notice that if the relevant activities are not made environmentally friendly as per the notice, necessary legal actions shall be taken where the DG may direct the utility authorities to disconnect the electricity, gas, telephone, and water connections. In case of any threat to public life due to environmental pollution, the DG may, as a matter of urgency, give the necessary instructions immediately. All these instructions issued by DG may specify the time limit for carrying out the relevant work.[90] Besides, if it appears to the DG that the actions or inactions of any person are directly or indirectly harming the ecosystem, i.e., the interdependence and balanced complexity of the elements of the environment, which assists and influences the conservation and development of plants and animals or any person or group, he shall determine the amount of such damage and can give the instructions to the person responsible for paying it and take appropriate corrective action or both, and he will be bound to follow such instructions.[91] The DG, with the notification for remedies of the loss or potential loss from any person who has suffered or is in danger of sufferings due to environmental pollution or environmental degradation, can also arrange for a public hearing.[92]

109. On the other hand, the BFD has the mandate to perform the following activities:

– Manage and conserve forest resources along with biodiversity & watershed management and development.

88. Section 4(2), the Bangladesh Environment Conservation Act, 1995 (Act No. 1 of 1995).
89. Section 6A, the Bangladesh Environment Conservation Act, 1995 (Act No. 1 of 1995).
90. Sections 4 (3) and 4A(2), the Bangladesh Environment Conservation Act, 1995 (Act No. 1 of 1995).
91. Section 7, the Bangladesh Environment Conservation Act, 1995 (Act No. 1 of 1995).
92. Section 8, the Bangladesh Environment Conservation Act, 1995 (Act No. 1 of 1995).

- Enforce laws and regulations for the protection and management of forest resources and wildlife as the custodian of the government forests.
- Contribute to meet the basic needs of current and future generations through sustainable management of the forest.
- Increase the importance of forests to economic development by creating forest-based employment opportunities and mass forestry activities by creating forest-based employment opportunities.
- Conserve natural habitats and restore degraded forests for biodiversity conservation.
- Ensure participatory forest management.
- Expand forest cover through massive afforestation and reforestation programmes in newly accreted land and other suitable areas including unclassified state forest.
- Assist and encourage forestry at government and non-government levels.
- Provide technical advice and assistance on tree planting and agroforestry.
- Support conventions, contracts and protocols promised by the government for international efforts related to global warming control, desertification, forest, wildlife, biodiversity and environment.
- Restore degraded forests and discarded land with the participation of local people.

110. It may be relevant to share here that the policymakers of the country have also established various boards and Commissions under various ministries with additional responsibilities to perform specialized functions. For example, Bangladesh Rubber Board was established in 2019 through the provisions of the Bangladesh Rubber Board Act, 2013 (Act No. 19 of 2013) to:

(a) formulate policies and plans for rubber cultivation and rubber industry and provide recommendations, advice and assistance to the Government in their implementation;
(b) identify land suitable for rubber cultivation in collaboration with all concerned ministries or departments;
(c) select suitable persons or institutions interested in rubber cultivation and to make recommendations to the Government for leasing or allotment of land in their favor;
(d) make necessary recommendations to the Government to take necessary legal action against the breach of the terms of the lease or allotment agreement;
(e) motivate the owners or, as the case may be, the allotted recipients to create a rubber plantation;
(f) provide necessary assistance to the owners or, as the case may be, the allotted recipients in obtaining loans and insurance facilities for the creation of rubber plantations and the establishment and development of the rubber industry;
(g) provide scientific, technical and economic assistance to the owners of rubber plantations or, as the case may be, to the allotted recipients;
(h) provide training to the owners, workers and employees of rubber plantations;

(i) advise the Government to discourage the production, import, marketing and use of harmful synthetic rubber materials;
(j) provide technical and financial assistance for the production of fruit, forest or medicinal trees and other auxiliary cash crops in unsuitable parts of rubber plantation land (above 35 degree slope or in waterlogged areas);
(k) provide necessary assistance for marketing or, as the case may be, export of the rubber produced;
(l) create and regularly update the database on any subject related to bar cultivation and rubber industry;
(m) observe and monitor the overall progress of rubber cultivation and rubber industry;
(n) take necessary welfare measures for the workers and employees involved in the rubber plantation and rubber industry;
(o) make recommendations to the Government for the establishment of a Rubber Research Institute for research on rubber cultivation and rubber industry;
(p) assist in the extraction, processing and marketing of rubber wood that has lost its life cycle;
(q) provide necessary assistance in rubber cultivation rehabilitation activities; and
(r) perform any other duty assigned by the Government from time to time.

111. Similarly, following the decision of the High Court Division of the Bangladesh Supreme Court in Writ Petition No. 3503/2009 regarding the protection of four main rivers which surround Dhaka, i.e., Buriganga, Turag, Balu and Shitalakkha, the National River Protection Commission Act, 2013 (Act No. 29 of 2013) was enacted to prevent illegal occupation of rivers, pollution of water and environment, pollution of rivers caused by industrial factories, illegal constructions and various irregularities and ensuring multidimensional use of rivers for socio-economic development including restoration of the normal flow of rivers, proper maintenance thereof and making them navigable. The Commission is statutorily responsible for recommending the government, namely:

(a) for coordination of the functions among all concerned Ministries or Divisions related with river;
(b) to free the rivers from illegal occupation and to prevent reoccupation;
(c) to evict illegal installations established on the rivers or on the banks of rivers;
(d) to keep the water of rivers free from pollution;
(e) regarding excavation of extinct or moribund rivers;
(f) for developing information store house relating to rivers;
(g) regarding the matter relating to the development of rivers;
(h) to ensure environmentally balanced and sustainable management of rivers;
(i) to take short-term and long-term scheme to conserve rivers;
(j) for taking actions to increase public awareness;

(k) after monitoring the activities regarding conservation of rivers and regular inspection;
(l) after reviewing practical uses of existing different laws and policies related with the conservation of rivers and if necessary to amend the Act and policies; and
(m) to keep the canals, water bodies and coastal areas of the country free from occupation and pollution.[93]

112. It may be relevant to share here that in the historic judgment which bestowed the rives the legal personality in Bangladesh, the National River Protection Commission was declared as the 'legal guardian' of the rivers in Bangladesh.

§5. Sources of Environmental Law

113. Environment-related problems are local, regional and international in nature, and so are the initiatives taken by various countries in this regard. The IEL, being part of public international law, shares the same sources of international law as incorporated in article 38 (1) of the Statute of the International Court of Justice. These are: international conventions, international customs, general principles of law recognized by civilized nations, judicial decisions and the teachings of the most highly qualified publicists of the various nations.

114. Though the governance of environmental issues at the international level was not entirely new and some bilateral and multilateral treaties or agreements were available, the Charter of the United Nations, 1945 did not include provisions directly on environmental issues. Subsequently, with the establishment of the United Nations Environment Programme (UNEP) in June 1972, as the main responsible body authorized, *inter alia*, to coordinate UN's environment-related activities, set the global environmental agenda, promote the coherent implementation of the environmental dimension of sustainable development, etc., situation started to evolve and various Multilateral Environmental Agreements (MEAs) have been introduced since then. Though a generally accepted definition of MEAs is difficult to share, many of the rules and principles of IEL are derived from MEAs, which are one of the most important authoritative sources of international law as reflected in article 38(1) of the Statute of the International Court of Justice.

115. Hundreds of international instruments focusing on different aspects of the environment and components such as biological diversity, chemicals and waste, climate and atmosphere, environmental governance, land and agriculture and marine and fresh water have been adopted by way of bilateral, regional and multilateral agreements and treaties.[94] Of these, a list of major IEL MEAs includes: the International Convention for the Prevention of Pollution from Ships, 1973; the World

93. Section 12, the National River Protection Commission Act, 2013 (Act No. 29 of 2013).
94. Access information on Multilateral Environmental Agreements, https://www.informea.org/.

Heritage Convention, 1975; the Convention on Wetlands of International Importance, 1975; the Convention on International Trade in Endangered Species of Wild Fauna and Flora, 1975 (CITES); the Convention on the Conservation of Migratory Species of Wild Animals, 1983; the Vienna Convention for the Protection of the Ozone Layer, 1985; the Vienna Convention for the Protection of the Ozone Layer, 1988; the Basel Convention on the Control of Transboundary Movements of Hazardous Wastes and their Disposal, 1989; the UNFCCC, 1992; the Convention on Biological Diversity, 1992; the International Plant Protection Convention, 1992; the United Nations Convention to Combat Desertification, 1996; the International Treaty on Plant Genetic Resources for Food and Agriculture, 2001; the Rotterdam Convention on the Prior Informed Consent Procedure for Certain Hazardous Chemicals and Pesticides in International Trade, 2004; the Stockholm Convention on Persistent Organic Pollutants, 2004; the Minamata Convention on Mercury, 2013; the United Nations Watercourses Convention, 2014.

116. It has already been shared that immediately after the Independence of the country in 1971, Bangladesh delegations led by A. Razzak, Ambassador Extraordinary and Plenipotentiary to Sweden attended the historic Stockholm Conference on the Human Environment, 1972. Since then, Bangladesh has signed, ratified, or accessed many of the MEAs containing provisions on the protection or preservation of environmental components. Though it is difficult to share a precise list of such MEAs, it should be appreciated that the total number of these MEAs shall be quite high as it has been reported that the country has already ratified or accessed ocean-related more than a hundred instruments and implemented around ninety of such instruments which were endorsed by the United Nations.[95]

117. In the absence of a precise list of such MEAs, a non-exhausted list, containing the main MEAs only, which are signed, acceded and ratified by Bangladesh, is shared below:[96]

1. The International Plant Protection Convention (Rome, 1951) [accessed on 1 September 1978].
2. The International Convention for the Prevention of Pollution of the Sea by Oil (London, 1954 (as amended on 11 April 1962 and 21 October 1969)) [entry into force on 12 December 1981].
3. The Plant Protection Agreement for the South East Asia and Pacific Region (as amended) (Rome, 1956) [accessed on 4 December 1974].
4. The Treaty Banning Nuclear Weapon Tests in the Atmosphere, in Outer Space and under Water (Moscow, 1963) [signed on 13 April 1985].

95. General Economic Division, Bangladesh Planning Commission, Ministry of Planning, Government of Bangladesh, 'Sustainable Development Goals Bangladesh Progress Report, 2020', June 2020, p. 186.
96. Source: United Nations Information Portal on Multilateral Environmental Agreements, Bangladesh, https://www.informea.org/en/countries/bd/party-status. For more, *see*, University of Oregon, International Environmental Agreements (IEA) Database Project on Bangladesh, https://iea.uoregon.edu/country-members/Bangladesh.

5. The Treaty on Principles governing the Activities of States in the Exploration and use of outer Space Including the Moon and Other Celestial Bodies (London, Moscow, Washington, 1967) [accessed on 14 January 1986].
6. The International Convention Relating to Intervention on the High Seas in Cases of Oil Pollution Casualties (Brussels, 1969) [ratified on 4 February 1982].
7. The Convention on Wetlands of International Importance especially as Waterfowl Habitat (Ramsar, 1971) ('Ramsar Convention') [ratified on 20 April 1992].
8. The Convention on the Prohibition of the Development, (Biological) and Toxic Weapons, and on Their Destruction (London, Moscow, Washington, 1972) [ratified on 13 March 1985].
9. The Convention Concerning the Protection of the World Cultural and Natural Heritage (Paris, 1972) [accessed on 3 August 1983 and ratified on 3 November 1983].
10. The Convention on International Trade in Endangered Species of Wild Fauna and Flora, 1973 [signed on 20 November 1981 and ratified on 18 February 1982].
11. The United Nations Convention on the Law of the Sea, 1982 [ratified on 10 December 1982].
12. The Convention for the Protection of the Ozone Layer (Vienna, 1985) [accessed on 2 August 1990 and ratified on 31 October 1990].
13. Montreal Protocol on Substances that Deplete the Ozone Layer (Montreal 1987) [accessed on 2 August 1990 and ratified on 31 October 1990].
14. London Amendment to the Montreal Protocol on Substances that Deplete the Ozone Layer (London, 1990, Copenhagen Amendment) [accessed on 18 March 1994, ratified on 16 June 1994].
15. The Convention on Early Notification of a Nuclear Accident (Vienna, 1986) [ratified on 7 January 1988, entry into force on 7 February 1988].
16. The Convention on Assistance in the Case of a Nuclear Accident of Radiological Emergency (Vienna, 1986) [ratified on 7 January 1988 and entry into force on 7 February 1988].
17. The Agreement on the Network of Aquaculture Centres in Asia and the Pacific (Bangkok, 1988) [ratified on 15 May 1990].
18. The Convention on the Control of Transboundary Movements of Hazardous Wastes and Their Disposal (Basel, 1989) [accessed on 1 April 1993].
19. The International Convention on Oil Pollution Preparedness, Response and Cooperation (London, 1990) [signed on 30 November 1990].
20. The United Nations Framework Convention on Climate Change (New York, 1992) [signed on 9 June 1992 and ratified on 16 February 1994].
21. The Convention on Biological Diversity (Rio De Janeiro, 1992) [signed on 5 June 1992 and ratified on 3 May 1994].
22. International Convention to Combat Desertification (Paris 1994) [signed on 21 June 1994 and ratified in October 1995].

23. The Convention on the Prohibition of Military or Any Other Hostile Use of Environmental Modification Techniques (Geneva, 1976) [accessed on 3 October 1979].
24. The Convention on the Conservation of Migratory Species of Wild Animals (Bonn, 1979) [signed on 1 September 2005 and entered into force on 1 December 2005].
25. The Agreement Relating to the Implementation of Part XI of the United Nations Convention on the Law of the Sea of 10 December 1982 on Fish Stocks (New York, 1994) [signed on 28 July 1996].
26. The Agreement for the Implementation of the Provisions of the United Nations Convention on the Law of the Sea of 10 December 1982 Relating to the Conservation and Management of Stradling Fish Stocks and Highly Migratory Fish Stocks (New York, 1995) [signed on 4 December 1995].
27. The Convention on the Prohibition of the Development, Production, Stockpiling and Use of Chemical Weapons and on their Destruction (Paris, 1993) [signed on 14 January 1993].
28. The United Nations Convention to Combat Desertification in those Countries Experiencing Serious Drought and/or Desertification, particularly in Africa (Paris, 1994) [signed on 14 October 1994 and ratified on 26 January 1996].
29. The Convention on Nuclear Safety (Vienna, 1994) [signed on 14 November 1995 and ratified on 21 September 1995].
30. Cartagena Protocol on Biosafety to the Convention on Biological Diversity [signed on 24 May 2000 and ratified on 5 February 2004].
31. The Minamata Convention on Mercury, 2013 [signed on 10 October 2012].
32. The United Nations Treaty on the Prohibition of Nuclear Weapons [signed on 20 September 2017].
33. The Stockholm Convention on Persistent Organic Pollutants (Stockholm, 2001) [signed on 23 May 2001 and ratified on 12 March 2007].
34. The Framework Agreement on International Solar Alliance (Marrakech, Morocco, 2016) [signed on 15 November 2016].

118. Bangladesh has signed the historic Paris Agreement on Climate Change on 22 April 2016 and ratified the Agreement on 21 September 2016. The Agreement entered into force on 4 November 2016. In the historic Paris Agreement to the UNFCCC adopted in the COP21, the global community pledged to reduce global warming within 1.5 to 2 degree Celsius above the pre-industrial level. In September 2015, Bangladesh submitted the Intended National Determined Contribution (INDC) to this Paris Agreement and committed to reduce the GHGs 15% by 2030. In that contribution, 12 million tons (5%) would be an unconditional reduction in GHS emission from a business as usual (BAU) level by 2030 and a further 24 million tons (10%) conditional reduction with the support from the international community.

119. Recently, in August 2021, the country updated the Nationally Determined Contribution (NDC) considering the year 2012 as the base year and pledged to reduce GHG emissions in Energy (power, transport, energy use in industry, residential, commercial, agriculture and brick manufacturing, and fugitive emission), Industrial Processes & Product Use (IPPU) (Cement and Fertilizer), Agriculture, Forestry and other Land use (AFOLU) (agriculture and livestock, forestry), and waste sectors (Municipal Solid Waste and wastewater). Interestingly, the country, following IPCC guidelines and stakeholder consultation, updated the target and committed to reduce GHS emission, i.e., 27.56 and 61.9 Mt CO_2e below BAU level unconditionally and in conditional scenario respectively in 2030.

120. Besides, the country is also a part of relevant initiatives taken regionally. Bangladesh is a member of the South Asia Co-operative Environment Programme (SACEP), which was created in 1981 to recognize environmental degradation caused by factors like poverty, over population, over consumption and wasteful production threatening economic development and human survival; integrate environment and development as essential prerequisites to sustainable development; and, act on cooperation in the South Asian region where many ecological and development problems transcend national and administrative boundaries. SACEP has been working in the area of biodiversity conservation, sustainable consumption and production, waste management, climate change, etc. This organization has been serving as the secretariat for the South Asian Sees Programme under the UNEP's Regional Seas Programme. Besides, one of the important contributions of SACEP is the adoption of the Malé Declaration on Control and Prevention of Air Pollution and its Likely Transboundary Effects for South Asia adopted at the Seventh meeting of the Governing Council of SACEP in April 1998.

I. Status of International Law in Bangladesh

121. Before any discussion on the national laws related to the environment and its various components, it will be significant to comprehend the status of international law in Bangladesh since IEL is a subset of public international law. The principle of IEL has officially been emerging in the last six decades, and the sources of environmental law in Bangladesh are derived from both the national legislation and in response to the obligations of the countries stemming from signing a party to multilateral environmental agreements.

122. Article 25 of the Bangladesh Constitution, 1972 provides that the 'state shall base its international relations on the principle of, *inter alia*, respect for international law and the principles enunciated in the United Nations Charter'. Therefore, this is a constitutional obligation upon the state to respect international law,[97] provided that a corresponding domestic legislation is enacted.[98] It will be relevant

97. *Professor Nurul Islam v. Bangladesh* [2000] 52 DLR (HCD) 413.

98. For a general discussion on the status of international law in Bangladesh; *see*, Kamal Hossain and Sharif Bhuiyan. *Bangladesh*, in *The Oxford Handbook of International Law in Asia and the Pacific*,

to share here that drawing on the spirits of different international instruments, Bangladesh has already enacted similar municipal legislation to give effect to the provisions of those international instruments.[99] However, it is to be remembered that since the provision on respect for international law was placed in article 25 which is encapsulated in Part II of the Constitution as a Fundamental Principles of State Policy meaning that the government will realize this gradually.

123. After the independence of the country, the Supreme Court first touched the issue of public international law in *Bangladesh v. Unimarine S.A. Panama*, 29 DLR (1977) 252, when the respondents-defendants claimed immunity of attachment of a foreign vessel before judgment as the said vessel was responsible for damage of 5,109 metric tons of wheat. While deciding the question of whether any private foreign entity, e.g., in this contested case, a foreign vessel, enjoys immunity and can be attached or not, Mr Justice KM Subhan held that: 'Immunity is available under the Public International Law to persons and properties of a classified person and mentioned in the list which is usually filed by foreign mission and International Agencies.' Dissatisfied with the decision of the HCD, the defendants moved to the AD with an appeal. The AD, though allowed the appeal and set aside the decision of the HCD considering the facts and interpreting the provisions of the domestic law, did not shed light on the public or private international law aspect of the issue in the judgment.

124. Subsequently, in the case of *Bangladesh v. Sombon Asavhan*, 32 DLR (1980) (SC) 194, when Thai fishing trawlers were captured by the Bangladesh Navy for illegally entering and fishing in the territorial waters of Bangladesh, while commenting on the application of Bangladesh Territorial Waters and Maritime Zones Act, 1974, Chief Justice Kemaluddin Hossain held that: '[t]he point touches upon International Law, since three foreign fishing trawlers are involved and they have been captured from a place over which Bangladesh claims sovereignty. We are, however, relieved from entering into long discussion of diverse laws, conventions, rules and practices of International Law since there is a complete code provided by our Municipal law. It is well settled that where there is municipal law on an international subject the national court's functions are to enforce the municipal law within the plain reading of the statute'.[100]

125. In the case of *Bangladesh National Women Lawyers Association (BNWLA) v. Government of Bangladesh*, 2011, 40 CLC (HCD) [4739]=1 BLD (HCD) (2011) 324, 18 BLC (HCD) (2013) 290, the HCD while framing directives/guidelines on

---

ed. Simon Chesterman, Hisashi Owada & Ben Saul (Oxford: Oxford University Press, 2019); Mohammad Shahabuddin (ed.). *Bangladesh and International Law* (London: Routledge, 2021); Sheikh Hafizur Rahman Karzon & Abdullah-Al-Faruque. 'Status of International Law under the Constitution of Bangladesh: An Appraisal.' *Bangladesh Journal of Law* 3, no. 1 (1999): 23–47; Christine Richardson & Md. Mostafa Hosain, 'Application of International Law in Bangladesh: An Analysis of the Supreme Court Judgments'. *Jagannath University Journal of Law* 1 (2015), 1–18.

99. *Unimarine S.A. Panama v. Bangladesh*, 31 DLR (AD) 112.

100. Sumaiya Khair. *Bringing International Human Rights Law Home: Trends and Practices of Bangladeshi Courts*. In *Asian Yearbook of International Law, Volume 17 (2011)*, 47–84, at p. 61.

'eve teasing' reiterated that '[w]hen there is a gap in the municipal law in addressing any issue, the courts may take recourse to international conventions and protocols on that issue for the purpose of formulating effective directives and guidelines to be followed by all concerned until the national legislature enacts laws in this regard'. While delivering the judgment, Mr Justice Sheikh Hassan Arif shared the highly regarded observation of Mr Justice Bimalendu Bikash Roy Chowdhury shared in the case of *Hussain Mohammad Ershad v. Bangladesh & others*, 21 BLD (AD) 2001, 69 where Justice Chowdhury stated as below:

> The national courts should not, I feel, straightway ignore the international obligations, which a country undertakes. If the domestic laws are not clear enough or there is nothing therein the national courts should draw upon the principles incorporated in the international instruments. But in the cases where the domestic laws are clear and inconsistent with the international obligations of the state concerned, the national courts will be obliged to respect the national laws, but shall draw the attention of the law makers to such inconsistencies.

126. Moreover, in the case of *Dr. Shipra Chaudhury and another v. Government of Bangladesh and others*, 2009, 38 CLC (HCD) [9178] = 29 BLD (HCD) (2009) 183, Justice Syed Mahmud Hossain opined that: 'Our courts will not enforce those Covenants [ICCPR and ICESCR] as treaties and conventions, even if ratified by the State, are not part of the corpus juris of the State unless these are incorporated in the municipal legislation. Therefore, this is generally the stand of the courts in Bangladesh regarding the implementation of the provisions of international instruments.[101] However, the court can look into these Conventions and Covenants as an aid to interpretation of the provisions of Part III, particularly to determine the rights implicit in the rights like the right to life and the right to liberty, but not enumerated in the Constitution.' In addition to this, in the case of *Anika Ali v. Rezwanul Ahsan*, 2011, 40 CLC (AD) [5145] =17 BLC (AD) (2012) 77, 17 MLR (AD) (2012) 49, Mr Justice Muhammad Imman Ali held that 'unless provisions of international instruments are contrary to our domestic laws, the beneficial provisions may profitably be referred to and implemented in appropriate cases'. Accordingly, in the case of *Allama Delawar Hossain Sayedee v. Bangladesh and others* (2009) 38 CLC (HCD) = 18 BLT (HCD) (2010) 188, it was held that since the provisions of article 13 of the Universal Declaration of Human Rights, 1948 were incorporated in the domestic laws of the country, such provisions shall be enforceable.

127. From the decisions of the Apex court of the country, it is evident that the international law doctrine of transformation or adoption, as opposed to the doctrine of incorporation, is followed in Bangladesh. As a result, signing an international treaty or multilateral agreement is not enough and in order to give effect to the provisions of the signed treaty, a corresponding national law is to be enacted. It can be seen that following this doctrine or adoption or incorporation, Bangladesh has already enacted some national laws to incorporate the provisions of international

101. *Robin Chowdhury @ Misba Uddin v. Anti-Corruption Commission and others* 2017 (1) LNJ 152.

laws.[102] Nevertheless, Bangladeshi courts are free to refer to the beneficial provisions of the international instruments in appropriate cases if they are not contrary to the national laws.

II. Sources of Environmental Law in Bangladesh

128. In order to understand the different legal issues covered in this monograph, it will be beneficial to have some background discussion on the legal system of the country.[103] Otherwise, for an outsider, some of the words, such as 'order' and 'regulation' as frequently used in the domestic legal arena, may create confusion.[104]

129. The legal system of Bangladesh is influenced by the English common law legal system which was instilled during the British colonial regime between 1757 and 1947, except for the personal and family disputes matters where the provisions of the religious laws are followed. Thus, family matters relating to the believers of different religions as practised in the country such as Islam, Hinduism, Christianity and Buddhism are mainly dealt with personal laws derived from the respective religious texts.

130. The Constitution of the People's Republic of Bangladesh, 1972 is the supreme law of the Republic, and it is not constitutionally possible to enact any law inconsistent with the provisions of the Constitution. If any law is found inconsistent with the provisions of the Constitution that other law shall, to the extent of the inconsistency, be void.[105] Being a country predominantly influenced by the English common law legal system, the Supreme Court of Bangladesh consisting of AD and HCD performs the duty to interpret the Constitution and other laws of the land.[106]

131. Article 152 of the Constitution of Bangladesh, 1972 defines 'law' as any 'Act, ordinance, order, rule, regulation, bye law (by-law), notification or other legal instrument, and any custom or usage, having the force of law in Bangladesh.' Of these, three types of laws, i.e., Acts of Parliament, Ordinance and Presidential

102. For example, Bangladesh signed the Convention on the Prohibition of the Development, Production, Stockpiling and Use of Chemical Weapons and on their Destruction, 1993 on 14.03.1993 and in order to give effect to the provisions of this Convention, Bangladesh enacted the Chemical Weapon (Prohibition) Act, 2006 (Act No. 37 of 2006). It will be pertinent to share here that the Preamble to this Act also clearly provides that since Bangladesh became the party to the Convention on the Prohibition of the Development, Production, Stockpiling and Use of Chemical Weapons and on their Destruction, it is necessary to enact a law and that is why this Law has been enacted.
103. For a detailed discussion on the historical background of the legal system of Bangladesh, *See*, *Bangladesh, represented by the Secretary, Ministry of Law, Justice and Parliamentary Affairs and others v. Bangladesh Legal Aid and Services Trust (BLAST)*, 8 SCOB [2016] AD 1.
104. For an updated overview of Bangladesh legal system, *see*, E. Karim. *UPDATE: The Legal System of the Peoples' Republic of Bangladesh* (July/August 2018), http://www.nyulawglobal.org/globalex/Bangladesh1.html.
105. Articles 7(2) & 26(2), the Constitution of the People's Republic of Bangladesh, 1972.
106. Articles 103(2)(a) & 110, the Constitution of the People's Republic of Bangladesh, 1972.

Orders, are treated as 'primary legislation', and the 'rules', 'regulations', bye-law (by-law) and notification can be considered as 'subsidiary legislation' in the Bangladesh context.

132. In this above definition of 'law', the word 'Act' means the Act of Parliament,[107] 'Ordinance' denotes the Ordinances promulgated by the President of Bangladesh when the Parliament stands dissolved, or the Parliament is not in session,[108] and 'Order' means Presidential Orders made after the independence of the country in 1972 and 1973. Along with these Presidential Orders, there are at least four Acting President's Orders made during and after the Liberation War in 1971, which will also be included in the definition of the word 'Order'.[109] These 'Orders' must not be confused with the orders pronounced by the court of laws,[110] statutory orders[111] and 'Orders' as included in the Code of Civil Procedure, where the word 'Order' is apparently used to mean various Chapters of the Schedules.

133. The Ordinances promulgated as per Article 93 of the Constitution of Bangladesh, 1972 deserve special mention in the legal history of Bangladesh as many such Ordinances were promulgated during the two martial law regimes from 15th August 1975 to 9th April 1979 and 24th March, 1982 to 11th November, 1986. These Ordinances were in force for more than twenty-five years. Subsequently, the Constitution (Fifth Amendment) Act, 1979 (Act No. I of 1979) validating the Martial Law was declared void in the judgment pronounced by the Appellate Division of the Supreme Court of Bangladesh (in Civil Petition for Leave to Appeal No. 1044-1045/2009). Similarly, the Constitution (Seventh Amendment) Act, 1986 (Act No. I of 1986) validating the Martial Law was also declared void in the judgment pronounced by the Appellate Division of the Supreme Court of Bangladesh (in Civil Appeal No. 48/2011). Since these Martial Laws were declared unconstitutional, all

107. There are more than 1,000 Acts of Parliament in force in the country. Hardbound copy of Bangladesh Code contains a total of 956 Acts, Ordinances and President's Orders enacted between September 1836 and January 2007. Part V, Ch. II (Arts 80–92) of the Constitution of Bangladesh, 1972 deals with the lawmaking process and financial procedure. The law-making process can be found at http://www.parliament.gov.bd/index.php/en/parliamentary-business/business-of-the-house/bill-and-legislation/legislative-procedure. *See also*, G. Murphy. 'How Legislation Is Drafted and Enacted in Bangladesh'. *Statute Law Review* 27 (2006): 133–149.
108. *See*, for reference, Art. 93 of the Constitution of Bangladesh, 1972. It should be noted that an Ordinance so made must be presented before Parliament at its first meeting following the promulgation of the Ordinance. Unless such Ordinance is earlier repealed, it shall cease to have effect at the expiration of thirty days after it is so presented or, if a resolution disapproving of the Ordinance is passed by the Parliament before such expiration, upon the passing of the resolution.
109. The Bangladesh (Collection of Taxes) Order, 1971 (Acting President's Order No. 1 of 1971), The Bangladesh (Administration of Banks) Order, 1971 (Acting President's Order No. 3 of 1971), The Bangladesh (Taking Over of Control and Management of Industrial and Commercial Concerns) Order, 1972 (Acting President's Order No. 1 of 1972), The Bangladesh (Administration of Financial Institutions) Order, 1972 (Acting President's Order No. 3 of 1972).
110. According to s. 2(14) and 2(2) of the Code of Civil Procedure, 1908 (Act No. V of 1908), 'order' means the formal expression of any decision of a Civil Court. An order is not a decree, which is the formal expression of an adjudication which conclusively determines the rights of the parties.
111. A statutory order means an order passed as required by law and if so passed it would have the force of law as if made by the legislature itself. *DCCI v. Secretary, Ministry of Works*, 39 DLR 145.

the Ordinances enforced and promulgated by Martial Law Proclamation between the period from 15 August 1975 to 9 April 1979 and from 24 March 1982 to 11 November, 1986 respectively have ceased to have an effect due to omission of articles 3A and 18, and 19 respectively of the Fourth Schedule to the Constitution of the People's Republic of Bangladesh regarding ratification and confirmation of the said Ordinances by the Constitution (Fifteenth Amendment) Act, 2011 (Act No. XIV of 2011).

134. As a result, the government has decided to make new laws in Bangla by way of necessary amendment and modification of such Ordinances as may be considered necessary after reviewing the necessity and relevance of such Ordinances promulgated. Accordingly, the government has been updating some of the Ordinances promulgated during these martial law regimes.[112]

135. However, some Ordinances promulgated during these martial law regimes have been maintained through the provisions of the Implementation of Certain Ordinances promulgated from 15th August 1975 to 9th April 1979 (Special Provisions) Act, 2013 (Act No. VI of 2013) and the Implementation of Certain Ordinances promulgated from 24th March 1982 to 11th November 1986 (Special Provisions) Act, 2013 (Act No. VII of 2013). As a result, one may still see some of these Ordinances available in the Bangladesh Code.

136. Rules and regulations, bye-laws (by-laws), etc., are regarded as delegated and subsidiary legislation. Parliament, by the provisions of an Act of Parliament, can delegate its lawmaking power to any person or authority to make statutory orders, rules, regulations, bye-laws or other instruments having a legislative effect.[113] Usually, the government Ministry that is in charge of implementing any law, by being empowered by the Parliament through a primary legislation, e.g., an Act of Parliament, frames subsidiary legislations such as orders, rules, regulations, bye-laws or other instruments having legislative effect containing detailed provisions in order to assist the stakeholders in the implementation of that law.

137. In *Raghib Rauf Chowdhury v. Bangladesh and others* 9 SCOB [2017] HCD, 34 at paragraph 37, it was held that the Parliament can delegate its power to any person or authority by an Act of Parliament, to make orders, rules, regulations, bye-laws or other instruments having a legislative effect. From a plain reading of Article 65 of the Constitution, it can be seen that unless and until the Parliament delegates its power to any authority or any department within the limit of the country, they cannot make any Rule and thus, the Parliament is the sole authority to enact a rule or law and only the Parliament can delegate its powers to any authority to formulate regulations or any guidelines.

---

112. For example, the Bangladesh Sangbad Sangstha Ordinance, 1979 (Ordinance No. XX of 1979) was repealed and updated by the Bangladesh Sangbad Sangstha Act, 2018 (Act No. LXV of 2018). Similarly, the Marine Fisheries Ordinance, 1983 (Ordinance No. XXXV of 1983) was repealed and updated by the Marine Fisheries Act, 2020 (Act No. 19 of 2020).
113. Proviso to Art. 65(1), the Constitution of Bangladesh, 1972.

138. The word 'regulation' may cause some confusion as the word is used mostly as subsidiary legislation in the legal arena of Bangladesh. However, there are some 'regulations' that have the status of primary legislation since historically primary laws were known as 'regulations'.[114] According to the Rules of Business and its Schedule I, i.e., Allocation of Business, these 'regulations' are framed by the administrative departments established under various ministries of the government.

139. All Bangladeshi existing primary laws are available in the Bangladesh Code containing laws since 1836.[115] Bangladesh Code was updated in 2006 in thirty-eight volumes. Some of the 'Regulations',[116] though they have the status of primary legislation, were not included in the Bangladesh Code as section 6 of the Bangladesh Laws (Revision and Declaration) Act, 1973 provides to include only the Acts of Parliament, Ordinances and President's Orders in the Bangladesh Code.

140. In the definition of 'law' under Article 152 of the Constitution, 1972, 'bye laws (by-laws)' are made by the statutory public authorities, i.e., any public or private body, such as the Bangladesh Rubber Board, which is established following the enactment of a statute; 'notification' means the Gazette notifications usually published by Bangladesh Government Press.[117] For this monograph, it will be pertinent to share that the DoE regularly publishes circulars and the BFD also publishes some Gazette declaring various places as, e.g., protected forests.

141. Generally speaking, the phrase 'legal instruments' denote the documents executed between parties such as deeds, contracts and agreements. These notifications and instruments have a binding effect between the executing parties if properly made following the proper legal requirements derived from the provisions of different domestic laws. In the case of *AZ Rafique Ahmed v. Bangladesh Council of Scientific and Industrial Research*, 31 DLR (1979) 222, when a body was created by a resolution of a Ministry, a question was raised whether a resolution is a law as it is not made in exercise of any lawmaking power of the President. The AD held

---

114. Under the Regulating Act, 1773 of British India, the Governor-General in Council sitting at Fort William in Bengal was empowered to make Regulation for good governance of the East India Company's settlement at Fort William and other subordinate factories and places. Accordingly, the Governor-General passed hundreds of Regulations between 1773 and 1833. Subsequently, the Charter Act, 1833 empowered the Governor-General in Council at Kolkata to make laws for the whole of India, and since then the laws passed by the Governor-General were called Acts. *See*, Bangladesh Law Commission Report No. 116 published in 2012.
115. Section 6 of the Bangladesh Laws (Revision and Declaration) Act 1973 provides that 'All Acts of Parliament, Ordinances and President's Orders in force in Bangladesh shall be printed in chronological order under the name and style of the Bangladesh Code.'
116. The Wills and Intestacy Regulation, 1799 (Regulation V of 1799); The Charitable Endowment, Public Buildings and Escheats Regulation, 1810 (Regulation XIX of 1810); The Government Indemnity Regulation (Regulation XI of 1822); The Alluvion and Diluvian Regulation 1825 (Regulation XI of 1825); The Revenue Commissioners Regulation, 1829(Regulation 1 of 1829); The Sati Regulation, 1829 (Regulation XVII of 1829); The Land Revenue (Settlement and Deputy Collectors) Regulation, 1833 (Regulation IX of 1833).
117. It may be relevant to share here that Gazettes are of two types: Weekly Gazettes and Extraordinary Gazettes. Matters of legal nature are normally in Extraordinary Gazettes. *See*, Bangladesh Government Press, https://www.dpp.gov.bd/bgpress/index.php/document/gazettes/140.

that the resolution is covered by the expression 'other legal instrument'. Finally, customary laws and usages, which are extensively followed, e.g., in the Chittagong Hill tracts region of the country, come 'within the ambits of law and as such they cannot be violated'.[118]

142. The Alluvion and Diluvian Regulation, 1825 (Bengal Regulation XI of 1825), apparently one of the oldest laws still in force, contains rules for the general information of individuals, guidance of Courts of Judicature, and for the protection of environmental components. While the Regulation provides for the settlement of the claims and disputes as to alluvial lands by clearly recognized and established usage, and also provides for how such claims and disputes are to be settled when there is no such established usage in sections 2 and 3, respectively, section 5 of the Regulation provides that '[n]othing in this Regulation shall be construed to justify any encroachments by individuals on the beds or channels of navigable rivers, or to prevent Zila Magistrate or any other officers of the Government who may be duly empowered for that purpose from removing obstacles which appear to interfere with the safe and customary navigation of such rivers, or which shall in any respect obstruct the passage of boats by tracking on the banks of such rivers, or otherwise'.

143. Bangla is the state language of the Republic.[119] In 1987, the *Bangla Bhasha Procholon Ain*, 1987 (Act No. 2 of 1987) (The Introduction of Bangla Language Act, 1987) was enacted, and it was provided that after the enactment of the law, everywhere in Bangladesh including in government offices, courts, semi-government and statutory public authorities, except in case of correspondence with foreign countries, examination and cross-examination in the court of laws and all other legal activities shall be written in Bangla.[120] Bangla is widely used as a language of business in subordinate courts. Whereas, in the Supreme Court, English is used as a language of business though it is reported that some members of the Bar and Bench have started using Bangla even in the Supreme Court. One may find that in many instances, honourable Judges of the Supreme Court have delivered Judgments in Bangla also and sometimes used the English equivalent of some of the terms which are not easily understandable or do not have equal words or expressions in Bangla.

144. Following the enactment of this law, it can be seen that since 1987, almost all the Acts of Parliaments have been enacted in Bangla. In 1998, the government asked for the opinion of the Law Commission of Bangladesh regarding the making

---

118. *Pruesiau Aug Marma and another v. Aungmra Shang Marma and another*, 14 SCOB [2020] HCD. Usages are also recognized in ss 2 and 3 of the Alluvion and Diluvian Regulation, 1825 (Bengal Regulation XI of 1825), which is apparently one of the oldest laws in force, containing rules for the general information of individuals as well as for the guidance of Courts of Judicature, in the country which provide for how the claims and disputes as to alluvial lands are to be decided when there are clearly recognized and established usage, and when there is no such established usage.
119. Article 3, the Constitution of the People's Republic of Bangladesh, 1972.
120. Section 3, the *Bangla Bhasha Procholon Ain*, 1987 (Act No. 2 of 1987).

or introduction of authentic texts of authorized translation of the original Bangladesh texts of all such laws.[121] The Law Commission recommended positively by stating that to attract foreign investment and to transact trade and commerce, exports and imports with foreign countries on a competitive basis, the laws, rules and regulations on trade, commerce, investment, exports, imports, industries, banking, etc., which are enacted or framed in Bangla hardly have any use. The Law Commission, by sharing that the availability of unofficial translations has no legal sanction or authenticity, further proposed to include the provision for making or introducing authentic English text.[122] As a result, some laws, having commercial or international implications, though were originally enacted in Bangla, are subsequently translated into English by the drafting wing of the Ministry of Law, Justice and Parliamentary Affairs, and only these versions of laws are treated as authentic texts of authorized translation.[123] On the other hand, some Acts of Parliaments that were enacted before 1987 in English were translated into Bangla later on due to their importance and wide use.[124]

---

121. The Law Commission of Bangladesh was established through the provisions of the Law Commission Act, 1996 (Act No. XIX of 1996). The Preamble of the Law provides that in the context of the changes in the socio-economic conditions of the country, introduction of free market economy and huge backlog of cases pending for trial in different courts, and for re-examination of the legal aspects of the fundamental human rights situation, and repeal of the obsolete laws for making provisions in respect of other matters of public importance including upgrading the standards of the legal education, and for making recommendation to the government for review and timely reform of the existing laws and enactment of new laws, as the case may be, it is expedient and necessary to establish a permanent Law Commission. The Law Commission is empowered, *inter alia*, to identify the causes for delay in the disposal of civil and criminal cases at various tiers of courts and to expedite disposal of the cases and to ensure justice as speedily as possible, to recommend amendment of the laws or enactment of new laws in appropriate cases after review and research of the relevant laws, to recommend on the legal matters referred by the government from time to time. *See*, s. 6, the Law Commission Act, 1996 (Act No. XIX of 1996).
122. The Law Commission, Government of the People's Republic of Bangladesh, Report on Necessity of English Translation of Law drafted in Bengali, Report No. 14, date of submission 14 May 1998.
123. For example, the Bangladesh Telecommunication Regulation Act, 2001 (Act No. XVIII of 2001) was originally enacted in Bangla, but it was subsequently translated into English. Similarly, the Companies Act, 1994 (Act No. 18 of 1994), the Copyright Act, 2000 (Act No. 28 of 2000), the Chemical Weapons (Prohibition) Act, 2006 (Act No. 37 of 2000), the Public Procurement Act, 2006 (Act No. 24 of 2006), the Right to Information Act, 2009 (Act No. 20 of 2009), the Trade Mark Act, 2009 (Act No. 19 of 2009), the Money Laundering Prevention Act, 2012 (Act No. 5 of 2012), the Breast-milk Substitutes, Infant Foods, Commercially Manufactured Complementary Foods and the Accessories Thereof (Regulation of Marketing) Act, 2013 (Act No. 35 of 2013), etc., were all enacted originally in Bangla, but later on translated into English. Nevertheless, it may be relevant to share here that, sometimes such authentic translation may not be able to present the content of the law in a clear manner. In the case of *Jamuna Television Limited and another v. Bangladesh and others*, 2005, 34 CLC (HCD) [8911] = 57 DLR (2005) 345, referring to the authentic English translation of the of the Bangladesh Telecommunication Act (Act No. 18 of 2001) shared by the then Attorney General, Md. Abdur Rashid J. mentioned: 'After the commencement of the Act, the Government . . . published a translation of the Act, which is known to be as Authentic English Text of the Act. However, in case of conflict between the Act and the said translation, the Act shall prevail. Learned Attorney-General read all relevant provisions of the English version. Sometimes, we found the translation led us to nowhere.'
124. For example, the Mines Act, 1923 (Act No. IV of 1923) was originally enacted in English. Later on, on 15 Nov. 2007, the Ministry of Law, Justice and Parliamentary Affairs published the Bangla translated version of the law. Similarly, some other laws which were originally enacted in English

145. Environment-related provisions can be found in both general and special law. For example, the main substantive criminal law of the country, i.e., the Penal Code, 1860 (XLV of 1860), contains general provisions on various types of pollution without mention of the word 'pollution'; whereas, the BECA, 1995 (Act No. 1 of 1995), a special law in relation to environment conservation, also contains provisions on pollution.[125] Again, being a special law, the BECA, 1995 (Act No. 1 of 1995) though contains provisions prohibiting the filling of wetlands (section 6E), an additional Act of Parliament, i.e., the Conservation of Playgrounds, Open Spaces, Parks and Natural Reservoirs in all Metropolitan, Divisional Cities and District Towns including Municipal Areas of the Country Act, 2000 (Act XXXVI of 2000) has also been enacted in this regard. Therefore, this will be relevant to share the differences between these two categories of law, i.e., general law and special law. According to the rules of interpretation of statutes, if there are any general laws and special laws on the same issue, the provisions of the special law will prevail. The same rule is also followed in Bangladesh, and therefore, even though one may find legal provisions on some issues in the domestic general law, the provisions of the specially enacted laws shall prevail. Similarly, if any legal remedy is ordinarily available under both general law and special law, the remedy prescribed by the special law must be sought in exclusion of the one available under the general law.[126] When a provision of law in a statute is amended by a subsequent-Amendment Act and such amended provision comes into force, the subsequent amended provision becomes part of the original statute.[127]

146. In relation to the content of this monograph, various directives, notifications, instructions and guidelines issued by the relevant ministries, administrative departments and regulators will be discussed. All these are crucial and binding on the subjects even though these are not included within the definition of 'law' under Article 152 of the Constitution of Bangladesh, 1972.

III. National Policies on Environmental Components

147. Bangladesh has adopted several national policies relating to the protection of various components of the environment. A list of some of the policies includes: the National Land Use Policy, 2001; the Coastal Zone Policy, 2005; the National Water Policy, 1999; the National Policy for Safe Water Supply and Sanitation, 1998; the National Fisheries Policy, 1998; the National Livestock Development Policy, 2007; the National Seed Policy, 1993; the National Agriculture Policy, 2010; the

---

were subsequently translated into Bangla. For example, the Bangladesh Small and Cottage Industries Corporation Act, 1957 (East Pakistan Act No. XVII of 1957), the *Bangladesh Sangbad Shangtha* Ordinance, 1979 (Ordinance No. XX of 1979), the Administrative Tribunal Act, 1980 (Act No. VII of 1981), the Civil Aviation Authority Ordinance, 1985 (Ordinance No. XXXVIII of 1985).

125. *See*, ss 3, 6 & 6D, the Bangladesh Environment Conservation Act, 1995 (Act No. 1 of 1995).

126. *DCCI v. Secretary*, Ministry of Works, 39 DLR 145.

127. *Mahfuzar Rahman v. Moshiur Rahman and others*, 2019 (Civil Revision No. 1199 of 2019).

National Plan for Disaster Management (2010–2015); and the National Environment Policy, 1992, which was recently updated in 2018.

148. In various parts of this monograph, various policies such as national policy on water, environment, forest and agriculture are discussed and therefore, an understanding of the legal status of the policy is necessary. Though it is difficult to explain the precise role and legal effect and status, these policies framed by the government play a very significant role in guiding various organs of government in running the state activities. Out of more than a hundred policies available in various sectors, two policies, i.e., the National Fisheries Policy, 1998 and the National Livestock Development Policy, 2007, could be identified which contain a provision on 'Legal status' of these policies. However, a closer look at the language of these provisions on 'Legal status' will reveal that these are merely the provisions on the scope of these Policies,[128] and there is no indication about the legal status of these Policies.

149. It will be pertinent to share that these national policies should not be confused with the 'Fundamental Principles of State Policy' as encapsulated in the Constitution of Bangladesh, 1972. The Fundamental Principles of State Policy are fundamental to the governance of Bangladesh. Constitutionally, these Principles are applied by the state in the making of laws. These Principles are also used as a guide to the interpretation of the Constitution and of the other laws of Bangladesh, and they form the basis of the work of the state and its citizens but are not judicially enforceable.[129]

150. Sometimes, an individual Department or organization can formulate a Policy on any issue containing detailed provisions on that issue, and such Policy provisions play an important role in regulating internal matters. For example, an organization can develop the ICT Policy containing provisions that the officers/staff of all levels, including subsidiary bodies, and all other granted users of ICT assets

128. **4. Legal status of the National Fisheries Policy.**

4.1 All the government and autonomous organizations, multi-national institutions, various non-governmental organizations, voluntary organizations, and persons who are working within the geographical territory of Bangladesh for the development of fisheries resources, harvesting and preservation, export-import or other businesses, related to the fisheries sector will be included in the National Fisheries Policy.

4.2 All the water bodies suitable for fisheries production and their fisheries resources and conservation, development and management will be under this policy.

3. Legal Status of the National Livestock Development Policy

All the government and autonomous organizations, multi-national institutions, NGOs, CBOs (community based organizations), and persons who are working within the geographical territory of Bangladesh for the management, development and conservation of livestock resources, import-export or other business related to the livestock sub-sector will be under the purview of National Livestock Development Policy.

129. Article 8(2), the Constitution of Bangladesh, 1972. The nature and judicial enforceability of these principles were evaluated in *Kudrat E-Elahi Panir v. Bangladesh*, 44 DLR (AD) 319.

should follow and define their responsibility for the protection and appropriate use of information, applications, computer system, and network.

151. Even though there are various policies, which are like plans or set of ideas the government uses in making decisions, their legal status is somehow uncertain. In *National Board of Revenue v. Abu Saeed Khan and others*, 2012, 41 CLC (AD) [8674] = 18 BLC (AD) (2013) 116, the AD of Bangladesh Supreme Court observed that: '[u]nless the policy or action is inconsistent with the Constitution and the laws, or arbitrary or irrational or by exercise of abuse of power, the court will not interfere. If the policy cannot be faulted on the grounds of arbitrariness/or irrationality or perversity or mala fide, judicial interference is impermissible even if it hurts the business interest of a party. The court cannot dictate either that a certain policy ought to have been adopted nor can it opine that a policy should be changed. An executive policy is not open to impeachment unless it infringes any constitutional or statutory provision. In economic regulation or tax matters, judicial restraint is necessary, and the judgment of the executive should not be interfered with'. Therefore, it is clear that the executives can formulate any Policy and implement the provisions thereof as long as they are not inconsistent with the Constitution or any statutory provisions. While the provisions of some of these Policies will be shared in different parts of this monograph discussing various environmental components, the salient features of some of the general policies are shared below.

IV. National Environment Policy, 2018

152. The National Environment Policy, 2018 was formulated with the vision of environmental protection, pollution control, biodiversity conservation and to ensure sustainable development by tackling the adverse effects of climate change. The National Environment Policy, 2018, while updating and replacing the provisions of the previous Policy available in this field, i.e., the National Environment Policy, 1992, was formulated to consider the following important matters:

- 1.1 to ensuring sustainable development by reducing population pressure on nature and natural resources;
- 1.2 to consider environmental protection as integral to all development activities aimed at meeting the needs of present and future generations;
- 1.3 to make the extraction, use and conservation of natural resources scientific;
- 1.4 to consider environmental impacts and risks in the extraction, use of natural resources;
- 1.5 to evaluate the ecosystem services while considering the economic contribution of natural resources to the national development plan;
- 1.6 to ensure the accessibility right and equity of the local people who are dependent on the natural resources and ecological services, and to prioritize the rights of the poor and underprivileged group of people in order to ensure the participation and equality of everyone concerned at the time of use of natural resources and ecological services;

1.7 to ensure the moderate use of water, land, natural gas and other natural resources and to take initiatives to prevent the waste of these in all the production processes and day-to-day activities;
1.8 to encourage the sustainable use of all resources, including new and renewable ones;
1.9 to strengthen food security and alleviate long-term poverty through biodiversity conservation;
1.10 to recover compensation from the person / organization responsible for environmental pollution by applying Polluter's Pay Principle;
1.11 to include provisions on environmental protection in all national policies, and to ensure the implementation of the provision of the environment policies at all levels of governmental and non-governmental activities;
1.12 to give priority to preventive measures over curative measures in order to protect the environment;
1.13 to take all development plans keeping in mind the adverse effects of climate change and to include adaptation and mitigation activities in the implementation;
1.14 to ensuring the sustainable use of ecosystem goods and services;
1.15 to implement 3R principle: reduce, reuse and recycle in the use of resources;
1.16 to implement environmental policy and all laws and regulations related to environmental protection, and to improve the institutional and legal capacity of institutions (government, local, private and technical) concerning the implementation and enforcement;
1.17 to ensure all types of disaster management including the impact of climate change, while constructing all types of infrastructure in the country;
1.18 to reduce short-lived climate pollutants harmful to public health and the environment;
1.19 to undertake development activities keeping in mind the concept of 'sustainable production and consumption' to meet the needs of present and future generations as an integral part of environmental protection;
1.20 to allocate funds required in all cases applicable for environmental protection and pollution control;
1.21 to undertake activities to expand the environment-friendly economy;
1.22 to include issues on environment and ecology conservation and development in the textbooks and syllabus of the school-college to give a comprehensive idea about these.

153. The National Environment Policy, 2018 was formulated to achieve the following objectives:

2.1 to ensure the natural balance and overall development of the country through environmental protection and sustainable management;
2.2 to expand adaptation activities to mitigate the adverse effects of climate change in the country;
2.3 to encourage the acquisition and introduction of low carbon emissions technologies in the country;

2.4 to identify and control all types of environmental pollution and degradation activities;
2.5 to ensure environmentally friendly development in all areas;
2.6 to ensure sustainable, long-term and environmentally friendly use of all natural resources;
2.7 to unveil and expand areas of mutual cooperation at regional and international levels in global environmental development;
2.8 to develop environmental education, capacity, public awareness and public opinion in environmental protection;
2.9 to adopt Public-Private Partnership in the development of environment;
2.10 to integrate and harmonize environmental policies and strategies among other policy disciplines in the interest of sustainable development;
2.11 to develop people capable of tackling all kinds of environmental and ecological problems, including climate change;
2.12 to ensure environmental impact assessment and strategic environmental assessment in all the necessary cases;
2.13 to discourage the artificial intrusion of alien and invasive species of animals and plants; and take decisions through adequate research, if necessary;
2.14 to be as actively involved as far as possible with all international environmental initiatives and to take necessary action at the local and national levels;
2.15 to take steps to alleviate poverty through environmental protection;
2.16 to strengthen observations on proper implementation of environmental laws and regulations.

Part I. Pollution Control

154. The socio-economic progress of Bangladesh, an independent state with a history of five decades and one of the most densely populated countries in the world, has been remarkable in recent times and has been acknowledged by various renowned international bodies and organizations. Immediately, after the independence of the country in 1971, the first example of a country that became independent based on 'right to self-determination' after the colonial framework, the policymakers of the country realized the importance of the protection of environmental components. Consequently, successive governments, especially the governments after the 1990s, took and have been taking various initiatives in this regard, often dubbed as improper and ill-coordinated, and poorly implemented, as evident from various initiatives taken to improve the legal and policy regime and systems for the protection of environmental components and pollution management in the country.

155. With all the domestic limitations, the country is one of the worst victims of climate change as well and thus has been suffering due to the activities of the developed and industrialized countries. In the latest Country Environmental Analysis 2018 published by the World Bank, it was revealed that in 2015, the total number of deaths and disability adjusted life years in the country was around 80,000 and 2.6 million respectively, and only in Dhaka, the figures were around 18,000 and 578,000 respectively annually. Some factors, e.g., air pollution, inadequate water, sanitation, and hygiene, arsenic in drinking water, and occupational pollutants in urban areas, etc., were found to be responsible for these.

156. The economic cost of this mortality is also huge – USD 1.40 billion and USD 310 million in all urban areas and Dhaka alone, respectively. These figures are again equivalent to 0.7% and 0.2% of Bangladesh's GDP respectively in 2015. However, the broader welfare impacts of mortality are enormous, i.e., USD 6.52 billion and USD 1.44 billion in all urban areas and Dhaka alone, respectively. These figures are equivalent to 3.4% and 0.7% of Bangladesh's GDP, respectively.[130] The estimated cost of mortality and its comparison with national GDP, as revealed by the World Bank in the aforementioned report (Table 6):

130. World Bank, Enhancing Opportunities for Clean and Resilient Growth in Urban Bangladesh: Country Environmental Analysis 2018, September 2018, Washington, DC, The World Bank Group, pp. 2–3, https://documents.worldbank.org/en/publication/documents-reports/documentdetail/585301536851966118/enhancing-opportunities-for-clean-and-resilient-growth-in-urban-bangladesh-country-environmental-analysis-2018.

Table 6 Estimated Cost of Mortality in Urban Bangladesh and Greater Dhaka (USD Billion) and National GDP (2015) Equivalences

	Urban Bangladesh				*Greater Dhaka*			
	Welfare Loss		*Foregone Output*		*Welfare Loss*		*Foregone Output*	
	Amount	*GDP Equivalent*	*Amount*	*GDP Equivalent*	*Amount*	*GDP Equivalent*	*Amount*	*GDP Equivalent*
PM2.5 air pollution ambient								
ambient	2.42	1.24%	0.49	0.25%	0.53	0.27%	0.11	0.06%
household	1.27	0.65%	0.25	0.13%	0.28	0.14%	0.06	0.03%
Inadequate water, sanitation and hygiene								
direct impact	0.43	0.22%	0.14	0.07%	0.09	0.05%	0.03	0.02%
indirect impact	0.08	0.04%	0.04	0.02%	0.02	0.01%	0.01	0.00%
Arsenic in drinking water	0.80	0.41%	0.18	0.09%	0.18	0.09%	0.04	0.02%
Occupational pollutants	1.52	0.78%	0.29	0.15%	0.34	0.17%	0.06	0.03%
TOTAL	6.52	3.35%	1.40	0.72%	1.44	0.74%	0.31	0.16%

Source: World Bank[131]

157. This Report proposed that a few initiatives such as enhancement of environmental policy and institutions at the national level and environmental management at the local level, strengthening the enforcement and accountability regime, leveraging of market-based instruments to protect the environment and unlock green financing, promotion of resource-efficient and cleaner production as a tool for reconciling environmental performance with competitiveness, and harnessing the power of public awareness, have the prospects to improve the situation.

131. *Ibid.*, at p. 3.

Chapter 1. General Law

158. People in this part of the world were aware of the protection of environmental components, and they used to protect these in ancient and medieval Bengal though due to religious faiths, customs and social practices, etc. Yet, interestingly, some forms of legal instruments aiming at the protection of environmental components were also available even in the year of AD 1204 when the ruling class introduced such provisions in the name of protection of the forest, forest resources and wildlife, etc., though the researchers believe that their intention was, *inter alia*, to collect revenue. [132]

159. Historically, after the invasion of this part by the British East India Company, several initiatives were taken to address the pollution issues. After the Mutiny of 1857, when the British Raj took over the ruling power, a few factors compelled the British rulers to introduce the British style laws in all sectors in this subcontinent, most importantly to ensure the safety and healthy lifestyle of the British officials and the local elites. The geographic location and characteristics of ancient Bengal were influenced by the presence of rivers and wetlands, and the weather influenced the British rulers to enact laws aiming at the protection of environmental components.

160. During this time, the colonial rulers established a network of rail communication for the easy administration and management of their authority. With the initiatives of the then British rulers, after the opening of the first railway line between Calcutta and the Raniganj coalfields in 1855, the number of coal-fuelled steam engines and other activities were increased, and a bulk amount of dense black smoke caused smoke pollution or nuisance due to the geographical setting and meteorological condition of the city. As a result, with the constant pressure of the British officials and local elites, one of the earliest air pollution laws, i.e., the Calcutta and Howrah Smoke-Nuisance Act of 1863, was enacted in this part of the world following similar laws enacted in the UK as a consequence of the industrial revolution.[133] This law was subsequently amended and updated by the Bengal Smoke Nuisance Act, 1905, which was enacted to amend the law relating to the abatement of nuisances arising from the smoke of furnaces or fireplaces in certain areas. This law of 1905 was subsequently adapted in Pakistan and finally in Bangladesh after the independence in 1971. The Smoke-Nuisances Act, 1905 (Act No. III of 1905) is still in force.[134]

---

132. *See generally*, Md. Mokarrom Hossan, *History and Development of Environmental Law, Policy and Organization in Bangladesh*, PhD Thesis, University of Dhaka, 2013.
133. Carlos Flick, 'The Movement for Smoke Abatement in 19th-Century Britain'. *Technology and Culture* (1980): 29–50; M. Akatsu. 'The Problem of Air Pollution During the Industrial Revolution: A Reconsideration of the Enactment of the Smoke Nuisance Abatement Act of 1821'. In *Economic History of Energy and Environment*, ed. S. Sugiyama. Monograph Series of the Socio-Economic History Society (Tokyo: Springer, 2015).
134. For a background history of the air pollution laws in ancient Bengal, *see*, Janine Wilhelm, *Environment and Pollution in Colonial India: Sewerage Technologies along the Sacred Ganges* (New York: Routledge, 2016), p. 164.

161. After the independence of Bangladesh in 1971, even in a war-ravaged situation coupled with various severe socio-economic challenges, the policymakers did not ignore the importance of the protection of environmental components. At the national level, the government either adapted the laws and maintained the institutions that were in existence during the Pakistan period or enacted new laws in this regard. Even in the international forum, Bangladesh delegations led by A. Razzak, Ambassador Extraordinary and Plenipotentiary to Sweden, attended the historic Stockholm Conference on the Human Environment, 1972.

162. Following the developments of the said Stockholm Conference, 1972, the government established the Department of Public Health Engineering and enacted the Water Pollution Control Ordinance, 1973. Later on, the Environmental Pollution Control Ordinance, 1977 (Ordinance XIII of 1977) was enacted and Environment Pollution Control Board was established. In 1989, the government established the Department of Environment merging the activities of the Department of Public Health Engineering and Environment Pollution Control Board.

163. With the establishment of the MoEF in 1989, now MoEFCC, the process of lawmaking to protect environmental components took an institutional shape. Immediately after the establishment of the Ministry, the National Conservation Strategy was drafted. During this time, the country experienced a major political shift. After the democratic journey resumed in the country in 1991, the government formulated the Environment Policy, 1992 which was recently modernized in 2018. The DoE, under the MoEFCC, has been functioning as the main government body in regulating pollution in the country. As a consequence of the Environment Policy, 1992, the BECA, 1995 was enacted, repealing the Environmental Pollution Control Ordinance, 1977 (Ordinance XIII of 1977).

164. Even though there are more than two hundred laws containing provisions on the protection of different aspects of the environment and environmental components, the BECA, 1995 and the subsidiary legislation framed as per the provisions of this Act, i.e., the Bangladesh Environment Conservation Rules, 1997, contain the broad and general provisions regarding the control and regulation of various types of pollution in the context of Bangladesh. Apart from the BECA, 1995 and the Environment Conservation Rules, 1997, a few other laws, e.g., the Easement Act, 1882 (Act No. V of 1882), which was enacted to define and amend the law relating to easements, i.e., 'a right which the owner or occupier of certain land possesses, as such, for the beneficial enjoyment of that land, to do and continue to do something, or to prevent and continue to prevent something being done, in or upon, or in respect of, certain other lands not his own', and licences contain provisions on various types of pollution. Some provisions of these laws will be discussed extensively in subsequent chapters.

Chapter 2. Air Pollution

§1. Introduction

165. Clean air is fundamental for human existence, and polluted air is responsible for many diseases leading to even the loss of human life as reflected in the findings of various evidence-based research. After the independence in 1971, due to socio-economic and political reasons, the air quality of Dhaka, the capital of Bangladesh, and other parts of the country was not a serious concern for the policymakers, and this continued until the mid-1990s. However, since the development activities and industrialization process started after the parliamentary democracy resumed in 1991, the air quality of the country, especially of Dhaka, started to deteriorate and the air pollution scenarios of Bangladesh have turned to be very alarming for the last couple of years.

166. In the latest Environmental Performance Index, 2020, developed by the Yale Center for Environmental Law & Policy, Bangladesh is placed at the bottom in terms of air pollution.[135] Similar are the findings of other indexes too. According to the very recently published World Air Quality Index Report, out of 106 countries, Bangladesh is ranked as the country with the poorest urban air quality in 2020.[136] It may be relevant to share here that when Bangladesh is projected in that way, i.e., country with the poorest urban air quality, where mainly the air quality of Dhaka was considered, the air quality of most of the other cities was generally acceptable, though the situation could be better and improved, which cannot be done overnight.

167. The air in Bangladesh is polluted both through, i.e., anthropogenic sources and natural sources. Some of the main contributing factors to the air pollution in Dhaka, according to the MoEFCC, are: (a) brick manufacturing fields; (b) various types of ongoing construction, reconstruction, and repair (roads, mega-development projects such as expressways, metro rails, etc., multistoried buildings at government and private levels); (c) commercial sand extraction and collection on roadsides or highways, transportation of sand, soil, cement, and other construction materials in trucks or lorries in an open condition; (d) waste from various sources, e.g., municipal waste on the streets, dumping drain-dirt on the streets, hospital wastes, etc.; (e) harmful smokes of unfit transports; and (f) lack of public awareness, etc.[137] Besides, cooking in rural and downtown areas of Bangladesh is mostly dependent on firewood and different other agricultural materials, which is an important factor of air pollution and deforestation, and thus has an adverse effect on the environment.

---

135. Z.A. Wendling et al. *2020 Environmental Performance Index* (New Haven, CT: Yale Center for Environmental Law & Policy, 2020). epi.yale.edu.
136. Air quality in Bangladesh, https://www.iqair.com/bangladesh.
137. Shonchita Sheetu, 'Air Pollution: Reasons Why Dhaka Tops the List Every Day'. *Dhaka Tribune*, 23 Jan. 2021, https://www.dhakatribune.com/bangladesh/2021/01/23/air-pollution-reasons-why-dhaka-tops-the-list-everyday.

168. Both the Constitution of Bangladesh and the environmental laws enjoined the government functionaries to take adequate measures to prevent environmental pollution, including air pollution.[138] The factories and industries that are one of the main sources of emissions need to obtain regulatory approval from the DoE. The DoE has also taken some initiatives. Yet, the problem persists, and the situation becomes unbearable at times, especially in Dhaka, which is the centre of almost everything. Apparently, though the research data revealed that the air quality of Dhaka is stable while economic activities have been ongoing and the number of sources was increased in many folds,[139] the air quality of Dhaka during the dry season, i.e., November to March, remains below the acceptable standard. A decade-long initiative, i.e., The Clean Air and Sustainable Environment (CASE) project that was started in 2010 and ended in June 2019 found, *inter alia*, that the air quality of the country is highly affected due to the meteorological changes in different seasons and gaseous pollutants were generally within the standards set by the government.[140]

169. It may be relevant to share that the appeals court for the Administrative Court of Bordeaux, France, has recently considered the issue of air pollution in Bangladesh and blocked the deportation of a Bangladeshi citizen who received a temporary French residency permit as he has been suffering from asthma and severe sleep apnoea. This is unprecedented, and observers and media around the world hailed this as the first recognition for 'climate refugees' or 'environmentally-impacted migrants'.

§2. Government Initiatives

170. The government has taken various initiatives to improve the air quality in urban areas. After the formulation of the Environment Policy, 1992, the BECA, 1995 was enacted and as the air quality of the country, especially of Dhaka, started to deteriorate, the government adopted the air quality standards in the Environment Conservation Rules, 1997 formulated under the BECA, 1995. Subsequently, the standard was updated and Bangladesh Ambient Air Quality Standard was adopted in July 2005.[141]

138. *Dr Mohiuddin Farooque (BELA) v. Bangladesh and others* 55 DLR 69.
139. Bilkis A. Begum & Philip K. Hopke. 'Ambient Air Quality in Dhaka Bangladesh over Two Decades: Impacts of Policy on Air Quality'. *Aerosol and Air Quality Research* 18, no. 7 (2018): 1910–1920.
140. CASE Projects, Ambient Air Quality in Bangladesh, 2012–2018, http://case.doe.gov.bd/index.php?option=com_content&view=article&id=5&Itemid=9.
141. Bangladesh Govt. Gazette S.R.O. No: 220-Law/2005 of 16 July 2005.

171. The present national air quality standards for Bangladesh are shared below:

Pollutant	*Objective*	*Average*
CO	10 mg/m^3 (9 ppm)	8 hours(a)
	40 mg/m^3 (35 ppm)	1 hour(a)
Pb	0.5 μg/m^3	Annual
NO_x	100 μg/m^3 (0.053 ppm)	Annual
PM10	50 μg/m^3	Annual (b)
	150 μg/m^3	24 hours (c)
PM2.5	15 μg/m^3	Annual
	65 μg/m^3	24 hours
O_3	235 μg/m^3 (0.12 ppm)	1 hour (d)
	157 μg/m^3 (0.08 ppm)	8 hours
SO_2	80 μg/m^3 (0.03 ppm)	Annual
	365 μg/m^3 (0.14 ppm)	24 hours (a)

Notes:[142]

(a) Not to be exceeded more than once per year.

(b) The objective is attained when the annual arithmetic mean is less than or equal to 50 ug/m3.

(c) The objective is attained when the expected number of days per calendar year with a 24-hour average of 150 μg/m3 is equal to or less than 1.

(d) The objective is attained when the expected number of days per calendar year with the maximum hourly average of 0.12 ppm is equal to or less than 1.

Source: Department of Environment, Government of Bangladesh.[143]

172. It is apparent that in developing the standard, Bangladesh mostly followed the standards set by the United States Environmental Protection Agency (US EPA) [for particulate matter (PM10, PM 2.5)[144], nitrogen dioxide (NO_2), sulphur dioxide (SO_2), carbon monoxide (CO) and Ozone (O3)] and the World Health Organisation (WHO) [for Lead (Pb)]. A comparative table of air quality standard of Bangladesh with that of the WHO and USEPA Guidelines is projected in Table 7.

142. μg/m^3 = microgram per cubic meter; ppm= parts per million.
143. Schedule II, the Environment Conservation Rules, 1997. Monthly Air Quality Monitoring Report Reporting Month: March 2021, http://case.doe.gov.bd/index.php?option=com_content&view=article&id=5&Itemid=9.
144. (PM10)= Particulate Matters with Aerodynamic Diameter less than 10 Micrometre; (PM2.5)= Particulate Matters with Aerodynamic Diameter less than 2.5 Micrometre.

Table 7 Bangladesh National Ambient Air Quality Standards Versus WHO Guideline Values and US EPA Standards[145]

Pollutant	*Averaging-Period*	*Bangladesh Standards*	*WHO Guideline Values (μg/m³)*	*US EPA Standards (μg/m³)*
CO	8-hour	10,000 μg/m³ (9 ppm)	10,000	10,000
	1-hour	40,000 μg/m³ (35 ppm)	30,000	40,000
Pb	Annual	0.5 μg/m³	0.5	-
NO_2	Annual	100 μg/m³ (0.053 ppm)	-	-
TSP	8-hour	200 μg/m³	-	-
PM_{10}	Annual	50 μg/m³	20	Revoked
	24-hour	150 μg/m³	50	150
$PM_{2.5}$	Annual	15 μg/m³	10	15
	24-hour	65 μg/m³	25	35
O_3	1-hour	235 μg/m³ (0.12 ppm)	-	235
	8-hour	157 μg/m³ (0.08 ppm)	100	157
SO_2	Annual	80 μg/m³ (0.03 ppm)	-	78
	24-hour	365 μg/m³ (0.14 ppm)	20	365

173. In 2004, the Ozone Depleting Substances (Control) Rules, 2004, were formulated under section 20 of the BECA, 1995 (Act No. 1 of 1995) to regulate the production, import, export, marketing, sale, display for the purpose of sale, storage, distribution or commercial use of ozone layer depleting substances. The Rules have listed a number of such substances and prohibited the import and export of these to and from Bangladesh without permission and obtaining proper licence following the conditions stipulated in rule 13.[146] Besides, the distribution without obtaining no objection certificate from the DoE (rule 6), purchase of such substances for unauthorized use (rule 7), new investment for the purpose of industrial production (rule 8), and the production of compressor without the permission of the Director General (rule 10) are also prohibited.

145. Richard Baldwin & David Calkins, *Bangladesh Urban Air Quality Management: An Institutional Assessment, 2007*, http://documents1.worldbank.org/curated/en/456251468210889617/689630ESW0P103010July070sent0to0DOE.doc.

146. Rules 4 & 5, the Ozone Depleting Substances (Control) Rules, 2004.

174. Chlorofluorocarbons (CFC), halons, methyl bromide, carbon tetrachloride (CTC), HCFC, hydro bromofluorocarbons (HBFCs) are ozone-depleting substances. Bangladesh has successfully phased out major ODSs such as CFCs, CTC, halons, and methyl bromide from their use in the commercial sector in 2010. CFC, which was used in refrigeration, air conditioning appliances, foam production, cleaning solvents, process agents and propellants, etc., was totally phased out in Bangladesh in 2012. The manufacturing of metred dose inhalers and HCFC-141b in manufacturing refrigerator foam as foam blowing agent was phased out in 2012 under the Public-Private Partnership (PPP) model with financial support from the Montreal Protocol Multilateral Fund through UNDP.

175. Subsequently, the government has amended different provisions of these Rules in 2014. For different words such as 'recovery', 'reclaiming', 're-cycling', and 'license' new definitions were adopted. Rule 4 was amended to prohibit the production of ozone-depleting substances, and the list of such objects is included in column 2 of Schedule 1 of the rules. Rule 5 was amended to include provisions relating to the export and import of ozone-depleting substances to and from Bangladesh, without having a licence relating to recovery, reclaiming, or recycling.

176. Since 2014, the government of Bangladesh has been addressing the issue of reduction of Short Lived Climate Pollutants—that is, black carbon, methane, tropospheric ozone, and some hydrofluorocarbons and adopted the first National Action Plan for Reducing Short Lived Climate Pollutants, 2014, followed by the second National Plan adopted in 2018. This Plan aims to reduce the emission of methane and black carbon by 20% and 53% respectively to assist the country in fulfilling its commitments under the Paris Agreement. Moreover, it has been anticipated that 16,300 air pollution-induced premature deaths can also be avoided.

177. The United Nations Environment Programme (UNEP) recognized Bangladesh for its achievement in phasing out major ODSs from the country on the eve of twenty-five years of the signing of the Montreal Protocol. The UNEP awarded a 'Certificate of Appreciation' to the country for achieving all reduction targets set out in the protocol in the 29th meeting of the parties.

178. Some additional legal and institutional measures have also been taken in this regard. Some of the significant measures were: '(a) removal of lead from the gasoline in 1999, (b) phase-out of 2-stroke 3-wheeled baby taxis from Dhaka in early 20's, (c) introduction of cleaner fuel CNG to transport sector in early 90's, (d) enlargement of the chimney height of the fixed chimney kiln (FCK) for brick production, and recently (e) adoption of new brick burning and control law – 2013 (revised) which prohibits energy-extensive FCKs in the brick manufacturing sector'.[147] The government completed the CASE project which was taken in 2010 to abate air pollution from the transport sectors and brick kilns through three government agencies: DoE, Dhaka City Corporation and Dhaka Transport Coordination

147. CASE Projects, Ambient Air Quality in Bangladesh, 2012–2018, p. 1 http://case.doe.gov.bd/index.php?option=com_content&view=article&id=5&Itemid=9.

Authority. In order to reduce the air pollution from using firewood in cooking, the government has also formulated the Bangladesh Country Action Plan for Clean Cookstoves aiming at distributing environment-friendly clean cook stoves, the use of which will reduce the pollution from cooking and achieve 100% clean cooking solutions by 2030.

§3. Domestic Laws on Air Pollution

179. There is no stand-alone law dealing with air pollution in the country like the Air Pollution Control Act, 1955 of the USA. Nevertheless, this issue is regulated through the provisions of some general law, e.g., the Penal Code, 1860 (XLV of 1860), the Smoke-Nuisance Act, 1905 (Act No. III of 1995), the sectoral law, e.g., the BECA, 1995 and special law, e.g., the Brick Manufacturing and Brick Kiln Establishment (Control) Act, 2013 (Act 59 of 2013). The industrial emission responsible for air pollution and air quality issues is generally covered through the provisions of the BECA, 1995 and the Bangladesh Environment Conservation Rules, 1997. The DoE has already adopted the Bangladesh National Ambient Air Quality Standards shared above which the relevant stakeholders need to follow. Besides, various industries are already categorized and accordingly, they need to obtain various types of licences and permissions before the establishment of theses. These industries need to follow the conditions of the licences and pollution standards. The operation of the vehicles that emit smoke or gas exceeding the standards set by the Rule causing injury to human health or the environment is prohibited except for the purpose of test operation for stopping the emission of such smoke or gas.[148] Anyone responsible can be fined up to BDT 5,000 (approximately USD 60) and BDT 10,000 (approximately USD 120) for the first and second offence respectively, and for every subsequent offences, an accused can be held liable for imprisonment for up to one year or fine up to BDT 20,000 (approximately USD 240) or both.[149]

180. For the ongoing development activities, bricks are fundamental though brick production is one of the main culprits in polluting the air in Bangladesh. Accordingly, the Brick Manufacturing and Brick Kiln Establishment (Control) Act, 2013 (Act No. 59 of 2013) was enacted, repealing the previous law that was enacted in 1989, i.e., the Brick Kiln (Control) Act, 1989 with the aim to regulate the manufacturing of brick and to impose restrictions on the establishment of brick factories to preserve and improve the environment and biodiversity. This Act of 2013, which came into force from 1 July 2014, defines ‘Brick Klin’ as a place or infrastructure where brick is produced and that place uses improved and energy-efficient technology and is capable of maintaining air pollution within the standard approved according to the Environment Conservation Rules, 1997. Thus, one of the purposes of the enactment of this law is to reduce emissions from the brick kilns aiming to improve the air quality of the country. The law provides that for the establishment of brick-making factories, a licence is to be obtained from the Deputy Commission of the

148. Section 6, the Bangladesh Environment Conservation Act, 1995 (Act no. 1 of 1995).
149. Section 15(1), the Bangladesh Environment Conservation Act, 1995 (Act no. 1 of 1995).

district where the factory is proposed to be set up.[150] The law imposes restrictions on the use of soil, wood, and coal in brick factories. It is provided that no person can use soil collected from agricultural land or hills or high lands as the raw material for the production of bricks, without the permission of the proper authority, and no person can collect soil from wetlands, unused ponds, lakes, rivers, islands, or abandoned places for the same purpose.[151]

181. The law bans the use of wood as fuel and restricts the use of coal that contains more sulphur, ash, and mercury than the permissible limit.[152] The law restricts the establishment of brick factories in residential, restricted, or commercial areas, City Corporations, municipal areas, or subdivisional headquarters, government or private-owned forests, sanctuaries, gardens, or water bodies, agricultural land, ecologically critical areas, degraded air sheds, and also in places that are within half a kilometre from hills or highlands, roads constructed by the local government, and engineering departments; within one kilometre from prohibited areas, special structures, rail lines, educational institutes, hospitals and clinics, research institutes; and within two kilometres from government forests, without the permission of the Divisional Forest Officer.[153] The law provides for punishment ranging from imprisonment up to five years and fines up to BDT 500,000 (approximately USD 5850) for the violation of different provisions of the law. After the enactment of the law, a considerable number of brick factories are already modernized, and environment-friendly technologies have already been installed. The regulators have also imposed fines on several brickfields for using, *inter alia*, firewood in these factories.

182. It may be relevant to share here that though the Bangladesh Labour Act, 2006 (Act No. XLII of 2006), which was enacted repealing the Factories Act, 1965, deals with the working condition of a premise in general including indoor air pollution, the law has not set any specific standard for such pollution. This is because these establishments need to obtain licences and permissions, including the environmental clearance certificates under the BECA, 1995, depending on their nature, and such provisions are included there.

183. Tobacco production and smoking pollute the air and thus have serious adverse environmental consequences. In order to address this issue, the Tobacco Products Marketing (Control) Act, 1988 was enacted. Section 3 of the Act of 1988 provided for the insertion of a statutory warning that smoking is dangerous for health. It was also provided that the warning must be printed on a packet or canned tobacco-based products on a prominent and distinct space of the container of the packet, which would be easily readable and understood. Similarly, section 3(2) of

150. Section 4, the Brick Production and Establishment of Factories (Control) Act, 2013 (Act 59 of 2013).
151. Section 5, the Brick Production and Establishment of Factories (Control) Act, 2013 (Act 59 of 2013).
152. Section 7, the Brick Production and Establishment of Factories (Control) Act, 2013 (Act 59 of 2013).
153. Section 8, the Brick Production and Establishment of Factories (Control) Act, 2013 (Act 59 of 2013).

the said Act stated that no advertisement of tobacco-based products shall be published, broadcast, or displayed without having the said warning in easily readable and understood Bengali engraved, written, or printed on a prominent part of the advertisement. In one instance, the petitioners moved to the HCD for the strict implementation of section 3 of the Tobacco Products Marketing (Control) Act, 1988 as this provision was not properly adhered to by the companies engaged in the tobacco business, and it was found that they were printing the statutory warning in obscure corners of tobacco packets and containers, and publishing the warning in such small size that it was barely readable.[154] Moreover, in advertisements with moving images in the movie theatres and those broadcast on television, the statutory warnings were shown so briefly and without any voice that they had little or no effect on the viewers. Unfortunately, these acts were not illegal. Mr Justice Mohammad Fazlul Karim, sharing the intoxicating and fatal effect of smoking or consumption of tobacco-related products, held that: '. . .it is abundantly clear that before a detrimental action can be taken there must be some law which permits that any action detrimental to life, body, liberty or property of a person can be taken. No such law is in existence in Bangladesh. Mere non-existence of such permissive law is not enough to take detrimental actions invading the right to life of a citizen for the State could not pass such law which are contrary to the fundamental rights of a citizen. There is no law permitting cigarette advertisement on the news media, bill boards or on the electronic medias and such advertisements have the effect of propagating and inducing people, particularly the younger generation to adopt smoking habit which results in endangering human life and environment. Thus, advertisement of cigarette and cigarette related products bidi on T.V/Radio, newspaper, phamplets, Billboard or through any other means are steps which can be termed detrimental to life and body of the people and in this view of the matter Article 31 of the Constitution is directly contravened by advertisements in any form of Telecasting and Board casting of cigarette/bidi commercial on the TV and Radio Bill boards, newspapers etc.' Finally, the HCD issued some directions.

184. This law of 1988 was subsequently repealed and updated. The Smoking and Tobacco Products Usage (Control) Act, 2005 (Act No. 11 of 2005), as amended by the Smoking and Tobacco Products Usage (Control) (Amendment) Act, 2013, is the principal law governing tobacco control in Bangladesh. The Act is comprehensive and covers smoke-free policies; tobacco advertising, promotion and sponsorship; and packaging and labelling of tobacco products, among other areas. The Smoking and Tobacco Products Usage (Control) Rules, 2015, are the implementing rules of the Act and provide further details regarding many provisions of the law. The 2005 Act was passed after Bangladesh became a party to the WHO Framework Convention on Tobacco Control, and was enacted as an addition to, not in derogation of, existing laws, e.g., the Railways Act, 1890 (Act No. IX of 1890) governing the smoking in railway compartments, at least to the extent that there were no contradictory provisions.

---

154. *Nurul Islam v. Government of Bangladesh* [Writ Petition No. 1825 of 1999 with Writ Petition No. 4521 of 1999].

185. Section 18 of the Act, 2005 has updated the provisions included in section 3 of Act of 1988 and provides for the insertion of a statutory warning on printed on packet or canned tobacco-based products on a prominent and distinct space of the container of the packet, which would be easily readable and understood that the smoking is dangerous for health. It is also provided in section 3(2) of the said Act that no advertisement of tobacco-based products shall be published, broadcast, or displayed without having the said warning in easily readable and understood Bengali engraved, written, or printed on a prominent part of the advertisement.

186. Despite the enactment of the Law, 2005, the provisions were not properly implemented. As a result, the Ministry of Local Government, Rural Development and Cooperatives issued implementation guidelines in March 2021 to ensure proper implementation of the Tobacco Control Act by local government administrations. These guidelines address retail licence requirements and location-based sales restrictions, among other measures.

§4. The Clean Air Bill, 2019

187. Even after all these initiatives were taken, the country has been in the headlines of global media due to the poor air quality. In response, an initiative was taken to enact a stand-alone law aiming to ensure cleaner air in the country. Accordingly, the Clean Air Bill, 2019, has been drafted with the assistance of leading and renowned NGOs of the country: Bangladesh Environmental Lawyers' Association (BELA) and Bangladesh University of Engineering and Technology (BUET), recognizing the protection of the environmental components as a fundamental principle of state policy as encapsulated in article 18A of the Constitution of Bangladesh, 1972. Various important provisions of the Bill were drafted to ensure an acceptable standard of air in different places of the country, environment and sustainable development, public health and citizen's right to life and clear air. The Draft Bill, containing several important relevant definitions, has statutorily recognized the application of the precautionary, sustainable development and polluter pays principles in the implementation of the law.[155] Besides, the Bill has included provisions empowering the government to declare an area as a degraded airshed or specially controlled area if it appears that the ambient air quality of an area exceeds the approved standard (section 11).

188. The Bill has included several provisions including air pollution emission standard (section 9), national air quality management plan (section 10), the formation of an advisory committee to assist the government and the Department of Environment in the implementation of the law (section 14), control of emission through transport vehicle (section 16), and air quality improvement fund (section 19). It is provided that the provisions of this proposed law will be in addition to the existing

155. Section 3, the Clean Air Bill, 2019.

laws on environment conservation, environment and air pollution; however, the provisions of this law shall prevail over the provisions of other laws if there is any conflict. It will be relevant to mention here that the proposed law aims to ensure clean air for the citizens and not to punish the wrongdoers and the implementation of many of the provisions of the law depends on future actions on the part of the regulators. Therefore, it will take a more considerable amount of time to see the real impacts of the law. It is a matter of fact that, even though the Bill was drafted in 2019, it has not been passed yet by Parliament, perhaps due to the COVID-19 pandemic-induced consequences. Interestingly, while the Clean Air Bill, 2019 awaits to be passed by the Parliament, the MoEFCC has recently released the draft of the Control of Air Pollution Rules, 2021, formulated under section 20 of the BECA, 1995 for the improvement of environment and sustainable development, prevention, control and reduction of air pollution for the protection of public health. This indicates that the policymakers prefer not to consider a new law, rather prefer to introduce the necessary legal provisions through the existing avenue available under the BECA, 1995.

189. It can be seen that the Draft Air Pollution Rules, 2021 provide that the DG of DoE shall, with the permission of the government, develop a standard containing the list of pollutants, procedure, process, guidelines, etc., and this standard needs to be observed (rule 3). Rule 4 of the Draft Rules, 2021 provides that after the entry into force of the Rules, the DG of DoE shall, with the authorization of the government, develop a national air quality management plan containing provisions on institutional workplan for strategic management and coordination; effective management of discharged air from the continuous, specific, uncertain sources and from permanent sources with chimney; effective management of Indoor Air Quality; management of control of risky pollutants; recognition and publicity of best practices in air standard management; clean, energy-efficient, fuel, processes; review of air standards; awareness, education, information and knowledge management regarding air standard; research about air pollution and assessment of its dangers; actions regarding sustainable financing for air standard management, etc. The Draft Rules empower the government to declare an area as degraded airshed in case the air quality of that place reduces and crosses the prescribed air standard, etc. (rule 5); develop Air Pollution Prevention Plan (rule 7); control of pollution of air from transport (rule 8) and waste (rules 11 & 17); specify functions of agencies/organizations/individuals responsible for construction, improvement and repair of roads, drain, buildings and other infrastructures, etc. (rule 10). The draft Rules also provide for the formation of National Executive Council for the Control of Air Pollution involving representatives from all relevant sectors (rule 15), have also included the polluter pay principle (rule 16) and provide for awards in recognition of contribution in reducing the air pollution (rule 18). The release of the Draft Rules is undoubtedly an important development even though there are some isolated provisions available in the domestic laws, and thus reflects the concerns of the policymakers to improve the air quality of the country to make the ongoing development activities sustainable and meaningful. However, as various provisions of the Draft Rules, if accepted, will require further action from the government and relevant agencies, the countrymen will require some more time to get the benefits of this legal development.

Chapter 3. Water Pollution

§1. Introduction

190. Bangladesh, a riverine country, is blessed to have more than 238 major rivers originating from the major transboundary rivers – Ganges, Brahmaputra, and Meghna.[156] These rivers, such as Padma, Meghna, Jamuna, Surma, and Karnaphuli – and other rivers criss-cross the country and form an integral part in shaping the geographic, social, economic, and cultural development while providing the major source of food, livelihood, and transport facilities for the people of this part of the world.

191. The free flow of the water of these rivers ensures rich biodiversity as the water is believed to be relatively less polluted. However, water pollution and a frequent outbreak of waterborne diseases in ancient periods have also been reported where the interruption of free flow of waters contributed indirectly in this regard as people had to build dams, though recklessly, to build and secure their accommodation affected due to natural calamities.

192. The rivers and other wetlands of the country have been being polluted for the last forty years, again as a consequence of improper development and urbanization. Studies found that pollutants discharged in the river have been causing serious pollution leading to adverse environmental consequences. As a result, the dissolved oxygen level was found to be almost nil in Buriganga, and several points in other rivers around Dhaka such as Turag, Balu, Sitalakhya, and Karnaphuli. Moreover, metal concentrations in sediments were found above the US EPA threshold value resulting in these metals being available in fish and agricultural products.[157] The situation has turned to be of grave concern in recent times for all except for the encroachers and landgrabbers. Various activities were reported in national dailies, and different organizations moved to the HCD to manage directions to stop such activities for the protection of the environment. As similar activities have been continuing, the HCD had to grant recently the rivers 'legal personality' and order the relevant authority to take various initiatives to improve the conditions of the rivers.[158]

193. In 2010, the UN General Assembly and the UN Human Rights Council on 'Human rights and access to safe drinking water and sanitation' have recognized the

156. *See generally*, River, Banglapedia, https://en.banglapedia.org/index.php/River.
157. Md Jamal Uddin & Yeon-Koo Jeong. 'Urban River Pollution in Bangladesh During Last 40 Years: Potential Public Health and Ecological Risk, Present Policy, and Future Prospects Toward Smart Water Management.' *Heliyon* 7, no. 2 (2021): e06107.
158. *Human Rights and Peace for Bangladesh v. Government of Bangladesh and others* (Writ Petition No. 13989 of 2016).

right to safe and clean drinking water and sanitation as a human right that is essential for the full enjoyment of the right to life and human rights.[159] The right to life is a constitutionally guaranteed right in Bangladesh, and after the insertion of Article 18A which provides for, *inter alia*, the preservation and safeguard of natural resources and wetlands, the government is bound to take coordinated efforts. Based on Bangladesh's commitment to UN SDGs, the country is bound to ensure Goal 6, i.e., the availability and sustainable management of water and sanitation for all. Bangladesh has enough legal and policy provisions on the prevention, reduction, and control of water pollution, though these are not properly implemented. Bangladesh has not signed the United Nations Convention on the Law of Non-Navigational Uses of Watercourse, 1997, which contains substantive provisions on the prevention, reduction, and control of pollution of an international watercourse.

§2. Causes of Water Pollution

194. Even with all the recent socio-economic success stories, the issue of water quality has been a serious concern for Bangladesh as contaminated water can have devastating effects on public health, agriculture, economy, biodiversity, and society. Earlier, people of independent Bangladesh used to use surface water for drinking and other household purposes. However, after the industrialization process started, primarily readymade garments industries, the surface water started to become contaminated as industries established on the bank of the rivers and wetlands started to discharge untreated industrial effluents, toxic chemicals, solid waste, sewage, etc., into the water. The textile, leather, sugar, agriculture, paper, construction and transport sectors are top polluters in Bangladesh.[160] Besides, for the huge population living in a small area, the farmers need to use fertilizers and pesticides, and this makes the water contaminated and such water is again used for irrigation purposes. As a result, the government started the process of installation of drinking water tube well for safe, sustainable and affordable water.

195. The installation of tube well for drinking water started in 1928 in this part of the world, and now, almost everyone in Bangladesh has the access to microbiologically safe drinking water, except for a small group of people living in coastal areas. Though the people of this part have been experiencing various waterborne diseases such as cholera and diarrhoea due to the use of contaminated surface water, the arsenic-contaminated groundwater became an issue of concern first in 1993 when the Department of Public Health Engineering detected such water in the tube wells of northern districts of Nawabganj.[161] As such contaminated water has serious

159. For an introduction to human right to water, *see*, Emanuele Fantini. 'An Introduction to the Human Right to Water: Law, Politics, and Beyond.' *Wiley Interdisciplinary Reviews: Water* 7, no. 2 (2020): e1405.

160. United Nations ESCAP, Tackling Water Pollution and Promoting Efficient Water Use in Industries, Regional Perspectives, Environment and Development Policy Brief, 2019/3, at p. 19.

161. Sk Akhtar Ahmad, Manzurul Haque Khan & Mushfiqul Haque. 'Arsenic Contamination in Groundwater in Bangladesh: Implications and Challenges for Healthcare Policy'. *Risk Management and Healthcare Policy* 11 (2018): 251.

consequences on the human health, this was reported as the 'largest poisoning of a population in history, with millions of people exposed'.[162] It may be relevant to share here that the provision of arsenic-free water to the citizens was brought before the apex court of the country and contested in the case of *Rabia Bhuiyan, M.P. v. Ministry of Local Government and Rural Development and Others*, 2007, 27 BLD (AD) 261.

§3. Water Administration and Governance

196. The management of water and construction of wetlands by the rulers for the inhabitants of this part of the world is deeply rooted in history. Yet, at the time of the partition of the subcontinent in 1947, the management of water resources did not get any institutional shape. Since 1757, when the British East India Company took over the administrative control of this part, the water administration and governance regime in this part witnessed five major shifts. The researchers revealed that between 1757 and 1947, the British colonial rulers attempted to introduce European urban water technologies, between 1948 and 1971 during the Pakistan period and between 1972 and 1995 during the first two decades of independent Bangladesh, the policymakers focused on strategic planning in various sectors, e.g., water supply, drainage, sanitation, etc. Between 1996 and 2005, influenced by the UN MDGs and encouraged by integrated water resources management, participatory approaches involving the communities and civil society increased. In the period between 2006 and 2016, the participatory approaches continued and experts from various disciplines, e.g., economics, social science, and engineering, etc., started to draft various relevant policies and management plans with different time frames, and initiatives have been taken for decentralized administrative systems in water governance in the lowest level of administration.[163]

197. Following the devastating flood of 1954 and 1955 in this part of the world, United Nations formed a mission and following the recommendations of that mission, the East Pakistan Water and Power Development Authority, 1959 (East Pakistan Ordinance No. 1 of 1959) was promulgated for the unified and coordinated development and utilization of the Water and Power Resources of East Pakistan, present Bangladesh, and the East Pakistan Water and Power Development Authority was established in January, 1959 with two wings, i.e., water wing and power wing. The Dhaka Water Supply and Sewerage Authority (WASA) was established in 1963 by the Local Government Engineering Department. Subsequently, in 1964, the first Master Plan relating to water was prepared and published to be used for the next twenty years. The Chittagong WASA was established in 1968.

162. Allan H. Smith, Elena O. Lingas & Mahfuzar Rahman. 'Contamination of Drinking-Water by Arsenic in Bangladesh: A Public Health Emergency'. *Bulletin of the World Health Organization* 78 (2000): 1093–1103.

163. To understand the historical and contemporary water resources management and governance approaches since 1757 till 2016; *see*, M. Tahmina Yasmin, A. Farrelly & Briony Cathryn Rogers. 'Evolution of Water Governance in Bangladesh: An Urban Perspective'. *World Development* 109 (2018): 386–400.

198. At the time of independence of the country in 1971, there was an Ordinance titled the East Pakistan Water Pollution Control Board Ordinance, 1970 (East Pakistan Ord. No. V of 1970), which was promulgated to control, prevent and abatement of pollution of waters of the then East Pakistan, present-day Bangladesh. The Ordinance of 1970 contained the definitions of some important terms such as 'pollution' and 'water'. That Ordinance of 1970 provided for the establishment of East Pakistan Water Pollution Control Board to 'formulate policies for the control, prevention and abatement of waters. . . and suggest measures for the implementation of these policies', and accordingly, the East Pakistan Water Pollution Control Board was established. After the independence of the country, various immediate priorities in a war-ravaged country had to be addressed. Yet, the Ministry of Water Resources was established in January 1972 as the main government agency responsible for the administration and management of water and water resources in Bangladesh. Immediately, after the establishment of the Ministry, the East Pakistan Water and Power Development Board Ordinance, 1959 was repealed through the enactment of the Bangladesh Water and Power Development Order, 1972 (President's Order No. 59 of 1972) on 31st May 1972. Accordingly, the Bangladesh Water and Power Development was established.

199. After the independence of the country, initiatives were taken to revise and update the Ordinance of 1970, and these were done through the provisions of the Environment Pollution Control Ordinance, 1977 (Ordinance No. XIII of 1977), which reconstituted the Water Pollution Control Board with similar mandates of that of the East Pakistan Water Pollution Control Board. One of the innovations of this Ordinance of 1977 was that an authorized officer could inspect buildings and lands to 'inspect and test any wastes, air, waters, soil, plants, materials of disposal system . . . and to afford all reasonable opportunities to such officers for such inspection, search and test' [section 7(3)(c)].

200. The National Environmental Policy, 1992 has many significant contributions in the development of environmental jurisprudence in Bangladesh. Following the provisions of this Policy, the National Environmental Management Plan was developed in 1995 and the BECA, 1995 was enacted which provides for the establishment of the DoE (sec. 3). This BECA, 1995 repealed the Environment Pollution Control Ordinance, 1977, but provides that notwithstanding such repeal, any action or action taken under the repealed Ordinance shall be deemed to have been made in accordance with the provisions of this Act, irrespective of the provisions of this Act (sec. 21).

201. The National Water Policy, 1999, formulated by the Ministry of Water Resources to 'guide management of the country's water resources by all the concerned ministries, agencies, departments, and local bodies that are assigned responsibilities for the development, maintenance, and delivery of water and water related services as well as the private users and developers of water resources' is an important breakthrough in the context of water management in the history of Bangladesh. Though the Policy, 1997 has not included any specific provision on water pollution, there are, however, several mentions of the term 'pollution', and it provides that these government bodies will take necessary action to prevent the water from being polluted and work with co-riparian countries in this regard.

202. The National Water Policy, 1999, under the heading 'Water Supply and Sanitation', stipulated that the government will empower and hold the municipalities and urban water and sewerage institutions responsible for regulating the use of water for preventing wastage and pollution by human action. Besides, the government will mandate local governments to make the people aware of water pollution and wastage.[164] The Policy also provides to strengthen the regulatory system for agricultural chemicals that pollute ground and surface water,[165] and further provides for the application and enforcement of the 'polluter pay' principle in case of industrial polluters for the clean-up of waterbodies polluted by them.[166] The Policy has not been amended so far.

203. For the proper implementation of this Policy, 1999, the Order No. 59 of 1972 was amended and updated in 2000 through the enactment of the Bangladesh Water Development Board Act, 2000 (Act No. 26 of 2000), and the Bangladesh Water Development Board was made a separate government agency responsible for proper development and efficient management of water resources of Bangladesh. Under section 5 of the Bangladesh Water Development Board Act, 2000, the Board has the power and is responsible, *inter alia*, to: (a) control the flow of water in all rivers, waterways and groundwater with the prior approval of the government and without infringing upon the legal rights of any person; (b) develop and implement appropriate standards and guidelines for the operation and maintenance of all water control infrastructure constructed in accordance with the provisions of section 6 of the law. Section 6 of the Law, while dealing with the functions of the Board, provides that in the light of the National Water Policy and National Water Master Plan adopted by the government and subject to other provisions of this section, the Board may, subject to the fulfilment of some conditions as mentioned in subsection (2) of section 6 of the Law, carry out both structure and non-structure related functions and undertake all the activities related to the formulation, implementation, management, maintenance and evaluation of necessary projects.

204. The list of structural related functions includes: (a) control and development of rivers and river basins and construction of reservoirs, barrages, dams, regulators or any other infrastructure for flood control, drainage, irrigation and drought prevention; (b) re-excavation of waterways, canals, etc., for the development of water flow or diversion of water flow to assist in irrigation, fish farming, shipping, forestry, wildlife conservation and overall development of the environment; (c) land conservation, land augmentation and recovery and control of river estuaries; (d) protection of river banks and protection of cities, markets, haats and places of historical and national importance from possible river erosion; (e) construction and

164. Section 4.6 Water Supply and Sanitation, the National Water Policy, 1997.
165. Section 4.7 Water and Agriculture, the National Water Policy, 1997.
166. Section 4.8 Water and Industry and Section 4.12 Water for the Environment, the National Water Policy, 1997.

maintenance of coastal dams; (f) prevention of salinity penetration and mitigation of desertification; (g) rainwater harvesting for irrigation, conservation of environment and extraction of drinking water.[167]

205. Under the same section 6 of the Law, the Board is responsible for undertaking some non-structural and ancillary functions such as: (i) flood and drought forecasting and warning; (ii) conduct research activities related to hydrology, and receive, store and distribute information and data related to it; (iii) afforestation, implementation of fisheries programmes and construction of roads on embankments on own lands within the infrastructure created by the Board in collaboration with the concerned agencies of the government for the protection and development of the environment; (iv) basic and practical research on the functions of the Board; (v) innovate, implement and manage various techniques and institutional structures related to organizing the beneficiaries, ensuring their participation in the project, project maintenance, and management and recovering the project cost to continue the benefits of the project implemented by the Board among the concerned beneficiaries.

206. In terms of water resources planning, the Master Plan Organisation (MPO) under the Ministry of Water Resources was created in 1983, and the National Water Plan project was taken to formulate a perspective plan (1985–2005) for the development of water resources. Subsequently, in 1986, a National Water Plan (NWP) was completed which was later updated in 1991. This NWP recommended the establishment of an Organization responsible for the planning of water resources. After the devastating flood in 1987 and 1988, the Bangladesh Water and Flood Management Strategy, which was approved in 1995, recommended to formulate a National Water Policy. Meanwhile, the existing MPO was renamed, and the Water Resources Planning Organisation (WARPO) was established in 1992 through the provision of a newly enacted law, i.e., the Water Resources Planning Act, 1992 (Act No. 12 of 1992) which was enacted to ensure the development of water resources and their proper development.

207. The Act of 1992 empowers the WARPO to: (a) formulate an environmentally balanced water resources master plan for the development of water resources; (b) determine national strategies and policies on the scientific use and conservation of water resources; (c) advise other agencies responsible to development, use and conservation of water resources, cooperate them in conducting surveys; and evaluate and review the issues arising out of the measures taken by such organization; (d) promote education, training and professional standards in the use of water resources; (e) collect and review information on the use of water resources and make arrangements for their dissemination; (f) organize and conduct international seminars, conferences and workshops on water resources nationally with the prior approval of the government; and (g) perform other duties related to water resources given by the government.[168] In 1999, the National Water Policy was formulated,

167. Section 6(1), the Bangladesh Water Development Board Act, 2000 (Act No. 26 of 2000).
168. Section 7, the Water Resources Planning Act, 1992 (Act No. 12 of 1992).

and the WARPO was authorized to play the main role in planning for the water resources of the country, including the coastal resources. The WARPO formulated the Coastal Zone Policy and has developed the National Water Resources Database and the Integrated Coastal Resources Database.

208. Other than the Bangladesh Water Development Board and the WARPO, two other bodies, i.e., River Research Institute and Bangladesh Haor and Wetland Development Board, and two other organizations, i.e., Institute of Water Modeling and Center for Environmental and Geographic Information Services under the Ministry of Water Resources perform an instrumental role in terms of river research and mathematical water modelling.

209. The National Policy for Safe Water Supply & Sanitation, 1998, the National Strategy for Water Supply and Sanitation, 2014 formulated by the Ministry of LGRD to ensure the people's access to safe water and sanitation services at an affordable cost contains some isolated provisions on water pollution. In the National Policy for Arsenic Mitigation and Implementation Plan, 2004 though there is no specific provision on water pollution, understandably the Policy provisions have been shaping citizens' access to safe water for drinking and cooking in the arsenic affected areas. All these Policies and Strategies provide for the decentralized management of water, which is yet to be achieved.

210. In 2013, a comprehensive law, i.e., the Bangladesh Water Act, 2013 (Act No. 14 of 2013), was enacted, following the provisions of the National Water Policy and the National Water Management Plan, 2004, to make provisions for integrated development, management, abstraction, distribution, use, protection, and conservation of water resources. This Law of 2013 has defined a few words such as 'water', 'water course', 'wetland', 'water resources', 'aquifer', 'ground water', 'surface water', 'khal', 'haor', 'baor', 'beel', and 'estuary'. According to the Law, 'water' means surface water, groundwater, seawater, rainwater and water in the atmosphere.[169]

211. The law, under section 4, provides for the establishment of the National Water Resources Council, headed by the Prime Minister. This Council, composed of members from all relevant ministries such as Ministry of: (a) Finance, (b) Agriculture, (c) Planning, (d) Local Government, (e) Law, Justice and Parliamentary Affairs, (g) Land, (h) Water Resources, (i) Foreign Affairs, (j) Fisheries and Livestock, (k) Shipping & Inland Water, (l) Environment, Forest and Climate Change, and government agencies such as Bangladesh Water Development Board, WARPO, Joint River Commission, Institute of Engineers, Institute of Diploma Engineers, etc., and one representation from NGO nominated by the Prime Minister, is the highest decision-making body relating to the water sector. The Law also provides for the establishment of an Executive Committee of the National Water Resources Council under section 9. Both the Council and the Executive Committee were formed immediately.

---

169. Sections 2(13) & 3 (1), the Bangladesh Water Act, 2013 (Act No. 14 of 2013).

212. As the farmers of the northern part of the country have been suffering due to the unavailability of sufficient irrigation water, the government has established a special body in this regard. A law, i.e., the Barind Multipurpose Development Authority Act, 2018 (Act No. 36 of 2018) was enacted for the overall development of the Barind area, i.e., all districts of the Rajshahi and Rangpur divisions and other areas declared as Barind area by the government. The Authority is responsible for, *inter alia*, developing surface and groundwater resources for irrigation purposes and ensuring their proper use; agricultural mechanization, seed production and supply and diversification of crops; planting and conservation of trees to maintain the balance of the environment; and construct and maintain limited roads for marketing of agricultural products.[170]

213. Moreover, two other government ministries, i.e., Ministry of Local Government, Rural Development and Corporations (LRGD) and Ministry of Agriculture, have been playing an important role in the governance of water in Bangladesh and thus ensuring the water remains free from pollution. Under LGRD, subordinate agencies such as Local Government Engineering Department, Department of Public Health and Engineering, Water and Sewerage Authority, local government administrations at various levels, e.g., City Corporations, municipal authorities, district council, upazila parishad, and union parishad through their mandates have been functioning to ensure the provisions of clean water for drinking and domestic use.

214. In an agro-based riverine country, the Ministry of Agriculture has been taking various initiatives in this regard through the Department of Agriculture Extension, Bangladesh Agriculture Development Corporation, Barind Multipurpose Development Authority. Besides, there are a few other government agencies responsible for ensuring the provision of clean and safe drinking water, and a list of such agencies includes: Planning Commission, Department of Agriculture, Bangladesh Inland Water Transport Authority, etc. Moreover, the roles that have been being played by the National River Protection Commission and River Research Institute are significant too. Finally, the roles of various NGOs such as WaterAid and development agencies such as UNICEF and World Bank in this regard should be appreciated as well.

§4. Domestic Legal Framework

215. A good number of laws, both general and special, primary and subsidiary, along with Policies, contain extensive provisions relating to various aspects of water governance and administration to ensure the water remains pollution free and thus safe and clean for drinking and household purposes. Relevant legal provisions can be found in the BECA, 1995, BEC Rules, 1997, National Environment Policy and Implementation Plan, 1992, the National Water Policy, Bangladesh Climate Change Strategy and Action Plan, National Strategy for Water Sanitation and Hygiene, the

170. Section 7, the Barind Multipurpose Development Authority Act, 2018 (Act No. 36 of 2018).

National Sustainable Development Strategy, National Adaptation Programme of Action and Bangladesh Delta Plan, 2100.

216. Section 3 of the Bangladesh Water Act, 2013 (Act No. 14 of 2013) stipulates that all rights over the surface water, groundwater, seawater, rainwater, and water in the atmosphere within the state territory shall vest in the state on behalf of the people, though all rights over the surface water on any private land, except for the land near to the bank of any water sources, shall remain with the owner of such land. However, the Executive Committee as established under section 9 of the Law can issue a protection order to the owner of such private land to prevent the wastage and misuse of water. This section further provides that the right to potable water, and water for hygiene and sanitation, shall be treated as the highest priority right.

217. Section 18 of the Act, 2013 sets the preferential uses of water in water-stressed areas and provides that in such areas, the availability of water shall be made in the following order: (1) as potable; (2) in households; (3) in agriculture; (4) in aquaculture; (5) for balancing ecosystem; (6) for wildlife; (7) for natural river flows; (8) in industry; (9) for salinity control; (10) for power generation; (11) for amusement; and (12) for other purposes. In addition, the law has provisions ensuring the normal flow of water (section 20), protection of flood control embankments (section 21), conservation of water sources and management (section 22), demarcation of water zones into industrial water zones, agricultural water zones, brackish water agricultural zones, and hatchery water zones (section 23), restriction on water storing (section 24), declaration of flood control zones and management (section 25), restriction on the abstraction of total water from any water source (section 26), and control of water pollution (section 28). The law provides for punishment ranging from imprisonment up to five years and a fine of up to BDT 10,000 (approximately USD 120) for the violation of different provisions of the law.

218. Section 28 of the Law, 2013, while defining 'water pollution' as direct or indirect harmful changes of physical, chemical and organic properties of water, provides that in the case of the prevention of water pollution, the provisions of the BECA, 1995 shall apply.

219. The Water Rules, 2018 were formulated on 16 August 2018. Rule 2 states that the government may, at times, fix the minimum amount of clean water, and the maximum distance of the water source based on the scientific data, and consider the geographical location for ensuring the right to water of the citizens. Whereas Rule 4 asserts, to enhance cooperation among different nations and organizations, the concerned bodies will collect the necessary information and data and preserve them in the National Water Resources Department. For violating the provisions of the Water Rules, 2018, the maximum fine is an amount of BDT 5 million (Rule 44).

220. The Participatory Water Management Rules 2014 were framed under section 25 of the Bangladesh Water Development Board Act, 2000 (Act No. 26 of

2000). These rules provide for the direct and active involvement of local stakeholders concerning a project on water resources and its design, maintenance, and evaluation. All of these projects are divided into three categories—small, medium, and large—which are again subdivided into other different categories. These rules also contain detailed provisions on how to elect members in different water management projects.

221. The National River Protection Commission Act, 2013 (Act 29 of 2013) was enacted to establish a commission to control illegal possession of and encroachment upon rivers, water and environmental pollution, river pollution caused by industries, to restore the normal flow of the rivers and to make rivers suitable for navigation and to ensure the multipurpose use of rivers in socio-economic development. The Commission, which consists of a chairman and five other members, is a statutory public authority and is responsible for making different guidelines and recommendations to the government to implement different objects of the law.

222. Concerning water, initiatives were taken to finalize the Water Policy to comply with the provisions of the Bangladesh Water Act 2013. The government has established the 'Bangladesh Haor and Wetlands Development Department' as an attached Department of the Ministry of Water Resources through Gazette Notification dated 7 February 2016 to ensure the coordinated development and proper management of unlimited natural resources in wetlands of the country.

I. Surface Water Pollution

223. The National Water Policy, 1997 has rightly identified that the surface water supplies in the rural areas of Bangladesh are generally polluted. The Bangladesh Water Act, 2013 (Act No. 14 of 2013) defines 'surface water' as any water on the surface of water sources. There is no special law on the regulation of surface water; however, as per section 28 of the Bangladesh Water Act, 2013 (Act No. 14 of 2013), the provisions of the BECA, 1995 shall be applicable in this regard.

224. The DoE can mark a place as a wetland, and such place shall not be filled or changed in any other way notwithstanding anything contained in any other law for the time being in force, though such restrictions may be relaxed by obtaining clearance from the DoE for the essential national interest.[171]

225. The BECA, 1995 has not included any specific provision on water pollution, instead the law has included some broad and general provisions. For example, it is provided that the DG of the DoE has the authority to conduct drinking water quality monitoring programmes, prepare reports, and give advice or, as the case may be, instructions to all concerned to follow the drinking water standards.[172] Under section 6A of the BECA, 1995, the DG can direct to stop the production, import,

171. Section 6E, the Bangladesh Environment Conservation Act, 1995 (Act No. 1 of 1995).
172. Section 4(2)(h), the Bangladesh Environment Conservation Act, 1995 (Act No. 1 of 1995).

marketing, sale, display for sale, storage, distribution, transportation for commercial purpose or commercial use of anything harmful for the environment. Though there is an indication that this provision deals mainly with the control of the rampant use of polythene which is one of the main culprits in creating various environmental problems, this provision can also be interpreted in relation to water pollution as polyethylene is responsible for waterlogs resulting in water pollution in the disaster-prone Bangladesh with an inadequate drainage system.

226. Under the BECA, 1995, the concept 'pollution' means the contamination or alteration of the physical, chemical, or biological properties, *inter alia*, of water, including change in the temperature, taste, odour, density, or any other characteristics. To know the standard physical, chemical or biological properties of water, the Environment Conservation Rules, 1997 (as last amended in 2017) have provided for the standard for both inland surface water and drinking water. The standard for inland surface water including the standards for the source of drinking water for supply only after disinfecting, water usable for recreational activity, source of drinking water for supply after conventional treatment, water usable by fisheries, water usable by various process and cooling industries, and water usable for irrigation is shared below:

Table 8 Standards for Inland Surface Water

Best Practice Based Classification	*Parameter*			
	pH	*BOD mg/l*	*DO mg/l*	*Total Coliform number/100 ml*
a. Source of drinking water for supply only after disinfecting	6.5–8.5	2 or less	6 or above	50 or less
b. Water usable for recreational activity	6.5–8.5	3 or less	5 or more	200 or less
c. Source of drinking water for supply after conventional treatment	6.5–.5	6 or less	6 or more	5000 or less
d. Water usable by fisheries	6.5–8.5	6 or less	5 or more	5000 or less
e. Water usable by various process and cooling industries	6.5–8.5	10 or less	5 or more	
f. Water usable for irrigation	6.5–8.5	10 or less	5 or more	1000 or less

Notes:

1. In water used for pisciculture, the maximum limit of the presence of ammonia as Nitrogen is 1.2 mg/l.

2. Electrical conductivity for irrigation water – 2250 μmho/cm (at a temperature of 25°C); Sodium less than 26%; boron less than 0.2%

Source: Schedule III to the Environment Conservation Rules, 1997.

227. The Department of Public Health Engineering under the Ministry of Local Government, Rural Development and Co-operatives is the national main agency responsible for the provision of drinking water supply, sanitation, and hygiene, and waste management except in Dhaka, Narayanganj, and Chottogram, where a different WASA performs these duties.

228. The Protection and Conservation of Fish Act, 1950 (East Bengal Act No. XVIII of 1950) empowers the government to formulate rules to be applied to any water or waters prohibiting 'the destruction of, or any attempt to destroy, fishes by the poisoning of waters or the depletion of fisheries by pollution by trade effluents or otherwise'.

II. Groundwater Pollution

229. The Bangladesh Water Act, 2013 (Act No. 14 of 2013) defines 'ground water' as any water underneath the soil which flows through aquifers and is abstractable onto the surface by the natural or artificial process. Since the surface water sources are generally polluted, the people of Bangladesh rely mostly on groundwater to meet their daily needs. Unfortunately, the groundwater in some places is also contaminated with arsenic and contains elevated levels of dissolved iron, manganese and boron.[173] Therefore, the Ground Water Management Ordinance, 1985 (Ordinance No. XXVII of 1985) was enacted to manage the groundwater resources for agricultural production. Under the said Ordinance, a licence has to be obtained to instal a deep tube well, shallow tube well, suction lift hand-pumped well or deep-set hand-pumped well used for irrigation or water supply. The Ordinance has not contained any pollution-related provision.

230. There are some general provisions available in the National Water Policy, 1999 and the Bangladesh Water Act, 2013, though these legal instruments do not provide 'effective guidelines on permission, extraction limit, monitoring, protection of quality, water harvesting procedure, and recharge mechanism'.[174] The previous Ground Water Management Ordinance, 1985 (Ordinance No. XXVII of 1985) was recently repealed and replaced by the Management of Ground Water for Agricultural Purpose Act, 2018 (Act No. 5 of 2018). Unfortunately, this law has not included any provision on pollution and therefore, as per section 28 of the Bangladesh Water Act, 2013 (Act No. 14 of 2013), the provisions of the BECA, 1995 shall be applicable.

173. Shama E. Haque. 'An Overview of Groundwater Quality in Bangladesh'. *Groundwater of South Asia* (2018): 205–232.

174. Shubhra Bhattacharjee et al. 'Groundwater Governance in Bangladesh: Established Practices and Recent Trends'. *Groundwater for Sustainable Development* 8 (2019): 69–81.

III. Marine Pollution

231. The word 'marine' indicates anything relating to sea or ocean which covers almost three-fourths of the earth and is the most valuable natural resource of the earth in all senses, e.g., food, job, transport, biodiversity, etc. Therefore, the marine environment demands sustainable development which is threatened due to reckless pollution.

232. Marine pollution is not a new issue, rather human beings have been discharging chemical contaminants into the ocean for long. The researchers traced that back in the 1500s, people started to release anthropogenic mercury from the mining into the ocean.[175] Marine pollution refers to the introduction of substances by humans into the marine environment, resulting in harm to living resources, presenting hazards to human health, downgrading the quality of seawater, and hindering marine activities such as fishing and swimming.[176] A good number of international and regional instruments have also been adopted in this regard.[177] Article 1 (1) (4) of the United Nations Convention on the Law of the Sea, 1982 (UNCLOS), which includes the causes and consequences of 'marine pollution', defines such pollution in the following manner:

> The introduction by man, directly or indirectly, of substances or energy into the marine environment, including estuaries, which results or is likely to result in such deleterious effects as harm to living resources and marine life, hazards to human health, hindrance to marine activities, including fishing and other legitimate uses of the sea, impairment of quality for use of sea water and reduction of amenities.[178]

---

175. Juan José Alava. 'Ocean Pollution and Warming Oceans: Toward Ocean Solutions and Natural Marine Bioremediation'. In *Predicting Future Oceans: Sustainability of Ocean and Human Systems Amidst Global Environmental Change*, ed. Andrés M. Cisneros-Montemayor, William W.L. Cheung & Yoshitaka Ota (Amsterdam, Netherlands: Elsevier, 2019), pp. 495–518.
176. C.R. Nichols & R.G. Williams. *Encyclopedia of Marine Science* (New York: Facts on File, Inc., 2009) 360.
177. For example, the Geneva Convention on the Continental Shelf, 1958; Geneva Convention on Fishing and Conservation of the Living Resources of the High Seas, 1958; Arctic Waters Pollution Prevention Act (Canada), 1970; Oslo Convention for the Prevention of Marine Pollution by Dumping from Ships and Aircraft, 1972; London Convention on the Prevention of Marine Pollution by Dumping of Wastes and Other Matter, 1972; International Convention for the Prevention of Pollution from Ships, 1973; Convention on the Protection of the Environment between Denmark, Finland, Norway and Sweden, 1974; Draft Rules on Sea Pollution, 1968; Draft Articles on Marine Pollution of Continental Origin, 1972; GESAMP definition, 1969; Paris Convention for the Prevention of Marine Pollution from Land-Based Sources, 1974; Convention on the Protection of the Marine Environment of the Baltic Sea Area, 1974; Convention for the Protection of the Mediterranean Sea Against Pollution, 1976; Kuwait Regional Convention for Co-operation on the Protection of the Marine Environment from Pollution, 1978; Convention for Co-operation in the Protection and Development of the Marine Environment of the West and Central African Region, 1981; Law of the Sea Convention, 1982.
178. The United Nations Convention on the Law of the Sea, opened for signature 10 December 1982, 1833 UNTS 3 (entered into force on 16 Nov. 1994). It may be relevant to share here that after studying at least sixteen international instruments on oceanic areas of international importance between 1954 and 1982, excluding conventions relating to pollution from specific substances, researchers

233. The United Nations Glossary of Environmental Statistics and international organization such as Organisation for Economic Co-operation and Development (OECD) has also included similar features in the definition of 'marine pollution'.[179] However, subsequently, the General Multilingual Environmental Thesaurus has expanded the definition. Accordingly, with the direct and indirect release, the accidental release of dangerous or toxic substances, e.g., industrial, commercial and urban wastewater, has also been included within the definition of the term.[180] From these definitions, some features of marine pollution can be revealed. These are: (a) the pollution must be induced by human beings directly or indirectly, (b) by the introduction of substances or energy, and (c) with such actions of the human being it must: (i) deteriorate and degrade the marine environment, (ii) harm the living resources, and (iii) endanger human health and marine lives.

234. Various factors, e.g., discharge of oil and radioactive materials, domestic sewage, pesticides, inorganic wastes, including pulp and paper wastes, military wastes, heat, detergents, solid objects, and dredging spoil and inert wastes have been contributing to making the marine environment polluted.[181] The United Nations Educational, Scientific and Cultural Organization (UNESCO) revealed that the agricultural run-off, discharge of nutrients and pesticides, and untreated sewage including plastics account for approximately 80% of marine pollution worldwide.[182]

235. Bangladesh is a coastal state and blessed to have the Bay of Bengal in the southern part of the country. Marine pollution, like other parts of the world, is a concern for the country as well. In the context of Bangladesh, the Republic is the owner of all lands, minerals, and other things of value underlying the ocean within the territorial waters, or the ocean over the continental shelf.[183] The Bangladesh National Programme of Action for Protection of the Coastal and Marine Environment from Land-Based Activities, 2006 identified at least fifteen main sources of coastal and marine pollution. These are: industrial waste (including ship Break yards), sewage disposal, solid waste management, agrochemicals and PoPs, deforestation, salinity intrusion, rapid urbanization, erosion in the coastal zone, extraction of coastal resources, gas oil, and mineral resources, shrimp farming, coastal fishing and fish processing, coastal tourism, land use change and climate change.

---

found that the definition on marine pollution as included in the UNCLOS, 1982 is comprehensive enough to cover all aspects. *See*, Tomczak Jr, 'Defining Marine Pollution: A Comparison of Definitions used by International Conventions'. Marine Policy (1984): 311.

179. United Nations Glossary of Environmental Statistics, https://unstats.un.org/unsd/environmentgl/gesform.asp?getitem=738 ; OECD, Marine Pollution, Glossary of Statistical Terms, 2001, https://stats.oecd.org/glossary/detail.asp?ID=1596.
180. Marine Pollution, General Multilingual Environmental Thesaurus, https://www.eionet.europa.eu/gemet/en/concept/5044.
181. H Rahman, *Legal Regime of Marine Environment in the Bay of Bengal* (New Delhi: Atlantic Publishers & Distributors (P) Ltd., 2007) 6.
182. United Nations Educational, Scientific and Cultural Organisation, *Facts and figures on marine pollution*, http://www.unesco.org/new/en/natural-sciences/ioc-oceans/focus-areas/rio-20-ocean/blueprint-for-the-future-we-want/marine-pollution/facts-and-figures-on-marine-pollution/.
183. Article 143, the Constitution of Bangladesh, 1972.

236. Various government agencies of the country have been dealing with various aspects relating to marine pollution. These are: MoEFCC, DoE, Department of Shipping, Department of Fisheries, Port Authorities of Chittagong, Mongla, and Payra, Mercantile Marine Department, Department of Explosives, Bangladesh Navy, and Bangladesh Coast Guard.

237. Bangladesh has signed or accessed and ratified most of the international instruments that address marine pollution. The country has also enacted a considerable number of domestic laws to address this challenge. Immediately after the independence of the country, the government enacted the Territorial Water and Maritime Zones Act, 1974 (Act No. XXVI of 1974) to declare the territorial waters, continental shelf, and other maritime zones of Bangladesh.

238. This Law of 1974 was substantially amended in 2021. Around forty new provisions are incorporated into the Law. Relevant definitions of the terms 'waste', 'marine pollution' and 'dumping of wastes', etc., have been incorporated. Accordingly, 'waste' includes any matter prescribed to be waste and any matter, whether liquid, solid, gaseous or radioactive, which is discharged, emitted or deposited in the environment in such volume, composition or manner as to cause an adverse effect. Besides, 'dumping of wastes' means, in the case of the sea, activities of discharging wastes, by dumping or throwing of wastes and other matters, conducted by or from vessels, aircraft, ships and offshore platforms or other man-made structures, causing marine pollution, which creates hazards to human health, harms living resources and marine biodiversity, damages amenities or interferes with other legitimate uses of the sea. Whereas 'marine pollution' means the introduction by man, directly or indirectly, of substances or energy into the marine environment including estuaries, which results or is likely to result in such deleterious effects as harm to living resources and marine life, hazards to human health, hindrance to marine activities including fishing and other legitimate uses of the sea, impairment of quality for use of sea water and reduction of amenities.[184]

239. The recently amended section 8 of this Law, 1974 empowers the government, with the aim to sustainably managing, preserving and protecting marine and coastal ecosystems, through preventing and controlling marine pollution, to take necessary measures to prevent and control marine pollution. Besides, the government is empowered, with a view to preserving the quality and ecological balance in the marine environment in the maritime zones under jurisdiction, *inter alia*, to prevent, reduce and control pollution from land-based sources, sea-based activities, by dumping or from vessels, from or through atmosphere, by plastics and microplastics; and to sustainably manage and protect marine and coastal ecosystem by strengthening their resilience and restoration.[185]

184. Sections 2(21), 2(10) & 2(5), the Territorial Water and Maritime Zones Act, 1974 (Act No. XXVI of 1974).
185. Section 8, the Territorial Water and Maritime Zones Act, 1974 (Act No. XXVI of 1974).

240. Under the Law of 1974, with the recent amendment of 2021, it is provided that the passage of a foreign vessel is not innocent and shall be considered as an offence if the vessel, while in the Territorial Sea, engages in, *inter alia*, any act of wilful pollution in contravention of the Convention and the Bangladesh Environment Conservation, Act 1995 (Act No. 1 of 1995).[186] Besides, the Law has inserted two new sections on the punishment for pollution (section 22) and punishment for failure to take measures to prevent pollution (section 23). Section 22 provides for punishment. Accordingly, the activities such as the damaging behaviours, which happened in areas outside the jurisdiction of Bangladesh, but cause pollution in areas under its jurisdiction; discharge of any types of pollutants or other substances that are prohibited by this Act; discharge of pollutants to sea without following the provisions of this Act or discharging pollutants exceeding the standard; causing of marine pollution incidents and without immediate measures to deal with due to accidents or other unexpected events; and any activity affecting directly or indirectly the marine environment in coastal areas, etc., are punishable offences.[187] However, section 23 provides for stricter punishments in the form of imprisonment which may extend to five years and/or fine of minimum 100 million BDT for failure to take measures to prevent pollution.

241. Before the introduction of the amendments in 2021, the Territorial Water and Maritime Zones Rules, 1977 were framed under which any act of wilful or serious marine pollution during the innocent passage of foreign ships through the territorial waters of Bangladesh is considered as prejudicial to the security or interest of the country. Through the recent amendment of 2021, the Law has also included provisions giving the government authority to preserve and protect the marine environment and to prevent and control marine pollution in the exclusive economic zone [sections 5(2)(c) & 5(4)(a)] and continental shelf [section 7A(f)].

242. It may be relevant to share that after the two historic judgments delivered by the International Tribunal for the Law of the Sea in the Dispute concerning the delimitation of the maritime boundary between Bangladesh and Myanmar in the Bay of Bengal (Bangladesh/Myanmar), 2012 and the 7 July 2014 Award of the Arbitral Tribunal in the Bay of Bengal Maritime Boundary Arbitration between Bangladesh and India, the government took the initiative to repeal and update the Territorial Water and Maritime Zones Act, 1974 and a draft titled the Bangladesh Maritime Zones Act, 2018 was released accordingly. Though the draft has not been passed yet, the Act of 1974 was substantially amended in 2021. Nevertheless, the Draft of 2018 has included extensive provisions on 'marine pollution'. As for the definition of 'marine pollution', the exact definition as included in article 1 (1)(4) of UNCLOS has been included. The draft law contains a complete chapter, i.e., Part X 'Marine Pollution and Environmental Protection' (sections 80–87), and includes provisions on Marine Pollution (section 81), Environmental Protection of Particularly Sensitive Sea Areas (PSSAs) (section 82) Control of Marine Pollution, Pollution Damage and Protecting Coastal Ecosystem (section 83), Enforcement with

186. Section 15(1)(d), the Territorial Water and Maritime Zones Act, 1974 (Act No. XXVI of 1974).
187. Section 22, the Territorial Water and Maritime Zones Act, 1974 (Act No. XXVI of 1974).

Respect to Pollution (section 84), Enforcement by Flag State (section 85), Legal Liability (section 86), Prevention and Control of Marine Environment Pollution by Coastal Construction Project (section 87).

243. In 1983, two other important laws were enacted. The Marchant Shipping Ordinance, 1983 (Ordinance No. XXVI of 1983) was promulgated to consolidate and amend the law relating to merchant shipping and almost all types of ships in the ports of Bangladesh and within the territorial waters of the country. Though the ships are responsible for polluting the marine environment as a consequence of their various activities, this law has not included any provision on pollution though the National Shipping Policy, 2000 contains various provisions on marine pollution.

244. Recently, the government has taken initiatives to repeal and update the law of 1983 and released a Draft in 2020 containing extensive provisions on marine pollution. The Draft contains a dedicated part, i.e., Part V on Prevention of Pollution (Chapter 40: General (sections 278, 279), Chapter 41: International Maritime Conventions on Pollution Prevention (sections 280, 281), Chapter 42: Regulations for Prevention of Pollution (sections 282–284), Chapter 44: Oil Pollution (sections 286–292), Chapter 45: Prevention of Pollution by Noxious Substances (sections 293-297), Chapter 46: Prevention of Pollution by Packaged Harmful Substances (sections 298–299), Chapter 47: Prevention of Pollution by Sewage (sections 300–301), Chapter 48: Prevention of Pollution by Garbage (sections 302–303)). The Draft, 2020 has not been converted into an Act of Parliament yet.

245. The Marine Fisheries Ordinance, 1983 (Ordinance No. XXXV of 1983) was promulgated containing provision, in section 29, prohibiting the discharge or deposit of waste or any other polluting matter in the marine reserves declared under the law. This Ordinance was repealed recently in 2020 through the enactment of the Marine Fisheries Act, 2020 (Act No. 19 of 2020). While the Territorial Water and Maritime Zones Rules, 1977 and the recently amended the Territorial Water and Maritime Zones Act, 1974 (Act No. XXVI of 1974) prohibit marine pollution by foreign ships, the Marine Fisheries Act, 2020 (Act No. 19 of 2020) contains provisions on pollution by local fishing ships. This Law prohibits the fishing by local fishing ships in the marine reserves (zone) or the high sea, i.e., the area beyond the territorial water and exclusive economic zone without the collection of licence or prior permission of the Director appointed and empowered by the government to implement the provisions of the law.[188] Such an act of fishing in the marine reserves or the high sea without a licence or permission is a punishable offence. According to this Law, such a licence can be suspended or cancelled if the fishing boat or ship is found to pollute the river or marine water, or environment.[189]

246. It was reported that a Bill titled the Bangladesh Marine Pollution Control Ordinance was drafted and was in the process of promulgation in 1984, though it

188. Sections 7 (1) and 21, the Marine Fisheries Act, 2020 (Act No. 19 of 2020).
189. Section 13 (1) (f), the Marine Fisheries Act, 2020 (Act No. 19 of 2020).

has not been passed by the Parliament and enacted yet.[190] Besides, in 2004, the Department of Shipping drafted a Marine Environment Conservation Bill, 2004 though this has not been enacted so far.

247. In the discussion on marine pollution, the issue, i.e., marine-based pollution, deserves special attention in the context of a coastal state like Bangladesh where around 29% of the total population of the country lives in the coastal zone, i.e., the area where land, ocean, and atmosphere interact with each other spreading in nineteen coastal districts, i.e., Jessore, Narail, Gopalganj, Shariatpur, Chandpur, Satkhira, Khulna, Bagerhat, Pirozpur, Jhalakathi, Barguna, Barishal, Patuakhali, Bhola, Lakshipur, Noakhali, Feni, Chittagong, and Cox's Bazar, divided into three parts, i.e., eastern, central and central. Coastal pollution from land-based (point and non-point) and sea-based sources, e.g., municipal waste from coastal cities and industrial wastes, wastewater treatment plants, untreated sewage-outfalls, untreated sewage-outfalls, partially treated/untreated industrial effluent outfalls, aquaculture effluents, runoffs from various sources, e.g., agriculture, shipbreaking, river, etc., oil spill, waste dumping from ships, etc., is a major concern for the country.[191] The government of Bangladesh has adopted various policy and institutional initiatives to protect the coastal zones. [192]

248. Following the government's initiatives started in 1999, the Coastal Zone Policy, 2005 was formulated to provide a policy framework for long-term integrated coastal zone management.[193] The Policy of 2005 provides for general guidance to at least fifteen relevant agencies and government bodies to develop the coastal zone in a manner so that a secure and conducive environment relating to life and livelihood can be provided to the communities living in the coastal areas since natural and man-made hazards including various forms of pollution affect these areas.[194] While framing provisions on 'Conservation and enhancement of critical ecosystems', in section 4.8.2, some general provisions on pollution control are

190. Regional Seas, United Nations Environment Programme, Environmental Problems of Marine and Coastal Area of Bangladesh: National Report. UNEP Regional Seas Report and Studies No. 75, https://www.unep.org/resources/report/environmental-problems-marine-and-coastal-area-bangladesh-national-report-unep.

191. Md Wahidul Alam & Xu Xiangmin. 'Marine Pollution Prevention in Bangladesh: A Way Forward for Implement Comprehensive National Legal Framework.' *Thalassas: An International Journal of Marine Sciences* 35, no. 1 (2019): 17–27.

192. A list of such initiatives include: the Off shore Islands Development Boards (1977–1982), the Bangladesh National Conversation Strategy (1987), the Coastal Environment Management Plan for Bangladesh (1987), the Coastal Areas Resources Development Plan (1988), the Special Parliamentary Committee on Coastal Area Development (1998–1990), the National Capacity Building Approach the ICZM initiative (1997), the Coastal Zone Policy (2005), the Tsunami Vulnerability Map (2005), the Coastal Development Strategy (2006), etc. *See*, Hafez Ahmad, 'Bangladesh Coastal Zone Management Status and Future Trends'. *Journal of Coastal Zone Management* 22, no. 1 (2019): 1–7.

193. For a background on integrated coastal zone management in the Bangladesh context, *see*, A.T.M. Shamsul Huda 'Interagency Collaboration for Integrated Coastal Zone Management: A Bangladesh Case Study'. *Coastal Management* 32, no. 1 (2004): 89–94.

194. These agencies are: Resources Planning Organization (WARPO), Bangladesh Water Development Board (BWDB), Local Government Engineering Department (LGED), Department of Fisheries

included. Accordingly, it is provided that: '[a]ll industrial units will be required to install built-in safeguards against pollution within a given timeframe and will help them in obtaining financial support from international bodies to carry out the adjustments. Units failing to comply with the pollution standards will be required to pay "green tax" for clean up of the environment polluted by them'.[195] The Coastal Development Strategy was also approved in 2006. As a result, the 7th Five Year Plan (2016–2020) has recently proposed an integrated coastal and ocean governance framework.

249. Realizing the importance and necessity to establish a specialized law enforcement agency, the Coast Guard Act, 1994 (Act No. 26 of 1994) was enacted to ensure the security of the maritime area and coastal areas of Bangladesh and to safeguard national interests in those areas. This Law of 1994 was updated in 2016 through the enactment of the Bangladesh Coast Guard Act, 2016 (Act No. IX of 2016), and the law provides for the establishment of a paramilitary force named 'Bangladesh Coast Guard' (section 4), which will be responsible to, *inter alia*, observe, monitor and prevent environment pollution-related activities [section 10 (h)].

250. There are three main seaports in Bangladesh in Chottogram, Mongla, and Payra. Though the Ports Act, 1908 (Act No. XV of 1908), enacted to deal with the administration and management of port affairs, the safety of shipping and conservation of ports and port-duties, fees and other charges, etc., does not contain any provision on pollution, both the Chittagong Port Authority Ordinance, 1976 (Ordinance No. LII of 1976) and the Mongla Port Authority Ordinance, 1976 (Ordinance No. LIII of 1976) enacted to establish the Chittagong and Mongla Port authorities respectively were amended in 1995 to include some broad and general provisions relating to pollution and make the throwing or allowing 'to fall into the water, shore, bank or land within the limits of the Port any goods, ballast ashes or any other thing whatsoever causing pollution of the water or environment' a punishable offence.[196] Similar provisions are also included in the law enacted to establish the Payra Port Authority.[197]

251. Both these above Ordinances of 1976 were repealed in 2022 through the Mongla Port Authority Act, 2022 (Act No. VII of 2022) and the Chattogram Port Authority Act, 2022 (Act No. VIII of 2022). While repealing and updating the previous Ordinances, relevant provisions were reviewed and included in the updated

(DoF), Forest Department (FD), Department of Livestock Service (DoLS), Department of Agricultural Extension (DAE), Directorate of Land Record and Surveys (DLRS), Department of Public Health Engineering (DPHE), Disaster Management Bureau (DMB), Department of Environment (DoE), Bangladesh Parjatan Corporation (BPC), Bangladesh Inland Transport Authority (BIWTA), Bangladesh Agricultural Research Council (BARC), and Coast Guard (CG).

195. Section 4.8.2(b), the Coastal Zone Policy, 2005.

196. Section 41A, the Chittagong Port Authority Ordinance, 1976 (Ordinance No. LII of 1976) [now repealed]; Section 41A, the Mongla Port Authority Ordinance, 1976 (Ordinance No. LIII of 1976) [now repealed].

197. Section 42, the Payra Port Authority Act, 2013 (Act No. 53 of 2013).

laws. It is provided that if: 'anyone or any ship discharges, or permits the discharge of any waste, ash, oil or greasy substance or any other substance on the beach, coast or land which pollutes the water and environment, and causes damage to the aquatic animals, plants etc. within the port territory, then the provisions of serial no. 10 (1) of table in section 15 (1) of the BECA, 1995 (Act No. 1 of 1995) shall apply'.[198] It may be relevant to share here that this provision of BECA, 1995 (Act No. 1 of 1995) provides for punishment of imprisonment for up to two years and fine up to BDT 200,000 for the first offence and imprisonment for up to ten years and fine up to BDT 1,000,000 for every subsequent offences.

252. Bangladesh is one of the lucrative destinations for Shipbreaking, and this industry has been contributing a lot to the economy of the country. Nevertheless, this has been reported frequently that this industry is one of the main contributors to marine pollution. Two different subsidiary laws, i.e., the Ship-breaking and Hazardous Waste Management Rules, 2010 and the Ship Breaking and Recycling Rules, 2011 have already been enacted to deal with various aspects of shipbreaking, including pollution.

253. The Department of Explosives, under the Ministry of Power, Energy and Mineral Resources, is responsible for regulating the manufacture, possession, use, sale, transport and importation of explosives, i.e., gunpowder, nitroglycerine, dynamite, guncotton, blasting powders, fulminate of mercury or other metals, includes fog signals, fireworks, fuses, rockets, percussion caps, detonators, cartridges, ammunition of all descriptions, etc. This Department can play an important role in monitoring the pollution while granting licences under the provisions of the Explosives Rules, 2004 for transportation and importation of explosives by sea through the seaports.

254. The Petroleum Act, 2016 (Act No. 32 of 2016), which was enacted to make provisions relating to the import, transport, storage, production, refining, blending, or reclaiming by recycling, marketing, and distribution of petroleum and other inflammable substances, prohibits the import, transportation, storage and distribution of petroleum without a licence obtained under the Petroleum Rules, 2018 formulated under the Act of 2016. The Rules, 2018 allow the import of petroleum only through the Chottagram, Mongla, Khulna, and Payra seaports.[199]

255. Bangladesh has experienced incidents of various limited-scale chemical and oil spillages having serious detrimental impacts on the environment. Besides, being a coastal state, Bangladesh has to suffer also due to the strategic location of the country in the Bay-of-Bengal. Recently in 2020, the MoEFCC has adopted the National Oil and Chemical Spill Contingency Plan following the provision of the international instruments, e.g., MARPOL, UNCLOS, etc., and the guidelines developed by SACEP, and the Regional Oil and Chemical Pollution Contingency Plan

198. Section 41, the Mongla Port Authority Act, 2022 (Act No. VII of 2022), and Section 41, the Chattogram Port Authority Act, 2022 (Act No. VIII of 2022).
199. Rule 22, the Petroleum Rules, 2018.

for the South Asian Seas containing provisions on response measures aiming to protect the environmental components. With this policy initiative, Bangladesh also has been concentrating on specialized equipment, e.g., vessel to be used as an oily waste reception vessel, dispersant, etc.

256. The Parliament has enacted the Bangabandhu Sheikh Mujibur Rahman Maritime University, Bangladesh Act, 2013 (Act 47 of 2013) to establish a specialized university for higher education and research on maritime affairs in Anwara, Chittagong, on the campus of the Bangladesh Marine Academy. The Law of 2013 provides that the University shall provide teaching and research on safe navigation management and administration, marine engineering and technology, oceanography, international maritime law, maritime strategy, maritime security, shipbuilding engineering and architecture, hydrography, sea resources, maritime legislation, and any other relevant issues in graduate and postgraduate level. With the establishment of a dedicated University, it can be anticipated that the University will play instrumental roles in shaping the policy of the government relating to marine pollution by undertaking various theoretical and empirical research.

Chapter 4. Waste

§1. Introduction

257. Waste is the natural consequence of various activities of life on earth and is increased with economic progress and development activities. While some kinds of wastes are generally degradable and recycled naturally, some are not. Such wastes can be in the natural environment for ages and may create additional concerns by way of a chemical reaction resulting in imbalances in the ecosystem and loss of biodiversity. Thus, waste management is a concern for most developing countries as the waste generation rate is ever increasing. Though it is believed that the developed countries have the financial and technological capabilities to manage the issue while continuing their development activities, there is frequent news that some of these countries have been exporting wastes in some of the developing or least developed countries in exchange for a negligible amount of money.

258. The issue of wastes and their management is, directly or indirectly, related to almost all UN sustainable development goals. Some of the SDGs, e.g., good health and well-being (goal no. 3); clean water and sanitation (goal no. 6); decent work and economic growth (goal no. 8); industries, innovation and infrastructure (goal no. 9); sustainable cities and communities (goal no. 11); responsible consumption and production (goal no. 12); climate action (goal no. 13); life below water (goal no. 14); life on land (goal no. 15) and peace, justice and strong institutions (goal no. 16), etc., are directly related.

259. World Bank estimates that 33% of the solid waste generated annually worldwide is not managed in an environmentally safe manner. Annually, 2.01 billion tonnes of municipal solid waste are generated worldwide where every human being on average generates 0.74 kilogram of solid waste.[200]

260. There are no reliable and official statistics or data about the amount of waste generated in Bangladesh every year though it is evident that the issue is serious and this has been increasing regularly in the absence of proper recycling and management facilities. Nevertheless, based on the World Bank's benchmark, i.e., 0.74 kg of solid waste per person per day, an estimation about the amount of waste generated in the densely populated Bangladesh can be anticipated where around 170 million people live in a small area of land and realizing the impact of waste on human health and the environment, the importance of waste management can be perceived. It has been reported that approximately 312 tons of one-time use plastic

200. The World Bank, What a Waste 2.0: A Global Snapshot of Solid Waste Management to 2050, https://datatopics.worldbank.org/what-a-waste/trends_in_solid_waste_management.html.

are produced each month, and almost 250 tons of non-recyclable plastic products are sold every month in Dhaka old town alone, and over 4,000 tons of single-use plastic are produced annually.[201]

I. Waste in General

261. Waste is the by-product of industrial activities which started in this part in the 1960s. As a result, Chapter III (section 13) of the Factories Act, 1965 (Act No. IV of 1965), though did not define 'waste', included a provision on waste in very general terms that every factory shall make effective arrangements 'for the disposal of wastes and effluents due to the manufacturing process carried on therein'. Subsequently, the definition of 'waste' was included in section 2 of the East Pakistan Water Pollution Control Ordinance, 1970 (Ordinance No. V of 1970) where 'waste' was defined as 'sanitary sewage, industrial discharges and all other liquid, gaseous, solid, radioactive, or other substances which may pollute or tend to pollute any waters'. The Ordinance, 1970 was subsequently adapted in Bangladesh, and finally, the BECA, 1995, in section 2, slightly revised the definition and defined 'waste' in more general terms as any liquid, gaseous, solid, radioactive substance, the discharge, disposal, and dumping of which may cause harmful change to the environment. The BECA, 1995 empowers the government, subject to the provisions of other laws and through the formulation of Rules, to reduce environmental harms, control the production, processing, holding, stocking, loading, logistics, transport, import, export, disposal, and dumping, etc., of hazardous waste, i.e., any substance the chemical or biochemical properties of which are such that their production, availability, release or uncontrolled transport is harmful to the environment.[202]

262. The Factories Act, 1965 was subsequently repealed by the Bangladesh Labour Act, 2006 (Act No. 42 of 2006), and this Act of 2006 reproduced the same provision of the previous law of 1965 using the same language regarding the disposal of wastes and effluents (section 54) and dirt and refuse [section 51(a)]. However, the Act, 2006 has also empowered the government to formulate Rules prescribing 'arrangements to be made in an establishment for disposal of its wastes and effluents or for requiring approval from prescribed authority for such arrangements' [section 351 (1)(a)(ii)]. Accordingly, the Bangladesh Labour Rules, 2015 were formulated containing provisions on removal of wastes (rules 40 & 47). Rule 40 provides that 'wastes should be removed in the box with lid as the appropriate measure so that bad smell or germs can't be spread from these', and 'metallic objects, wastes with terrible odor, chemical wastes and medical wastes should be removed in separate boxes every day'. On the other hand, rule 47 provides that arrangements of removing the wastes and liquids following the provisions of the existing law and direction of the country and the clearance issued by the concerned

201. Mehedi Al Amin, 4,000 tons of single-use plastic produced annually, https://www.dhakatribune.com/bangladesh/environment/2018/11/15/4-000-tons-of-single-use-plastic-produced-annually.

202. Section 2, the Bangladesh Environment Conservation Act, 1995 (Act No. 1 of 1995).

environment and health authorities should be submitted to the inspector and the inspector, considering the health of worker's, may include additional measures to remove the wastes. Besides, it is also provided that: '[a]ll drains carrying wastes and water should be constructed with impervious materials with strong and durable lids so that there will be regular water flow and those wastes should be removed after making free from pollution'. Both these requirements need to be fulfilled to get the clearance certificate from the inspector.

263. As waste, and often hazardous waste, is a natural by-product of human development activities, this issue is automatically covered in most of the development plans and strategies in every country, including Bangladesh. As a result, one may notice that the provisions on waste management are included in national policies of Bangladesh such as the National Policy for Water Supply and Sanitation, 1998; the National Industrial Policy, 2005; National Renewable Energy Policy, 2008; and the National Agriculture Policy, 2018. Relevant provisions can also be found in the National Environmental Management Action Plan, 1995; Urban Management Policy Statement, 1998; National Urban Policy, 2006 (Draft); Private Sector Infrastructure Guidelines, 2004; Dhaka Environment Management Plan, 2005; National CDM Strategy, 2005; National Sanitation Strategy, 2005; Bangladesh Climate Change Strategy and Action Plan, 2009; Dhaka Structure Plan, 2016–2035 (Draft), etc.

264. In the context of Bangladesh, many laws can be identified containing direct and indirect provisions on the management of different types of waste, including hazardous and dangerous waste. A list of such laws include: the BECA, 1995 (including its various amendments, last amended in 2010); the Bangladesh Environment Conservation Rules, 1997 (including its various amendments, last amended in 2017); the Bangladesh Environment Courts Act, 2010; the Medical Waste Management and Processing Rules, 2008; the Ship Breaking and Ship Recycling Rules, 2011; the Ozone Layer Depleting Substances (Control) Rules, 2004; the Animal Slaughtering and Control of Standard of Meat Act, 2011; the Local Government (City Corporation) Act, 2009; the Local Government (Municipal Corporation) Act, 2009; the Pesticides Management Act, 2006; the Public Health (Emergency Provisions) Ordinance, 1944; the Criminal Procedure Code, 1898 (empowers the Magistrate to take actions to control public nuisance); the Penal Code, 1860; the Bangladesh Labour Act, 2006 (dealing with the cleanliness of the factory premises); the Pure Food Act, 2013 (containing provisions prohibiting the spoiled and expired food for selling); the Town Improvement Act, 1953; the Chattogram Development Authority Act, 2018; the Khulna Development Authority Act, 2018; the Rajshahi Town Development Authority Act, 2018; the Dhaka Metropolitan Police Ordinance, 1976; the Chittagong Metropolitan Police Ordinance, 1978; the Khulna Metropolitan Police Ordinance, 1985; the Rajshahi Metropolitan Police Act, 1992; the Gazipur Metropolitan Police Act, 2018; the Rangpur Metropolitan Police Act, 2018; the Water Supply and Sewerage Authority Act, 1996 (area under the jurisdiction of Dhaka), etc.

265. The Bangladesh Environment Conservation Rules, 1997 have included the standards for waste from industrial units or projects waste in Schedule 10. Besides, various other legal and policy documents have also been adopted in this regard. A list of such documents includes: Lead Acid Battery Recycling and Management Rules, 2006; the Ship Breaking and Recycling Rules, 2011; National Information and Communication Technology Policy; Import Policy Order, 2015–2018; and Export Policy Order, 2015–2018. The government has also issued several statutory orders and instructions prohibiting the reprocessing of lead-acid batteries. The tax-related various laws, e.g., the Municipal Committee (Taxation) Rules, 1960; the Paurashava Model Tax Schedules, 1985; the Municipal Corporation (Taxation) Rules, 1936; the Municipal Corporation Model Tax Schedules, 1985, etc., have also empowered the government or the statutory authority to make legal provisions which can directly or indirectly be linked to waste management.

266. Moreover, some of the relevant laws are in the drafting stage, and some of these, e.g., the Solid Waste Management and Handling Rules (first drafted in 2005 and revised in 2010 and 2017, yet not finalized), are unfortunately taking a huge amount of time which may indicate government's genuine willingness to make legal provisions to regulate this sector.

267. Polyethylene plastic waste has been a real challenge and concern for Bangladesh for decades. These are cheap and easily available but one of the most notorious agents in environment management. After the deadly floods of 1988 and 1998, when plastic was found to be the main reason for blocking the sewage system, the government of Bangladesh, being the first country in South Asia, took the initiative to ban the production and use of polythene plastic bags in 2002. In 2010, the government even enacted a law titled the Mandatory Use of Jute in Product Packaging Act, 2010 (Act No. 53 of 2010) to ensure mandatory use of jute wrappers in the supply and distribution of certain products to prevent environmental pollution caused by the use of artificial wrappers. Jute is environment-friendly, and the law provides that the manufacturers may not sell, distribute or supply packaging materials other than materials made of 75% jute fibre (section 4). At least nineteen products, i.e., paddy, rice, wheat, maize, fertilizer, sugar, spices, turmeric, onion, ginger, garlic, coriander, pulses, potato, flour, crude flour (ata) and rice bran, poultry feed and fish feed were selected for this law, and it is provided that in the packaging of these products, the jute-made packaging materials must be used failing to which will make the package processor, seller, distributor and supplier liable to imprisonment for up to one year or fine up to BDT 50,000 for the first offence and the punishment will be double for the subsequent commission of the same offence (sections 13–14).

268. Thus, it is evident that though some provisions are available law in the domestic laws and the law enforcement agencies have been taking some isolated drives, this ban and use of polythene has not been properly and strictly implemented as the rampant use of plastic in different forms and ways could be identified. The price of the available alternatives has also been a factor and discourages businesses to replace polythene plastic bags with an alternative. Realizing this issue of lenient implementation of the law, very recently, BELA moved to the HCD with a writ petition and in response, the HCD directed the government to ban single-use plastic products, e.g., drinking straws, cotton buds, cigarette butts, food packaging, food containers, bottles, plates, plastic cutlery and plastic bags, in the coastal areas, hotels, motels and restaurants.[203]

269. Waste management is a real concern for all, and Bangladesh is not an exception. Different countries have come up with some innovative solutions emphasizing 3R, i.e., reduce, reuse, and recycle strategy. Some countries have imposed an additional tax to discourage people from throwing waste outside, and some countries have been reusing waste to generate energy. Bangladesh has also started some pilot projects using which some wastes are recycled and reused in different manners.

II. Dangerous Waste [Hazardous Waste]

270. The BECA, 1995, sharing the characteristics, has defined 'hazardous waste' in broad and general terms in section 2 as any waste which, due to its own physical or chemical quality or due to exposure to any other waste or substance, is capable of causing poisoning, bacterial infection, combustion, explosion, radioactivity, corrosion or any other damage. For 'hazardous wastes or materials', the Ship Breaking and Recycling Rules, 2011, as formulated by the Ministry of Industries, have also accepted the definition of the BECA, 1995. The major hazardous waste generating sectors in the country are: iron and steel industry (re-rolling mills), textile industry, fertilizer industry, refineries, chemical industry, tanneries, and healthcare institutions.[204]

271. Bangladesh is a signatory to important and relevant international instruments on hazardous waste management, i.e., the Basel Convention on the Control of Transboundary Movements of Hazardous Wastes and their Disposal and Stockholm Convention of Persistent Organic Pollutants (POPs). Bangladesh, after joining the Basel Convention on 1 April 1993, banned the import of all kinds of waste through the Import Policy Order and enacted the BECA, 1995 which is the principal legislation on hazardous waste management in the country. The recently amended Territorial Water and Maritime Zones Act, 1974 (Act No. XXVI of 1974) has included a new provision on punishment for throwing nuclear or hazardous wastes.[205] Besides, relevant and important provisions are also incorporated in the

---

203. *BELA v. Ministry of Environment, Forest and Climate Change and others*, [Writ Petition No. 14941 of 2019 (20 Jan. 2020)].

204. Bangladesh Hazardous Waste Assessment Report – 2016, p. 5, https://wwwcdn.imo.org/localresources/en/OurWork/PartnershipsProjects/Documents/Ship%20recycling/WP2a%20Hazardous%20Waste%20Assessment%20Report.pdf.

205. **17. Punishment for throwing nuclear or hazardous wastes.-** If a master of a foreign vessel discharges or permits to discharge any nuclear or other dangerous, noxious or harmful substance or hazardous waste in the Internal Waters and Territorial Sea, it shall be an offence and the master of

Hazardous Waste and Ship Breaking Waste Management Rules, 2011, and the government has also prepared the Bangladesh Standards and Guidelines for Sludge Management, 2015. Important provisions of these legal instruments are shared below.

A. *Hazardous Waste and Shipbreaking Industry*

272. The shipbreaking industry in Bangladesh is believed to offer many economic opportunities and has been projected to be very prospective though this was not recognized as industry till 2006.[206] Bangladesh has been building ships for different purposes and exporting those to different parts of the world. The country is one of the largest shipbreaking nations in the world where end-of-life ships come from developed countries.[207] Being a coastal area, people of this part of the world used to know the technique to build ships and boats since ancient times as testified by Ibn Batuta, the great Moroccan traveller, who visited this part in the fourteenth century and Caesar Frederick who revealed Chittagong as the 'centre of building ocean-going vessels in the 15th century'.[208] Several references to ships can be found in mediaeval folklore and literature, e.g., *Chandimangal* and *Manasamangal*. Various terracotta engraved in ancient temples also gives an indication about the types of ships people of this part used to build to sail to Ceylon, Java, Sumatra, China and Japan 'in pursuit of their colonizing ambition, commercial interests, and artistic and religious mission'.[209] Besides, in the seventeenth century, one complete fleet of warboats was built for the Sultan of Turkey by the manufacturers of Chittagong.[210] After the mid-seventeenth century, shipbuilding activities in Bengal 'encountered three successive long-run cycles': (i) a phase of decline in the second half of the seventeenth century as the European merchant navy steadily took over the Indian Ocean trade, (ii) a complete collapse when the English East India Company started to govern Bengal, and (iii) recovery again in the 1760s under British capital and ruining by the 1840s.[211]

---

the vessel shall be punishable with imprisonment for a term which may extend to 7 (seven) years or with fine which may extend to BDK 110 crore but shall not be less than BDK 80 crore or with both.

206. Shawkat Alam and Abdullah Faruque. 'Legal Regulation of the Shipbreaking Industry in Bangladesh: The International Regulatory Framework and Domestic Implementation Challenges'. *Marine Policy* 47 (2014): 46–56.
207. Food and Agriculture Organization of the United Nations and United Nations Environment Programme, *Global assessment of soil pollution - Summary for policy makers* (2021), at p. 20, Rome, FAO, https://doi.org/10.4060/cb4827en.
208. Shipbuilding Industry, Banglapedia, https://en.banglapedia.org/index.php/Shipbuilding_Industry.
209. Radhakumud Mookerji. *Indian Shipping: A History of the Sea-Borne Trade and Maritime Activity of the Indians from the Earliest Times* (London: Longmans, Green and Company, 1912), pp. 155–160.
210. Shipbuilding Industry, Banglapedia, https://en.banglapedia.org/index.php/Shipbuilding_Industry.
211. Indrajit Ray, *Bengal Industries and the British Industrial Revolution (1757–1857)*, Routledge, London, pp. 171–172, 2011.

273. It was reported that Chittagong Steel House first scrapped a Greek ship in 1964, and the commercial shipbreaking in Bangladesh was started in 1974 at Karnafully Metal Works Ltd.[212] However, due to some serious concerns, e.g., the management of hazardous waste, human health and environmental implications and occupational health hazards, the country was in global news headlines. As a result, various legal, regulatory and policy initiatives have already been taken.

274. In *Bangladesh Environmental Lawyers Association (BELA) v. Bangladesh*, 2009, 38 CLC (HCD) [8173]=7 LG (HCD) (2010) 118, in a dispute regarding the import of a scrap oil tanker named Atlantia/New Atlantia (IMO No. 7709136), Justice Md. Imman Ali, while instructing the DoE to take immediate necessary steps to ensure closure of all the shipbreaking yards without clearance certificate and sharing some general guidelines in relation to import of ship for breaking purpose, held that: '[w]e may mention that in issuing the above order it is not our intention to totally prohibit the import of vessels for the purpose of breaking in this country, but the government should take steps to prioritise the interests of the public and the interest of the environment as against commercial interest of ship breakers. We can only say that human life and posterity is worth much more than immediate small commercial benefit. The harm caused by shipbreaking might not be so intolerable if the vessels were decontaminated prior of importing the same and if sufficient infrastructure, precautionary and security measures are put in place to deal with hazardous working conditions and for handling and management of harmful waste materials which will inevitably be produced by the process of dismantling. It is our view that the purpose of the law has always been to ensure the safety and security of the persons working in the ship-breaking yards as well as other manufacturing industries and also to protect the environment and if sufficient measures are taken to ensure all of this, then there is no reason why ship-breaking should not continue'.[213]

275. The main and relevant legal provision in this area can be found in the Bangladesh Ship Recycling Act, 2018. Besides, some other relevant provisions are included in the Ship Breaking and Recycling Rules, 2011; the Hazardous Waste and Ship Breaking Waste Management Rules; the Inland Shipping Ordinance, 1976; the Bangladesh Shipping Corporation Order, 1972; the Bangladesh Merchant Shipping Ordinance, 1983; etc. The provisions of these Laws generally provided that the owner, importer of the ship, and the owner of the shipyard where any ship is cut or shipbreaking activities are going on should ensure that no environmental pollution and human health risk arise out of the ship-cutting or shipbreaking activities.

276. The Bangladesh Ship Recycling Act, 2018 (Act No. 8 of 2018) was enacted for the overall development, management and promotion of the ship recycling

212. Dr. Md. M. Maruf Hossain & Mohammad Mahmudul Islam. *Shipbreaking Activities and Its Impact on the Coastal Zone of Chittagong, Bangladesh: Towards Sustainable Management*. Chittagong: Young Power in Social Action, 2006: 5.
213. Similar views were also expressed in *Bangladesh Environmental Lawyers Association (BELA) v. Bangladesh represented by the Secretary, Ministry of Environment and Forest and 18 others*, 2010, 39 CLC (HCD) [7831] = 16 BLC (HCD) (2011) 123.

industry. The provisions of this law are in addition to the other legal provisions in force in the country (section 3). It is prohibited to establish a shipyard in any place other than the zones established by the government (sections 4 & 5), and violation of this provision is a punishable offence under the law (section 25). It is permitted to recycle and break down imported or locally collected ships in permitted zones (section 6). The law provides for the establishment of a Board, under section 8, to oversee the ship recycling industry and to ensure the implementation of the Hong Kong International Convention for the Safe and Environmentally Sound Recycling of Ships, 2009 and other international instruments. The Board may also issue guidelines based on relevant international law and conventions for the implementation of these at the national level (section 7). Subject to the provisions of this law, the Board shall also take necessary actions for the coordination among different ministries, organizations, or departments to continue the ship recycling activities acceptably as per the provisions of environmental laws (section 11).

277. Chapter five of the law (sections 17–20) is especially relevant as it deals with environmental protection, and the protection and security of workers. According to section 17, for the sake of protection of the environment, safety, and security of the workers, the government may, in the light of existing laws, issue guidelines, instructions, and regulations for the collection, preservation, and management of all types of wastes produced from the ship reprocessing activities. The government will establish, within three years of the enactment of this law, the Treatment Storage and Disposal Facility (TSDF) to manage the waste produced from the ship recycling activities.

278. Chapter seven deals with the punishment and trial of various offences under the law. The list of offences includes: establishment of shipyard without permission (section 25), import or collection of local ships for recycling without the non-objection certificate (section 26) or release order (section 27) from the Board, creation of forged certificate or documents (section 28), the running of ship recycling business outside the zone (section 29), etc. The offences committed under this Act shall be bailable, non-cognizable and compoundable (section 34).

279. Various agencies of the government, e.g., the Ministry of Labour and Employment, Ministry of Industries, Department of Environment, Ministry of Science and Technology, and Ministry of Power, Energy and Minister Resources have been dealing with different aspects relating to the shipbreaking activities having their mandate under various laws, e.g., the Bangladesh Labour Act, 2006 and the Bangladesh Labour Rules, 2015; the Labour Welfare Foundation Act, 2006 and the Labour Welfare Foundation Rules, 2010; National Occupational Health and Safety Policy, 2013; the Ship Breaking and Recycling Rules, 2011; the BECA, 1995; the Hazardous Waste and Management of Shipbreaking Waste Rules, 2011; the Atomic Energy Regulation Act, 2012; the Petroleum Act, 2016; the Petroleum Rules, 2018; the Explosives Act, 1884; the Explosives Rules, 2004; the Gas Cylinder Rules, 1991; the Gas Tank Rules, 1995; the Bangladesh Ship Recycling Act, 2018 (Act No. 8 of 2018), etc.

280. Of these government agencies, two ministries, i.e., Ministry of Industry and MoEFCC play a vital role. While the Ministry of Industry is more concerned about the regulation of the industry, the DoE considers the environmental aspects of the industry. Interesting, both these ministries formulated two different subsidiary legislation in 2011 to cover these two aspects. The Ministry of Industries framed the Ship Breaking and Recycling Rules, 2011 following the Directives issued by the HCD in *Bangladesh Environmental Lawyers Association (BELA) v. Bangladesh*, 2009, 38 CLC (HCD) [8173] = 7 LG (HCD) (2010) 118 (Writ Petition No. 7260 of 2008, 24 May 2011). While developing the Rules, the Ministry of Industries considered the provisions of the Petroleum Act, 1934; the Explosive Act, 1934; the BECA, 1995; the Labour Act, 2006; Import Policy Order; ILO Guidelines for safety and health in shipbreaking activities; the Hong Kong International Convention for Safe and Environmentally Sound Recycling of Ships, 2009; and the Basel Convention on Hazardous Waste, 1989.

281. Under the Import Policy Order 2015–2018, except: (a) iron and steel waste and scrape; (b) aluminium waste and scrape; (c) cullet scrape of glass; (d) copper waste and scrape; (e) recovered paper and paper board waste and scrape; and (f) break acrylic of scrape and waste, the import of all wastes/scraps is prohibited.[214]

282. The Ship Breaking and Recycling Rules, 2011 provide that: 'the Ministry of Shipping, Government of Bangladesh and the respective Port Authorities or the concerned Department of the Government reserve the right to give specific exemptions for undertaking recycling/breaking of ships grounded at any other sea front other than a recognized ship recycling plot or yard with the consent of Ministry of Industries. These rules do not apply to the ships, which are grounded and defined as a wreck. For removal of the wreck, rules under the Merchant Shipping Ordinance, 1983 shall apply'. The Rules, 2011 contain extensive provisions on waste and provide for the formation of a Ship Building and Ship Recycling Board (SBSRB) as One Stop Service provider under the Ministry of Industry. The Rules, 2011 empower the SBSRB to provide NOC (No Objection Certificate) to facilitate letter of credit to import scrap vessel by evaluating and examining Ship's detail, MOU and inventory of HW (Hazardous Waste) as per import policy order; oversee hazardous waste/materials generation and its disposal; waste generated report in précised form to be submitted to SBSRB every after dismantling of each ship; facilitate, establish, commission and operate treatment, Stowage, Disposal Facilities and central incineration plant for common use of hazardous wastes/materials; oversee yard activity relating to worker's safety, adequate measures and facilities to handle, manage and dispose of hazardous wastes/materials in the shipbreaking yards (rule 3).[215]

283. The MoEFCC, as the competent authority under the Basel Convention on the Control of Transboundary Movements of Hazardous Wastes and their Disposal,

214. The Import Policy Order 2015–2018, Chapter five: General Provisions for Industrial Import; clause-35, 36 & 37.
215. Rule 3, Ship Breaking and Recycling Rules, 2011.

has been submitting national reports regularly, and the latest one was submitted in 2019. To the MoEFCC, the relevant law relating to hazardous waste management is the Hazardous Waste and Management of Shipbreaking Waste Rules, 2011, formulated under the BECA, 1995, which prohibits the import of any ship violating the provisions of the Basel Convention (rule 17). Rule 18 of the Rules, 2011 prohibits the illegal traffic of hazardous substances or hazardous waste. It is provided that: '(1) any consignment or lot of hazardous substances or hazardous waste is deemed to be illegal movement if: (a) It is not authorized by the government; or b) Received consent of the government with misinformation or by deceiving; or c) any discrepancy between documents and consignments; (2) The exporter (from foreign country) is bound to take back illegally exported hazardous substances or hazardous waste on its own cost within 30 days from the date of reaching outer anchorage of the destination/export port; (3) In case, if the Illegal consignment could not be returned, the entire consignment will be confiscated and destroyed; the cost of destruction will be borne by the exporter or by Bangladeshi importer'.

284. With all these concerns, it is a matter of hope that the stakeholders in the shipbreaking industry have taken some initiatives in improving the safety practices, and the findings of the empirical research have confirmed this.[216] Recently, there was an interesting development in the UK having far-reaching implication regarding the dismantling of end-of-life vessels by the shipping companies in the UK. In the decision of *Hamida Begum (on behalf of MD Khalil Mollah) v. Maran (UK) Limited* [2021] EWCA Civ 326, it was held that in such a case, an UK company could owe a duty of care to the shipbreaking workers in Bangladesh. In this case, the widow of Mohammad Khalil Mollah died while working in a shipyard in Chattogram, Bangladesh. The Appellant, an English company, agreed to provide agency and shipbreaking services in respect of a vessel, on which the deceased was working. Lord Justice Coulson of the Court of Appeal of England and Wales, sharing the judgment of another decision in a case coincidentally involving Bangladesh where water samples were collected from wells used for supply of drinking water and negligent issue of report that the water was safe to drink when it was in fact contaminated with arsenic,[217] found the appellant responsible 'for sending the ship to Chattogram, knowing that this would expose workers such as the Claimant's husband to the risk of death or serious injury as a result of the negligence of the shipbreaker which employed him'.

B. Solid Waste

285. Solid waste is a concern for the country also. The Bangladesh Environment Conservation Rules, 1997 has included the standard of sewage discharge in Schedule 9, and the standards are shared below:

---

216. Moutushi Tanha et al. 'Shipbreaking in Bangladesh: Organizational Responses, Ethics, and Varieties of Employee Safety.' *Journal of Safety Research* (2021).

217. *Sutradhar v. Natural Environmental Research Council* [2006] UKHL 33, [2006] 4 All ER 490.

Table 9 Standards for Sewage Discharge
[See Rule 12]

Parameter	*Unit*	*Standard Limit*
BOD	milligram/l	40
Nitrate	milligram/l	250
Phosphate	milligram/l	35
Suspended Solids (SS)	milligram/l	100
Temperature	Degree Centigrade	30
Coliform	number per 100 ml	1000

Notes:

(1) This limit shall be applicable to discharges into surface and inland waters bodies.

(2) Sewage shall be chlorinated before final discharge.

286. The National Clean Development Mechanism Strategy, 2004 prepared by the DoE identified that the waste sector has the prospect of attracting finance in the country. The National Renewable Energy Policy, 2008 provides for the promotion of the production of biogas from waste. In 2010, the government adopted the National 3R Strategy for Waste Management. The Local Government administration, e.g., the City Corporations and municipalities are responsible for solid waste management activities. The DoE has been promoting Zero Discharge Policy and has been issuing conditional environmental clearance and renewal certificates to encourage industries to follow this. Though some projects have been taken in this regard, the government has been suffering from financial constraints, lack of qualified human resources and technological support, and lack of coordination among various government bodies. In 2005, the National Solid Waste Management Rules, 2005 were drafted, though they were not finalized. It is reported that the Draft was updated, and the Draft Solid Waste Rules, 2021 are now under review.

III. Nuclear or Radioactive Waste

287. The issue of nuclear waste management was a serious concern for all, especially after the Fukushima disaster. Bangladesh has been constructing her first two reactors 2,000 megawatt nuclear power plant in Rooppur, Ishwardi, Pabna since 2013 with the technical help of Russia's State Nuclear Energy Corporation, Rosatom. The country has also been considering the possibility of constructing another nuclear power plant with the technical support of Japan.[218] Earlier, the country

218. For a historical background of the Rooppur Nuclear Power Plant, *see*, Md Shafiqul Islam, Shafiqul Islam Faisal & Sadia Khan. 'Development and Strengthening of the Nuclear and Radiation Safety Infrastructure for Nuclear Power Program of Bangladesh'. *Nuclear Engineering and Technology* 53, no. 5 (2021): 1705–1716.

signed relevant international legal instruments, adopted the Nuclear Power Action Plan, created an independent regulatory body, i.e., the Bangladesh Atomic Energy Regulatory Authority – through the provisions of the Atomic Energy Regulation Act, 2012.[219] Initially, there was no provision on nuclear waste management, though the issue has been addressed recently as Bangladesh Atomic Energy Commission, responsible for regulating nuclear wastes in the country, signed a contract with a subsidiary of Rosatom.

288. Bangladesh Atomic Energy Commission, established through the provisions of the Bangladesh Atomic Energy Commission Order, 1973 (President's Order No. 15 of 1973) as repealed by the Bangladesh Atomic Energy Commission Act, 2017 (Act No. 23 of 2017), is now responsible for the promotion of the peaceful uses of atomic energy in Bangladesh, the discharge of international obligations connected therewith, the undertaking of research, the execution of development projects involving nuclear power stations, etc. Initially, the Commission, being the largest scientific and technical organization under the Ministry of Science and Technology, did not have any regulatory power and was mainly responsible for doing all acts and things, including research work, necessary for the promotion of the peaceful uses of atomic energy in the fields of agriculture, medicine, industry, development of related technology and electronic equipment and appliances, and for the execution of development projects involving nuclear power stations and the generation of electric power thereat, and to carry out space and upper atmosphere research.[220]

289. In 2012, the law, i.e., the Bangladesh Atomic Energy Regulation Act, 2012 (Act No. 19 of 2012) was enacted containing extensive provisions, *inter alia*, on nuclear waste management. The law defines 'radioactivity' as the decay of an unstable nucleus through disintegration or emission of nuclear particles; 'radioactive material' as any material in which radioactivity is present more than the authorized limit; 'radioactive waste' as any such material, in whatever physical form, remaining from practices or interventions and for which no further use is foreseen and: (i) that contains or is contaminated with radioactive material and has an activity or activity concentration higher than the limit set for clearance from regulatory requirements; and (ii) exposure to which is not excluded from the scope of applicable regulations. Chapter 3 of the Act, 2012 deals with the process of authorization, and provides that authorization holder, operator or foreign operator cannot exempt the authorized use, design, construction, commission, operation of any nuclear facility, and stop the disposal of nuclear waste without taking the permission of the authority [section 18(1)]. Besides, an authorization holder is responsible for maintaining a physical inventory of, *inter alia*, radioactive waste and spent fuel,

219. Bangladesh National Report of 2017 submitted under the Convention on Nuclear Safety, p. 13.
220. The functions of the Commission were originally included in s. 6(1), the Bangladesh Atomic Energy Commission Order, 1973 (President's Order No. 15 of 1973), were subsequently updated and included in s. 10 of the Bangladesh Atomic Energy Commission Act, 2017 (Act No. 23 of 2017).

and ensure safety measures for the control or mitigation of environmental pollution caused by the emission or exclusion of radioactive waste or sources in the environment (section 23).

290. Under section 36 of the Act, 2012, the original producer shall be responsible for the safe management and security of radioactive waste from the time of transfer of radioactive waste production to the transfer of radioactive waste management facility. Besides, the authorized person or organization for the management of radioactive waste shall ensure the following, namely: (a) the availability of qualified personnel and adequate funding for safety and security during the active life of the installation and during decommissioning; (b) to have provisions relating to finance which shall enable proper institutional control and monitoring system at the discretion of the authorities at the discretionary period even after the closure of the disposal facility. It is further provided that to manage the radioactive waste a few things need to be done: (a) keep the subcriticality intact; (b) ensure removal of residual heat; (c) reduce the effects of ionizing radiation on radiation workers, the public and the environment; (d) consider the properties affecting nuclear safety, such as toxicity, combustibility, explosiveness and other hazardous properties. Most importantly, the management of the used fuel and its security responsibilities shall rest on the authorized person or inventor producing the used fuel until it is supplied to the receiving agency in accordance with the agreement, and the authorized person or inventor shall ensure availability of qualified personnel and adequate funding for safety and security activities. Finally, by emphasizing on storage and disposal of used fuel management and production and classification in different categories including details of demand related to radioactive waste management and import of radioactive waste, it is provided that the content and scope of documents related to radioactive waste management, waste management equipment, details of related accounting requirements shall be determined by regulations.

291. Bangladesh Government has recently approved the National Policy on Radioactive Waste and Spent Nuclear Fuel Management, 2019 following the country's obligations under the Convention on Assistance in the Case of Nuclear Accident or Radiological Emergency, the Convention on Nuclear Safety, the Comprehensive Nuclear-Test-Ban Treaty Organization, the Convention on Physical Protection of Nuclear Material, the International Convention for the Suppression of Acts of Nuclear Terrorism, the Convention on Early Notification of a Nuclear Accident, the Nuclear Non-Proliferation Treaty, the Additional Protocol to Safeguards Agreement, the Supplementary Agreement of Provision of Technical Assistance by the IAEA. Accordingly, the government plans to establish a company, i.e., 'Radioactive Waste Management Company', under the Bangladesh Atomic Energy Commission aiming at the management of radioactive wastes used in all sectors in the country, e.g., nuclear power plants, medical industries, agriculture, livestock, etc. As per the National Policy on Radioactive Waste and Spent Nuclear Fuel Management, 2019, Bangladesh will store the waste for a limited period in a sealed environment and will not treat or dispose of such waste, rather will send it back to Russia.

292. The government has also formed eight subgroups for the proper functioning of the Rooppur Nuclear Power Plant and of these sub-groups: (i) the International Obligations, Legal and Regulatory Aspects and Nuclear Safety and Security, and (ii) Nuclear Fuel Cycle and Management of Radioactive Waste and Decommissioning are relevant for the purpose of this monograph.

293. It will be relevant to share here that in the recently amended Territorial Waters and Maritime Zones Act, 1974 (Act No. XXVI of 1974), a new provision containing punishment for throwing nuclear or hazardous wastes has been included. It provides that it shall be an offence: '[i]f a master of a foreign vessel discharges or permits to discharge any nuclear or other dangerous, noxious or harmful substance or hazardous waste in the Internal Waters and Territorial Sea' and for this, the master of the vessel shall be punishable with imprisonment for a term which may extend to seven years or with fine which may extend to minimum 800 million BDT to maximum 1100 million BDT.

IV. Electronic Waste

294. It is difficult to provide an authoritative legal and regulatory definition of the concept 'electronic waste' or e-waste, also referred to as waste generated from electrical and electronic equipment (EEE), i.e., WEEE or e-scraps. Nevertheless, it is widely accepted that e-wastes are generated from the end-use of all kinds of EEE which are discarded by the owners as waste without the intention of reuse. With the progressive development of our living standard on this earth, people have been using a burgeoning amount of diversified EEE, devices, and gadgets, developed using various chemicals, for various purposes. As the research and development activities are an ongoing process in this market-oriented capitalist time, the way these devices and gadgets are developed within the context of existing technological development, most of these EEEs become obsolete within a limited period, and only a small portion of these can be recycled. As a result, the waste generated from end-used disposed of EEE or e-waste, if not properly managed, can make the environmental components polluted by releasing toxic substances and emitting greenhouse gases.

295. At the international level, there are differences in regulatory moves in terms of EEE that should be included within the definition of WEEE or e-waste. Nevertheless, the legal and regulatory issues relating to e-waste are generally discussed within the provisions of hazardous waste. The Basel Convention on the Control of Transboundary Movements of Hazardous Wastes and their Disposal, 1991 has contained provisions on e-waste under both the hazardous and non-hazardous waste in Annex VIII and Annex IX of the Convention, respectively. Nevertheless, most importantly, to be treated as e-waste, the WEEE needs to release some toxic chemical substances or components such as lead, nickel-cadmium, and chromium.

296. The European Directive on WEEE, on the other hand, has included an extensive indicative list of WEEE. The List has included ten types of WEEE, deriving from the components/metals/substances which are assembled and used to produce EEE, within the definition and these are: (1) large household appliances; (2) small household appliances; (3) IT and telecommunications equipment; (4) consumer equipment and photovoltaic panels; (5) lighting equipment; (6) electrical and electronic tools (except large-scale stationary industrial tools); (7) toys, leisure and sports equipment; (8) medical devices (except all implanted and infected products); (9) monitoring and control instruments; and (10) automatic dispensers.[221]

297. Electricity is the hallmark of the second industrial revolution. With the advancement of our living standard especially after the Third Industrial Revolution led by ICT tools, applications and services, our reliance and fascination for these consequently increase the amount of WEEE. Recent studies revealed that in 2019, 53.6 Mt e-waste was generated globally. Of these, Asia, Europe, Africa, America and Oceania produced 24.9 Mt, 12 Mt, 2.9 Mt, 13.1 Mt and 0.7 Mt, respectively. Of these, only 17.4% of e-waste was collected officially and recycled.[222]

298. With the economic progress of Bangladesh along with the policy initiatives of the successive governments aiming to harness the benefits of digitalization after the resumption of the democratic government system in the 1990s, the use of EEE has increased in many folds and so is the WEEE. One recent study revealed that in 2018, the amount of e-waste was 0.40 million tons, and the amount will reach 4.62 million tons by 2035 with an annual growth rate of around 20%.[223] Each year, about 0.17 million tons of e-waste are generated, where around 296,302 TV sets are scrapped. Around 70%–80% of these wastes are generated from locally manufactured products. Such e-waste recycling activities cause the death of 15% of child workers and the rest with long-term illnesses.[224] Of these, as the country can recycle only a small fraction of generated WEEE, the remaining unrecycled WEEE ultimately ends in the environment and releases different chemicals. This invites serious consequences having human health and environmental implications.

299. There was no direct and specific binding legal instrument to regulate the e-waste in the Bangladesh context, though the government formulated the National 3R (Reduce, Reuse & Recycle) Strategy containing provisions, *inter alia*, on e-waste. To address this issue, the government initiated the process of drafting such

221. The European Directive on waste electrical and electronic equipment (WEEE) [Directive 2012/19/EU of the European Parliament and of the Council of 4 July 2012], Annex I.
222. Global E-Waste Monitor, 2020, https://www.itu.int/en/ITU-D/Environment/Pages/Spotlight/Global-Ewaste-Monitor-2020.aspx.
223. Department of Environment and Centre for Environmental and Resource Management, Bangladesh University of Engineering and Technology, 'Assessment of Generation of E-Waste, Its Impacts on Environment and Resource Recovery Potential in Bangladesh', Final Report, June, 2018, p. E-6.
224. Editorial, the Daily Observer, E-waste management rules – 2017, 8 November, 2017, https://www.observerbd.com/details.php?id=104758.

a law almost a decade ago in 2009. Finally, the DoE has drafted the E-Waste Management Rules, 2017 under the BECA, 1995. The draft Rules proposed 'extended responsibilities' for the manufacturers or assemblers, businessmen, repairers, and consumers. The draft Rules also contain proposals that the manufacturers or assemblers of the electrical and electronic goods/parts can ask to deposit up to 5% of the actual price of the goods for the recycling purpose. A consumer can claim such deposit money with interests after the end-use of the product. In 2019, the DoE updated the draft and finally the Rules have recently been approved by the government in June 2021.

300. The Hazardous Waste (e-Waste) Rules, 2021 were formulated to regulate the production, marketing, sale and purchase, import, export, and storage of electric and electrical goods listed in Schedule I and their storage, repairing, processing, transportation of these for research in the laboratory. Accordingly, Schedule I to the Rules includes a comprehensive list of the household appliance (e.g., washing machine, dishwasher, microwave oven, vacuum cleaner, toaster, television, DVD player, camera, etc.), monitoring and control instruments (smoke detector, engineering/environmental survey instruments, etc.), medical equipment, automatic machine, IT and telecommunication equipment. It will be pertinent to mention here that the provisions of this Rule shall not apply to nuclear wastes [rule 1(3)].

301. The Rules, 2021 have defined 'e-waste' as any electrical and electronic goods the economic life of which has been expired or the needs or utilities of which has been over or anything that has been rejected from the manufacturing process or disposed of as unnecessary. The Rules have included provisions relating to the responsibilities of the manufacturer or assembler (rule 3); dealer, business owner or shopkeeper (rule 4); repairing service provider (rule 5); collection service centre (rule 6); individuals or group of individuals (rule 7); crusher (rule 8); and reprocessor (rule 9). Of them, the manufacturers or assemblers need to take a lot of responsibilities.

302. The Rules, 2021 provide that every e-waste manufacturer, assembler, large importer, business owner or shopkeeper, storekeeper, transporter, repairer, collection centre, crusher, reprocessor, auctioneer, and exporter need to register with the DoE following the specified forms (rule 10) and need to submit an annual report (rule 16). The manufacturer, collection centre, transporter, crusher, repairer, and anyone who will make EEE for reuse will have to take the responsibility and will be liable for any kind of environmental and public health-related harms (rule 21). Besides, the manufacturer, assembler, crusher, and reprocessor must obtain the environment clearance certificates (rule 12) and these should be transported in an environment-friendly manner (rule 18). Moreover, the manufacturers of electronic and electric goods must not use dangerous chemicals exceeding the standard mentioned in Schedule 3 to the Rule. Additionally, the manufacturer, assembler and large-scale importer need to set a target for the collection of WEEE, which is shared below:

303. The target for the collection of WEEE by the manufacturer, assembler and large-scale importer is as follows:

Serial No.	*Year*	*The Target for the Collection of WEEE (Number/Weight)*
(1)	(2)	(3)
1.	In the 1st year from the date of implementation of the Rule	10% of the e-waste generated from the planned production
2.	In the 2nd year from the date of implementation of the Rule	20% of the e-waste generated from the planned production
3.	In the 3rd year from the date of implementation of the Rule	30% of the e-waste generated from the planned production
4.	In the 4th year from the date of implementation of the Rule	40% of the e-waste generated from the planned production
5.	In the 5th year onwards from the date of implementation of the Rule	50% of the e-waste generated from the planned production

Source: Schedule II, the Hazardous Waste (e-Waste) Rules, 2021.

304. The Rule, 2021 further provides that the manufacturer, business owner or shopkeeper, collection centre, crusher, repairer, or reprocessor can store the WEEE for a maximum of 180 days (rule 13). Old and used EEE cannot be imported and such EEE which were donated or granted cannot be brought (rule 15), though these can be exported with the permission of the DoE if there are no mechanisms available for their reprocessing or reuse (rule 19). The Rule has empowered and authorized various bodies, e.g., DoE, City Corporations, municipalities, and other government agencies responsible for ensuring occupational health and safety while imposing some responsibilities on them to implement the Rules.

V. Medical Waste

305. Health is wealth and is recognized as a human right. To attain this right, medical or healthcare services are provided, and wastes are generated in different stages of these services consequentially. Medical wastes, also known as healthcare waste or hospital waste, or biomedical waste, can be general and infectious, solid or liquid. According to the World Health Organization, healthcare wastes are categorized as *infectious* (materials containing pathogen in sufficient quantities that can cause diseases, if exposed, e.g., swabs, bandages, and disposable medical devices), *pathological* (e.g., human tissues, organs or fluids), *sharps* (e.g., disposable needles, syringes, saw, blades, broken glass, nails, etc.), *pharmaceuticals* (outdated and contaminated drugs and chemicals returned from wards), cytotoxic (highly hazardous substances, e.g., drugs used for cancer treatment and their metaboliters), *radioactive* (solids, liquids and gaseous wastes, e.g., toxic goiter) and non-hazardous or general waste.[225] In the management of medical wastes, three principles are followed: the polluter pay principle, the precautionary principle, and the proximity principle.

306. In Bangladesh, the right to health is constitutional and legally recognized.[226] The basic provision of health is covered by article 15 of the Constitution, and the improvement of public health is recognized as one of the primary duties of the state through article 18(1) of the Bangladesh Constitution, 1972. Though these provisions are within the FPSP and thus are not judicially enforceable, the Supreme Court has, from time to time, expanded the scope of these FPSP and interpreted that the right to health within the meaning of the right to life, which is guaranteed through articles 31 and 32 of the Constitution as discussed earlier.[227]

307. Being a developing country, the government hospitals have been providing the citizens medical or healthcare services. There are around 654 government hospitals and 5,055 private hospitals and clinics with 141, 903 beds in total, along with an additional 9,061 diagnostic centre beds. These generate a huge amount of biomedical waste. Recently, the researchers reported that in Dhaka every day per bed generates on an average 1.63–1.99 kg medical waste.[228] In another study, it was found that the average waste generation rate is 1.9 kg per bed per day or 0.5 kg per patient per day, and of these wastes, 77.4% were non-hazardous, while 22.6% were found to be hazardous.[229]

308. Apart from the general provisions available in the 7th 5-year Plan (FYP), National Environment Policy, 2018; the BECA, 1995 (as amended till 2010); the Environment Conservation Rules, 1997 (as amended till 2017); the Environment Court Act, 2010, some of the relevant legal and policy direction regarding the medical waste management can be found in the Medical Waste (Management and Processing) Rules, 2008; the Manual for Hospital Waste Management 2001; the Guidelines on Infection Prevention and Control (IPC) and Biosafety 2016; and the Environmental Assessment and Action Plan for Health, Population and Nutrition Sector Development Program (HPNSDP), 2011–2016; National 3R Strategy for Waste Management.

---

225. Health-care waste, World Health Organisation, https://www.who.int/news-room/fact-sheets/detail/health-care-waste.
226. Md. Ershadul Karim, 'Health as Human Rights under National and International Legal Framework: Bangladesh Perspective'. *Journal of East Asia & International Law* 3 (2010): 337.
227. *Chairman, National Board of Revenue (NBR) v. Advocate Zulhas Uddin Ahmed and others* (2010)15 MLR (AD) 457.
228. Md Mostafizur Rahman, Md Bodrud-Doza, Mark D. Griffiths, and Mohammed A. Mamun. 'Biomedical waste amid COVID-19: perspectives from Bangladesh.' *The Lancet. Global Health* 8, no. 10 (2020): e1262.
229. M. Manzurul Hassan et al. 'Pattern of Medical Waste Management: Existing Scenario in Dhaka City, Bangladesh.' *BMC Public Health* 8, no. 1 (2008): 1–10.

309. The Medical Practice and Private Clinics and Laboratories (Regulation) Ordinance, 1982 (Ordinance No. IV of 1982), which was promulgated to regulate medical practice and functioning of private clinics and laboratories, provides that private clinics need to obtain a licence and to get the licence, an important condition, i.e., 'proper accommodation with a hygienic environment for the patients', needs to be ensured.[230] A local NGO named Prism Bangladesh Foundation has been assisting the City Corporations in Dhaka, Rangpur, Rajshahi, Narayangong, Savar, Jessore, and Sylhet in collecting and discharging solid medical waste.

310. To address the problem of medical waste management and processing, the Medical Waste (Management and Processing) Rules, 2008 were formulated under the BECA, 1995 which defines medical waste and includes clinical wastes as well as 'any solid, liquid, gaseous or radioactive material which is discharged, thrown away or piled up (dumped) during the medical procedure, vaccination, diagnosis or medical research and causes a harmful change in the environment'. The provisions of the Rules, 2008 are applicable to all places where healthcare services are provided. These are: all public and private hospitals, consultation chambers, private clinics, nursing homes, pathological laboratories, dispensaries, pharmacies, blood banks.[231] Schedule II to the Rules, 2008 has also classified the producers of medical wastes into two categories: large-scale procedures (hospitals, health clinics, pathological laboratories, blood banks, elderly nursing homes, etc.) and small-scale producers (e.g., ambulance and mortuary service).

311. A list of medical wastes is also included in the Schedule I to the Rules, 2008, and classified medical wastes into eleven categories, i.e., general wastes (non-harmful/germfree/non-infectious), anatomical wastes, pathological wastes, chemical wastes, pharmaceutical wastes, infectious/wastes containing germs, radioactive wastes, sharp wastes (infectious/non-infectious), reusable general wastes (non-harmful/germfree/non-infectious), liquid wastes (infectious/non-infectious) and pressurized wastes. The Medical Waste Management Rules, 2008 include some general provisions on the management of waste generated from the electronic equipment used in the medical sector other than nuclear or atomic waste. The Rules, 2008 provide for the establishment of an Agency for the implementation of the provisions (rules 3 & 4). The Rules, 2008 also provide for licences for the collection, management, and processing of medical wastes and without obtaining such licences, these activities cannot be run. However, the City Corporations and municipalities can do these activities without such licence. The provisions of these Rules may also be considered for the management of medical e-wastes.

230. Sections 8 and 9 (a), the Medical Practice and Private Clinics and Laboratories (Regulation) Ordinance, 1982 (Ordinance No. IV of 1982).

231. Rules 1 (3) & 2(1)(h), the Medical Waste (Management and Processing) Rules, 2008.

Chapter 5. Soil Pollution

312. Soil is the foundation of the agri-food system and provides the larger share of the food we eat. In an authoritative report published in 2015, the Food and Agriculture Organization of the United Nations (FAO) and the Intergovernmental Technical Panel on Soil (ITPS) identified ten major threats to the world's soils. These are: erosion, loss of soil organic carbon and biodiversity, pollution, acidification and sodification, salinization, nutrient imbalance, compaction, sealing, and waterlogging.[232] Realizing the importance of the protection of soil from various types of pollutants, UNEP's governing body, i.e., the United Nations Environment Assembly, adopted a Resolution on Managing Soil Pollution to Achieve Sustainable Development.

313. Bangladesh is blessed to have one of the most fertile soils in the world. However, the soil of the country has been contaminated due to the release of heavy metal and metalloid pollution from various sources such as tanneries and brick kiln industries.[233] Soil pollution has severe consequences in an agro-based country like Bangladesh.

314. This issue of protection of soil from pollution is specially covered in various policies. The National Land Use Policy, 2001 contains some broad provisions which can be interpreted to have connections with sustainable land use activities and environmental protection. The draft of the National Land Policy was released in 2016 and is not finalized yet. The National Agriculture Policy, 2018 was formulated for sustainable agriculture and the protection of soil from contaminations.

315. There are general legal provisions on the protection of soil contamination from various types of pollution as can be found in the environment protection-related laws such as BECA, 1995. A special law aiming to regulate the lease activities relating to the complexities of the sand estate, extraction of sand and land from the sand estate, and the marketing of so was enacted in 2010 titled the Balumohal and Soil Management Act, 2010 (Act No. 62 of 2010). However, the provisions of this law shall not be applicable if sand and land from the sand estate are explored for non-commercial purposes.[234] The law, in section 2, has defined 'soil' as clay or sand mixed with clay other than mottled clay, shale or clay and China clay (Fire clay or White clay); 'sand' as all types of sand except mineral sand and silica sand, 'mineral sand' as sand rich in heavy minerals (such as Zircon, Rutile, Ilmenite, Monazite, etc.) as prescribed by the Department of Energy and Mineral Resources; 'silica

232. Food and Agriculture Organization of the United Nations and United Nations Environment Programme, *Global assessment of soil pollution - Summary for policy makers* (2021), Rome, FAO, https://doi.org/10.4060/cb4827en.
233. M. Mominul Islam et al.. 'Heavy Metal and Metalloid Pollution of Soil, Water and Foods in Bangladesh: A Critical Review'. *International Journal of Environmental Research and Public Health* 15, no. 12 (2018): 2825; Food and Agriculture Organization of the United Nations and United Nations Environment Programme, *Global assessment of soil pollution – Summary for Policy Makers* (2021), Rome, FAO, https://doi.org/10.4060/cb4827en.
234. Section 7, the Balumohal and Soil Management Act, 2010 (Act No. 62 of 2010).

sand' means the amount of silicon-di-oxide rich sand prescribed by the Department of Energy and Mineral Resources and 'Balu Mahal' or sand estate means any open space, tea garden or river bed, which is declared as Balumhal by the Deputy Commissioner under this Act, while the environment is intact and the sand or soil which is extracted or extracted is preserved.

Chapter 6. Noise Pollution and Vibrations

§1. Introduction

316. The word 'noise' is derived from the Latin term 'nausea'. Sound is the reconfirmation of the existence of life, but any sound becomes noise when it is unpleasant. Noise pollution is a general concern for any country, both developed and developing, and Bangladesh is not an exception.[235] Noise pollution can be either natural or man-made, and the sources of noise can broadly be classified as: (a) *industrial or occupational noise* and (b) *community noise* (also known as environmental, domestic, or residential noise), i.e., noise emitted from any sources other than industrial workplaces.[236] 'Industrial or occupational noise', related to noise generated from industrial operations, can be continuous or intermittent.

317. Noise becomes 'pollution' (also referred to as 'sound pollution'), when it exceeds permitted levels proposed by the responsible international bodies and adopted by the municipal authorities. [237] Noise is measured in decibels (dB), and to the World Health Organization, 45 dB is a safe level for residential areas.[238] 60 dB sound levels can cause temporary deafness in people, while 100 dB sound levels can cause permanent deafness. The legal issues relating to vibrations are covered through the provisions of the noise.

318. With some exceptions to marine and occupational noise pollution and the standards set by WHO, there is no international instrument that directly, explicitly, and comprehensively addresses this as this is seen primarily as a domestic rather than transboundary problem. Realizing that sound, at some point, is unbearable or unpleasant for living beings, including human beings, and various other environmental components, and can cause adverse effects and can be hazardous for both

235. *See generally*, Md. Ershadul Karim, Mohammad Abu Taher & Mohammad Ataul Karim, 'Noise Pollution in Dhaka and the Constitutional Right to Life'. *Australian Journal of Asian Law* 21, no. 2 (2021): Article 5: 67–84.
236. Preface, Guidelines on Community Noise (World Health Organization 1999).
237. For example, rule 2(r) of the Noise Pollution (Control) Rules 2006, as enforced in Bangladesh, defines 'noise pollution' as a noise which is above the level of sound mentioned in Schedule 1 or 2 and which is, or may be, harmful to the environment. Schedule 1 deals with the standard limits of noise in silent, residential, mixed, commercial and industrial zones during daytime (6.00 am to 9.00 pm) and night time (9.00 pm to 6.00 am). The noise limits, set in the *dB(A)Leq*, are: silent zones (50 daytime: 40 night time), residential (55:45), mixed (60:50), commercial (70:60), industrial (75:70). According to Schedule 2, the authorized noise limit for all types of motor vehicles and inland water transport is 85–100 dB(A).
238. Guidelines for Community Noise, World Health Organization, 1999.

physiological and psychological health, various countries have already set the permittable level of noise through general and special laws to minimize noise levels so that noise generated from various sources can be kept to an acceptable level.[239]

§2. Noise Pollution in Bangladesh

319. Like other types of pollution, the sound levels in Bangladesh were not a serious problem in the first two decades after the independence of the country in 1971. However, the situation has been getting worse since the 1990s, and it is, particularly in major cities, most importantly in Dhaka, almost unbearable due to improper and uncoordinated ongoing development activities and a failure to decentralize the service sectors to different parts of the country. Accordingly, the sound levels, even in residential areas and near institutions such as schools and hospitals, are beyond the permissible limit, and more than double the limit in some cases.[240]

§3. Noise and Transport

320. Transport is one of the main causes of noise pollution. Before the enactment of the Road Transport Act 2018, the relevant law on road transport, that is, the Motor Vehicles Ordinance, 1983, already contained provisions on the prohibition of installation and use of horns and other sound-producing devices without the permission of the relevant authority. Since the law was found ineffective in ensuring a safe road transport system, the government took the initiative to revise and update the law and proposed a new Road Transport and Traffic Bill in 2011. The government took a considerable amount of time to pass this Bill into law, and finally the law was hurriedly passed in 2018 in response to a movement for road safety started after the tragic death of two students in a bus accident. Because control of noise pollution from transport was not the main concern for the government in enacting this law, it mostly reproduced the provisions on noise pollution as available in the Motor Vehicles Ordinance, 1983 but with fines increased from BDT 100 (approximately USD 1.18) in the 1983 law to BDT 10,000 (approximately USD 117.96).[241] There is, however, no scope for civil remedies in the Act, and, therefore, no victim of noise pollution from road transport can get any individual compensation.

---

239. For example, the Protection of the Environment Operations Act 1997 [Australia], the Environmental Quality Act 1974 [Malaysia], the Environmental Protection Act 1997 [Nepal], the Noise Regulation Law, 1968 [Japan], the Noise Control Act 1972 [USA], the Control of Pollution Act 1974 [UK], the Dutch Noise Nuisance Act 1979 [the Netherlands], the Noise Pollution (Regulation and Control) Rules 2000 [India].
240. *See generally*, Md. Ershadul Karim, Mohammad Abu Taher & Mohammad Ataul Karim. 'Noise Pollution in Dhaka and the Constitutional Right to Life'. *Australian Journal of Asian Law* 21 no. 2 (2021): Article 5: 67–84.
241. Section 88, the Road Transport Act 2018.

321. This new Act provides that vehicles cannot be designed without following technical specifications, for example, car horns (section 40). Government or authorized bodies set the noise level limit and vehicles, except for emergency vehicles such as ambulances and fire service vehicles, cannot make noise beyond this set limit (section 45). The use of horns in silent zones is prohibited. This section also provides that the provisions of the BECA, 1995 and the Rules framed thereunder must be followed as far as possible to achieve the objectives of this section. Thus, due to the use of the words 'as far as possible', it can be inferred that the provisions of the Road Transport Act, 2018 enjoy primacy or a superior level of protection over environmental law provisions. The success of this section, however, depends on the framing of subsidiary legislation, which is yet to be formulated.

322. In addition to road transport, inland ships, railways, and aircraft, etc., also create a considerable amount of noise. While inland ships are prohibited from creating noise pollution on inland water,[242] the railways, that create a huge amount of noise, are not properly regulated. The Railways Act, 1890, one of the oldest laws in force in the country, does not contain any provision on noise pollution and unfortunately, noise caused by railways is also beyond the scope of the Noise Pollution Rules 2006.[243]

323. Historically, in 1911, the Indian Aircraft Act was enacted, and the law applied to the whole of British India, including the present-day Bangladesh, containing provisions on technical matters, e.g., the manufacture, possession, use, sale, export, and import of aircraft, registration, licensing, etc. Part II of the said law prohibited flying over cities and towns which may be dangerous to public safety by reasons of low altitude or proximity to persons or dwellings.

324. Part XVI of the Civil Aviation Rule, 1984, framed under the Civil Aviation Ordinance, 1960, contains provisions on Aircraft noise (Rules 276–79). An aircraft, whether registered in Bangladesh or a foreign country, needs to obtain a noise certificate issued and validated by the Chairman of Civil Aviation confirming that the aircraft complies with the noise requirements specified in Annex 16 to the Convention on International Civil Aviation Organisation. Though this Ordinance of 1960 was repealed and updated in 2017 through the provisions of the Civil Aviation Act, 2017 (Act No. 18 of 2017), the Rule of 1984 is still valid as per section 48 of the newly enacted law of 2017.

§4. Occupational Noise

325. There is no domestic law that specifically regulates occupational noise in the Bangladesh context. The Bangladesh Labour Act, 2006 (Act No. 42 of 2006) though contains various provisions on the protection of workers, e.g., protection of

242. Section 60A, the Inland Shipping Ordinance, 1976 (Ordinance No. LXXII of 1976).
243. Rule 1(2), the Noise Pollution (Control) Rules 2006.

health (Chapter V, sections 51–60), safety (Chapter VI, sections 61–78A), and special provisions relating to health, health rules and safety (Chapter VII, sections 79–88), etc., the Law does not contain specific provisions on occupational exposure to noise. The same is the case with the Labour Rules formulated under the Labour Act, 2006. However, it is provided that if there is an establishment with more than forty female workers, then one or more suitable rooms should be allocated and maintained for them, and such room/s should not be close to a place where excessively noisy works are carried out.[244] Although this seems to be a beneficial provision for childcare and female workers taking rest breaks, it was not meant for workers exposed to occupational noise, and, given the population density in the city, the proper implementation may not be possible. Besides, though sections 82 and 83 of the Act provide that noise-induced hearing loss is a notifiable disease,[245] for which regular, frequent, and timely information is necessary for the prevention and control of the disease, these provisions cannot be interpreted in a way that these deal with occupational noise in Bangladesh context.

326. It may be relevant to share here that the International Labour Organization adopted the Working Environment (Air Pollution, Noise and Vibration) Convention, 1977 (No. 148), which has not been ratified by Bangladesh.

§5. Noise in Residential Areas

327. Some of the domestic laws contain general provisions prohibiting noise in residential areas. This issue is covered through the provisions of the Easement Act, 1882, and the Penal Code, 1860, the two oldest laws still in force in Bangladesh.[246] The Easements Act, 1882, s 7 (b) provides that every owner of immovable property has the right to his or her physical comfort not being interfered with materially and unreasonably by noise or vibrations caused by any other person. Besides, the owner of an easement right is also entitled to enjoy the easement rights without any disturbance.[247]

328. The improper use of any land and building that causes nuisance is also prohibited.[248] The Bangladesh National Building Code, 2015 also contains some broad provisions on sound and noise management. Although no specific limit of noise is suggested, Rule 17(4) of the Dhaka Metropolitan Building (Construction, Development, Preservation and Removal) Rules 2008 provides that in a residential area, it

244. Section 94(3), the Bangladesh Labour Act 2006.
245. A notifiable disease is one for which regular, frequent, and timely information regarding individual cases is considered necessary for the prevention and control of the disease. Noise-induced hearing loss is considered as notifiable disease. *See*, Item 30, Schedule II, the Bangladesh Labour Act 2006.
246. *See*, for example, ss 268, 290 and 291, the Penal Code, 1860.
247. Chapter IV, the Easements Act 1882.
248. Section 3A, the Building Construction Act 1952.

is prohibited to produce noise pollution between 6.00 pm and 6.00 am, and it is strictly prohibited to use stone crushing machines at any time.[249]

§6. Noise Pollution under Special Law

329. The issue of noise is regulated through the provisions of some special laws.[250] The BECA, 1995 contains the general provisions on noise pollution. The law includes 'noise' within the definition of 'environmental pollutant' under s 2(e).[251] The same law, in section 20, empowers the government to make Rules on the standards for noise. Accordingly, the Environment Conservation Rules of 1997 provide for the standard sound levels for different places, such as silent zones, residential areas, mixed zones, commercial areas, and industrial areas. Schedule 4 of the 1997 Rules provides for 'standards for sound', and sets the sound level for both day (between 6.00 am to 9.00 pm) and night (9.00 pm to 6.00 am) at: 45 dBa and 35 dBa respectively in silent zones; 50 dBa and 40 dBa in residential areas; 60 dBa and 50 dBa in mixed zones; 70 dBa and 60 dBa in commercial areas; and 75 dBa and 70 dBa respectively in industrial areas. It also provides that in silent zones, the use of horns and loudspeakers is prohibited.

330. Schedule 5 of the 1997 Rules provides for the standard sound levels for motor- or machine-run water transport. In framing the Rules, policymakers seem to have seriously considered the issue of noise and therefore included a provision that industrial units that produce sound beyond permissible limits will not be permitted in commercial areas. Under the Rules, it is the responsibility of the authorized persons to inform the Director General about the environmental pollutants, including noise, that exceed the standard limit.[252] However, these Rules do not prescribe the actions of the Director General after receiving such information from the authorized person. Therefore, there is still scope for improper implementation of the law.

331. After the Rules of 1997 were formulated, the government attempted to revise the law on noise pollution almost ten years later and formulated the Noise Pollution (Control) Rules 2006 under section 20 of the BECA, 1995. The provisions of these Rules override any other law in force,[253] though they exempt several activities that are responsible for generating an extreme level of noise, including

249. Unfortunately, the Rule does not define 'residential area'. However, Rule 2(3) of the Noise Pollution (Control) Rules 2006 defines 'residential area' as an area where people live with family members. Based on this definition, and considering that Dhaka is one of the most densely populated cities in the world, it will be difficult to find any area under Dhaka City Corporation authority that is not a 'residential area', although there are some places within the City Corporation which are treated as commercial areas or industrial areas.

250. For example, the Bangladesh Environment Conservation Act, 1995; s. 45 of the Road Transport Act, 2018; Schedule 1 of the Noise Pollution (Control) Rules, 2006.

251. Similarly, s. 60A of the Inland Shipping Ordinance 1976 provides that excess of noise exceeding the standard noise level can pollute inland waters.

252. Rules 17, the Environment Conservation Rules 1997.

253. Rule 3, the Noise Pollution (Control) Rules, 2006.

sound generated from religious institutions and activities, official activities of law enforcement bodies, air transport, and railways.[254]

332. The Noise Pollution Rules, 2006 have higher standard noise levels at day and night than the Environment Conservation Rules 1997, that is, 50 dBa and 40 dBa respectively in silent zones and 55 dBa and 45 dBa in residential areas. The same standard noise level, however, is maintained for mixed zones, and commercial and industrial areas. Except for silent zones, where motor honking is prohibited within a 100-meter radius of a hospital, school, or office, it is permissible to exceed the noise level with the authorization of the authority, as specified in Schedule 3, for other activities, such as sport, social, cultural, and political activities.[255] Various local government authorities are responsible for placing and preserving standard signs and signboards in different zones. Under Schedule 3, different bodies are empowered for granting permission to use instruments that exceed the standard noise level in different places, that is, village, municipal, upazilla (subdistrict), district and city corporation areas.

333. The Rules have also considered the issue of noise pollution in the residential area generated from the construction works. Use of machinery in construction works, including machinery to crush brick or rock and concrete mixers, within the 500 meters of residential areas, is prohibited between 7.00 pm and 7.00 am.[256] Rule 14 creates a legal obligation to provide security devices for workers inside factories or using machinery that creates continuous noise above the standard limit. The law has provisions to sentence first-time offenders to up to one month's imprisonment or a fine of BDT 5,000, or both. Second-time and subsequent offenders can be sentenced to up to six months' imprisonment or a BDT 10,000 fine, or both. But lack of proper enforcement of this law has resulted in Dhaka being seriously exposed to noise pollution, which results in a rapidly decreasing quality of life.

334. To enforce the Rules, it is provided under Rule 16 that, where there is a noise that exceeds the standard level, anyone can inform a relevant officer by telephone, orally, or in writing. After investigation, the officer can issue an order to stop the noise. In addition to the Noise Pollution Control Rules, 2006 and other laws, police officers in metropolitan areas such as Dhaka are authorized to control noise pollution[257] under sections 25, 27, and 28 of the Dhaka Metropolitan Police Ordinance, 1976. The Police Commissioner, under section 31 of the 1976 Ordinance, can issue a written order to prohibit, restrict, regulate or impose conditions on the carrying on of any premises of any trade, avocation or operation resulting in, or accompanied by, noise that creates annoyance, disturbance, discomfort or injury or risk of annoyance, disturbance, discomfort or injury to the public or to any person who lives, or occupies the property, in the vicinity.

---

254. Rule 1(2), the Noise Pollution (Control) Rules, 2006.
255. Rule 9(1), the Noise Pollution (Control) Rules, 2006.
256. Rule 11, the Noise Pollution (Control) Rules, 2006.
257. *See*, for example, Chittagong Metropolitan Police Ordinance 1978 (s. 33), the Khulna Metropolitan Police Ordinance, 1985 (s. 33).

§7. REMEDIES AVAILABLE

335. Noise is a nuisance and therefore, the provisions on nuisance discussed above can also be considered. Accordingly, government agencies and public servants can take action if any of the provisions discussed above are violated. Police officers are under a statutory duty to prevent public nuisance.[258] Even in the case of 'public nuisance', where there are no special damages, the Attorney General, or two or more persons with his written consent, may institute a suit for a declaration and injunction or such other relief as may be appropriate to the circumstances of the case.[259] A District Magistrate or any other Executive Magistrate can also take initiative and order the removal of a nuisance from a public place, and any such order made by a Magistrate cannot be questioned in any Civil Court.[260] Such magistrates are also empowered to order any person not to repeat or continue a public nuisance.[261] The mobile courts, as constituted under the Mobile Court Act, 2009 (as amended in 2016), can also take action on noise pollution covered in various laws.

336. In addition, various other avenues are available using which an aggrieved person can seek legal remedies against noise pollution. An initial assessment of the provisions of the existing Bangladeshi laws reveals that an aggrieved person or victim, an organization, or specified government officials can take initiatives to reduce the level of noise pollution. An aggrieved person can claim both civil and criminal remedies under the laws discussed above. He or she can also apply for a perpetual injunction to minimize noise pollution under the Specific Relief Act.[262] In some cases, an aggrieved person can file a criminal case in the Chief Metropolitan Magistrate court under s 290 of the Penal Code, 1860, and s 30 of the Printing, Presses and Publications (Declaration and Registration) Act 1973.[263]

§8. NOISE POLLUTION AND THE COURT OF LAW

337. Although the issue of noise pollution is serious and unbearable at times in district and divisional cities, this has not been the main issue of contention in any reported landmark cases decided by the Supreme Court of Bangladesh, which oversees and guarantees fundamental rights under the Constitution of Bangladesh. The High Court Division has, on a very few occasions, indirectly discussed the issue of noise pollution. In *Dr. Mohiuddin Farooque v. Bangladesh & others*,[264] the petitioner Dr Farooque moved to the HCD for directions to restrict, *inter alia*, the use of audible signalling devices in motor vehicles, which emit unduly harsh, shrill,

258. Section 23 of the Police Act 1861 and s. 15(c), the Dhaka Metropolitan Police Ordinance, 1976. Similar provisions can be found in other metropolitan police laws.
259. Section 91, the Code of Civil Procedure, 1908 (Act V of 1908).
260. Section 133, the Code of Criminal Procedure, 1898 (Act V of 1898).
261. Section 143, the Code of Criminal Procedure, 1898.
262. Illustration (s), s 54, the Special Relief Act, 1877.
263. *Delwar Ali Khan & another v. Sajedul Haque* (1986) 38 DLR (AD) 52.
264. Writ Petition No 300 of 1995 (Vehicular Pollution Case).

loud or alarming noises. The HCD, after citing instances of improper implementation of relevant municipal laws, issued several directions, including stricter implementation of laws to restrict noise generated from motor vehicles.[265] In relation to a case on shipbreaking, the High Court Division found that the workers in shipbreaking sites are affected by the excessive noise associated with grinding, hammering, metal cutting and breaking the metal bodies of vessels.[266] The High Court Division also considered the issue of excessive noise in relation to a case on the Jaflong stone quarry.[267] Earlier, the court had also commented on the use of microphones and loudspeakers at all times of the day during the election campaign.[268] More recently, in relation to a writ petition on ongoing commercial activities in Dhanmondi Residential Area, Dhaka, the High Court Division reiterated that commercial activities create noise pollution.[269]

338. In some cases, the HCD has ruled indirectly on noise pollution, and accordingly, punitive measures were taken by the law enforcement agencies. In August 2017, for example, an NGO, Human Rights and Peace for Bangladesh, filed a writ petition to the HCD arguing that the use of hydraulic horns in motor vehicles violates the provisions of the Motor Vehicles Ordinance, 1983. The Divisional Bench of the HCD, led by Justice Quazi Reza-Ul Hoque and Justice Mohammad Ullah, issued a ruling asking the Bangladesh Road Transport Authority and Dhaka Metropolitan Police to take the necessary steps to stop the use of hydraulic horns in motor vehicles in Dhaka city and thereby prevent noise pollution. The court also asked the government to seize the instruments used for pneumatic horns and directed the government to enforce restrictions on imports of pneumatic horns, and to seize vehicles with such horns. As it was subsequently reported by the Bangladesh Road Transport Authority and the Dhaka Metropolitan Police that even though they had seized a huge number of hydraulic horns in the city, some people were still using them, the HCD then ordered the vehicle owners' association and drivers' organizations in Dhaka to surrender all hydraulic horns to the local police station within fifteen days, so that these could be dismantled and destroyed, given that their use is prohibited by law.

---

265. *Ibid.*
266. *Bangladesh Environmental Lawyers Association (BELA) v. Bangladesh* (2009) 7 LG (HCD) 118.
267. *Bangladesh Environmental Lawyers Association (BELA) v. Government of Bangladesh and others* (2010) 30 BLD (HCD) 185.
268. *Bangladesh Environmental Lawyers' Association v. Election Commission & others* (1994) 46 DLR (HCD) 235.
269. *Professor Dr. AFM Masud and another v. The Secretary, Ministry of Housing & Public Works, Bangladesh Secretariat, Shahbag, Dhaka and others* (Writ Petition No 1058 of 2011).

Chapter 7. Radiation (Nuclear and Non-nuclear)

339. Radiation is included within the definition of 'environment pollutant' under section 2 of the BECA, 1995 (Act No. 1 of 1995) and there the general provisions of the BECA, 1995 shall be applicable concerning radiation. Radiation-related important provisions are also included in the Bangladesh Atomic Energy Regulation Act, 2012 (Act No. 19 of 2012), which was enacted repealing the previous law available in this regard, i.e., the Nuclear Safety and Radiation Control Act, 1993 (Act No. 21 of 1993). While the law of 1993 was enacted to ensure nuclear safety and to control radiation, the law of 2012 was enacted to regulate the peaceful uses of atomic energy.

340. The law of 2012 has included the definitions of several terms such as radioactivity, radioactive substance, radioactive radiation, and radioactive waste materials in section 2. Accordingly, 'radioactivity' means the fusion of unstable atomic nuclei through fission or the dispersion of atomic particles, and 'radioactive substance' means any substance the radioactivity of which exceeds the approved level of radioactivity; whereas 'radioactive radiation' means ionizing radiation originating from radioactivity, apparatus, and processes; and 'radioactive waste material' means waste material created as a result of atomic or radiation processes, the radioactivity of which exceeds the approved level of radioactivity.[270] This Law of 2012 contains an extensive provision on radiation.

341. The Nuclear Safety and Radiation Control Rules, 1997 formulated under the Nuclear Safety and Radiation Control Act, 1993 following the IAEA basic safety standards no. 115 contain provisions on the protection of workers and the public from radiation. The Medical Waste (Management and Processing) Rules, 2008 also contain provisions on the management of medical waste containing radioactive materials.

342. It may be relevant to share here that under the 1993 law, the Bangladesh Atomic Energy Commission had no regulatory power. As a result, Dr M. Farooque, as the Secretary General of the Bangladesh Environmental Lawyers Association, moved to the HCD to stop the release of a consignment of imported skimmed milk power imported by Danish Condensed Milk Bangladesh Limited from M/S Datraco B.V. Netherland (Holland) containing radiation above the permitted level. While Justice Kazi Ebadul Hoque of the HCD commented that the fundamental right to life as guaranteed by article 31 and 32 of the Constitution of Bangladesh, 1972 'extends to the protection of health and strength of workers, their means of livelihood, enjoyment of pollution free water and air, bare necessities of life, facilities

270. Section 2, the Bangladesh Atomic Energy Regulation Act, 2012 (Act No. 19 of 2012).

for education, development of children, maternity benefit, free movement, maintenance and improvement of public health by creating and sustaining conditions congenial to good health and ensuring the quality of life consistent with human dignity', he did not comment on the issue of radiation as the matter was then pending in a lower court.[271]

343. Under Article 16 of the Import Policy Order, 2015–2018, subject to some exceptions, e.g., in case of import of tobacco and alcohol products, spices and medicine, etc., and in case of foods where the Ministry of Food stipulates for a different procedure, it is mandatory to test the radioactivity levels in case of import of milk, milk food, milk products, edible oil and other goods, edible vegetable seeds and grains produced in any country. It is also provided that without the collection of the clearance certificate(s) obtained from the Bangladesh Atomic Energy Commission mentioning that the radioactivity level in the imported foodstuff is within the acceptable limit, the Customs Authority shall not release the goods.

271. *Dr. Mohiuddin Farooque v. Bangladesh, represented by the Secretary, Ministry of Commerce, Government of the People's Republic of Bangladesh, Bangladesh Secretariat and others,* 48 DLR (HCD) (1996) 438= 25 CLC (HCD) [7650].

Chapter 8. Noxious Substances

344. In this world, whatever we see, touch and feel are composed of chemicals, and our life without chemicals cannot be imagined. While most of the chemicals save lives, easy to handle, some are not. Being an agricultural country where a huge number of people live in a small territorial land, Bangladesh needs to rely on the use of chemicals, e.g., fertilizers and pesticides for better food production. Besides, being one of the fastest-growing economies of South Asia in recent times, Bangladesh imports a huge amount of chemicals and chemical products.

345. Globally, several international instruments have been adopted to regulate the management of chemicals. Bangladesh has signed and ratified some of these international instruments and has also enacted domestic law to give effect to these. A list of such instruments includes: Basel Convention on Hazardous Wastes, the Rotterdam Convention on Prior Informed Consent, the Montreal Protocol on the Protection of Ozone Layer, Minamata Convention on Mercury, Chemical Weapons Convention, and International Health Regulation. Besides, the country signed the Stockholm Convention to protect humans and environment from persistent organic pollutants and SAICM Convention on the management of chemicals throughout their lifecycle, though these are not ratified yet.

346. Like other parts of the world, successive Bangladesh governments have enacted a few laws to regulate and govern the chemicals used in various sectors in the country. Several government bodies are involved in the regulation and governance of pesticides in Bangladesh. Certain aspects of storage, transportation and regulation of noxious substances can be found in the Explosives Act, 1884, the Petroleum Act, 2016, etc. The country enacted the Fire Prevention and Extinction Act, 2003 (Act No. 7 of 2003), which provides to take special permission for noxious substances and warehouses. However, it is evident from several chemical-induced fires in recent times that this provision is not strictly implemented.[272]

347. Under the Dangerous Cargoes Act, 1953 (Act No. V of 1953), which was enacted to make provisions for the safety of ports in respect of the transit, working, and storage of dangerous cargos, i.e., any goods listed as explosives in the Comprehensive Classified List of Government Explosives, petroleum, and any other dangerous goods classified by the government, etc., the government is empowered to make necessary orders for securing the safety of any port and preventing or dealing with explosions and fires on vessels carrying dangerous cargoes within the limits of any port, and generally for the transit working and storage of dangerous cargoes and matters incidental thereto.[273]

---

272. For a list of chemicals induced major incidents in Bangladesh, *see*, Sultana Razia Syeda. 'Framework for Sound Management of Chemicals: Toward a Sustainable Chemicals Industry in Bangladesh'. *ACS Chemical Health & Safety* 27, no. 5 (2020): 288–298.
273. Section 3, the Dangerous Cargoes Act, 1953 (Act No. V of 1953).

348. The production, import, storage, distribution, marketing, transportation, and sale of essential fertilizer used in agricultural activities are prohibited without registration with the government and such activities without the registration are punishable offences under the Fertiliser Management Act, 2006 (Act No. 6 of 2006).[274] Section 14 of the law contains a specific provision on the production, storage, distribution, sale or possession of unauthorized or environmental pollutant fertilizers. It is provided that if such activities are conducted, then an inspector, appointed under section 9 of the Act, will collect the sample in the presence of one witness, can order to suspend such activities for a maximum of ten days, and will report to the Deputy Director of the District Agriculture Extension Department. Following some other procedures, the Deputy Director can order the owner to destroy the remaining pollutant fertilizer at his own cost and can further fine up to BDT 200,000 and/or order for rigorous imprisonment up to two years.

349. The Poisons Act, 1919 (Act No. XII of 1919), which was enacted to consolidate and amend the law regulating the importation, passion and sale of poisons, has not defined 'poison'. The Pesticides Act, 2018 (Act No. 24 of 2018), which repealed and updated the Pesticides Ordinance, 1971, was enacted to regulate the import, manufacture, formulation, sale, distribution and use of pesticides, i.e., any substance or mixture of substances used or represented as a means for preventing, destroying, repelling, mitigating or controlling, directly or indirectly, any insect, fungus, bacterial organism, nematodes, virus, weed, rodent, or other plant or animal pest, but does not include a substance which is a 'drug' within the meaning of the Drugs Act, 1940.

350. The Agriculture Pests Ordinance, 1962 (East Pakistan Ordinance No. VI of 1962) was promulgated to provide for the prevention of the spread of agricultural pests, insects, or weeds in Bangladesh. Accordingly, the government may prohibit the employment of such methods of cultivation responsible for spreading agricultural pests generally or to any particular crop, or the transport or sale of any infested crop.[275] An occupier of land in which any crop is cultivated is responsible for carrying out the preventive measure in spreading the agricultural pests, etc.[276]

351. The principal substantive criminal law, i.e., the Penal Code, 1860 (XLV of 1860) contains various provisions relating to noxious food or drink (sections 272 & 273), drug (sections 274 & 275), and making the atmosphere noxious to health (section 278). Similar provisions dealing with the penalty for adulteration of, or sale of adulterated food, drink, drugs or cosmetics can also be found in the Special Powers Act, 1974 (section 25C). Besides, the Cantonments Act, 2018 (Act No. 27 of 2018) contains provisions on noxious vegetation (section 143), the Sarais Act, 1867 (Act No. XXII of 1867) imposes responsibility on the keeper of a Sarai to remove all noxious vegetation on or near the Sarai [section 7(4)]. Similar provisions on noxious vegetation can be found in the City Corporation-related laws. Moreover, the

274. Sections 8, 10, 11, 12, the Fertiliser Management Act, 2006 (Act No. 6 of 2006).
275. Section 3, the Agriculture Pests Ordinance, 1962 (East Pakistan Ordinance No. VI of 1962).
276. Section 4, the Agriculture Pests Ordinance, 1962 (East Pakistan Ordinance No. VI of 1962).

Post Office Act, 1898 (Act No. VI of 1898) prohibits the transmission of any articles, explosive, dangerous, filthy noxious or deleterious substance by post (section 19). Back in 1914, the Destructive Insects and Pests Act, 1914 (Act No. II of 1914) was enacted to prevent the introduction of any insect, fungus, or other pests, which is or may be destructive to crops, which includes all agricultural or horticultural crops and all trees, bushes, or plants. However, this law of 1914 was repealed in 2011 through the enactment of the Plant Quarantine Act, 2011 (Act No. 5 of 2011), which was enacted 'to make provisions, in the context of international traffic in plants and plant products, for preventing the introduction of insects or pests into, and spread thereof within, Bangladesh and for the matters relating to phytosanitary and other measures incidental and ancillary thereto'. Section 6(1) of this Act, 2011 provides that the: 'import or export of any plants or plant products which have the potential threat to introduce any pest into plants and plant products may be prohibited, restricted or otherwise controlled subject to the conditions mentioned in the import or export policy order issued by the Government, from time to time, under the Imports and Exports (Control) Act, 1950 (Act No. XXXIX of 1950)'.

352. The National Marine Fisheries Policy, 1998 identified that the water bodies are damaged, and the environment is polluted due to the unplanned discharge of wastage. Therefore, discharge of harmful municipal and industrial wastes directly into the water bodies will be considered a punishable crime, and measures will be taken to control and limit the use of harmful chemical fertilizers, insecticides, and other agrochemicals in the agricultural fields. The government has been working on updating this Policy, and the final draft of the National Marine Fisheries Policy, 2018 is under consideration.

353. The Marine Fisheries Act, 2020 (Act No. 19 of 2020), which repealed the Marine Fisheries Ordinance, 1983 (Ordinance No. XXXV of 1983) and was enacted to make provisions for the management, conservation, and development of marine fisheries of Bangladesh, contains various provisions on noxious substance. Under section 27 of the Act of 2020, the use and carry of explosives, poison, or other noxious substances for killing, stunning, disabling, or catching fish are prohibited and are punishable offences.

354. In Bangladesh, the issue of rampant and uncontrolled use of various types of chemicals in food products, fruits, vegetables, consumer goods, and chemicals, etc., has been reported frequently for the last couple of years where the writers used to pen down columns in different media mentioning the severe consequences of contaminated foods on the human health and the environment. As a result, various regulatory bodies have been running law enforcement drives and destroying adulterated or contaminated goods and products. These actions of the law enforcers received both positive and negative reactions from the business entities and the public. While the consumers reacted positively, the business entities expressed their grief as some of them were claiming to follow the standards and used the acceptable level of chemicals in various products.

355. There was, unfortunately, no institution in the country with proper and world-class facilities to confirm the level of chemicals used in various products. As a result, when the members of the law enforcement agencies used to destroy the confiscated goods due to the alleged excessive use of chemicals beyond the permissible limits, they were also having problems because of the protest of the business community. Bangladesh Council of Scientific and Industrial Research (BCSIR), under a centre, i.e., Bangladesh Reference Institute for Chemical Measurements (BRICM), was functioning to solve this problem. BRICM became a member of the International Bureau of Weights and Measures (*French*: (Bureau International des Poids et Mesures (BIPM)), Asia Pacific Metrology Programme in 2012. BRICM is also the scientific partner of the UN Organisation for the Prohibition of Chemical Weapons.

356. In 2020, the government enacted a special law entitled the Bangladesh Reference Institute for Chemical Measurements Act, 2020 (Act No. 15 of 2020) to establish an independent statutory institute for conducting activities as a reference laboratory on chemical metrology, research, services and other related activities. Chemical metrology is the science of chemical measurements, and the Institute is statutorily authorized to do the following activities, *inter alia*, namely to:

(a) provide measurement and reference measurement services;
(b) provide proficiency testing and Inter-Laboratory comparison services;
(c) develop, validate and transfer chemical measurement systems;
(d) provide assistance in establishing traceability by keeping contact with chemical metrology-related international and other regional organizations, e.g., International Bureau of Weights and Measures (Bureau International des Poids et Mesures BIPM), Asia Pacific Metrology Programme, and other similar domestic, regional, and international organizations and by participating in the technical committees of those institutions;
(e) upgrade the examination services of the domestic laboratories to the international level by providing proficiency testing, Inter-Laboratory comparison, and calibration services and assist in making comparable and acceptable with the international units introduced by International Committee for Weights and Measures and mentioned in BIPM.
(f) collect, manufacture, preserve and distribute or sell the national reference containing meteorological traceability regarding chemicals, cosmetics, pharmaceuticals, food, beverage, climate and environment, clinical, microbiological, gaseous, petroleum, polymers, nanomaterials, and a variety of organic, inorganic material measurement;
(g) provide the reference value of the chemical, biological, inorganic, microbiological, etc., substances used in objects;
(h) provide the instrumentation and calibration services;
(i) provide reference measurement-based bioequivalence and active pharmaceutical ingredients (API) calculation services;
(j) set up of organic and inorganic reference specimen bank to introduce matrix-matched reference materials;

(k) introduce the reference measurement-based 'chemical poisoning and risk assessment management';

(l) serve as the Technical Support Organization of the various regulatory bodies involved in chemical measurement such as: Bangladesh Standards and Testing Institute, Drug Administration, Bangladesh Safe Food Authority, Department of Environment, and similar agencies by coordinating their provided services;

(m) assist the government in making policies by taking fundamental and applied research, application of research results and through the management, coordination, and control of these activities;

(n) develop and publish Guidelines based on similar guidelines issued by metrology-related international organizations such as the International Union of Pure and Applied Chemistry (IUPAC), International Organization for Standardization (ISO), BIPM, APMP Association of Officials of Analytical Chemist (AOAC).

Chapter 9. Rational Use of Energy

357. Energy is the foundation of any development. Of the various sources available for energy generation, the process followed in the production and use of energy using the fossil fuel sources such as coal and gas is though cheaper compared to their renewable energy sources (RES) such as solar, wind, and biomass, fossil fuel sources are responsible for GHGs emissions responsible for global warming leading to climate change. Bangladesh is blessed to have some fossil fuel sources, i.e., gas and coal. However, these are not sufficient to meet the needs of the country, and therefore, the country needs to import raw materials.

358. Bangladesh's success in recent times in energy production is remarkable though there are some concerns as the government has been continuously providing indemnity. Article 16 of the Constitution of Bangladesh, 1972 provides that 'the State shall adopt effective measures to bring about a radical transformation in the rural areas through the promotion of an agricultural revolution, the provision of rural electrification, . . . so as progressively to remove the disparity in the standards of living between the urban and the rural areas'. With the aim to provide electricity to all by 2020, the present government took initiatives to generate 10% energy using RES through the adoption of the Renewable Energy Policy of Bangladesh, 2008. Energy generated using RES is environment friendly and promotes 3Ds, i.e., decentralization, decarbonization, and democratization.[277]

359. Government bodies, various international organizations, and researchers have been reporting the suitability and prospects of the use and exploitation of RES in Bangladesh regularly.[278] The government of Bangladesh has signed the historic Paris Agreement to the UNFCCC, became a signatory of the International Renewable Energy Agency, the international organization that supports countries in their transition to a sustainable energy future, and the International Solar Alliance's Framework Agreement. According to the World Bank, Bangladesh has the largest off-grid solar power programme in the world, which enables 20 million people to access electricity.[279] The largest solar power plant of Bangladesh, a 100 Mega Watt project, constructed in Mongla, Bagerhat district, is going to start supplying electricity to the national grid in December 2021.

---

277. Md Ershadul Karim et al. 'Energy Revolution for Our Common Future: An Evaluation of the Emerging International Renewable Energy Law'. *Energies* 11, no. 7 (2018): 1769.
278. Mohammad Ruhul Amin Bhuiyan, Hayati Mamur & Jahanara Begum. 'A Brief Review on Renewable and Sustainable Energy Resources in Bangladesh'. *Cleaner Engineering and Technology* 4 (2021): 100208; Mohammad Ershadul Karim et al. 'Renewable Energy for Sustainable Growth and Development: An Evaluation of Law and Policy of Bangladesh'. *Sustainability* 11, no. 20 (2019): 5774; M. Sazib Mollik et al. 'Prospects, Progress, Policies, and Effects of Rural Electrification in Bangladesh'. *Renewable and Sustainable Energy Reviews* 65 (2016): 553–567.
279. The World Bank, Bangladesh Solar Home Systems Provide Clean Energy for 20 million People, Press Release, 8 Apr. 2021, https://www.worldbank.org/en/news/press-release/2021/04/07/bangladesh-solar-home-systems-provide-clean-energy-for-20-million-people.

360. Various legal, regulatory, policy, and institutional initiatives have been taken in this regard. A list of these includes: the National Energy Policy, 1996 (updated in 2004); the Bangladesh Energy Regulatory Commission Act, 2003; the Sustainable and Renewable Energy Development Authority Act, 2012; the Rural Electrification Board Act, 2013; the Bangladesh Energy and Electricity Research Council Act, 2015; the Electricity Act, 2018, etc.

361. The Bangladesh Power Development Board, an entity under the Ministry of Power, Energy and Mineral Resources, even after serious protest from the stakeholders and environmental activists, decided to establish a 1,320-megawatt coal-generated thermal power plant, known as Maitree Super Thermal Power Project, at Rampal in the Bagerhat district, through a joint venture project with an Indian company, National Thermal Power Corporation. One of the main concerns of environmental activists is that this initiative will endanger the environment and ecological balance of the largest mangrove forest in the world, the Sundarbans, which was declared a world heritage site by the UN Educational, Scientific and Cultural Organization in 1997, and the Sundarbans Reserved Forest, which is also listed as Wetlands of International Importance under the Convention on Wetlands of International Importance Especially as Waterfowl Habitat (Ramsar Convention) in 1992.

362. Millions of people depend on the Sundarbans, and therefore, to protect this forest, stakeholders have demonstrated protest regularly to convince the government to reconsider the decision of setting up the power plant near this forest. The protesters even moved to the HCD, though the attempt was unsuccessful. Subsequently, the government published a 676-page environmental impact assessment final report of the project. The stakeholders seriously criticized the report as instead of focusing on the environmental impact of the project on the Sundarbans, the report primarily focused on environmental management.

363. The Bangladesh Energy and Electricity Research Council Act, 2015 (Act No. II of 2015) was enacted on 2 February 2015 to identify diversified use of energy and electricity, preservation of energy and its transformation ensuring its safety, and to ensure technological competence in the energy and electricity sector. The law provides for the establishment of a statutory authority named Bangladesh Energy and Electricity Council (BEEC) to be responsible to: (a) develop, coordinate, review and evaluate short- and long-term research plans; (b) develop and implement the annual action plan on energy and electricity research; (c) encourage research and development activities on development, preservation and efficient use of energy and electricity, etc. (sections 3, 4). The law also contains provisions for the appointment of one Chief Executive (section 8), meeting of the governing body (section 9), the establishment of one Advisory Council to attain the objectives of this law (section 12), meeting of the Advisory Council (section 13), formation of International Expert Panel consisting of internationally renowned Bangladeshi citizens or Bangladeshi expatriate scientists, professional, industrial entrepreneurs or academics (section 14), etc.

Part II. Nature Conservation and Management

364. Bangladesh is rich and diversified in flora and fauna. The rich biodiversity of the country has a tremendous effect and impact on the cultural heritage, livelihood, economy, rural lifestyle, and traditional healthcare of the citizens of the country. 45.6% of the domestic labour force is engaged in the agriculture sector. Agriculture biodiversity, forest, and related services, fisheries, livestock, tourism sectors contribute 17.22%, 1.43%, 3.30%, 2.5%, and 2.1% respectively of the total GDP.[280]

365. The biogeographical location of Bangladesh at the cross-road of the Indian, Himalayan, and Indochinese Subregions of the Oriental Realm or Regions helps the densely populated Bangladesh to support a vast assemblage of biodiversity making the country a home for a wide diversity of wildlife.[281] This is officially reflected in the recent IUCN's Red List of Threatened Species; the first one was assessed in 2000.

Table 10 Major Wildlife Species of Bangladesh Compared to the World

	Number of Species in World	*Number of Species Reported from Bangladesh*
Mammals	5,515	133
Birds	10,424	711
Reptiles	10,272	173
Amphibians	7,448	64
Freshwater Fishes	33,200	653
Sub-total-vertebrates	156,859	1,734
Crustaceans	47,000	185
Butterflies	18,000	323

280. Department of Environment, Ministry of Environment and Forests, National Biodiversity Strategy and Action Plan for Bangladesh 2016–2021, pp. xiii-xiv.
281. Bangladesh Forest Department and International Union for Conservation of Nature and Natural Resources, Red List of Bangladesh: volume 1: Summary, 2015, p. 5, https://www.iucn.org/content/red-list-bangladesh-volume-1-summary.

	Number of Species in World	*Number of Species Reported from Bangladesh*
World Totals	131,859	2,242
% of the World	–	1.70

Source: Bangladesh Forest Department and International Union for Conservation of Nature.[282]

366. In order to protect these and to ensure their sustainable uses and management, the country has already adopted many legal, policy, and institutional measures. While a handful number of laws, regulations, legal regimes, and institutional arrangements were already in place before the independence of the country in 1971 and after the endorsement of the World Conservation Strategy, 1980, several initiatives were taken to develop the National Conservation Strategy document for Bangladesh. All these started to evolve in a better-coordinated manner when the country signed the Convention on Biodiversity, 1992 (CBD) on 05 June 1992 and ratified the same on 03 May 1994. Various initiatives were taken, e.g., the National Environment Policy, 1992 was formulated, and following this Policy, the BECA, 1995 was enacted.

367. In 2005, the Ministry of Environment and Forests first adopted the National Biodiversity Strategy and Action Plan for Bangladesh (NBSAP). Subsequently, in 2011, Article 18A was inserted in the Constitution of Bangladesh, 1972, which encourages the state to take initiatives to protect and improve the environment and to preserve and safeguard the natural resources, biodiversity, wetlands, forests, and wildlife for the present and future citizens. Accordingly, inspired by the Aichi Biodiversity Targets (CBD Strategic Plan for Biodiversity 2011–2020), the NBSAP (2016–2021) was prepared by the DoE. The NBSAP (2016–2021) contains fifty activities under twenty headlines, e.g., Status of Biodiversity Loss in Bangladesh, Importance of Biodiversity, Mainstreaming of Biodiversity and NBSAP, National Targets and Activities towards Implementing NBSAP, Capacity Development of Implementation of NBSAP, Resource Mobilization towards Implementation of NBSAP, Coordination and Monitoring and Reporting of NBSAP, etc., aiming at biodiversity conservation.

368. The Forest Department, with the technical support from IUCN Bangladesh and financial support of the BCCT Fund, has developed the Bangladesh National Conservation Strategy (2016–2031) covering areas such as land resources, water resources, forest resources, biodiversity fauna, and biodiversity flora, inland fisheries, coastal and marine resources, livestock resources and energy and minerals. In the management of the resources of these areas, the government has also identified some national resources dependent sectors such as crop agriculture, industry (large,

282. Bangladesh Forest Department and International Union for Conservation of Nature and Natural Resources, Red List of Bangladesh: volume 1: Summary, 2015, p. 6, https://www.iucn.org/content/red-list-bangladesh-volume-1-summary.

small, and cottage), power, rural development, transport and communications, and urbanization, housing, and settlement planning. Besides, some supporting sectors are also identified, and these are: human resources, gender, health and sanitation, disasters and disaster management, environment and international obligations, environmental education, and awareness, information and communication technology, monitoring and coordination mechanisms for the implementation of the National Conservation Strategy, etc. It is anticipated that the Strategy, once completed, will foster development in the country through the conservation, development, and enhancement of natural resources within the framework of sustainable development. It is further expected that this Strategy (2016–2031) will create a conducive policy environment and strategy for conservation, development, and enhancement of natural resources in the country.

369. After the adoption of this Strategy (2016–2031), the government of Bangladesh has enacted the Bangladesh Biodiversity Act, 2017 (Act No. 2 of 2017) to ensure sustainable use of biodiversity and its components, fair and equitable distribution of benefits from the use of biodiversity and related knowledge. The enactment of this law is very significant as this was overdue for quite a long time. The country has signed all the 'Big 5' wildlife conservation treaties, including the Convention on Biological Diversity in 1992 and ratified in 1994. Subsequently, after the ratification of CBD, the National Committee on Plant Genetic Resources proposed a draft of the 'Biodiversity and Community Knowledge Protection Act of Bangladesh' in 1998, though the draft was not accepted. Later on, the country formulated the NBSAP first in 2004 which was subsequently updated following Aichi Biodiversity Targets as discussed above. Hence, given the fact that while the NBSAP has no binding legal effect, the enactment of the Bangladesh Biodiversity Act, 2017 is an important development in the protection and conservation of biodiversity in Bangladesh.

370. The enactment of the Bangladesh Biodiversity Act, 2017 is timely and justified on various grounds. First, the conservation of biodiversity is included in article 18A under 'Fundamental Principles of State Policy' Part in the Constitution of the People's Republic of Bangladesh, 1972. Also, the country is rich in terms of traditional knowledge on biological resources and the conservation of biodiversity. Moreover, being a party to the CBD, Bangladesh is internationally committed to conserving biodiversity, sustainable use of its various components, and proper and equitable distribution of benefits arising out of the use of related knowledge. The law is a special law and has its overriding effect since the provisions of this law shall prevail over provisions available in any other law in force (section 3).

371. The Act is divided into 9 chapters and 51 sections. 'Biological diversity' in the Act is defined as the variability among living organisms, which are parts of the overall environment, and includes species diversity, genetic diversity, and ecosystem diversity in land, aquatic and marine environment [section 2 (11)]. 'Biological resources' are defined as plants, animals, and microorganisms or parts thereof, their genetic material and genetic resources included within the by-products (excluding value-added products or ingredients) or any other biotic component included within any ecological system, with actual or potential use or practical value to the human being, but does not include human genetic material [section 2(13)]. 'Sustainable use' is defined as the use of components of biological diversity in such a manner that does not lead to the long-term decline of the biological diversity, thereby maintaining its potential to meet the needs and aspirations of present and future generations [section 2 (15)].

372. Chapters 3 (sections 8–27) and 4 (sections 28–29) of the Act include provision for the formation of biodiversity-related committees, specifying their roles and responsibilities, at various levels, i.e., national (section 8), metropolitan areas (section 13), district (section 16), upazilla (section 19), municipal areas (section 22), unions (section 25), and even in grassroots level (Chapter 4, sections 28–29). The Act also provides for the establishment of biodiversity-related technical committee (sections 11–12) and has also specified the functions and responsibilities of these committees and their meeting procedures.

373. Section 4 of the Act seems to be the most significant, as it specifies that without the prior permission of the National Committee, it is prohibited for any non-resident Bangladeshi, foreigner, organization not registered in Bangladesh to collect or take in possession of any traditional knowledge relating to biodiversity and biological resources. They are not even allowed to make any commercial use of biodiversity or biological resources, and conduct any bio-survey, bio-use or bio-experiment activities or any related research, or be involved in the exploration activities of any biodiversity or bio-resources exploration, or transfer or send any research result obtained from biodiversity or bio-resources to any person or organization. Nevertheless, if any research is published in accordance with the government rules and regulations, that can be presented or published in any seminar or workshop (section 5).

374. Section 6 of the Act makes it specific that if anyone wishes to apply for intellectual property rights in or outside Bangladesh, for any innovation derived from the use of biological resources, it will require to take prior permission from the National Committee. It is further stated that the National Committee can, while considering the application for granting the intellectual property rights, impose necessary conditions on the fee or royalty or both on benefit sharing or on the equitable distribution of financial profits received from the commercial use of that right [section 6 (2)]. Detailed procedure for application for conducting research on biological resources or for intellectual property rights is mentioned in section 7 of the Act.

375. Section 30 in Chapter 5 of the Act provides for equitable distribution of a portion of genetic or biodiversity resources. It says that the National Biodiversity Committee, while approving the application before the distribution of benefits, may consider various things. The Committee can inform the local authority and legal claimer of resources in the case of use of traditional knowledge relating to biological and genetic resources, and, based on their agreed conditions, may grant the intellectual property rights to the claimant if it is certain or grant the rights jointly; may ensure the handover of technology on the development of biological diversity in favour of the local community, etc. The law empowers the government to frame and time to time update the national action plans on biodiversity to ensure their preservation, development, and sustainable use (section 31).

Chapter 1. Monuments and Landscapes

§1. Introduction

376. Ancient monuments have historic, cultural, and economic values and thus are relevant in the discussion of environmental law as some of these can be ecologically critical also. Internationally there is only one instrument, i.e., the UNESCO Convention for the Protection of the World Cultural and Natural Heritage, 1972 (WHC, 1972), that contains provisions on the protection of 'world natural heritage' and 'world cultural heritage', i.e., monuments, groups of buildings and sites. The global community reached the consensus to introduce the WHC, 1972 to protect these natural and cultural heritages, which are of 'outstanding interest', as the 'deterioration or disappearance of any item of the cultural or natural heritage constitutes a harmful impoverishment of the heritage of all the nations of the world' and these are threatened with destruction due to man-made and natural causes.[283]

377. The WHC, 1972 considers the following as 'cultural heritage':

> *monuments*: architectural works, works of monumental sculpture and painting, elements or structures of an archaeological nature, inscriptions, cave dwellings and combinations of features, which are of outstanding universal value from the point of view of history, art or science;
> *groups of buildings*: groups of separate or connected buildings which, because of their architecture, their homogeneity or their place in the landscape, are of outstanding universal value from the point of view of history, art or science;
> *sites*: works of man or the combined works of nature and of man, and areas including archaeological sites which are of outstanding universal value from the historical, aesthetic, ethnological or anthropological points of view.[284]

378. Besides, the WHC, 1972 considers the following as 'natural heritage':

> natural features consisting of physical and biological formations or groups of such formations, which are of outstanding universal value from the aesthetic or scientific point of view;
> geological and physiographical formations and precisely delineated areas which constitute the habitat of threatened species of animals and plants of outstanding universal value from the point of view of science or conservation;
> natural sites or precisely delineated natural areas of outstanding universal value from the point of view of science, conservation or natural beauty.[285]

---

283. Preamble, the UNESCO Convention for the Protection of the World Cultural and Natural Heritage, 1972.
284. Article 1, the UNESCO Convention for the Protection of the World Cultural and Natural Heritage, 1972.
285. Article 2, the UNESCO Convention for the Protection of the World Cultural and Natural Heritage, 1972.

379. Following the operational guidelines, which provide for a total of ten criteria (six criteria for cultural and four criteria for natural heritage) for evaluating the 'outstanding universal value', the Intergovernmental Committee for the Protection of World Cultural and Natural Heritage decides such sites as cultural or natural heritage.

380. Recognizing the importance of cultural and natural heritage, the WHC, 1972 has incorporated some individual and collective duties and rights for the individual state parties that are members to this international treaty, where these sites are situated, and the international community collectively.[286] The list of some of these duties include: the adoption of a general policy to give 'the cultural and natural heritage a function in the life of the community and to integrate the protection of that heritage into comprehensive planning programmes', setting up of services for the protection of these heritages with an appropriate human resources, the conduct of scientific and technical studies and develop training facilities to enable the state party capable to 'counteracting the dangers that threaten its cultural or natural heritage', and 'to take the appropriate legal, scientific, technical, administrative and financial measures necessary for the identification, protection, conservation, presentation and rehabilitation of this heritage'.[287] Bangladesh joined the WHC, 1972 on 3 August 1983, and the provisions of this international instrument came into effect after three months on 3 November 1983.

381. Only three sites, i.e., the Sundarbans, the Buddhist Vihara at Paharpur, and the Mosque City of Bagerhat, are listed in the UNESCO World Heritage Sites though some other sites also deserve special recognition. Accordingly, the government has taken initiatives to develop a 'tentative list' to include Halud Vihara, Jaggadala Vihara, Lalbagh Fort, Mahasthangarh, and the Lalmai-Mainamati Group of monuments, which if listed will be subsequently be considered to be included in the list of UNESCO World Heritage Sites.

382. From the latest data, it can be seen that except for the Dhaka division, there are a total of 411 archaeological sites or protected immovable antiquity in the country where 148 sites are located in Rajshahi, 89, 61, 56, 22, 18, and 17 sites are located in Khulna, Chottogram, Rangpur, Barishal, Mymensingh and Sylhet division, respectively.[288] It can be predicted that there are 98 sites and monuments in Dhaka since it has been reported that the Department of Archaeology maintains a total of 509 sites and monuments.[289]

---

286. Articles 5 & 6, the UNESCO Convention for the Protection of the World Cultural and Natural Heritage, 1972.
287. Article 5, the UNESCO Convention for the Protection of the World Cultural and Natural Heritage, 1972.
288. Protected Monument List, Department of Archaeology, Government of Bangladesh, http://www.archaeology.gov.bd/site/page/5db06c33-7e57-471c-a344-12fefee84740/-.
289. The Daily Star, 'Nominate Heritage Sites in Bangladesh: Dept of Archaeology Asks Public', https://www.thedailystar.net/country/news/nominate-heritage-sites-bangladesh-dept-archaeology-asks-public-1859764.

§2. Protection of Ancient Monuments: Legal Developments

383. The history of the legal protection of ancient monuments in this part of the world is considerably old and officially started, like any other legal development as introduced by the colonial rulers, with the visit of Sir William Jones as a Puisne Judge of the Calcutta Supreme Court in 1783 when he founded a society in January 1784 to enquire 'into the history and antiquities, arts, sciences and literature of Asia'. In 1848, the Lieutenant of the Royal Engineers of the Government of India, Alexander Cunningham urged the government to preserve the ancient monuments of India. Subsequently, in 1878, the Indian Treasure Trove Act (Act VI of 1878) was enacted, and the post of a 'Curator of Ancient Monuments' was created to prepare a classified list of ancient monuments of India and to advise the government so that the government could decide their repairment. Later on in 1904, following the model of similar laws as enforceable in then England, Greece, and Italy, Lord Curzon, as the greatest friend of Indian archaeology, took the initiative to enact the Ancient Monuments Preservation Act, 1904 (VII of 1904) with the aim 'to ensure the proper upkeep and repair of ancient buildings in private ownership excepting such as were used for religious purposes; to prevent the excavation of sites of historic interest by ignorant and unauthorized persons; and to secure control over the traffic in antiquities'.[290] With the aim to search for ancient remains, their unearthing, preservation, and protection, the Department of Archaeology was established in 1947. Until 1971, there were 152 archaeological sites, 4 sites museums, and 3 libraries cum museums in the country.[291]

384. Land-related first legal instrument under the British colonial regime was adopted in 1857, i.e., the Act 6 of 1857 though there was no provision on the acquisition of land for a public purpose, and therefore, Act 22 of 1863 was subsequently enacted. Both these laws were then consolidated by enacting Act No. 10 of 1870, and this law of 1870 was subsequently replaced by the Land Acquisition Act of 1894.[292] After the independence of Bangladesh in 1971, this Land Acquisition Act, 1894 was repealed and replaced by the Acquisition and Requisition of Immovable Property Ordinance, 1982, which was finally repealed by the Acquisition and Requisition of Immovable Property Act, 2017 (Act No. 21 of 2017). The Land Acquisition Act, 1894 contained important provisions on the acquisition and requisition of property or protected immovable antiquity for the public purpose such as properties of historic importance.[293]

290. *See*, 'Archaeology in India', Ministry of Education, Department of Archaeology, Government of India, 1950, pp. 1–15. *See also*, for reference, s. 10(4), the Antiquities Act, 1968 (Act No. XIV of 1968).
291. Department of Archaeology, Banglapedia, https://en.banglapedia.org/index.php/Department_of_Archaeology.
292. For a background of this Law, *see*, Atul M. Setalvad. 'A Study into Certain Aspects of the Land Acquisition Act, 1894'. *Journal of the Indian Law Institute* 13, no. 1 (1971): 1–69.
293. *See*, for reference, s. 16(1), the Antiquities Act, 1968 (Act No. XIV of 1968).

§3. Legal Protection of Ancient Monuments

385. Under article 24 of the Bangladesh Constitution, 1972, the state is empowered to adopt measures for the protection against disfigurement, damage, or removal of all monuments, objects, or places of special artistic or historic importance or interest. Ancient monuments can be treated as the property of the Republic under Article 143(1) of the Constitution of Bangladesh, 1972 which provides that there shall vest in the Republic all things of value underlying any land of Bangladesh and any property located in Bangladesh that has no rightful owner.

386. Rule 3 of the Environment Conservation Rules, 1997 empowers the government to declare ancient monuments as ecologically critical areas (ECA). Successive governments have taken various initiatives to protect ancient monuments within a clear legal and policy framework though there are reports that some of these are demolished in the name of development, and some are neglected with improper protection. Various laws contain important provisions on the protection of monuments and landscapes. For example, the Antiquities Act, 1968, was enacted for the preservation and protection of antiquities, i.e.: (i) any ancient product of the human activity, movable or immovable, illustrative of art, architecture, craft, custom, literature, morals, politics, religion, warfare, science or of any aspect of civilization or culture; (ii) any ancient object or site of historical, ethnographical, anthropological, military or scientific interest; and (iii) any other ancient object or class of such objects declared by the government, by notification in the Official Gazette to be an antiquity for this Act.[294] Under the Antiquities Act, a subsidiary law in the form of a Rule was framed in 1986. It has been reported that the government has taken initiatives to update the very old Antiquities Act, 1968, and a draft of the law containing some pragmatic provisions was released in 2015. Accordingly, it is provided that any kind of construction works that cause environmental pollution having a severe impact on these monuments need to take prior permission.

387. Chapter 3 of the Bangladesh National Building Code, 2015 contains provisions on the conservation and rehabilitation of historical and cultural heritage. Even the exploration or leasing of mining activities are not permitted in archaeological sites.[295]

388. The Apex court of the country has also ruled in favour of such protection from time to time. In *Human Rights and Peace for Bangladesh v. Bangladesh*, 2012 (Writ Petition No. 9592 of 2010), the HCD in response to a petition relating to the protection of Mohasthangor ancient monument and prevention of all types of construction work near the monument mentioning the historical importance of the site, Justice A.H.M. Shamsuddin Choudhury stated that- '[t]his Mohasthangarh Monument is not only significant for the history of Bangladesh, it also infuses profound importance in tracking and tracing the history of this subcontinent. It is a relic of a

294. Long Title and s. 2(c), the Antiquities Act, 1968 (Act No. XIV of 1968).
295. Rule 46, the Mines and Mineral Resources Rules, 2012.

highly developed city, subsequently ruined, that exited few centuries ago, and was used as the capital during the Gupta, Pal and Sen dynasties. It tells us of the exquisiteness of the civilisation that we have inherited. This represents an iconic symbol of or pride. The people of Bangladesh have emotional attachment to this place. For centuries, tourists from within and abroad had been visiting this place of immense historic attraction. It is pitiable, grotesque and weird that by constructing buildings in the vicinity of the place of profound sanctity, the beauty and the grandiose character of this monument is being irretrievably devastated and waned. Construction of buildings so close to this monument is posing as a stumbling block on the way of protecting this monument and is thereby putting its very existence in peril. If it is allowed to be perished, a glorious part of our history of civilisation, we deserve to be proud of, shall be effaced. Such construction is axiomatically without lawful authority and is violative of the provisions contained in Section 12(c) of the Antiquities Act, 1968', and finally directed the respondents to take infallible and inviolable steps to prevent all kinds of advancement or encroachment upon the Mohasthangarh Monument area.

389. Similar activities, i.e., building construction activities adjunct to Lalbagh Fort, were also brought before the attention of the HCD. In *Human Rights and Peace for Bangladesh v. Bangladesh*, 2011 (Writ Petition No. 9988 of 2010), the petitioner challenged the inactions of RAJUK in stopping building construction activities in areas adjacent to protected Lalbagh Fort, which has a very significant and important role, not only in the history of Bangladesh but also in the history of this subcontinent. It was also found that 'in recent years a few people have taken possession of the property which belongs to this protected historical monument and they are constructing buildings violating the provisions of law, which is illegal and without lawful authority. The matter involves interest of the common people as this historical place belongs to the common people of Bangladesh and the Government is under a duty to protect the interest of the people by protecting the historical places'. Justice A.H.M. Shamsuddin Choudhury further stated that: '[t]his Fort is no doubt a place of immense historic importance. Built by Moghal Prince Mohammad Azam, it is the only Moghal relic of significant importance in Bangladesh. It stands as a snazzy vestige of Moghal architectures, a rare display of our heritage. It is sombrely that the goons are out there to dissipate this invaluable monument that stands as a memento of our history, and worse even is the culpable non-feasance of those functionaries who are bounden with statutory obligations to protect this Fort and other places of historic importance which are on the way to total dissipation due to greedy foray of the grabbers'. Finally, the HCD directed the local police station, 'RAJUK, the City Corporation and the Department of Archaeology to immediately evict all squatters, demolish all structures erected within the Forts land or the surrounding area that has been designated as protected area and to maintain incessant vigilance to ensure protection of the Fort.'

390. The petitioners also moved to the HCD to protect the 'Bhitargarh Fort', built in the sixth century at present Bhitargarh Mouja & Sonarban Mouja of Amarkhana Union, Panchagarh Sadar Thana, District-Panchagarh. The fortified city of

Bhitargarh is not only significant for the history of Bangladesh but also bears importance in the history of this subcontinent as it was found that there had been inhabitants even before sixth century and the city was the centre of the trade route of Tibbat, Bhutan, Sikkim and Asham. In *Human Rights and Peace for Bangladesh v. Bangladesh*, 2013 (Writ Petition No. 5357 of 2011), it was found that: 'By constructing buildings within the perimeter and adjacent to its perimeter of Bhitargarh, the existence of this archaeological site is being dangerously affected and construction of buildings on this place is hampering the protection of this place and is making it endangered. So, such construction is without any lawful authority and unlawful under the Antiquities Act, 1968.'

391. The position of the HCD was slightly different in *Dr. Mahmuda Khatun v. Government of Bangladesh*, 2017 (Writ Petition No. 10472 of 2011), a case relating to the protection of Labsha Mosque, Shatkhira, an antique of 130 years old and also a public place which is now under the government and protection of the government of Bangladesh. When some people were trying to construct another Mosque, i.e., Labsha Jaminderbai jama Mosque near the Labsha Mosque area as the Labsha Mosque could not provide sufficient space for the devotees, the petitioners approached the relevant authorities as the 'Labsha mosque is not only significant but also it has very importance in the history of the country. The adjacent to its perimeter of the Labsha Mosque, the beauty of this monument is being dangerously affected, if construction of building so closer to this Monument is going on it will hamper the protection of this monument and making it endangered. Therefore, the construction is without any lawful authority and unlawful as per section 12C of the Antiquities Act, 1968.' However, considering that the construction has already been started and that the area is densely populated, the HCD held that: '[t]he Labsha Mosque since already been declared under Antiquity Act cannot be destroyed nor can be damaged. It is to be protected. However, in view of densely populated area the Respondent . . . can construct the Labsha Jaminderbai jama Mosque in consultation with the Directorate General of Archeological Department keeping/ preserving the Archeological Mosque as it is'.

§4. LANDSCAPE

392. Tragic causalities due to landslides after heavy rain and flood were quite regular in the southern part of Bangladesh as some people were found to cut hills recklessly in the name of development or housing projects. The Building Construction Act, 1952 (East Bengal Act No. II of 1953), which was enacted to provide for the prevention of haphazard construction of buildings and excavation of tanks and cutting of hills which are likely to interfere with the planning of certain areas in Bangladesh, provides that, without the prior permission of the Authorised Officer, it is prohibited to cut or raze any hill within the area to which this Act applies. Moreover, the law was subsequently amended in 1990 to insert a provision through which it is provided that no such permission shall be granted unless it can be satisfied that:

(a) the cutting or razing of the hill shall not cause any serious damage to any hill, building, structure or land adjacent to or in the vicinity of the hill; or
(b) the cutting or razing of the hill shall not cause any silting of or obstruction to any drain, stream or river; or
(c) the cutting or razing of the hill is necessary in order to prevent the loss of life or property; or
(d) the cutting of the hill is such as is normally necessary for the construction of dwelling house without causing any major damage to the hill; or
(e) the cutting or razing of the hill is necessary for the public interest.[296]

393. The BECA, 1995 (Act No. 1 of 1995) was also amended in 2010 to insert a new provision prohibiting the hill cutting, and it is provided that except in the essential national interest and with the permission and clearance of the DoE, cutting and/or razing of hills and mounds by anyone or organization owned or occupied by private or government or semi-government or autonomous organization is prohibited.[297]

§5. Parks and Reserves

394. Some municipal laws, both general and special, contain provisions on parks and reserves. The Public Parks Act, 1904 (Act No. II of 1904) was enacted for the regulation of public parks and gardens in Bangladesh, though the law does not contain any substantive provisions except giving authority to the government to extend boundaries of the park (sec. 3), an exhibition of copies of notifications and rules in the park (sec. 5) and give the government powers to make further rules.

395. The City Corporations as established in Barishal, Chottogram, Comilla, Dhaka (North), Dhaka (South), Gazipur, Khulna, Mymensingh, Narayanganj, Rajshahi, Rangpur, and Sylhet through the provisions of section 41 and Third Schedule to the Local Government (City Corporations) Act, 2009 (Act No. 60 of 2009) containing extensive provisions on the protection of various components of the environment are authorized to take various initiatives in this regard. Accordingly, these City Corporations are empowered and responsible for taking initiatives regarding public health, unhealthy buildings, waste collection and management, toilets and urinals, infectious diseases, water supply and drainage system, bath and washing places, declaration of a public water reservoir, production of food and beverage, city planning, Master Plan, land development projects, regulation of building construction, trees, park, garden and forest, open space, etc. Similar provisions are also available in the Local Government (Pourshava) Act, 2009 (Act No. 58 of 2009), the Local Government (Union Parishad) Act, 2009 (Act No. 61 of 2009). Besides, the Upazila Parishad Act, 1998 (Act No. 24 of 1998), Zila Parishad Act, 2000 (Act No. 19 of 2000) also contain similar general provisions on the protection of the various environmental components.

---

296. 3C, the Building Construction Act, 1952 (East Bengal Act No. II of 1953).
297. Section 6B, the Bangladesh Environment Conservation Act, 1995 (Act No. 1 of 1995).

396. After the most extensive and devastating flood from July to September 1998, the government enacted the Conservation of Playground, Open Space, Park and Natural Water Reservoir in the Metropolitan, Division, and District Towns Act, 2000 (Act No. 36 of 2000). This law is a special law; i.e., the provisions of this law will prevail over the provisions of other laws and subsidiary laws enacted thereunder in force for the time being, e.g., the Canal Act, 1864, the Irrigation Act, 1876, etc. (section 3). Looking at the apparent and unplanned development activities that have been going on throughout the country, it can be said that there are some limitations to this law. The implementation of this law largely depends on the declaration of the places as 'Playground, Open Space, Park, and Natural Water Reservoir' and the release of the Master Plan prepared and finalized by the development authorities such as RAJUK, Development Authorities in Chottogram, Khulna, Rajshahi or such other division, district and municipal authorities. The law provides for punishment, etc., which are criminal in nature, and accordingly, the authority in charge can destroy any unauthorized establishments without any compensation and can confiscate any establishments constructed, avoiding the provisions of this law.

397. Bangladesh National Zoo, a body under the Ministry of Fisheries and Livestock, has been functioning without any clear legal framework. Initially, it was known as Dhaka Zoo and in 2015, it was named as Bangladesh National Zoo. Besides, there are two safari parks in Gazipur and Cox's Bazar, and the government has also taken an initiative to establish another in Moulvibazar.

398. Though the absence of a domestic framework was not a serious issue in the management of the activities of the zoos in the country, the government has to face various challenges to import endangered wild animals to run the zoos. This is because, without a national law, it is difficult to be a member of the World Association of Zoo & Aquarium, which has been guiding, encouraging, and supporting the zoos around the world regarding animal care and welfare, environmental education. As a result, the government has taken the initiative to enact a law that has been in the process of drafting for a decade and could not be finalized due to the conflicts between the Ministry of Fisheries and Livestock and the MoEFCC regarding the lead ministry. Moreover, it was believed that there were some provisions in conflict with Wildlife (Conservation and Security) Act, 2012. A draft of the law was released in 2017, and it has been reported that the Bangladesh Zoo Act is in the final stage of enactment as the Cabinet has approved the Draft in August, 2021. Accordingly, once the law is in force, the provisions of the law will be used to manage government-run two zoos, i.e., the Bangladesh National Zoo and the Rangpur Zoo, and the zoos run by private persons and organizations.

Chapter 2. Protected Areas

399. Ecological restoration is one of the significant and widely practised approaches in restoring the ecosystem which is damaged, degraded, or destroyed due to irresponsible human activities having adverse impacts and effects on the ecology. ECA, also referred to as 'areas of critical environmental concern' and 'environmentally critical areas' in the USA and 'environmentally sensitive areas' in the UK, has been emerging and getting traction in the discussion of environmental law as a policy option aiming to protect the designated areas due to their environmental, biological, and ecological importance.

400. Bangladesh has signed or accessed all the relevant international legal instruments, i.e.: (a) the Ramsar Convention on Wetlands of International Importance Especially as Waterfowl Habitat, 1971; (b) the United Nations Educational, Scientific and Cultural Organization Convention for the protection of the world cultural and natural heritage, 1972; (c) the Convention on Biological Diversity, 1972 and 2010 Aichi Targets following the decision of the Conference of Parties; (d) the Convention on the Conservation of Migratory Species of Wild Animals, 1979; and (e) the UNFCCC, 1992 and the 2015 Paris Agreement dealing with, specifically or indirectly, ecological restoration.

401. The land-based ECAs, including sites of both natural importance and cultural heritages, can legally be protected through the provisions of the BECA, 1995. The 'ecologically critical area', under BECA, 1995 means 'an area, declared under section 5 of this Act, which is rich in unique biodiversity or important in environmental considerations and needs to be preserved or protected from destructive activities'. Apparently, the provision on places of cultural heritage is not mentioned explicitly, though there are scopes to include these places by interpreting that these places are important 'to be preserved or protected from destructive activities'.

402. Under section 5 of the BECA, 1995, the government, if satisfied to the extent that, due to the environmental degradation, the ecological system (ecosystem) of any area has reached a critical stage or there is any such apprehension then, may, by making official gazette notification, declare any area as ecologically critical areas and take immediate steps for its protection. Besides, the government can also release a list of permitted and prohibited activities in the said notification. In all such gazette notifications, there shall be a legal description and specifications of such areas including the boundaries and maps and these descriptions, specifications, boundaries, and maps will be displayed in that area and will be treated as the documentary description. After the declaration of such ECA, the government shall take the management plan for such areas. Moreover, section 7 of the BECA, 1995 contains provisions on remedial measures for injury to the ecosystem also.

403. Rule 3 of the Environment Conservation Rules, 1997, formulated under BECA, 1995, provides that while declaring any area as ECA, the government shall consider some factors such as human habitat, ancient monument, archaeological site, forest sanctuary, national park, game reserve, wild animals habitat, wetland, mangrove, forest area, biodiversity of the relevant area, and other relevant factors.

404. Some provisions were, thus, already included in section 5 of the BECA, 1995 regarding the declaration of ecologically critical area, and remedial measures. However, with the 2010 Aichi Targets following the decision of the Conference of Parties of the CBD, Bangladesh also amended the existing provision of the BECA, 1995. Through this provision, though the DoE has been given the primary authority to declare any place as ECA, the Department of Forest under the MoEFCC, and the Department of Fisheries under the Ministry of Fisheries and Livestock also play a significant and instrumental role in declaring and management of the ECA. Subsequently, the Constitution was amended in 2011 to include the provisions on article 18A, which mandates the state to 'endeavour to protect and improve the environment and to preserve and safeguard the natural resources, bio-diversity, wetlands, forests and wildlife for the present and future citizens'.

405. The Management of Ecologically Critical Area Rules, 2016 were also framed under the BECA, 1995. The Rules include provisions for the establishment of the National Committee (Rule 3), District Committee (Rule 6), Upazilla Committee (Rule 9), Union Co-ordination Committee (Rule 12), and Village Conservation Team (Rule 13). The Rules specify functions and responsibilities for these committees – National Committee (Rule 4), District Committee (Rule 7), and Upazilla Committee (Rule 10) specifying their composition, roles, and functions. The Rules provide that before declaring any place as 'ecologically critical area', the draft of the notification must be published on the websites of the respective Ministry and Department and in two Bengali Newspapers seeking the opinion of the stakeholders and interested persons at least 60 days before the issuance of the notification (Rule 17). The Rules further provide for a list of restricted or banned activities in the ecologically critical areas (Rules 18); restriction on change in classification of land types (Rules 19); site-specific management and development planning in ecologically critical areas (Rules 21) and public-private coordinated management modalities (Rules 22), etc.

406. In order to protect the environment, the ecosystem, natural and ecological balance of the largest sea beach area of Cox's Bazar, the government declared the area as ECA and prohibited any change of the nature of the land and water of that area through a Gazette Notification on 19.04.1999 issued under section 5 of the BECA, 1995. However, some people were already granted long-term leases of lands for the construction of 1–5 star hotels and motels in the Hotel/Motel Zone of Cox's Bazar. As per the terms of the lease, the petitioners paid the consideration money, obtained the necessary permission from the relevant authorities, and started the construction works, while some have already completed the construction works in the leasehold land as per the agreement. Nevertheless, after the gazette notification of 19.04.1999 through which the area was declared as ECA, the long-term leases of lands were cancelled through a memo dated 12.01.2010 as any construction works in that area would frustrate the purpose of the gazette notification of 19.04.1999. In the case of *Mahbubul Anam and others v. Ministry of Land & ors.* 13 SCOB [2020]

AD 8, the memo of 12.01.2010 was challenged as the petitioners had to suffer huge financial loss due to the cancellation of their leases. Justice Muhammad Imman Ali, though ordered for the compensation for such decision of the government, approved the cancellation of the lease on the ground that the area has been declared as ECA and noting the 'apparent policy of the Government to protect the environment and the natural resources of this country'. Mr Justice Ali also envisaged that: '. . . we hope that in the days and years to come the Government will adhere to the policy of preservation of the ecological balance and protection of the natural resources of our country not only for our future generations, but also to ensure protection of the environment from degradation and the harmful effects of climate change. Certainly, this much we owe to our progeny. It would indeed be a travesty of justice if the petitioners having been deprived of their business opportunities, the plots are leased out to others for the purpose of construction and commercial development'.

407. The Protected Areas Management Rules, 2017 under the Wildlife (Conservation and Security) Act, 2012 (Act No. 30 of 2012) were also formulated. The Rules include provision for the establishment of several committees with the active involvement of the stakeholders, their respective functions and responsibilities as well as operational modalities. A list of these committees includes: (i) co-management committee (rules 4), (ii) general committee of the co-management committee (rules 5, 6, 7), and (iii) executive committee of the co-management committee (rules 8, 10, 11). The Rules, 2017 further include provision for the establishment of people's forum (rules 15), village forum (rules 18), and community petrol team (rules 19) as well as their respective functions, responsibilities, and meeting procedures.

408. Besides, the Bangladesh Tourism Protected Areas and Special Tourism Zones Act, 2010 (Act No. 31 of 2010), enacted to declare tourism protected areas and special tourism zones for the management, development, and growth of the tourism industry and services sector in Bangladesh and to regulate the unplanned construction and activities in the areas having tourism potential, provides that the Tourism Department, after identifying and preserving any area where there is already tourism activities or have the potential for tourism activities, can declare any place as 'tourism protected areas'.[298] Through this provision, Bangladesh Parjatan Corporation, the official tourism organization of the government can also take initiatives to protect the archaeological sites in Bangladesh.

409. The government has already declared a few places as protected areas. Of the 38 protected areas in Bangladesh, 8 are coastal and marine protected areas covering around 4.5 thousand km^2 within the jurisdiction of national territorial

298. Preamble, ss 4–6, the Bangladesh Tourism Protected Areas and Special Tourism Zones Act, 2010 (Act No. 31 of 2010).

water.[299] Though Bangladesh was committed to declaring 10% of her exclusive economic zone (EEZ) by 2020 as per the Aichi target fixed at the CBD's Nagoya COP, the country was only successful to declare around 5.5% EEZ of its territorial water. A total of 475, 17, 11, 20, 28, 4, 33, 437 and 165 species of fish, marine reptiles, marine mammals, birds, crabs (including brackish water and freshwater), lobster, shrimp, marine and brackish water mollusk, and marine algae and seaweed respectively were identified in the expanded area of EEZ part of the Bay of Bengal.[300]

410. The southern side of the Dublarchar island in the Bay of Bengal, an area of 1,738 square kilometres with an average depth of 900 metres is the spawning and breeding area of: (1) five globally endangered dolphins—for example, Irrawaddy dolphins, pink dolphins, bottlenose dolphins, and so on; (2) eight species of whales, including fin whales, humpback whales, common sperm whales, killer whales, bryde's whale, and so on; (3) finless porpoises, and (4) different types of sharks—for example, hammerhead sharks, tiger sharks, catsharks, blacktip sharks, and so on. The government of Bangladesh declared this area to be the country's first marine protected area, Swatch of No Ground, to safeguard whales, dolphins, sea turtles, sharks, and other oceanic species under the Wildlife (Conservation and Security) Act, 2012. Fishing and other offshore commercial activities are restricted in this protected area.

411. In order to protect the species in these areas, e.g., whales, dolphins, turtles, sharks, and other marine animals, the government established the first marine protected area 'the Swatch of No Ground Marine Protected Area' under the Bangladesh Wildlife (Conservation and Security) Act, 2012 and 'Middle Ground and South Patches' of Bay of Bengal under the Marine Fisheries Ordinance, 1983, which was recently repealed by the Marine Fisheries Act, 2020 (Act No. 19 of 2020), section 29 of which provides that the government may, by notification in the Official Gazette, declare the following areas within the marine fisheries of Bangladesh as Fisheries Sanctuary or Marine Protected Areas: (a) areas within the marine fisheries of Bangladesh which are endangered or at risk of extinction of aquatic flora and fauna; or (b) areas where marine life is declining. However, the government can take actions to formulate, monitor, control, and supervise the natural breeding grounds and habitats of aquatic flora and fauna in such fish sanctuaries or marine protected areas to create opportunities for natural reproduction and to expand scientific review and research works.

---

299. General Economic Division, Bangladesh Planning Commission, Ministry of Planning, Government of Bangladesh, 'Sustainable Development Goals Bangladesh Progress Report, 2020', June 2020, pp. 184–185.
300. International Union for Conservation of Nature, National Framework for Establishing and Managing Marine Protected Areas (MPAs) in Bangladesh, 2015, at p. 12, https://portals.iucn.org/library/sites/library/files/documents/2015-054.pdf.

Chapter 3. Protection and Management of Species

§1. Introduction

412. The history of the protection and management of wild animals in this subcontinent through the binding legal instrument is quite old. At least two laws, i.e., the Elephant Preservation Act, 1879 (Act No. VI of 1879) and the Indian Fisheries Act, 1897 (Act No. IV of 1897) can be identified that were enacted in the eighteenth century by the British colonial rulers. The Elephant Preservation Act, 1879 prohibited the killing, injury and capture, and attempt to kill, capture and injure of wild elephants; though these activities were permitted for the purpose of self-defence, or, preventing wild elephants if they were found to injure houses or cultivation, or up to, or in the immediate vicinity of, any main public road or any railway or canal or, with proper licence. On the other hand, under the Indian Fisheries Act, 1897, the use of explosives and poisons for the destruction of fish in inland waters and on the coast was prohibited.

413. Apart from these two above-mentioned laws aiming to protect two specific species, the legal provisions relating to the protection of wild birds and animals were first introduced in the Indian subcontinent in 1912 when a law was enacted titled the Wild Birds and Animals Act, 1912 following similar laws available in the UK. This law generally covered the protection of all wild animals. In 1932, a special law, i.e., the Bengal Rhinoceros Preservation Act, 1932 (Bengal Act No. VIII of 1932) was enacted to provide for the preservation of wild rhinoceros. It was provided that unless for self-defence, the killing, injury, or capture or attempt to kill, injure or capture a wild rhinoceros was prohibited, though these could be done with a licence.

414. These laws were adapted by Pakistan after the separation in 1947 and thus were applicable to this part of the world being a part of the then Pakistan. Some of the Pakistani provinces then enacted provincial laws following these laws, e.g., on fisheries and wild birds and animals. However, during that time, any such specific laws were not in this part enacted except for the protection and conservation of fish, i.e., the East Bengal Protection and Conservation of Fish Act, 1950 (East Bengal Act XVIII of 1950), which was enacted repealing the Indian Fisheries Act, 1897.

415. Immediately after the Independence of Bangladesh in 1971, to provide for the preservation, conservation, and management of wildlife, the government of Bangladesh enacted the Wild Life (Preservation) Order, 1973 (President's Order No. 23 of 1973), which was revised in 1974 and the laws relating to elephant wild birds and animals, and Rhinoceros, enacted in 1879, 1912 and 1932 respectively were repealed. This Law of 1973 was finally repealed, and modernized by incorporating significant provisions by the Wild Life (Conservation and Security) Act, 2012 (Act No. 30 of 2012).

416. The previous law of 1973 defined 'wild life' as any vertebrate creature, other than human beings and animals of usually domesticated species or fish, and includes the eggs of birds and reptiles. From the definition, an important feature of 'wild animals' could be noticed; i.e., these can live independently without the help or care of the human being. For IUCN, this definition of the term 'wildlife' was very narrow and contained provisions to protect vertebrate species only, and therefore, a huge number of marine species such as corals and molluscs were not adequately protected.[301] Hence, the Wildlife (Conservation and Security) Act, 2012 (Act No. 30 of 2012) has defined 'wild animal' very generally as 'different types and species of animals or different stages of their life cycle, the source of which is considered as wild'.

417. As different methodologies are used, there are noticeable differences in the findings in different reports and research finds regarding the number of wildlife species in Bangladesh. Officially, there are 138 mammals, 690 birds, 171 reptiles, 64 amphibians, 253 freshwater fishes, 141 crustaceans, 175 protozoa, 29 porifers, 102 cnidaria, 10 ctenophora, 76 echinodermatas and 5000+ arthropods.[302] IUCN Bangladesh first released the 'IUCN Red List of Threatened Species Bangladesh' in 2000. After fifteen years, the list was updated including two invertebrate groups: crustaceans and butterflies. In the updated list, a total of 1,619 animal species belonging to seven groups – mammals (138), birds (566), reptiles (167), amphibians (49), freshwater fish (253), crustaceans (141), and butterflies (305) – were assessed for over thirty months. 390 species are categorized as threatened, where 56 are found as Critically Endangered, 181 are Endangered, 153 are Vulnerable and sadly, 31 species have been classified as Regionally Extinct.[303]

418. It was also reported that Bangladesh is blessed with a total of 34 kinds of amphibians, having 109 classes of reptiles, 301 species of resident birds, 176 types of migratory birds, 143 genera of rag rant birds. Unfortunately, so far, a total of 30 kinds of birds, 120 kinds of inland mammals, and 3 kinds of marine mammals have been extinguished.[304]

419. In order to protect the remaining animals from extinction, one of the steps taken by the government is to declare some places as protected areas. The government has declared 19,663.16 sq km areas of Dhaka (partial), Chittagong and Sylhet division and 27,717.26 sq km areas Khulna, Barisal, and Dhaka (partial) divisions as Specialised Landscape Zone and Vulture Safe Zone for the preservation and reproduction of the White-rumped Vulture and *Gyps bengalensis*.

---

301. International Union for Conservation of Nature, National Framework for Establishing and Managing Marine Protected Areas (MPAs) in Bangladesh, 2015, at p. 17, https://portals.iucn.org/library/sites/library/files/documents/2015-054.pdf.
302. Bangladesh 6th National Report for the Conservation on Biological Diversity, 15th November, 2019, Dhaka, Bangladesh.
303. Bangladesh: Red List reports 31 Regionally Extinct and 390 Threatened animal species, https://www.iucn.org/news/bangladesh/201607/bangladesh-red-list-reports-31-regionally-extinct-and-390-threatened-animal-species.
304. Kalid Hasan, *The wildlife scenario in Bangladesh*, https://www.observerbd.com/details.php?id=124889.

420. Tigers and elephants are very significant for Bangladesh. After the last tiger census in 2004, a systematic national tiger survey conducted using hidden cameras in 2015 found only 106 Royal Bengal tigers (*Panthera tigris tigris*) on the Bangladesh side of the Sundarbans, though the number was 440 in the last census. Even though the declination rate is alarming, experts are of the view that the numbers of tigers are declining for two main reasons: tiger poaching for traditional Asian medicine is rampant, and instead of the footprint as used in the last census, this time a better methodology (hidden camera) was used.[305] After the census result was published, it was reported that at least six tiger poachers were killed during a shootout.[306] The IUCN has conducted a status survey on an elephant during 2013–2016 and officially declared that there are 268 elephants which all reside in the southeastern forest areas of Bangladesh. The number of elephants has increased from 178 in 2004.

421. It has already been shared that the government has enacted the Wildlife (Conservation & Security) Act, 2012 (Act No. 30 of 2012). Under the Act, 2012, several rules have already been formulated and these are: the Wildlife Crime Control Rule, 2015; the Deer rearing Rule, 2015; the Crocodile rearing Rule, 2015; the Snake Farm Management Rule, 2015; the Elephant rearing Rule, 2015; the Cage bird rearing Rule, 2015; and the Crab rearing and Management Rule, 2015, etc.

422. The MoEFCC framed the Deer and Elephant Raising Rules, 2017 under the Wildlife (Conservation and Security) Act, 2012 (Act No. 30 of 2012) replacing the Bangladesh Spotted Dear (Axis Deer) Raising Policy, 2009 and Bangladesh Elephant Raising Policy, 2011. Under the Rules of 2017, it is prohibited to farm, manage and raise deer or elephants without obtaining a licence from the licensing authority. Even anyone who has been running these activities by taking licence under the previous Policies of 2009 and 2011 needs to obtain a new licence under the new Rules of 2017 within one year from the date of application of the Rules, 2017 (rules 4). After obtaining the licence, a farm owner or amateur needs to obtain a possession certificate to possess deer or elephant within his ownership or possession (rules 7). Without obtaining a grazing certificate, any farm owner cannot graze an elephant in the government forest area (rules 9). The Rules, 2017 have also stipulated some conditions that need to be satisfied for raising deer or elephants (rules 12). It is prohibited to purchase, gift, exchange, or any other kind of transfer of deer or elephant without the written permission of the licensing authority (rules 13).

423. The Wild Life (Conservation and Security) Act, 2012 (Act No. 30 of 2012) empowers the government to establish a wildlife Rescue Centre to provide medical

305. Scientific American, *Bangladesh Has 75 Percent Fewer Tigers Than Expected*, http://blogs.scientificamerican.com/extinction-countdown/bangladesh-tigers/.
306. Ed Payne and Sugam Pokharel, *6 Bengal tiger poachers killed in Bangladesh, police say*, http://edition.cnn.com/2015/08/11/world/bangladesh-tiger-poachers/.

service, food, shelter, and safety to any injured, seized, confiscated, abandoned, or donated wildlife and make guidelines for the disposition of wildlife from the Rescue Centre to nature.[307]

424. In order to protect the wild animals, provide compensation for causalities caused by wild animals, i.e., tiger, crocodile, and elephant, and to rehabilitate injured, the Compensation for Causalities Caused by Wildlife Policy, 2010 was formulated under the provisions of the Bangladesh Wild Life (Preservation) Order, 1973 (President's Order No. 23 of 1973). Though the law of 1973 was subsequently repealed and replaced by the Wild Life (Preservation and Security) Act, 2012 (Act No. 30 of 2012), the provisions of the Policy will remain effective. Pertinent to mention here that this Policy, 2010 was formulated so that people show sympathy to the wild animals that suddenly come to the locality. It is provided that anyone including government employees having the authority to enter the government forest area if affected by the wild animals beyond the territory of government forests will receive compensation up to BDT 1,00,000 in case of death, up to 50,000 in case of injury and up to BDT 25,000 if the property is damaged. However, if anyone enters the government forest without permission and is affected by the wild animals will not get any compensation. The Policy provides for the procedure to be followed in claiming compensation in such instances.

425. Bangladesh has categorized biodiversity under three broad ecosystem diversity, i.e., territorial, inland waters, and coastal and marine ecosystem hosting forty protected areas, thirteen ecologically critical areas, and twenty-five bioecological zones. Bangladesh signed the CBD, 1992 and signed and ratified the Cartagena Protocol on Biosafety to the Biological Diversity Convention which aims to ensure the safe handling, transport, and use of living modified organisms resulting from modern biotechnology that may have adverse effects on biodiversity on 24 May 2000 and 5 May 2004 respectively, and signed the Nagoya Protocol on Access to Genetic Resources and Fair and Equitable Sharing of Benefits arising from their Utilization to the Biological Diversity Convention which aims to share the benefits arising from the utilization of genetic resources in a fair and equitable way on 9 June 2011, though the country has not ratified the same yet.

426. Accordingly, the DoE has already developed necessary subsidiary laws in the form of rules, regulations, guidelines, frameworks, etc., in order to address the potential risks of genetically modified organisms (GMOs). A development project 'Implementation of the National Biosafety Framework' has also been taken in this regard.

427. The Bangladesh National Biotechnology Taskforce has approved the National Biotechnology Policy 2012 Plan of Action. The National Institute of Biotechnology under the Ministry of Science and Technology has published the National Database on Biotechnology Research and Personnel containing a list of

---

307. Section 30, the Wild Life (Conservation and Security) Act, 2012 (Act No. 30 of 2012).

plant, animal, fisheries, environmental, microbial, medical, and molecular biotechnology research projects that are going on in the country and the details of the biotechnology personnel.

428. The Biosafety Guidelines of Bangladesh, 2007 did not contain any reference on the elements necessary to conduct an environmental risk assessment for an open release (e.g., for commercial cultivation) of a genetically engineered plant. Therefore, the Guidelines for the Environmental Risk Assessment (ERA) of Genetically Engineered Plants containing technical or scientific terms and terminologies were developed to provide the scientists/researchers and biosafety regulatory officials a practical elaboration to the risk assessment framework by detailing the types of information that will be informative for environmental risk assessment of genetically engineered plants, both imported and domestically developed, in the country.

429. In 2016, the government permitted the Contained Field Trial (CFT) of 'Pro-Vitamin A' rich GR-E BRRI Golden Rice 29 in Bangladesh Rice Research Institute (BRRI) following certain conditions. It is further notified that certain conditions are to be followed, *inter alia*: (a) CFT has to be conducted maintaining the highest-precautions as per the rules and regulations contained in the Cartagena Protocol on Biosafety and international standards; and (b) all sorts of transboundary movement, handling, transport, and packaging activities should be conducted according to the Biosafety Guidelines of Bangladesh and Cartagena Protocol on Biosafety, etc.

§2. Protected Areas

430. Chapter IV of the Wild Life (Conservation and Security) Act, 2012 (Act No. 30 of 2012) contains provisions relating to protected areas in sections 13–23. Accordingly, the government may, by notification in the Official Gazette, in the light of national forest policy and forest master plan, and considering natural, geomorphological features, biodiversity, and environmental significance, declare any Government forests or part of such forests or any Government land or wetland or any specified area as a sanctuary to be called as a wildlife sanctuary, bird sanctuary, elephant sanctuary or wetland dependent animal sanctuary or, marine protected area, specifying the demarcation, for the conservation of forest and habitat of wildlife.[308] The government can also declare any government forests as a national park (section 17), safari park, ecopark, botanical garden and wild animal breeding centre (section 19), landscape zone or corridor, buffer zone and core zone (section 20), special biodiversity conservation area (section 22) and national heritage, memorial tree, sacred tree and kunjaban (section 23). Moreover, with the application of the owner, any land or wetland needed for the protection of traditional or cultural value or use of any animal or plant can be declared as a community conservation area (section 18).

308. Section 13 (1) & (2), the Wild Life (Conservation and Security) Act, 2012 (Act No. 30 of 2012).

431. Few activities such as: (a) land cultivation; (b) establishment or undertaking of any industrial operation; (c) harvest, destruction or collection of any plant; (d) setting of fire; (e) unauthorized entry into a sanctuary with any weapon without the permission; (f) disturbance or threatening of any wildlife, or use of chemicals, explosives or any other weapon or substances which may destroy wildlife habitat; (g) introduction of any exotic animal or plant; domestic animal or allow any domestic animal to stray; (h) dumping of any materials detrimental to wildlife; (i) exploration activities for extraction of minerals; (j) felling of any plant or part thereof except silvicultural operations required for natural regeneration of plants; (k) diversion or pollution of the watercourse; or (m) introduction to any alien and invasive plant species are prohibited in the sanctuaries.[309] Similarly, for example, Rule 13 of the Protection and Conservation of Fish Rules, 1985, was also amended to prohibit the catch, carry, transport, offer, sell, barter, exposure, or possession of all kinds of fish in the designated Hilsa fish sanctuary area on 20 November (SRO No. 269-Law/2014).

432. The DoE is primarily responsible for declaring protected areas. Besides, there are government agencies that also play an instrumental role in this regard. These are: the Ministry of Fishes and Livestock, the Ministry of Environment and Forests, the Bangladesh Fisheries Research Institute, Bangladesh Navy and Coast Guard, Bangladesh Fishery Development Corporation, etc.

433. Till 2015, there were thirty-eight Protected Areas (PA), including seventeen National Parks, twenty Wildlife Sanctuaries, one Marine Protected Area, and two Vulture Save Zones. Two RAMSAR sites namely Tanguar Haor and Sundarbans were declared in 1992. In addition to this list, five East Asian Australasian Flyway Partnership (EAAFP) sites have been declared in 2010 to conserve migratory birds and their habitat, namely Sonadia, Nijhum Dweep, Tanguar Haor, Hakaluki Haor, and Hail Haor.[310] The UNESCO World Heritage site, the Sundarbans, is the home to the rare Irrawaddy, Ganges dolphins, a wide range of fauna, the Bengal tiger, and endangered species such as the estuarine crocodile and the Indian python.

434. The Wild Life (Conservation and Security) Act, 2012 (Act No. 30 of 2012) has introduced provisions for the import, export, and re-export of wild animals and plants. Accordingly, the import and export of any wild animal or parts thereof, trophy, uncured trophy, or plants mentioned in schedule IV to the Act, 2012 is generally prohibited and are only allowed if a few conditions are fulfilled before the import and export of these; i.e., export or import is permitted only with proper licence, through customs port of entry only and CITES certificate, collected from the Chief Conservator of Forests (Chief Wildlife Warden) and the Conservator of Forests, Wildlife & Nature Circle (Additional Chief Wildlife Warden) who act as the CITES Permit Management authority in Bangladesh, should be produced, where

309. Section 14 (1), the Wild Life (Conservation and Security) Act, 2012 (Act No. 30 of 2012).
310. Dr. Tapan Kumar Dey & Md. Golam Rabbi, *Guideline Book on Wildlife Law Enforcement in Bangladesh*, Preface (Bangladesh Forest Department, Ministry of Environment and Forests, 2015).

applicable.[311] However, for the import of such animals and parts thereof, etc., a quarantine certificate issued by the appropriate authority of the country of import is to be produced.[312]

§3. Wildlife Crime

435. Wildlife crimes are included in the list of Transnational Organized Crimes by the United Nations Office on Drugs and Crime. Bangladesh has signed and ratified the major international law instruments on biodiversity conservation such as CBD, CITES, Convention on Migratory Species, Ramsar Convention on Wetlands, etc. Besides, Bangladesh has also enacted relevant legislation and formulated policies, e.g.: (a) the National Conservation Strategy; (b) the National Environment Management Action Plan; (c) National Biodiversity Strategy and Action Plan (2016–2021); (d) the Coastal Zone Policy, 2005; (e) Coastal Zone Strategy; (f) Bangladesh Climate Change Strategic Action Plan; (g) Bangladesh Fisheries Policy; (h) National Water Policy; (i) National Tourism Policy, etc.

436. Yet, after all these initiatives, wildlife trafficking is also growing at an alarming rate, and the country is being used as a route. Under section 31 of the Wild Life (Conservation and Security) Act, 2012 (Act No. 30 of 2012), the government can establish a wildlife crime control unit comprising custom officers, members of law and order enforcing agency at any place in Bangladesh including strategic air, land, and seaports to ensure strict compliance and effective implementation of wildlife-related international convention, protocol, treaty, etc. Chapter VIII of the Act, 2012 (sections 32 & 33) contains provisions regarding investigation and seizure of hunted, acquired, or captured wild animals without licence or animals reproduced from it during captivity; dead or dying wild animals on account of an accident; such wild animals or parts thereof, trophy or uncured trophy, meat, part of the body or any plant mentioned in schedule IV or parts or derivatives thereof, not registered under this Act or for which no licence has been received or not imported or exported following proper legal rules; weapons, articles or tools used in committing an offence; weapons, articles or tools used in committing an offence. Generally, the authorized officer shall follow the provisions of the Code of Criminal Procedure, 1898 (Act V of 1898), the principal legislation of criminal procedure, as far as possible and as long as the provisions of Act V of 1898 are not inconsistent with the provisions of the Act, 2012 for search, seizure or inspection in this regard.

437. Chapter nine (sections 34–46) of the Wild Life (Conservation and Security) Act, 2012 (Act No. 30 of 2012) contains a few general and specific provisions relating to crimes regarding general and specific wildlife such as tiger, elephant (section 36), cheetah, lam cheetah, hoolock, sambar deer, crocodile, gharial, whale or dolphin (section 37), birds or migratory birds (section 38). The law also provides for punishment for filing a false case for harassment or illegal seizure (section 42).

311. Sections 28 & 29, the Wild Life (Conservation and Security) Act, 2012 (Act No. 30 of 2012).
312. Section 28(2), the Wild Life (Conservation and Security) Act, 2012 (Act No. 30 of 2012).

All the offences under this law are generally non-cognizable, bailable, and compoundable except for the offence relating to the killing of a tiger and elephant, i.e., offences relating to the killing of these two elements will be cognizable and non-bailable (section 43).

438. Accordingly, the Wildlife Crime Control Unit involving Police, Customs, Coast Guard, and Forest Department was established for controlling illegal killing and trafficking of wildlife. In five years between 2010 and 2015, a total of 375 offenders were arrested with 177 mammals, 7483 birds, and 13902 reptiles.[313] A total of 37,039 wild animals and birds were seized between June 2012 and November 2016. Of the total seizure, the highest 19,359 were reptiles, while 16,979 were birds. A total of 374 wildlife offences were recorded in those five years, and only 566 offenders, mostly small traffickers, were taken to custody.[314]

439. It may be relevant to share here that to assess a country's response to wildlife and forest crime, the CITES Secretariat, with the help of the International Consortium on Combating Wildlife Crime (ICCWC), has developed two complementary tools: i.e., the ICCWC Wildlife and Forest Crime Analytic Toolkit and the ICCWC Indicator Framework for Combating Wildlife and Forest Crime. This Analytic Toolkit was first implemented in Bangladesh in 2012, and officials from the relevant government agencies of Bangladesh, being a signatory of the CITES, have already been trained upon these toolkits.

---

313. Pinaki Roy, *Wildlife trafficking sees sharp rise: Bangladesh used as route*, http://www.thedailystar.net/frontpage/wildlife-trafficking-sees-sharp-rise-152602.

314. Nawaz Farhin, Wildlife trafficking still high, Dhaka Tribune, https://www.dhakatribune.com/bangladesh/nation/2017/03/02/wildlife-trafficking-still-high.

Chapter 4. Agricultural Resources

440. Being an agrarian country, in Bangladesh, 'agriculture' includes many things such as 'crops production, vegetables, fruits and various kinds of flowers firming, establishment and maintenance of dairy farms, livestock and poultry farming, fish firming and forestry'.[315] Since the independence of the country in 1971, successive governments have already taken and have been taking various legal and regulatory initiatives and institutional arrangements.

441. The National Agriculture Policy, 2018 was framed with the aims to establish agriculture as a profitable sector, and ensure nutrition and food security in Bangladesh. Additionally, the Policy emphasizes socio-economic development by increasing and diversifying the production of crops, boosting farmers' income, producing quality foods, and promoting the marketing strategy. Intending to achieve the goals, the Policy stresses women's empowerment, research activities, and the application of ICT and nanotechnology in the field.

442. The Seeds Act, 2018 (Act No. 6 of 2018) was enacted to update and re-enact the provisions of the Seeds Ordinance, 1977 (Ordinance No. XXXIII of 1977) and to make provisions regulating the production, sale, conservation, import, export, exchange or supply of any crop, and to set their standards. The law provides for the establishment of a National Seed Board (section 3), Seed Laboratory (section 12), and Seed Certification Agency (section 13). Moreover, in order to implement the provisions of the law, the government can appoint qualified persons as seed inspectors (section 18) and seed analysts (section 21).

443. The law further provides that the government will regulate the quality standard of any saleable seed or seeds to be used for agriculture (section 7), can classify the seeds on the basis of their sources (section 9), and can set the necessary standards of the seeds in consultation with the National Seed Board (section 10). The seed dealers will have to obtain licence after making an application following the prescribed procure and payment of fees to conduct the business (section 8), and they cannot sell, conservation, and do the business of import, export, exchange, or supply unless the seeds are registered with the Board (section 11). It is an offence to create obstacles or to prevent the seed inspectors from discharging his duties under this law, and for such activities, anyone can be punished with imprisonment for a term, not more than ninety days, or with fine, not exceeding to BDT 50,000 or both (section 24). Assisting anyone in committing offences under this law is also an offence, and for that anyone will be liable to get a similar amount of penalty (section 25), and for the repetition of the offences under the law, anyone will receive the double amount of prescribed punishment (section 26).

444. After the adoption of two similar policies adopted in 1993 and 1998, the government formulated the National Seed Policy, 2018. Intending to establish a

315. Section 2 (1), the Bangabandhu National Agriculture Award Trust Act, 2016 (Act No. XLVII of 2016).

business-oriented seed industry that could compete in the international market too after fulfilling the national demand of seeds, the Policy aims to set a realistic and timely framework for the development of agriculture, farmers, and the seed sector by creating a planned and stable investment atmosphere for the non-government entrepreneurs.

445. For the regulation of import, manufacture, reproduction, sale, distribution, and use of pesticides by repealing the Pesticides Ordinance, 1971 (Ordinance No. II of 1971), the Pesticides Act, 2018 (Act No. 24 of 2018) was enacted. It is prohibited to import, produce, start package, sell, store, or advertise any kind of pesticide without registration of the pesticide brand (section 4). The registration of the pesticide brand will remain valid for three years (section 6), and such registration can be cancelled on various grounds (section 8). It is important to note that even after having a licence for any specific pesticide, one must have a separate licence also for conducting the business of import, produce, package, sell, store, or advertise any pesticide (section 9). It is mandatory to use sustainable tags or labels in Bangla in a prescribed manner, and without doing so, no pesticide can be preserved for sale, opening, advertisement, etc. (section 16). Addition of any false information while advertising about any pesticide is a punishable offence (section 29).

446. The Weather Act, 2018 (Act No. 28 of 2018) was enacted to provide proper weather and climate forecasts, reduction of disasters, protection of public life and property, and affording some other stable, integrated, objective-oriented and timely weather-related services. The law provides for the establishment of the Bangladesh Meteorological Directorate which will be responsible for, *inter alia*, making necessary planning, acquiring, and installing modern equipment, implementation of meteorological services, and relevant policies. While doing so, the Meteorological Directorate, in particular, follows the standards set by the World Meteorological Organization (WMO). Additionally, the Directorate shall represent Bangladesh in the concerned global forum by sharing information regarding the weather, climate change, and environment (Section 6). The law contains provisions for the weather forecast and warning (Chapter 6), climate (Chapter 7), earthquake (Chapter 8).

447. The Management of Underground Water for Agriculture Purpose Act, 2018 (Act No. 5 of 2018) was enacted to update and re-enact the provisions of the Ground Water Management Ordinance, 1985 (Ordinance No. XXVII of 1985). The law is a special law, and the provisions of the law shall prevail over the provisions of other laws (section 3). The law provides for the establishment of an Upazila Irrigation Committee in every Upazila, the second lowest tier of the local government in Bangladesh (section 4). It is provided that a licence is to be obtained from the Upazila Council, and without the permission of this Council, no tube well can be installed anywhere for agriculture (section 5), and the existing tube wells without licence have to obtain one immediately after the entry into force of the law (section 6). The law also contains provisions on the procedure to apply for the licence to instal tube well (section 5), suspension (section 7), and cancellation of such licence (section 8). It may be relevant to share here that to implement the provisions of this law, the Underground Water Management Rules, 2018 were also formulated.

448. Considering the present-day need for livestock property, the Bangladesh Livestock Research Institute Act, 2018 (Act No. 53 of 2018) was enacted by repealing the Livestock Research Institute Ordinance, 1984. Among others, the precise objectives of the Act are: to conduct research to identify the solutions of the major problems of the country's livestock resources; make agreements with national-international organizations and donor agencies; manage other functions required for fulfilling the purposes of this Act (Section 10). Within the next three months after the end of a financial year, the Institute shall submit an annual report to the government on their activities. Of course, the government may, if necessary, ask to send the report of the activities of the Institute at any time, and the Institute is bound to obey any direction of the government.

Plant Variety Act

449. The genetic resources in Bangladesh are threatened due to the introduction of modern varieties, changing cropping patterns, climate change, pest resurgence, rapid urbanization and industrialization. Bangladesh has signed the CBD, Nagoya Protocol, and the Regional Agreement with the Asian Food and Agriculture Cooperation Initiative.

450. Bangladesh has also signed the International Treaty on Plant Genetic Resources for Food and Agriculture, 2009 and thus recognizes 'the enormous contribution that the local and indigenous communities and farmers of all regions of the world, particularly those in the centres of origin and crop diversity, have made and will continue to make for the conservation and development of plant genetic resources which constitute the basis of food and agriculture production throughout the world'.[316] Under article 9 (2) of this Treaty, 2009, Bangladesh is required to take measures, subject to its national legislation, 'to protect and promote Farmers' Rights, including: a) protection of traditional knowledge relevant to plant genetic resources for food and agriculture; b) the right to equitably participate in sharing benefits arising from the utilization of plant genetic resources for food and agriculture; and c) the right to participate in making decisions, at the national level, on matters related to the conservation and sustainable use of plant genetic resources for food and agriculture'.

451. From the Country Report under article 9 of the International Treaty, 2009, it can be seen that the government has collected and conserved rice (20), mango (8), litchi (4), guava (4), jackfruit (4), jute, taro (7), potato (6), chilli (4), palm (2), brinjal (8), cucumber (2), lime & lemon (3), pineapple (4) and banana (5) as GI corps. Moreover, there are more than 11,000 accessions of 137 crops in Bangladesh Agricultural Research Institute (BARI) gene bank; more than 8,000 accessions of rice including wild relatives in BRRI gene bank; around 6,000 accessions of jute and allied fibre crops in Bangladesh Jute Research Institute (BJRI) gene bank; about

316. Article 9.1, the International Treaty on Plant Genetic Resources for Food and Agriculture, 2009.

3,000 accessions of cotton in CDB gene bank and a considerable number of germplasm of various crops are being conserved. Besides, variety development programme of every research institute has been strengthening exploiting local plant genetic resources.

452. Bangladesh has taken various measures; some of these were initiated even before joining the International Treaty, 2009, though the joining has propelled the shaping of the initiatives taken early. Back in 1998, the National Committee on Plant Genetic Resources proposed a bill for the government to consider the protection of plant varieties, biodiversity, and community knowledge.

453. Various organizations/institutions are involved in protecting the plant variety. These are: Bangladesh Agricultural Research Council (BARC), Department of Agriculture Extension (DAE), BARI, BRRI, Bangladesh Agricultural Development Corporation (BADC), Bangladesh Institute of Nuclear Agriculture (BINA), BJRI, Bangladesh Sugar Crop Research Institute (BSRI), Cotton Development Board (CDB), Bangladesh Agricultural University (BAU), Sher-e Bangla Agricultural University (SAU), Bangabandhu Sheikh Mujibur Rahman Agricultural University (BSMRAU).

Chapter 5. Forests

454. The forests in Bangladesh cover 12.8% of the total area of the country.[317] Forests in Bangladesh are divided into: reserved forests, protected forests, acquired forests, vested forests and private forests.[318] The Forest Act, 1927 (Act No. XVI of 1927) was enacted to consolidate the law relating to forests, the transit of forest-produce and the duty leviable on timber and other forest-produce. The law has not included any definition of the term 'forest', but under the Private Forests Ordinance, 1959 (East Pakistan Ordinance) (Ordinance No. XXXIV of 1959), 'forest' includes any land recorded as forest in a record-of-rights prepared under Chapter IV of the State Acquisition and Tenancy Act, 1950 (E.B. Act XXVIII of 1951) or such other land containing tree growth as may by notification be declared as forest by the government.[319] To Bangladesh Forest Department, 'forest' means 'Land spanning more than 0.5 hectares with trees higher than 5 meters (exception for the *Ceriops decandra* with a height of 2 meters) and a canopy cover of more than 10 percent, or trees able to reach these thresholds in situ. It does not include land that is predominantly under the rural settlement, agricultural or urban land use therefore trees grow outside forest land are considered as non-forest trees.'[320]

455. 'Forest-produce;, as per the provisions of the Forest Act, 1927 (Act No. XVI of 1927), includes –

- (a) the following whether found in, or brought from, a forest or not, that is to say: – timber, charcoal, cuatchouc, catechu, wood-oil, resin, natural varnish, bark, lac, mahua flowers, mahua seeds, kuth and myrabolans, and
- (b) the following when found in or brought from, a forest, that is to say –
  - (i) trees and leaves, flowers and fruits, and all other parts or produce not hereinbefore mentioned, of trees,
  - (ii) Plants not being trees (including grass, creepers, reeds and moss), and all parts or produce of such plants,
  - (iii) wild animals and skins, tusks, horns, bones, silk, cocoons, honey, and wax, and all other parts of produce of animals, and
  - (iv) peat, surface, soil, rock and minerals (including limestone, laterite, mineral oils and all products of mines or quarries).[321]

317. Government of Bangladesh, 'Tree and Forest Resources of Bangladesh: Report on the Bangladesh Forest Inventory', 2019, Ministry of Environment, Forest and Climate Change, Dhaka, Bangladesh. *See also*, Matieu Henry, Zaheer Iqbal, Kristofer Johnson, Mariam Akhter, Liam Costello, Charles Scott, Rashed Jalal et al. 'A multi-purpose National Forest Inventory in Bangladesh: design, operationalisation and key results.' *Forest Ecosystems* 8, no. 1 (2021): 1–22.
318. Forest Department, Ministry of Environment and Forests, Government of Bangladesh, Forest Investment Programme, 2017, pp. 10 & 21.
319. Section 2(5), the Private Forests Ordinance, 1959 (East Pakistan Ordinance) (Ordinance No. XXXIV of 1959).
320. Forest Department, Definition of Forest for Bangladesh, http://bforest.gov.bd/site/page/eca2a291-b487-4c7a-8ce0-dbe5069524ac/-.
321. Section 2 (4), the Forest Act, 1927 (Act No. XVI of 1927).

456. Under the Private Forests Ordinance, 1959 (East Pakistan Ordinance) (Ordinance No. XXXIV of 1959), 'forest-produce' includes:

(a) the following whether found in, or brought from a forest or not, that is to say –
   (i) timber, charcoal, caoutchouc, catechu, wood-oil, resin, natural varnish, bark, lac, mahua flowers, mahua seeds, kuth and myrabolans, and
   (ii) wild animals and skins, tusks, horns, bones, silks, cocoons, honey and wax, and all other parts or produce of animals, and
(b) the following when found in, or brought from a forest, that is to say –
   (i) trees and leaves, flowers and fruits, and all other parts, or produce not hereinbefore mentioned, of trees,
   (ii) plants, not being trees (including grass, creepers, reeds and moss), and all parts or produce of such plants,
   (iii) surface soil and rock (excluding salt rock and mineral rock), and
   (iv) fish, tortoise, oysters, shells, sponge, conch, all crustacea and mollusca and all parts of produce of such fauna.

457. Historically, before the partition of the Indo-Pak subcontinent based on religion in 1947, the forests, both reserved and prospective reserve, in this part of the world used to be administered by the Forest Circles of the Bengal and Assam Forest Departments. The management of forest, as an important component of the environment in the modern sense, came under regulatory protection since 1864 when a conservator of the forest was appointed and the first notification regarding reserve forest was issued on 14 December 1864.[322]

458. People of this part of the world were aware of some forms of forest management for long, and the British rulers first introduced forest management through civil administration. During this time, the system of forest protection through the Indian Forest Service was started for economic or commercial reasons, i.e., to conserve valuable timber, e.g., teak, to be used for the British Navy and sleepers and wood for the railways required for the purpose of colonial control lacking 'boarder social or environmental considerations'.[323] In 1855, just before the Mutiny in 1857 that demised the East India Company shifting the absolute power to the British Raj, Governor-General Lord Dalhousie drafted the influential Forest Minute, through which the state was given absolute power to claim the absolute ownership of forests and in 1856 appointed a trained German forest officer, Dietrich Brandis, to manage the forests of this part.

---

322. Banglapedia, Environmental Laws, http://en.banglapedia.org/index.php?title=Environmental_Laws.

323. 'A Condensed History of the Indian Forest Service To 1947', *The Commonwealth Forestry Review* 50, no. 2 (144) (June 1971), pp. 108–112; Gregory A. Barton & Brett M. Bennett. 'Environmental Conservation and Deforestation in British India 1855–1947: A Reinterpretation.' *Itinerario* 32, no. 2 (2008): 83–104.

459. After the mutiny in 1857, when the British Government, through the Secretary of State for India, took charge of ruling this part, the Inspector General of Forests was appointed in 1863 and the Indian Forest Act, 1865 (VII of 1865) was passed, which was improved significantly, repealed and replaced in 1878 by the Act VII of 1878. The first Forest Policy was framed in 1894, and finally, the law of 1878 was replaced by the Forest Act, 1927 (Act XVI of 1927).[324] In 1945, the Bengal Private Forest Act, 1945 (Act XI of 1945) was enacted to provide for the conservation of private forests and for the afforestation in cases of wastelands in Bengal,[325] which was subsequently repealed in 1966.[326] Between 1947 and 1962, a Provincial Forest Department used to perform the duties relating to the conservation of forest. This law of 1927 was adapted in Pakistan and finally, in Bangladesh, and the Law is still in force in Bangladesh. Subsequently, the law was amended in 1990 to incorporate deterrent penalties for certain forest offences and in 2000 to include provisions for social forestry.[327] The Forest Act, 1927 (Act XVI of 1927), though has not included the definition of the term 'forest', contains provisions on Reserved Forests (Chapter II, sections 3–27), Village-Forests and Social Forestry (Chapter III, sections 28–28B), Protected Forest (Chapter IV, sections 29–34). In 1959, the Private Forests Ordinance, 1959 (East Pakistan Ordinance) (Ordinance No. XXXIV of 1959) was promulgated.

460. After the independence, the first National Forest Policy was framed in 1979, and this was subsequently replaced by the Forest Policy of 1994. The government has recently drafted the National Forest Policy, 2016 and has finalized the updating of the Draft to replace the previous Forest Policy of 1994. The principle objectives of the Policy are, *inter alia*, to intensify efforts to ensure that 20% of the country's area is under forests and tree cover, including 100% of state forests, 80% of hill land areas, 30% of terrain land areas, and 10% of plain land areas, by 2035 through afforestation, reforestation, social forestry, and ecological restoration and sustainable forest management programmes involving the stakeholders.

461. After the partition of the Indo-Pak subcontinent in 1947, when present Bangladesh became part of Pakistan, the first hill forest inventory was developed in 1960 and 1961 covering the Kassalong and Rankhiong forests and Sangu-Matamuhuri reserved forests, respectively, and the inventory of Sundarban reserved forests was prepared in 1960. After the independence of the country in 1971, various types of inventories, covering various areas, were developed. The list of some of these includes: inventory of the pulpwood plantation in Kaptai, Chittagong Hill Tracks (1983), inventory covering Sitapahara Reserve, Chittagong Hill Tracks (1984), Kassalong and Rankhiong forests, Chittagong Hill Tracks (1985), inventory

324. 'A Condensed History of the Indian Forest Service To 1947', *The Commonwealth Forestry Review* 50, no. 2 (144) (June 1971): 108–112.
325. For a brief description of the law, *see*, Herbert Howard. 'The Bengal Private Forests Act (Act XI of 1945)'. *Empire Forestry Review* 25, no. 2 (1946): 222–224.
326. Section 64, the Private Forests Ordinance, 1959 (East Pakistan Ordinance) (Ordinance No. XXXIV of 1959).
327. Forest Department, Ministry of Environment and Forests, Government of Bangladesh, Forest Investment Programme, 2017, p. 67.

of the mixed hardwood-teak plantations, Chittagong Hill Tracks (1985), the High Forest in the Chittagong Districts (1985), the forest inventory of the Sundarbans (1985), the Maturing Mangrove Plantations of the Coastal Afforestation Project (1987), inventory of Forest Resources of Southern Sylhet Forest Division (1988), forest inventory of the Sal Forests of Bangladesh covering Sal forests of Central and Northwest Bangladesh, i.e., Dhaka, Tangail, Mymensingh, Rangpur divisions. The first village forest inventory of Bangladesh covering all districts except Chittagong Hill Tracks was prepared in 1980–1981. However, the first-ever national forest and tree resources assessment was conducted by Bangladesh Forest Department covering forest and tree cover area in 2007.

Reserve Forests

462. Chapter II (sections 4–27) of the Forest Act, 1927 (Act No. XVI of 1927) contains detailed provisions as to reserved forests. Section 3 of the Law, 1927 empowers the government to 'constitute any forest-land or waste-land or any land suitable for afforestation which is the property of Government, or over which the Government has proprietary rights, or to the whole or any part of the forest-produce of which the Government is entitled, a reserved forest'.

463. Under section 4 of the Forest Act, 1927 (Act No. XVI of 1927), the government is the final authority to declare and acquire land for reserve forests.[328] Nevertheless, there are provisions for filing objections against the declaration of a reserve forest, and the plaintiff must challenge once the notification for declaration is issued.[329] As per the provisions of sections 2, 4, 29 and 34 of the Forest Act, 1927 (Act No. XVI of 1927), the government can declare certain land as protected and reserved forest; subsequent settlement is not tenable in law.[330] There are adequate provisions for a remedy against wrongful inclusion of lands as reserved forest under the Forest Act, 1927 using which an aggrieved party may seek remedies. Otherwise, the plaintiff cannot get any relief when no such remedy as provided under the Forest Act 1927 is sought.[331]

464. Certain activities, under section 26 of the Forest Act, 1927 (Act No. XVI of 1927), are prohibited in reserved forests. It is provided that:

(1) Any person who, in a reserved forest:
  (a) kindles, keeps or carries any fire except at such seasons as the Forest Officer may notify in this behalf.
  (b) trespasses or pastures cattle, or permits cattle to trespass;

328. *Abu Musa being dead his heirs Md. Nurul Islam and others v. People's Republic of Bangladesh represented by the Secretary, Ministry of Forests,* 1 MLR (1996) (AD) 355.
329. *Md. Nurul Islam and others v. Bangladesh and others*, 17 BLD (AD) 91.
330. *Government of Bangladesh, represented by the Deputy Commissioner, Gazipur and others v. Abdur Rahman and others* 14 MLR (2009) (AD) 147.
331. *The Province of East Pakistan (Now Bangladesh) v. Shamser Ali Khan & others* 40 DLR (AD) (1988) 202.

(c) causes any damage by negligence in felling any tree or cutting or dragging any timber;
(d) quarries stone, burns lime or charcoal, or collects, subjects to any manufacturing process, or removes, any forest-produce other than timber;

or who enters a reserved forest with firearms without prior permission from the Divisional Forest Officer concerned, shall be punishable with imprisonment for a term which may extend to six months and shall also be liable to fine which may extend to BDT 2,000, in addition to such compensation for damage done to the forest as the convicting court may direct to be paid.[332]

465. It is further provided that any person who:

(a) makes any fresh clearing prohibited by section 5; or
(b) removes any timber from a reserved forest; or
(c) sets fire to a reserved forest, or, in contravention of any rules made by the government in this behalf, kindles any fire, or leaves any fire burning, in such manner as to endanger such a forest;

or who, in a reserved forest

(d) fells, girdles, lops, taps or burns any tree or strips off the bark or leaves from or otherwise damages the same;
(e) clears or breaks up any land for cultivation or any other purpose or cultivates or attempts to cultivate any land in any other manner;
(f) in contravention of any rules made in this behalf by the government, hunts, shoots, fishes, poisons water or sets traps or snares; or
(g) establishes saw-pits or saw-benches or converts trees into timber without lawful authority,

shall be punishable with imprisonment for a term which may extend to five years and shall not be less than six months, and shall also be liable to fine which may extend to BDK 50,000 and shall not be less than BDK 5,000, in addition to such compensation for damage done to the forest as the convicting court may direct to be paid.[333]

Protected Forests

466. Chapter IV (sections 29–34) of the Forest Act, 1927 (Act No. XVI of 1927) contains detailed provisions as to protected forests. It is provided that the government may, by notification in the Official Gazette, declare any forest-land or waste-land which is not included in a reserved forest, but which is the property of

332. Section 26 (1), the Forest Act, 1927 (Act No. XVI of 1927).
333. Section 26 (1A), the Forest Act, 1927 (Act No. XVI of 1927).

Government, or over which the government has proprietary rights, or to the whole or any part of the forest produce of which the government is entitled a 'protected forest'. However, before such declaration, the nature and extent of the rights of Government and of private persons in or over the forest-land or waste-land or char-land comprised therein should generally be enquired.[334] Some activities, as outlined in section 33, are prohibited in the protected forests and are stipulated as punishable offences. These are: quarrying of any stone, burning of any lime or charcoal, collection and/or removal of any forest-produces other than timber, leaving the burning of any fire kindled in the vicinity of any protected forest, causing any damage by negligence in felling any tree or cutting or dragging any timber, trespassing or pasturing cattle and entering into a protected forest with firearms without prior permission of the Divisional Forest Officer. Besides, setting fire to a protected forest without authorization, burning trees, unauthorized use of land in the protected forests for the purpose of cultivation, shooting, hunting, etc., of wild animals, birds and fishes, etc., are prohibited and listed as punishable offences. The government can also ban the cutting of trees in the protected forest. For example, in order to protect biodiversity, the government has banned the cutting of trees in protected and natural forests from 1 January 2016 to 31 December 2022.

467. If anyone is found guilty, he will be liable to punishment. Nevertheless, it is to be noted that the charge of illegal possession of forest timber has to be established with reliable and consistent evidence. Inordinate delay in lodging FIR without satisfactory explanation makes the prosecution version doubtful.[335] According to section 82 of the Forest Act, 1927 (Act No. XVI of 1927), the claim on account of difference between the original auction sale price and resale value being liquidated amount as the price of forest-produce is recoverable as Government arrear revenue under the Public Demand Recovery Act, 1913, through certificate proceeding and not by Civil Court decree.[336]

Private and Vested Forests

468. 'Private forest' is that forest which is not the property of the government or over which the government has no proprietory right, whereas 'vested forest' means a forest of which the control has been vested in a Regional Forest Officer by a notification under section 6(2) or under section 7 or under section 11 and includes any forest deemed to be or managed as, a vested forest under this Ordinance. [337] Under the Private Forests Ordinance, 1959, the owner of a private forest needs to submit a working plan aiming at the conservation of such private forest [section 3(1)] and that working plan once approved cannot be violated [sections 4 & 6]. Besides, the

334. Section 29, the Forest Act, 1927 (Act No. XVI of 1927).
335. *Mobarakullah (Md.) and another v. The State*, 9 MLR (2004) (HC) 208.
336. *Md. Humayun Kabir and others v. Certificate officer, Perojpor*, 1 MLR (1996) (HC) 340.
337. Sections 2(14) & 2 (19), the Private Forests Ordinance, 1959 (East Pakistan Ordinance) (Ordinance No. XXXIV of 1959).

land in the private forest cannot be leased without the previous sanction of the government [section 5], and the violation of the working plan relating to the private forest is a punishable offence [section 6(1)]. If the owner of a private forest is convicted a second time for the failure or neglect to carry out any of the terms and conditions of the working plan in respect of such forest, the government may, by a notification, direct that the control of such forest shall be vested in such Regional Forest Officer for such period as may be specified in such notification.[338]

469. Section 29 provides that any person who:

(a) fells, girdles, lops, taps, or burns any tree in a controlled or vested forest or strips off the bark or leaves from, or otherwise damages, any such tree,
(b) Quarries any stone, or burns any lime or charcoal, or collects, subjects to any manufacturing process, or removes any forest-produce from a controlled or vested forest,
(c) breaks up or clears for cultivation or any other purpose any land in a controlled or vested forest,
(d) sets fire to a controlled or vested forest, or kindles a fire without taking all reasonable precautions to prevent its spreading to any portion of such forest, or
(e) permits cattle to damage any tree in a controlled or vested forest,

shall be punishable with imprisonment for a term which may extend to six months, or with fine which may extend to five hundred taka, or with both.

Village Forests and Social Forestry

470. Chapter III of the Forest Act, 1927 (Act No. XVI of 1927) also deals with village forests (section 28) and social forestry (section 28A). Under section 28, the government may assign to any village community the rights of government to or over any land which has been constituted a reserved forest, and may cancel such assignment. All forests so assigned shall be called village forests.

471. On any land, under section 28A, which is the property of the government or over which the government has proprietory rights, and on any other land assigned to the government by voluntary written agreement of the owner for the purpose of afforestation, conservation or management through social forestry, the government may establish a social forestry programme. Such a programme is established when the government by one or more written agreements assigns rights to forest-produce or rights to use the land, for the purposes of social forestry, to person assisting the government in management of the land.[339] Social forestry in the country was introduced in 1980s and has been benefiting poor community and helping in the expansion of the forest cover of the country, though there are some concerns too.

338. Section 7, the Private Forests Ordinance, 1959 (East Pakistan Ordinance) (Ordinance No. XXXIV of 1959).
339. Section 28A, the Forest Act, 1927 (Act No. XVI of 1927).

Researchers found that this programme was suffering from various institutional deficiencies such as 'organization, skilled manpower, legitimate usufruct rights, peoples' participation from policy to implementation and clear budgetary arrangements'.[340]

472. In order to remove some of these deficiencies, the Social Forestry Rules, 2004 were farmed. Accordingly, depending on the nature of the forestry, the government can enter into an agreement for a minimum 10 to maximum 40 years, and in the selection of the beneficiary of such forestry, a group of people such as landless, someone having less than 50 decimal of land, distressed women, underdeveloped communities, poor indigenous people, poor forest villager, unwealthy freedom fighter or his unwealthy heir will get priority.[341] The Rules also contained detailed provisions on the functions and duties of the parties to the agreement (rules 17 & 18) and calculation of income generated from such forestry (rule 20).

340. Nur Muhammed et al. 'Reckoning Social Forestry in Bangladesh: Policy and Plan Versus Implementation'. *Forestry* 78, no. 4 (2005): 373–383.
341. Rule 6, the Social Forestry Rules, 2004.

Chapter 6. Fish Resources

473. The geographic location of Bangladesh and extremely rich inland water and river system are suitable for fish production. Being one of the leading rice and fish producers in the world, rice and fish are, thus, treated as the staple food of the countrymen. The fishery sector in Bangladesh is broadly classified into three subsectors: inland capture, inland culture, and marine fisheries. Besides, based on the depth of fishing operation, the habitat of coastal and marine fisheries is divided into artisanal (fishing up to 40 m in depth) and industrial fisheries (fishing beyond 40m in depth).[342]

474. The success of Bangladesh in freshwater fish production has already been recognized. The Food and Agriculture Organisation (FAO) considers Bangladesh as one of the leading inland fish producers in the world. In 2018 and 2019, Bangladesh became the third largest inland fish producer in the world, just behind two huge countries: China and India. Studies revealed that between 2000 and 2016, aquaculture production increased from 712,640 and 2,060,408 metric tonnes, and as a result, the revenue from fish exports has also increased from USD 34.08 billion in 2010 to more than USD 46.60 billion.[343] From the latest report of FAO, it is evident that the country produces 1.22 million tonnes of inland freshwater fish, which is 10% of the global catch in 2018.[344] The country is also one of the major aquaculture fish producers. In 2018, Bangladesh produced 1405.4 thousand tonnes of aquaculture fish, which is 2.93% of the total production, making the country the fifth-largest in this sector. In terms of marine and coastal aquaculture finfish production and crustaceans, Bangladesh ranked 12th and 8th respectively in 2020. Besides, Bangladesh is also blessed to have sea fish from the Bay of Bengal.

475. The recent decision of the International Tribunal for Law of the Sea (ITLOS) regarding the Bangladesh-Myanmar maritime boundary, 2012 and the decision of the Arbitral Tribunal of the UNCLOS on India-Bangladesh maritime boundary, 2014 established sovereign rights on more than 118,813 km^2 area of Territorial Sea and 200 nautical miles (nm) of Exclusive Economic Zone (EEZ) and all kinds of living and non-living resources under the continental shelf up to 354 nm from the Chittagong coast. After a similar dispute with India was resolved, Bangladesh has now an exclusive economic authority over more than 19 thousand km^2. In Bangladeshi marine waters, fish resources are extracted in three tiers: (1) up to 40 m in depth from the coastline where normal fishing boats operate; (2) from 40 m to 200 m in depth where mid-water trawlers operate; and (3) from 200 m in depth to the end of the EEZ where longliner trawlers run.[345]

---

342. Mohammad Mahmudul Islam et al. 'Exploitation and Conservation of Coastal and Marine Fisheries in Bangladesh: Do the Fishery Laws Matter?'. *Marine Policy* 76 (2017): 143–151.
343. Md Mostafa Shamsuzzaman et al. 'Fisheries Resources of Bangladesh: Present Status and Future Direction'. *Aquaculture and Fisheries* 2, no. 4 (2017): 145–156.
344. Food and Agriculture Organization of the United Nations, The State of World Fisheries and Aquaculture: Sustainability in Action, 2020, at p. 20.
345. Mohammad Mahmudul Islam et al. 'Exploitation and Conservation of Coastal and Marine Fisheries in Bangladesh: Do the Fishery Laws Matter?.' *Marine Policy* 76 (2017): 143–151.

476. Some of the major constraints for coastal and marine fishery resources in Bangladesh include: overexploitation, conflicts between artisanal and industrial fisheries, pollution, widespread poverty, extreme weather conditions, inappropriate knowledge of fish stock, destructive fishing methods, overcapitalization, the middleman in the fish chain, subjective insecurity due to illegal fishing and sea piracy, and climate change and variability.[346]

477. The government has formulated several national policies aiming at the protection of different aspects of fishing and relevant activities. Fish-related legal provisions can be found in the Permanent Settlement Regulation 1, 1793; the Private Fisheries Protection Act, 1889; the Tank Improvement Act, 1939; the State Acquisition and Tenancy Act, 1950; the Fish and Fish Products (Inspection and Quality Control) Ordinance, 1983; the Fish Hatchery Act, 2010 and Rules 2011; the National Fisheries Policy, 1998; the Joladhar (Wetlands) Act, 2000; the Fish Feed and Animal Feed Act, 2010; the Fish Hatchery Rules, 2011; the National Jalmahal Policy, 2009; the National Shrimp Policy, 2014; the National Cage Fishing in the Jalmahal (Flowing River and in Other Water Reservoir) Policy, 2019; the Fish Quarantine Act, 2018; the Fish and Fish Products (Inspection and Standard Control) Act, 2020; and Rules of 1997.

478. The list of some of the laws that contain provisions relating to marine fisheries includes: the Protection and Conservation of Fish Act, 1950; the Protection and Conservation of Fish Rules, 1985; the Marine Fisheries Act, 2020; the Marine Fisheries Rules, 1983 [the Marine Fisheries Ordinance, 1983, which was enacted after the country signed the United Nations Conservation on the Law of the Sea]; the Territorial Waters and Maritime Zones Act, 1974; the Territorial Waters and Maritime Zones Rules, 1977; the BECA, 1995; and the Environment Conservation Rules, 1997.

479. These laws prohibit different harmful fishing practices and gears, a ban on activities having an adverse impact on the fishery habitat quality, the specification of size for harvestable species, the specification of mesh size for fishing gear, and the prohibition on the entry of unauthorized foreign vessels. These laws empower the government to take various measures regarding the conservation of coastal and marine resources (e.g., by way of establishment of the marine reserve).[347]

480. The Fish and Fish Products (Inspection and Quality Control) Rules, 1997, framed under section 3 of the Fish and Fish Products (Inspection and Quality Control) Ordinance, 1983 (Ordinance No. XX of 1983), were amended in 2014 to specify the acceptable use of chemicals during fish cultivation, production, transport, marketing, preservation, import, and export.

---

346. Mohammad Mahmudul Islam et al. 'Exploitation and Conservation of Coastal and Marine Fisheries in Bangladesh: Do the Fishery Laws Matter?'. *Marine Policy* 76 (2017): 143–151.
347. *Ibid.*

481. The Fish Quarantine Act, 2018 (Act No. 68 of 2018) was enacted for the prevention and control of the spread of harmful bacteria inside Bangladesh during the international transport of fishes, fisheries products, and beneficial microbes. This law also attempts to secure a healthy environment for the fisheries commodity by imposing control over the contamination of fish and fish imports. It is a punishable offence to import, produce, reserve, carry or sell any fish, fish products, beneficial germs, or packing products by infringing any provision of this Act.

482. The Bangladesh Fisheries Research Institute Act (Act No. 69 of 2018) was enacted to repeal the Fisheries Research Institute Ordinance, 1984, and react a new law in its place to meet the current need. Section 3 of the law confers the legal personhood upon the institute; accordingly, it can dispose of all kinds of activities by its name; can sue and be sued. Section 7 of the Act states that the Institute shall conduct and coordinate research on fisheries for the promotion or marketing of fish production, the management, processing, and safe food.

483. The Institute has the mandate to organize different seminars, conferences, training sessions, and workshops on fisheries, and try organizing the joint research programmes in collaboration with national-international universities and research institutions. It will attempt publishing research journals in fulfilling the purpose of this law and conduct other necessary functions with the prior approval of the government. Section 18 affirms that the institute will submit a detailed annual report of all its activities to the government at its earliest convenience.

Chapter 7. Subsoil and minerals

484. Article 143 of the Bangladesh Constitution while specifying the property of Bangladesh provides in clause (1) that: (a) all minerals and other things of value underlying any land of Bangladesh; and (b) all lands, minerals, and other things of value underlying the ocean within the territorial waters, or the ocean over the continental shelf, of Bangladesh shall vest in the Republic of Bangladesh. The main mineral resources of Bangladesh are: natural gas, coal, peat, limestone, white clay, glass sand, hard rock, gravel, and mineral sand. Bangladesh had only one oil reserve discovered in Haripur, Sylhet, which produced only about 0.544 million barrels of oil during 1987–1994.[348]

485. Four stages, i.e., exploration, production, transmission, and distribution, complete the whole process in this regard. The Bangladeshi legal regime earlier did not cover the environmental issues adequately during the exploration phase, which may be due to the fact that when the law was enacted the environmental issues did not receive adequate legal attention. For example, the Bangladesh Petroleum Act, 1974 (Act No. LXIX of 1974), which was enacted to provide for the exploration, development, exploitation, production, processing, refining, and marketing of petroleum, i.e.: (i) any naturally occurring hydrocarbon, whether in a gaseous, liquid or solid state; (ii) any naturally occurring mixture of hydrocarbons, whether in a gaseous, liquid or solid state; or (iii) any naturally occurring mixture of a hydrocarbon or hydrocarbons, whether in a gaseous, liquid or solid state, and one or more of the following, that is to say, hydrogen sulphide, nitrogen, helium, and carbondioxide, provides that it shall be the duty of any person engaged in any petroleum operation to, *inter alia*, consider factors relating to the ecology and environment.[349] However, even after having this provision, the country, unfortunately, experienced some major gas blowouts in Magurchara and Tengratilla.

486. The Bangladesh Petroleum Corporation Act, 2016 (Act No. VIII of 2016) was enacted repealing the previous law in this regard; i.e., the Bangladesh Petroleum Corporation Ordinance, 1976 (Ordinance No. LXXXVIII of 1976). Within the scope of the law, the existing Bangladesh Petroleum Corporation as it was established under Ordinance No. LXXXVIII of 1976 shall remain in operation and will be responsible for continuing their duty in relation to import, refining, and processing of crude petroleum; blending of lubricants, import, export, and marketing of petroleum products including by-products and lubricants (but excluding natural gas), and will also perform the other responsibilities under the Bangladesh Petroleum Act, 1974 (Act No. LXIX of 1974).

487. The existing Petroleum Act, 1934 was updated by enacting the Petroleum Act, 2016 (Act No. XXXII of 2016) in order to consolidate and update provisions

---

348. A. Al Faruque. 'Bangladesh: Legal Framework on Mineral Exploration'. In *Encyclopedia of Mineral and Energy Policy*, ed. G. Tiess, T. Majumder & P. Cameron (Berlin, Heidelberg: Springer, 2018). https://doi.org/10.1007/978-3-642-40871-7_151-1.
349. The Long Title, ss 2(c) and 6(1)(c), the Bangladesh Petroleum Act, 1974 (Act No. LXIX of 1974).

on import, transport, storage, production, refining, blending, or reclaiming by means of recycling, distribution and marketing of petroleum and other inflammable substances in Bangladesh. The law bars anyone to import, transport, store and distribute Class 1 type petroleum without licence or observing the conditions mentioned in the licence (section 4). The law further provides that licence will not be required for the storage or transport of up to 2,000 litre of Class 2 & 3 petroleum. Similarly, up to 25 litre of Class 1 type of petroleum can be stored, transported, or imported for purposes other than sale (section 6).

488. The Mining Settlements Act, 1912 (Act No. II of 1912) was enacted to provide for the better control and sanitation of mining settlements in Bangladesh. The Mines Act, 1923 (Act No. IV of 1923) was enacted to amend and consolidate the law relating to the regulation and inspection of mines. Similarly, the Mines and Mineral Resources (Regulation and Development) Act, 1992 was enacted repealing the Minerals (Regulation and Development) Act, 1967 to regulate the mines and mineral resources.

489. The Mines and Mineral Resources Rules, 2012, formulated under section 4 of the Mines and Mineral Resources (Control and Development) Act, 1992, contain some important provisions relating to the protection of the environment. Other than exploration licence, lease of mines and silica sand, ordinary rock and sandstones, a person needs to obtain licence, under the Rules, for the lease of quarry following the formalities specified in the Rules. The Rules provide that the government can impose general or special conditions for conducting such activities in any reserved or protected forest.[350]

490. The licence holders need to give a thirty days' notice to the Divisional Forest Officer if the exploration, mining, or quarrying activities are conducted in any reserved or protected forest.[351] It is prohibited to cut any tree or hill in any government land without the permission of the Director General, Mineral Resources Development Bureau.[352] The licence holder is responsible for paying reasonable compensation for the damage to the environment.[353] If during the exploration or operation time, water becomes contaminated, the licence holder needs to take initiatives to prevent this and to separate the harmful elements from that water so that the contaminated water cannot harm the fish, seedlings, agriculture, and environment.[354] Rule 42, while dealing with the control of environmental pollution, provides that a licence holder needs to take the following steps to control environmental pollution:

- follow the provisions of the BECA, 1995 and the Environment Protection Rules 1997 and other instructions issued by the authority from time to time;

350. Rule 25, the Mines and Mineral Resources Rules, 2012.
351. Rule 19(2), the Mines and Mineral Resources Rules, 2012.
352. Rule 20, the Mines and Mineral Resources Rules, 2012.
353. Rule 18 (2), the Mines and Mineral Resources Rules, 2012.
354. Rule 39, the Mines and Mineral Resources Rules, 2012.

- take and implement steps to prevent or avoid pollution so that the emissions from solid and liquid waste, harmful gases or high sounds do not pollute the environment;
- take necessary steps to prevent the land degradation and deterioration in the quarry and mine area;
- plant trees suitable for making boundaries in all sides of the quarry or mine areas;
- fill in the excavated area in an environment-friendly manner, and if it is not possible to fill in then that place needs to be converted into an area suitable for fish farming.

491. Even after these provisions, Bangladesh has already experienced a few disasters caused by the minerals.

Chapter 8. Other Sectors

492. In the case of *Human Rights and Peace for Bangladesh and others v. Bangladesh and others*, 2009 (Writ Petition No. 3503/2009), the petitioners moved to the HCD with a public interest litigation by being concerned about the pollution of the four rivers flowing around Dhaka city, i.e., Buriganga, Turag, Balu and Shitalakkha and their almost dying conditions due to land grabbing, illegal encroachments, and earth filling. The HCD found, from various documents and newspaper reports, *inter alia*, that: (1) The amount of normal flow of the water of these four rivers, i.e., Buriganga, Turag, Balu, and Shitalakkha, has been reduced at an alarming rate, especially the rivers Buriganga, Turag, Balu have lost their previous status, and become very narrow. Other than pollution and encroachments, one of the important reasons behind this situation is the failure to protect the sources of these rivers. (2) These rivers are filled with enough silt. (3) Moreover, the illegal land grabbers have been doing businesses of sand and bricks, and encroaching the rivers by making semi-structured infrastructures, buildings, and housing projects.

493. Mr Justice ABM Khairul Haque of the HCD, while delivering the judgment in Bangla, observed, *inter alia*, that: Bangladesh is a land of rivers, and rivers are her life. Once upon a time, these rivers saved this country from the attack of foreign enemies. The rivers are invaluable resources. Bangladesh is very green with enough crops along with enough fresh water and fertile because of these rivers. The land of Bangla was built on these alluvial rivers. In that alluvial soils, nature grants an unlimited amount of food crops with a minimal amount of labour. Once, these rivers were one of the means of our lives. The fishermen used to capture a considerable amount of fish, and that is why fishes are one of the staple foods of Bengalese. These rivers were the main way of transport and supplied enough sources of literature. Through these ways, since antiquity, these rivers have been supporting the lifeline of the peoples of this country. Justice Haque, while sharing the references from the Holy Quran, also stated that the citizens are the owners of all the rivers of Bangladesh, and all the liabilities and responsibilities of these, on behalf of the citizens, lie on the government. The government is generally the owner of these rivers. Finally, the HCD issued some instructions and gave some directions for the recovery of these biologically dead rivers.[355]

494. In the case of *Bangladesh Environmental Lawyers Association (BELA) v. Government of Bangladesh and others*, 2020 (Writ Petition No. 1683/2004), the petitioners filed a writ petition to protect the agricultural lands, wetlands, low lands of Pirojpur Union, Sonargoan Upazilla, Narayangonj from unauthorized earth filling by the Unique Property Development Limited, which did not obtain the environment clearance certificate for its so-called Sonargaon Resort City. As the environment clearance certificate was not obtained, the DoE imposed a fine of BDT 5 million, which the respondent paid and thus admitted their mistakes. Moreover,

355. *Human Rights and Peace for Bangladesh and others v. Bangladesh and others*, 2009 (Writ Petition No. 3503/2009).

the DoE asked the respondent to submit the EIA for the project and to stop all activities before submission of the EIA. The respondent did not submit the EIA but continued all the activities of the project, violating the repeated instructions of the DoE. As a result, the victim villagers moved to the HCD and prayed to direct the HCD to prevent the aforesaid area from further earth filling, to assess the damage caused to the villages by earth filling already done, and to compensate the villagers for the said activities. An injunction was issued to prevent the respondent from further continuing the earth filling in that area, and the respondents were directed to take necessary steps for the removable of the sands/earth from the agricultural lands, wetlands, part of the Meghna river.

495. It may be relevant to share here that subsequently in 2015, these four rivers, due to their critical ecological conditions, were declared as ECA by the DoE. Subsequently, following the recent practices of some other countries, the HCD, in response to a writ petition filed by Human Rights and Peace for Bangladesh, declared the 'Turag' river as a legal person to save it from encroachment. Accordingly, the rights of the Turag river will be protected in similar manner the way the rights of the natural persons are protected through the exercise of their constitutional rights. The division bench of Justice Moyeenul Islam Chowdhury and Md. Ashraful Kamal while declaring this status about the 'Turag river' held that this same status will be applicable for all rivers across the country. Though, with this judgment, Bangladesh has joined the growing list of countries such as Columbia, India, and New Zealand that have recognized rivers as the holders of natural rights, the judgment has also raised a few concerns regarding the implementation of the HCD's directive keeping in view the livelihood of the poor and marginalized people who have been living on these rivers.[356] It is a matter of fact as hundreds of thousands of industries have been functioning on the bank of the rivers of Bangladesh that will be affected once the directives and instructions of the judgment are implemented, an appeal has already been preferred in the AD.[357]

496. In the 'river as a legal person' case, the Supreme Court of Bangladesh linked the legal rights of the rivers to the public trust doctrine and the human right to a healthy environment.[358] While delivering the most comprehensive judgments with specific and detailed directions by any court in the world, the HCD assigned the National River Protection Commission as the legal guardian to act as the parent to protect the rights of waterbodies, e.g., canals and rivers. The HCD also ordered to treat river grabbing as a crime, remove illegal structures from rivers and amend the law and punish the wrongdoers who are responsible for the deterioration of the natural flow of the rivers.[359]

---

356. *Human Rights and Peace for Bangladesh v. Government of Bangladesh and others* (Writ Petition No. 13989 of 2016).
357. *Nishat Jute Mills Limited v. Human Rights and Peace for Bangladesh (HRPB) and others* [2019] (Civil Petition No. 3039 of 2019).
358. Mohammad Sohidul Islam & Erin O'Donnell. 'Legal Rights for the Turag: Rivers as Living Entities in Bangladesh'. *Asia Pacific Journal of Environmental Law* 23, no. 2 (2020): 160–177.
359. United Nations ESCAP, Tackling Water Pollution and Promoting Efficient Water Use in Industries, Regional Perspectives, Environment and Development Policy Brief, 2019/3, at p. 14.

497. It can be seen that with this stand shared in the judgment, the HCD attempted to introduce an 'environmental personhood' approach in the country. This approach, famously proposed in the 1970s by American academic Christopher D. Stone, is fast becoming an international movement. In this approach, natural entities are granted similar legal status to that of corporations, with three primary rights: to sue and be sued (legal standing), to enter contracts, and to take legal action to protect themselves. However, there are some concerns too. If all the rivers are granted legal personhood, then the damages caused by the rivers should also be considered. Therefore, a better approach may be to assign a community to protect the river.[360]

360. Should rivers have legal rights? https://law.unimelb.edu.au/news/MLS/should-rivers-have-legal-rights; Mohammad Sohidul Islam and Erin O'Donnell. 'Legal rights for the Turag: rivers as living entities in Bangladesh.' *Asia Pacific Journal of Environmental Law* 23, no. 2 (2020): 160–177.

Part III. Zoning and Land Use Planning

§1. Introduction

498. Land use planning has huge impacts and consequences on the protection and preservation of environmental components. It is believed and documented that the inhabitants shaped the legal framework containing the laws and rules on land use and management, and thus, this is the most ancient type of law in this part of the world. In the ancient period, though the land was believed to be the common property of the community, during the time of Kautilya and Manu, people and their heirs could take possession of land for cultivation purposes by clearing the jungle and paying rent or revenue to the king at a specified rate. This system, i.e., the enjoyment of lands for cultivation purposes by paying rent or sharing crops, was also continued when Aryans defeated the non-Aryans and even till the thirteenth century when ancient Bengal was conquered by Bakhtiar Khalji. During the Mughal time, the land revenue system was systematized. Subsequently, like other parts of this region, the colonial rulers brought the country's land under state authority and management.[361]

499. Like many other sectors, the planning of town and urban governance was started by the East India Company that enacted the Improvement in Towns Act, 1858 (Act 26 of 1858) which called for contributions to support the municipal commission to introduce urban improvements. Bengal Presidency adopted a similar law in the 1850s, and 'a new regime of municipal record keeping and control over building activity in towns and cities was inaugurated'.[362] After the deadly outbreak of plague in Bombay in 1896–1900 and due to the huge number of slums in Calcutta, the concept of improvement trusts emerged so that these trusts could buy land in the vicinity of cities and develop these for the poor with a steady wage.[363] In 1912, the Calcutta Improvement Trust was established.

500. Historically, Dhaka (former Dacca, a name that originated from a Hindu temple *Dhakeshwari*), the capital of Bangladesh, has been one of the most important cities in the Indo-Pak subcontinent since the Mughal time and was the capital of the Muslim Mughal Dynasty of Bengal province (AD 1608–1639 and AD

361. For the historical background of Land Laws in Bangladesh, *see*, Land Laws, Banglapedia, https://en.banglapedia.org/index.php?title=Land_Laws.
362. Howard Spodek. 'City Planning in India under British Rule'. *Economic and Political Weekly* (2013): 53–61, at p. 55.
363. *Ibid.*, at pp. 57–58.

1660–1704), and the first municipality was constituted in Dhaka in 1864 under the British control. Subsequently, Dhaka became the capital of Eastern Bengal and Assam province (AD 1905-AD 1912), of East Bengal province (1947), and East Pakistan (1956). In 1917, Patrick Geddes, after a short visit to Dhaka, proposed the first, though very brief, Master Plan for Dhaka containing 9 chapters in 22 pages. That plan of Geddes though considered the geographical conditions of the then Dhaka failed due to its incomplete sketchy nature lacking details.[364]

501. After the end of the colonial rule, when present Bangladesh became the part of the then Pakistan in the name of East Pakistan, a law titled the Town Improvement Act, 1953 (Act No. XIII of 1953) was enacted for the development, improvement, and expansion of the town and municipalities and certain areas in their vicinity, and the Dhaka Improvement Trust (DIT) was established under this law to undertake development activities in Dhaka and Narayanganj.[365] In 1959, the second Master Plan was formulated by the British planners, Minoprio, Spencely, and MacFarlane. Their plan containing fifteen chapters, including transport, public buildings, population, housing, education, open spaces, commerce, industry, public utility services, land for special purposes, planning administration and implementation, and legislation, also could not be successful due to, *inter alia*, rapid population growth.[366]

502. The DIT was renamed as Rajdhani Unnayan Kartipakkha (Capital City Development Authority) (RAJUK) in 1987 through the Town Improvement (Amendment) Act, 1987, and this is a statutory public authority under the Ministry of Housing and Public Works. This RAJUK, since its inception, has been playing important roles towards sustainable development and protection of environmental components by way of planning the city, designing various development projects and approving the building designs, etc.

503. Almost three decades after the independence of Bangladesh, another Master Plan, Dhaka Metropolitan Development Plan 1995–2015 (DMDP), under section 73 of the Town Improvement Act, 1953, was prepared in 1995 and gazetted in 1997. This Master Plan, containing three levels of planning, i.e., the Structure Plan, the Urban Area Plan, and the Detailed Area Plan, was not also implemented properly, and therefore, another Master Plan, Dhaka Structure Plan, 2016–2035 was formulated. In the case of *Metro Makers and Developers Limited and others vs. Bangladesh Environmental Lawyers' Association Limited (BELA) and others*, 2012, 41 CLC (AD) [8366] = 65 DLR (AD) (2013) 181, 2 LNJ AD (2013) 222, Justice Surendra Kumar Sinha of the AD described the Dhaka Master plan:

364. Bayezid Ismail Choudhury & Peter Armstrong. 'The Failure of the 1917 Geddes Master Plan and 1959 Minoprio, Spencely, Macfarlane Master Plans: Some Reflections'. *Journal of Social and Development Sciences* 4, no. 10 (2013): 449–460.
365. Subsequently, in 1987, the Tongi Municipalities was also included.
366. Bayezid Ismail Choudhury & Peter Armstrong. 'The Failure of the 1917 Geddes Master Plan and 1959 Minoprio, Spencely, Macfarlane Master Plans: Some Reflections'. *Journal of Social and Development Sciences* 4, no. 10 (2013): 449–460.

In 1997 RAJUK prepared a fresh Master Plan known as Dhaka Metropolitan Development Plan (DMDP) for the Dhaka city and its surrounding area, which was published in Gazette notification on 3rd August, 1997 identifying few areas of flood plains, rivers, water bodies, Sub-Flood Flow Zone (SFFZ) etc. to protect the safety, health, and welfare of the common people from negative environmental impact and to protect and preserve natural drainage system to ensure their continual and proper functioning. Any interference with the same as earmarked in the said Master Plan will have devastating environmental effect for which the Master Plan in clear terms prohibited residential, commercial and industrial developments in those Zones, including raising the level of the land plain through earth filling in Flood Flow/Sub- Flood Flow Zones. The said Master Plan in categorizing the land use pattern for the city, identified 19 Spatial Planning Zone (SPZ) out of which 17 comprising area between Savar and Dhansona in the west and present Dhaka established area at the east which is low lying area across Torag river and its canals and is designated as Flood Flow/Sub- Flood Flow Zone area within which Ameen Bazar area under Savar Police station has fallen as part of Sub- Flood Flow Zone. The DMDP has identified that there have been many private development schemes approved by RAJUK especially in the Ameen Bazar area on the south of Dhaka-Aricha Road which will have a considerable negative impact on the environment and DMDP recommends that all such development permits issued by RAJUK for the development of housing within this area should be withdrawn and that no new ones be allowed. Moreover, conditions and restrictions have been imposed in DMDP and also by section 5 of Ain of 2000 prohibiting change of nature of any land that has been earmarked as natural reservoir including Flood-Flow zone.

504. It will be pertinent to share here that the British Government enacted the Land Acquisition Act, 1894 containing provisions on urban planning, and this law was in force in independent Bangladesh till 1982. Then this law was repealed and replaced by the Acquisition and Requisition of Immovable Property Ordinance, 1982 (Ordinance No. II of 1982), which was recently repealed and replaced by the Acquisition and Requisition of Immovable Property Act, 2017 (Act No. 21 of 2017).[367] It may be relevant to share here that land can be acquisitioned for very special purposes too, and the government usually does so by making a special law. For example, for the purpose of making the Jamuna and Padma Bridge, the government enacted special laws, i.e., the Jamuna Multi Purpose Bridge Project (Land Acquisition) Act, 1995 (Act No. 14 of 1995) and the Padma Multi Purpose Bridge Project (Land Acquisition) Act, 2009 (Act No. 31 of 2009), respectively.

505. The government has also enacted the Bangladesh Investment Development Authority Act, 2016 (Act No. 36 of 2016), through which the development authority established has been given some statutory power and authority to the use of land

367. Section 50(1), the Acquisition and Requisition of Immovable Property Act, 2017 (Act No. 21 of 2017).

and planning. Similar provisions can also be found in the Bangladesh Export Processing Zones Authority Act, 1980 (Act No. XXXVI of 1980), which provides for the establishment of Bangladesh Export Processing Zones Authority. Moreover, the Cantonments Act, 2018 (Act No. 27 of 2018), which was enacted to repeal and update the Cantonments Act, 1924, contains some provisions on planning.

506. Generally, the local government administrations in the country, e.g., City Corporations, district, upazila, union parishad administration, have been playing instrumental roles concerning zone and land use planning, and they have been enjoying relevant powers and authorities through the provisions of statutes through which they are constituted. These laws are: the Zila Parishad Act, 2000 (Act No. 19 of 2000), which applies to all district administration except for the three districts of the Chattogram Hill Tracts, i.e., Khagrachari, Bandarban and Rangamati;[368] the Upazilla Parishad Act, 1998 (Act No. 24 of 1998); the Local Government (City Corporation) Act, 2009 (Act No. 60 of 2009); the Local Government (Pourshava) Act, 2009 (Act No. 58 of 2009); the Local Government (Union Parishad) Act, 2009 (Act No. 61 of 2009). A very clear pattern in terms of incorporation of legal provisions in these laws can be noticed. Accordingly, these local government administrations are given power or authority to conduct the planning of all construction works, development plan, constructions of public ways, culverts, bridges, tree plantations, maintenance of the park, playground, and open space, etc.

507. In some cases, the government has also constituted development authorities for the proper development of important cities. Accordingly, laws like the RAJUK Law, i.e., the Town Improvement Act, 1953 (East Bengal Act No. XIII of 1953), enacted for the proper development of Dhaka, similar laws have also been enacted for other important cities too, e.g., the Cox's Bazar Development Authority Act, 2016 (Act No. 07 of 2016); the Rajshahi Development Authority Act, 2018 (Act No. 5 of 2018); the Chattogram Development Authority Act, 2018 (Act No. 31 of 2018); the Khulna Development Authority Act, 2018 (Act No. 32 of 2018); and the Gazipur City Development Authority Act, 2020 (Act No. 13 of 2020) containing similar provisions aiming at the proper development of that city. These city development authorities are responsible for developing the Master Plan, framing the development plan and its implementation, establishment of entertainment and tourism centres, maintenance of government roads and drains, etc. These laws also contain provisions on various offences, e.g., use of land violating the provisions of Master Plan, construction of building, wetlands, hill cutting, filling of low land and the flow of water and their punishments, etc.

508. In many cases, the planning or ever-going development activities create a lot of problems for the public at large. This is a general problem in most of the cities that these activities are done without proper coordination. Interestingly, almost

368. It will be pertinent to share here that these three districts are governed by the Rangamati Hill Tracts Act, 1989 (Act No. 19 of 1989), the Khagrachari Hill Tracts Act, 1989 (Act No. 20 of 1989), the Bandarban Hill Tracts Act, 1989 (Act No. 21 of 1989).

a century ago, the Highways Act, 1925 (Act No. III of 1925) was enacted to provide for the regulation and safety of traffic on Government roads in Bangladesh, for the prevention of obstruction and encroachments, and of nuisances on or near such roads, for the preservation of such roads, and the temporary closing of such roads for repairs or other works, or public purposes. The law has defined 'Government road' as 'a road vested in the Government, or under the control and administration of the Works Department of the Government, and includes- (a) the slope, berm, borrow-pits and side-drains of any such road; (b) all lands and embankments vested in, or under the control and administration of, the said Works Department, and attached to a Government road; (c) all bridges, culverts or causeways built on or across any Government road; and (d) all fences and posts on any Government road or any land attached to a Government road, and all roadside trees on such land'.[369] Thus, this definition categorically includes all the roads except the private ones. The law authorizes the government or any officer on behalf of the government to temporarily close any government road to repair such road, or to construct any sewer, drain, culvert, or bridge, or for any other similar public purpose.[370] The law also provides that before so doing, the government is bound, where possible, to provide other reasonably sufficient means of access to holdings adjacent to such road or part, if no such means of access already exist.[371]

509. As per the provisions of section 4 of this Act, 1925, the Highways (Security, Protection and Restriction of Movement) Rules, 2001 were formulated containing provisions on the declaration of road protection corridor (rule 3), restriction of movement on the highway (rule 4), adherence to authorized point and traffic signs to access and exit from highway (rule 5), restrictions on the use of highways by adjacent landowners or occupiers (rule 6), restriction on the stoppage of motor vehicles on the highways (rule 7), restriction of destructive use of highways (rule 8). It is provided that the violations of the provisions of these rules shall be treated as an offence, and a person shall be liable to pay a fine of BDK 10,000, and for the continuation of violations, simple imprisonment for a period of up to six months and a fine of BDK 100 for each day.[372] It has been reported that the government has taken initiative to revise and replace the existing Highway Act, 1925, and a draft of the law was released in 2019, which has not been finalized yet.

510. The landmark judgment, i.e., *Dr. Mohiuddin Farooque v. Bangladesh*, 48 DLR 1996, often cited as FAP-20 case, was related to flood action plan though the judgment is celebrated as it has established the clear foundation of 'person aggrieved' or person having '*locus standi*' to bring a matter of public interest in the superior court of the country.

---

369. Section 2, the Highways Act, 1925 (Act No. III of 1925).
370. Section 3, the Highways Act, 1925 (Act No. III of 1925).
371. *Ibid.*
372. Rule 11, the Highways (Security, Protection and Restriction of Movement) Rules, 2001.

§2. MASTER PLAN

511. Master Plans play a crucial role in the development of any city in a planned manner. Various laws of Bangladesh contain provisions on Master Plan for the improvement of the town, and these were started institutionally through the enactment of the Building Construction Act, 1952 and the Town Improvement Act, 1953, i.e., after the independence of India and Pakistan from the British rule in 1947. It may be relevant to share here that in the UK, a similar law, i.e., the Town and Country Planning Act, 1947, was enacted to enable the local authority to consider environmental factors while approving any development proposals.

512. Section 5(c) of the Building Construction Act, 1952 (East Bengal Act No. II of 1953) defines 'Master Plan' as the 'plan prepared and approved under any law for the time being in force for the utilisation of any land anywhere in Bangladesh'. Provisions relating to Master Plan can also be found in the laws relating to various development authorities established, e.g., in Cox's Bazar, Rajshahi, Chottogram, Khulna, Gazipur.[373]

513. Section 73(2) of the Town Improvement Act, 1953 (East Bengal Act No. XIII of 1953) provides that: 'The Master Plan shall include such maps and such descriptive matter as may be necessary to illustrate the proposals aforesaid with such degree of particularity as may be appropriate, between different parts of the area, and any such plan may, in particular, define the sites of proposed roads, public, and other buildings and works, or fields, parks, pleasure-grounds, and other open spaces or allocate areas of land for use for agricultural, residential, industrial or other purposes of any class specified in the Master Plan.' In 2000, a law titled 'Conservation of Playground, Open Space, Park and Natural Water Reservoir in the Metropolitan, Division, and District Towns Act, 2000 (Act No. 36 of 2000)' was also enacted containing provisions on making Master Plans popular (section 4). These Master Plans are developed for the improvement of the three cities, i.e., the Capital of the Republic, Narayanganj, and Tongi Municipalities, and can be altered for improvement. However, the conversion of open spaces and parks to be enjoyed by all allottees of a planned township into residential plots is not an improvement by any means.[374] Sections 73–75 of the Town Improvement Act, 1953 contain provisions on the preparation, publication of Master Plan, and the use of land contrary to Master plan with the permission of the Chairman of the RAJUK.

514. In *Ms. Syeda Rizwana Hasan v. Bangladesh and others*, 2010, 39 CLC (AD) [8508] = 9 ADC (2012) 816, 18 BLC (AD) (2013) 54, it was held that: '. . .a master plan is nothing but a guide for proposed future land use recommending the

373. For example, Chapter III, ss 13–15, the Cox's Bazar Development Authority Act, 2016 (Act No. VII of 2016), Chapter III, ss 12–15, the Rajshahi Development Authority Act, 2018 (Act No. III of 2018), Chapter III, ss 11–14, the Chottogram Development Authority Act, 2018 (Act No. 31 of 2018), Chapter III, ss 11–14, the Khulna Development Authority Act, 2018 (Act No. 32 of 2018), Chapter III, ss 11–14, the Gazipur Development Authority Act, 2020 (Act No. 13 of 2020).

374. *Rajdhani Unnayan Kartipakhya and another v. Mohshinul Islam and another*, 53 DLR (AD) (2001) 79 = 2001, 30 CLC (AD) [881].

development of the area and zoning. It generally surveys land use as it exists and recommends it for future planning. In the Act, the expression "Master Plan" has not been defined. There is, however, reference to "Master Plan" in sections 73, 74, and 75. Section 73 speaks about the preparation of a "Master Plan" in respect of an area for carrying out the development of the land in phases. It is said, a master plan includes maps and such descriptive matters to illustrate the sites of proposed roads, public and other buildings, fields, parks, pleasure grounds, and other open spaces. A master plan must be published in the official gazette by the Government after it has been prepared by the authority. There is also a provision for filing an objection against the master plan by any person aggrieved by the preparation of the same and the Government may modify it if there is merit in the objection. Though this "Master Plan" is a piece of conclusive evidence after it is approved by the Government as provided therein but it can also be amended or altered by the *Katripakkha* under section 74(2) from time to time with the approval of the Government. Section 75 relates to the use of land within the "Master Plan" area for any purpose other than that laid down in the master plan by any person with the prior permission of the authority'.[375]

515. Many decisions and initiatives of RAJUK were contested in the superior courts; some were on the ground of protection of environmental components when the RAJUK attempted to change the Master Plan. In *Mohshinul Islam v. Rajdhani Unnayan Kartripakkha and others*, 52 DLR (HCD) (2000) 12, the allottees of Uttara Model Town objected to the change of the original Master Plan/Layout of Uttara Model Town by RAJUK. The court pointed out that 'there is growing concern for maintaining open space like public parks in the urban areas for protecting health and hygiene of the inhabitants of the area and the authorities cannot deprive them of such facility. We have already noticed from the provisions of the Town Improvement Act, 1953 that the RAJUK should provide parks, open spaces, playgrounds, or similar amenities and cannot deprive the residents of an improvement scheme like Uttara or Gulshan from such facilities on the plea of providing residential plots to the growing number of town dwellers. Maintaining a healthy environment in a residential area is a prime necessity of the day and vacant spaces in the development schemes are kept under the requirement of law for maintaining a healthy environment for the residents and RAJUK cannot deprive the residents of such facilities on any plea whatsoever.'

516. In reaching to the Judgment, the court considered the decision of the case of *Giasuddin vs. Dhaka Municipal Corporations,* 17 BLD 577, 49 DLR 199, where a Division Bench of HCD held 'A public Park is necessary for protecting health and hygiene of the habitants of the area providing open space with the garden. Trespassers cannot be allowed to occupy the same on the plea of their indispensable accommodation to protect their life to the detriment of health and hygiene of the inhabitants of the area and the Corporation is under a legal obligation to evict such

375. *Ms. Syeda Rizwana Hasan v. Bangladesh and others*, 2010, 39 CLC (AD) [8508] = 9 ADC (2012) 816, 18 BLC (AD) (2013) 54.

unauthorised occupants from the park and other facilities meant for public convenience and for maintaining the environment free from pollution and degradation.' In the case of *Miah Fazal Din vs. Lahore Improvement Trust,* 21 DLR (SC) 225, it has been held that if the modification of a sanctioned scheme completely alters the nature of the scheme or radically changes it as to render the sanctioned scheme materially different then the modification must be republished on the general principles.

517. In the Writ Petition No. 2931 of 2009, Justice Zinat Ara and Justice J.N. Deb Choudhury considered the legality of changing the RAJUK's Master Plan/ Layout Plan of the Gulshan Model Town. In the original plan, there was a Children Park, which was used by the community people. Violating the Master Plan, the authority allotted the park to Bangladesh Squash Racquets Federation, which compelled the petitioner to move to the court. The subject matter of the petition was the legality of the said lease and not the importance of preservation of the park from an environmental perspective. As a result, the court spelt out that 'we are of the view that the park shown in the layout plan of RAJUK ought not be converted for the use of any other purpose and it must be maintained as a park for the use of public'.

518. In *Rajdhani Unnayan Kartipakkhya and others v. Dr. AK Shamsul Islam & others*, 2003, 32 CLC (AD) [5315] = 63 DLR (AD) (2011) 129, the RAJUK wanted to alter the original layout plan of sector 9 of Uttara Model Town to create new plots for allotments of some interested persons as residential plots. RAJUK also drew a new plan abolishing the spaces specified for a park, primary school, car park, community centre, mosque, playground, commercial zone, etc., without informing the respondents. They moved to the HCD and the HCD declared the newly created layout plan without any legal effect and ordered RAJUK to restore all civil facilities mentioned in the original plan. RAJUK was not happy with the decision and preferred an appeal in the AD where the AD maintained the decision of the HCD. Justice Mohammad Fazlul Karim held that: '[t]he open space is thus preserved and protected under the law particularly for the protection of the environment and designed to maintain the ecological balance in the vicinity to keep the city life free from the continuing pollution out of various city hazards. Thus, by abolishing open spaces and other consequential civic amenities reserved under a layout plan which are essential features of the development of a residential area under the Town Improvement Act for the residents of the area would tend to endanger the lives of the inhabitants of the area, making the same unfavourable for rural habitation. Thus, by modifying the existing layout plan thereby abolishing the spaces specified and reserved for the essential civic facilities for the residents of the locality has definitely deprived them of the promised facilities attached to the allotment of plots to them thereby endangering the healthy living conditions of the residents of the sector 9 resulting in making the area unfavourable for habitation. In view of the above, the subsequent modified layout plan depriving the civil amenities to the inhabitants of the locality is of no legal consequence'.

519. In the recently published judgment on *Metro Makers and Developers Limited and Others v. Bangladesh Environmental Lawyers' Association Limited (BELA) and Others*, 65 DLR (AD) (2013) 181, the AD considered the legality of a particular housing project—that is, the Modhumati Model Town Project started by the land development company, Metro Makers and Developers Limited (MMDL), in violation of the Master Plan, DMDP, where a few areas around the Dhaka city were identified as flood plains, rivers, water bodies, subflood flow zones (SFFZ) and so on to protect the safety, health, and welfare of the common people from negative environmental impact and to protect and preserve natural drainage system to ensure their continual and proper functioning.

520. The DMDP prohibited in clear terms residential, commercial, and industrial developments in those zones, including raising the level of land through earth filling in flood flow/SFFZs. Despite such a clear prohibition, the MMDL started a development project near Ameen Bazar within mouza Bilamalia and Baliarpur, which were situated within SPZ 17(3) and earmarked as an SFFZ and started to fill the earth in the substantial part of the zone with a goal of implementing an unauthorized satellite township under the name Modhumati Model Town (MMT) and also started through regular media advertisements to offer to sell housing plots in the said projects.

521. The RAJUK did not prevent the project but categorically rejected the plan. BELA undertook a field survey and, after finding serious illegalities, took the case to court. The protection of the environment received the highest attention in the judgment delivered by the AD, and the said housing project was declared unlawful, and the MMDL was directed to restore the wetlands to their original position. The AD observed, *inter alia*:

> Right to life includes right to protection and improvement of environment and ecology. Even if there could not have been any law imposing restriction relating to the use of the nal lands in the areas in question which operate as reservoir of flood and rain water. If these lands are filled up it will cause serious problem in draining out water resulting from flood and rain and the affected people can compel the authorities through judicial review to take steps to preserve and protect health, environment and ecology in the Metropolitan areas. The fundamental right of the third party purchasers cannot override the fundamental right of overwhelming number of residents of the metropolis under Articles 31 and 32 of the Constitution (per Justice Syed Mahmud Hossain, at paragraph 126).

522. The court further held that the purchaser who was the bona fide purchaser for value should not have any remedy from the court—that is, 'the right to life of overwhelming number of residents of Dhaka City cannot be overlooked and the third party purchasers cannot claim any relief dehors the fundamental right of the residents of Dhaka City under articles 31 and 32 of the Constitution'. However, the court instructed the MMDL to compensate them. This is undoubtedly a groundbreaking judgment in the history of the country when the mushroom-like real estate companies of the country have been in a race to grab most parts of the capital city and its vicinity. After that, the High Court Division has intervened in several similar housing projects such as the Asian City Housing Project in Dakkhinkhan, and the Rajuk Purbachal Housing Project.

523. In *M Saleem Ullah, Advocate and others Vs. Bangladesh, represented by the Secretary, Ministry of Housing and Public Works and others* (2003) 55 DLR 1, it was held that 'the State is bound to protect the health and longevity of the people free from threats of man-made hazards unless that threat is justified by law and as such action of authorities in converting open space for the park into residential plots is violative of the fundamental right guaranteed under article 31 and 32' and the action of the respondents in convening the open space meant for a park is without any lawful authority as the same is violative of fundamental rights and detrimental to the health and well-being of the people of the area. In *Giasuddin v. Dhaka Municipal Corporation,* 1997 BLD 577 = 49 DLR 199, it was held: 'A Public Park is necessary for protecting health and hygiene of the inhabitants of the area providing open space with garden.'

524. The case *Bangladesh Paribesh Andolan and another v. Bangladesh, represented by the Secretary, Ministry of Works and others*, 2004, 33 CLC (HCD) [4810] = 58 DLR (2006) 441 is important in various respects. In this case, the issue of *locus stadi* was raised when the petitioner challenged the construction of residences for the Speaker and Deputy Speaker within the National Assembly Area in violation of the original plan and the Building Construction Act, 1952.

§3. Environment Impact Assessment

525. There is no real conflict between the development activities with the provisions of the environmental law. To continue the development activities, some innovative tools, e.g., environmental impact assessment (EIA) and strategic environmental assessments (SEAs), were introduced. EIA and SEAs are considered as the 'most commonly known, used, and globally widespread, environmental planning and management tool'.[376] EIA is 'a process of evaluating the likely environmental impacts of a proposed project or development, taking into account interrelated socio-economic, cultural and human-health impacts, both beneficial and adverse'.[377] EIA aims to predict the environmental impacts of any project or development activity during the planning and design stage of the project, find ways to reduce the adverse impact, if any, shape the projects considering the environmental impacts, and share the predictions and alternatives to the decision makers.[378]

376. UN Environment (2018). Assessing Environmental Impacts- A Global Review of Legislation, Nairobi, Kenya.
377. What is Impact Assessment? Convention on Biological Diversity, https://www.cbd.int/impact/whatis.shtml.
378. *Ibid.*

526. Different countries have included different stages to conduct EIA in their legislation. Historically, the system of EIA was first introduced in the USA by the President Richard Nixon administration through the provisions of the National Environmental Policy Act, 1969 where it was provided that the proponents of any development projects that involved US federal land, federal tax dollar or federal jurisdictions had to submit an environmental impact statement explaining in detail the impacts of the proposed project on the physical, cultural and human environments, together with the statement if any alternative is available. The law also provided for the required mitigation measures for each impact and a monitoring programme to ensure the actual working of these mitigation measures.

527. At the international level, the Stockholm Declaration on the Human Environment, 1972, included the idea of EIA indirectly in principles 14 & 15 specifying the importance of planning in making a balance between environment and development. The European Economic Committee recommended its members the EIA in 1985. In January 1987, the UNEP released the 'Goals and Principles of Environmental Impact Assessment' containing three goals and thirteen principles. The recommendation of the European Economic Committee became a requirement in 1989.[379] Principle 17 of the Rio Declaration on the Environment and Development, 1992 provides for the conduct of EIA for proposed activities that may have a significant adverse impact on the environment. Subsequently, the provisions on EIA have been included in the United Nations Convention on the Law of the Sea, 1982, the Convention on Biological Diversity, 1992 and the UNFCCC.[380] By 1996, more than hundred countries in the world adopted legislation containing provisions on EIA, and EIA commitments are included in major international instruments.[381] However, the UN SDGs have not included an explicit provision on EIA.

528. In the context of Bangladesh, the idea of EIA was first included, though indirectly and implicitly, in section 12 of the BECA, 1995, which provides that '[n]o industrial unit or project shall be established or undertaken without obtaining, in the manner prescribed by rules, an Environmental Clearance Certificate from the Director General'. The Environment Conservation Rules, 1997 contain provisions on categorization of industries and development projects based on actual and prospective pollution, the requirement of EIA and environmental management plan, the procedure for getting environmental clearance, standards on air, surface water, groundwater, drinking water, industrial effluents, emissions, noise, and vehicular exhaust. It may be relevant to share here that a survey of industries that are responsible for polluting the environment was already conducted in 1986.[382]

379. Rabel J. Burdge. *A Brief History and Major Trends in the Field of Impact Assessment*, Impact Assessment 9, no. 4 (1991): 93–104, DOI: 10.1080/07349165.1991.9726070.
380. *See generally*, UN Environment (2018). Assessing Environmental Impacts- A Global Review of Legislation, Nairobi, Kenya.
381. Neil Craik. *The International Law of Environmental Impact Assessment: Process, Substance and Integration* (Cambridge, UK: Cambridge University Press, 2008), at p. 4.
382. *Dr Mohiuddin Farooque and other v. Bangladesh and others* (Writ Petition No 891 of 1994).

529. In Bangladesh, the EIAs are conducted in six stages: screening, scoping, baseline data generation, impact assessment, mitigation of impacts, environment management plan.[383] The DoE first published the EIA Guidelines for Industries in 1997. Since February, 2015, EIA is required for every project undertaken by the MoEFCC and recently, the DoE has updated the EIA Guidelines for Industries in February 2021.

530. One of the significant contributions of the Rules, 1997 is that this has classified various industries and development projects, for an environment clearance certificate, in places other than export processing zones (public/private), in different categories, i.e., Green, Orange A, Orange B, and Red based on location, the size and the severity of potential pollution. The category Orange is again classified into: Orange A, Orange B.[384] Of these categories, industries within the Green categories do not need to require any environmental examination and EIA as these are believed to be relatively pollution-free and an Environmental Clearance Certificate (ECC) to be obtained from the DoE is sufficient to run the business for regulatory purpose. Examples of industries in this category are assembling and manufacturing TV, Radio, telephones, clocks, and watches, etc., book-binding, etc.

531. For the industries in the Orange A category, before obtaining an ECC, along with the general information about the industry, a feasibility report, a process flow diagram and a schematic diagram of waste treatment facilities need to be submitted. Examples of industries in this category are: sawmill/wood sawing, printing press, restaurant, cinema hall, etc.

532. For the industries in Orange B category, to obtain an ECC, documents such as no objection certificate from the local authority, initial environment examination report, process flow diagram, layout plan, feasibility report of the industrial unit or project, emergency plan, outline of the relocation, rehabilitation plan, together with an Environmental Management Plan need to be submitted. Examples of industries in this category are jute mill, edible oil, glass factory, plastic products, bricks/tiles, perfumes, cosmetics.

533. The industries in the Red Category have the prospects to cause significant adverse impacts on the environmental components and therefore need to submit an EIA report, though it is possible to obtain an initial site clearance based on initial environment examination. For the projects and activities listed in the Red Category, the entrepreneurs need to submit an initial environmental evolution together with EIA.[385] However, they must submit the EIA report along with an Environmental Management Plan and other necessary documents to get the ECC. Examples of

383. Department of Environment, Ministry of Environment, Forest and Climate Change, Government of the People's Republic of Bangladesh, EIA Guidelines for Industries, February 2021, at p. 4.
384. In *Bangladesh Environmental Lawyers Association (BELA) v. Bangladesh*, 2009, 38 CLC (HCD) [8173]=7 LG (HCD) (2010) 118, the import of a scrap oil tanker named Atlantia/New Atlantia (IMO No. 7709136) was contested and the HCD instructed the DoE to take immediate necessary steps to ensure closure of all the shipbreaking yards without clearance certificate.
385. Rule 7, the Environment Conservation Rules, 1997.

industries in this category are tannery, urea fertilizer, all mining projects (coal, limestone, hard rock, natural gas, mineral oil, etc.), chemical dyes, polish, varnish, enamel, etc.

534. The EIA-related provision of the BECA, 1995 was amended and expanded in 2010. It is provided in section 12 that:

> 12. (1) No industrial establishment or project may be taken up in any area without obtaining an environmental clearance certificate, in the manner prescribed by rules, from the DG.
> (2) In the case of an industrial establishment or an adopted project established immediately before the coming into force of this Act, an environmental clearance certificate shall be obtained immediately after the enactment of the Bangladesh Environmental Protection (Amendment) Act, 2010.
> (3) In case of expansion of any industrial establishment or project, an environmental clearance certificate shall be obtained in the manner prescribed by the rules.
> (4) The rules on environmental clearances shall include in detail, among other things, environmental impact assessment report, preparation of environmental management plan, verification of public opinion, availability of public information on all these matters, formation and working procedure of clearance committee, minimum requirements of clearance, appeal etc.
> (5) The Department shall update the list of industrial establishments and projects for granting environmental clearance by 31st March of each year and determine the minimum qualifications and responsibilities of the concerned persons or organizations in preparing environmental impact assessment reports or environmental management plans of various industrial establishments and projects and will prepare, approve and update the list in this regard.

535. The ECC remains valid for three years for Green category industries and one year for other categories. The DoE can cancel an ECC though a notice must be served to explain the position. Failing to give notice before the cancellation of the licence is against the principle of natural justice and thus will be declared illegal in the court of law. In the case of *Abu Jafar Md. Nurul Islam v. DG, Department of Environment, Government of Bangladesh and others*, 2003, 32 CLC (HCD) [3897] = 56 DLR (2004) 1, various aspects of an 'environmental clearance certificate' were evaluated. In this case, though it was not required according to the provisions of the law, i.e., under the provisions of the Environment Conservation Rules, 1997, the petitioners obtained the ECC from the DoE to run a Muri (puffed rice) factory by submitting the necessary papers, e.g., processes flow diagram, Chalan form and layout plan, etc., and obtained the ECC valid for one year with the option for renewal. Subsequently, the petitioner took the initiative to start the factory by taking necessary permission from the Investment Board, Department of Fire Service & Civil Defence, and Dhaka City Corporation.

536. Unfortunately, after six months, without given any chance of explanation, the petitioner was asked to stop manufacturing 'Muri' within seven days and to shift the factory elsewhere, as on enquiry it was found that the petitioner violated the terms of the ECC. The petitioner claimed that there was a land dispute with his neighbour who used his personal connections to cancel the certificate though the petitioner apparently did not violate any provisions of the certificate. On the other hand, the respondents shared that the petitioner violated a few provisions of the certificate, e.g., fire fighting devices were not installed, cautions were not taken to protect the human health hazards, water was wasted, the business was creating noise, and air pollution. Moreover, the respondent demanded that the case is not maintainable as the petitioner did not use the option of appeal to the DoE as per section 14 of the BECA, 1995 which provides for an appeal against any notice, order, or direction passed under the said Law to the appellate authority constituted by the government.

537. Justice Md. Abdul Wahhab Miah, after reading sections 8, 10 and 11 of the BECA, 1995 and Rule 5 of the Environment Conservation Rules, 1997 found that a procedure has been laid down to file a complaint to the DG about the creation of any environment pollution by an industry, factory or industrial project and how to dispose of the same which also include giving hearing to the owner of the industry or factory concerned. More significantly, proviso to section 4 (3) of the BECA, 1995 has made it mandatory upon the Director General to give written notice to the owner of the industry-factory concerned giving him chance to take necessary step to rectify the environmental hazard. Finally, Justice Abdul Wahhab Miah found that '. . .the hasty manner in which the impugned action has been taken in clear defiance of the relevant provision of the law. . .' as the getting of a notice regarding the cancellation of a licence is 'an absolute legal right'.

538. In *Government of Bangladesh and others vs. Tajul Islam,* 49 DLR (AD) 177, it has been held that the cancellation of a licence is a serious matter adversely touching a serious pecuniary interest; more than that, it affects a fundamental right of a citizen to conduct any lawful trade or business subject to certain restrictions imposed by law, the court would always insist that an authority exercising such a drastic power of cancellation acts strictly according to law and always with fairness.

§4. Marine Spatial Planning and Coastal management

539. Bangladesh is blessed to have the sea, one of the main sources of all resources, on the southern side of the country. After the maritime boundary disputes with neighbouring India and Myanmar were resolved, Bangladesh can explore the potential of the blue economy.

540. The emerging concept 'blue economy' refers to the sustainable use of ocean resources for economic growth, improved livelihoods, and ocean ecosystem health, and encompasses activities such as climate change, renewable energy, tourism, fisheries, maritime transport, and waste management.[386] This concept of 'blue economy' is larger and wider than the concept of 'ocean economy' and advocates for the sustainable management, protection, and preservation of the oceans in a coordinated manner for the shake of present and future generations and therefore, this supports all the goals listed in the UN Sustainable Development Goals, especially 'life below water' (SGD 14). In 2013, the Commonwealth Blue Charter was adopted to help the commonwealth countries, including Bangladesh, work together to protect the ocean. Ten topics, i.e., commonwealth clean ocean alliance, coral reef protection and restoration, mangrove ecosystems and livelihoods, marine protected areas, ocean acidification, ocean and climate change, ocean observation, sustainable aquaculture, sustainable blue economy, and sustainable coastal fisheries are selected in this regard.

541. Through two national-level workshops held in 2014 and 2017 organized by the Ministry of Foreign Affairs, 26 sectors related to the blue economy were identified. These are: shipping, coastal shipping, seaports, passenger ferry services, inland waterway transports, shipbuilding, ship recycling industries, fisheries, aquaculture, coastal aquaculture and mariculture, marine acquaintance products, marine biotechnology, oil and gas, sea salt production, ocean renewable energy, tidal energy, blue energy (osmosis) and biomass, aggregate mining (sand, gravel, etc.) and marine mineral mining.

542. In the relatively new branch of public international law, IEL, marine spatial planning (MSP) is also relatively a new concept though the legal essence of this concept can be traced to the Law of the Sea Conventions, 1958, and the idea was then further expanded in the United Nations Convention on Law of the Sea, 1982 and in the Convention on Biological Diversity, 1992. In simple terms, MSP is a coordinated public process backed by political will aiming to protect the marine and surrounding environment. By controlling human activities to ensure the rational use of marine space, it is done in a way, so that the ecological, economic, and social objectives can be achieved.

543. MSP is thus neither a single sector planning and management nor conservation planning only. Besides, this does not deal with ocean zoning or one-time planning; rather, such planning has some unique characteristics; i.e., this is ecosystem-based, area-based, integrated, adaptive, strategic, and participatory.[387] MSP has the prospect of ensuring the sustainable use of marine resources by preventing marine pollution caused due to various reasons. Thus, any discussion on MSP covers issues such as maritime zoning, transportation, management of marine fisheries resources, mineral resources, marine environment, etc.

---

386. The World Bank, What is the Blue Economy?, https://www.worldbank.org/en/news/infographic/2017/06/06/blue-economy.
387. Marine Spatial Planning, International Oceanographic Commission- United National Educational, Scientific and Cultural Organisation, http://msp.ioc-unesco.org/about/marine-spatial-planning/.

544. Since the concept has been emerging, there is still no formal MSP in Bangladesh, except the Institute of Marine Sciences and Fisheries of the University of Chittagong has started to develop the spatial database and developed the 2nd edition of the map titled 'Maritime Province of Bangladesh' in 2017. The issue of MSP, though will be very challenging due to the socio-economic conditions and huge population of the country, is significant for a coastal state like Bangladesh and in a context when the country has been emphasizing to be benefitted from the blue economy initiatives.[388]

545. In the absence of any formal MSP, some of the initiatives taken by the government can be considered. Keeping in mind the relationship between the general laws, sector, and special laws, including the subsidiary legislation enacted thereunder, it should be remembered that all the planning-related general legal provisions will also be applicable in this regard. Yet, a tentative list of relevant laws in this regard will include: the Constitution of Bangladesh, 1972; the Territorial Waters and Maritime Zones Act, 1974; the Bangladesh Petroleum Act, 1974; the Bangladesh Export Processing Zones Authority Act, 1980; the BECA, 1995 and Rules, 1997; the Bangladesh Protected Tourism Area and Special Tourism Zone Act, 2010 and Rules, 2010; the Sustainable and Renewable Energy Development Authority Act, 2012; the Coast Guard Act, 2016; the Biodiversity Act, 2017; the Marine Fisheries Laws, 2020.

546. In 1974, the Territorial Waters and Maritime Zones Act, 1974 (Act No. XXVI of 1974) was enacted to declare the territorial waters and maritime zones. However, due to the long disputes regarding the limits of the territorial waters with the neighbours, Bangladesh could not exploit the full benefits of the sea. Fortunately, after the settlement of the maritime boundary dispute with India and Myanmar, all the barriers were removed, and Bangladesh is now free to enjoy the share of the sea without any objections from any end.[389] The issue of ocean management has been included in the 7th Five Year Plan (2016–2020), and a 'Blue Economy Cell' has been established in June 2016, which was formally launched in January 2017 under the Energy and Mineral Resources Division of the Ministry of Power, Energy and Mineral Resources. The Cell was established to exploit the potentials of the maritime areas of Bangladesh by coordinating the activities of different ministries, though there is no significant progress of the Cell even in the last four years due to lack of human resources and financial support.

547. A non-exhaustive list of various Policies can also be shared that contain relevant provisions in this regard that should be considered in making any planning in the coastal areas of the country. These are: the Coastal Zone Policy, 2005; Bangladesh Environment Policy and Implementation Plan; National Fish Policy;

---

388. Md. Ashraful Alam, 'Marine spatial planning for Bangladesh: learning from the Great Barrier Reef Marine Park, Australia.' PhD Thesis, Western Sydney University (2020).
389. International Tribunal for the Law of the Sea, Dispute concerning delimitation of the maritime boundary between Bangladesh and Myanmar in the Bay of Bengal (Bangladesh/Myanmar), https: //www.itlos.org/index.php?id=108 ; Bay of Bengal Maritime Boundary Arbitration between Bangladesh and India, [2010–2016], Award (7 Jul. 2014), https://pca-cpa.org/en/cases/18/.

National Tourism Policy, 1992; National Energy Policy; National Water Policy and National Shipping Policy; Private Economic Zone Policy; etc.

548. The Cox's Bazar Development Authority Act, 2016 (Act No. VII of 2016) was enacted to establish an authority to ensure planned development in the world's longest unbroken natural sea beach, Cox's Bazar. The law provides for the establishment of 'Cox's Bazar Development Authority' (section 3) with the mandate to undertake a number of activities to attain the objectives and purposes of the law (section 6). The law provides for punishment for a number of offences, e.g., for the construction or renovation of any building, for digging any pond or wetland, sand mining, or hill cutting, committed within the Cox's Bazar area under the scope of the law (section 24).

Part IV. Liability Questions

§1. Introduction

549. The emergence of IEL, as an independent branch of public international law and the independence of Bangladesh as an independent state, is contemporary. While the formal journey of the IEL is believed to be started with the UN Conference on the Human Environment and the establishment of the UNEP in 1972, Bangladesh became an independent state in 1971. When the 1992 Rio Earth Summit has influenced countries to make concerted efforts to enact environmental laws, Bangladesh also joined the movement as the country reinstated the parliamentary democracy in 1991, formulated the Environment Policy, 1992, enacted the BECA, 1995 and also enacted a law to establish specialized environmental courts. As the UN Conference on Sustainable Development, 2012 shifted the focus on the implementation of environmental laws, Bangladesh has also made noticeable progress in terms of economic and human development. Accordingly, as one of the worse victims of climate change, the policymakers of Bangladesh have also taken some pragmatic initiatives balancing many other development needs of the country, though the country was placed in the 'fair or limited' category by the Environmental Performance Index, developed by the Yale Center for Environmental Law & Policy based on three mutually reinforcing rights, i.e., the right to free access to information on the environment quality and problems, the right to participate meaningfully in decision-making and the right to see enforcement of environmental laws or compensation for harm.

550. In the First Global Report of the Environmental Rule of Law, 2019, it is provided that 'environmental rule of law provides an essential platform underpinning the four pillars of sustainable development-economic, social, environmental, and peace' and with environmental rule of law, which is instrumental for sustainable development, 'well-designed laws are implemented by capable government institutions that are held accountable by an informed and engaged public' to 'lead to a culture of compliance that embraces environmental and social values'.[390] According to the United Nations, environmental rule of law shared all the three components of rule of law, i.e., law consistent with fundamental rights, inclusively developed and fairly effectuated and properly implemented and complied with.[391]

390. UN Environment, Environmental Rule of Law, First Global Report, 2019, p. 1, https://www.unep.org/resources/assessment/environmental-rule-law-first-global-report.

391. *Ibid.*, p. 8.

The same document has also identified some of the challenges regarding the implementation and enforcement of environmental laws and regulations. These are: lack of clear standards or necessary mandates, adoption of the laws without considering the national and local needs, financial constraints of the implementing ministries, lack of support to the civil society moves.

551. In order to protect various environmental components, Bangladesh has adapted, amended or enacted more than two hundred general, sectoral, and special laws, containing both procedural and substantive provisions, and the number has been growing continuously. This part will try to explore and unwrap important provisions of environmental components related provisions.

552. Before delving deep into the relevant statutory provisions, it may be relevant to share that the Constitution of Bangladesh, 1972, as the supreme law of the land and various other domestic laws have encapsulated several provisions that bestow several rights to the citizens and others. While remedies can be sought for the violations of some of these rights, the rights incorporated in the Constitution, 1972, e.g., fundamental rights in Part III (Articles 26–44) can be judicially enforceable, subject to some exceptions, such as public order, public health, security of the state, and decency or morality against the state apparatus. The constitutional remedies under Articles 44 and 102 are available for the violation of such rights, and a citizen can move to the HCD to enforce such rights if violated by the government bodies and agencies. Besides, the Constitution, 1972 ensures that the fundamental rights (subject to the provisions on emergency) are not amendable by way of insertion, substitution, repeal, or by any other means,[392] and any laws or policies inconsistent with fundamental rights shall stand void.[393]

553. In contrast, the FPSP as included in Part II (Articles 8–26), including the provisions of article 18A, which encourages the state to take initiatives to protect and improve the environment, is not judicially enforceable. Instead, the FPSP which are 'fundamental to the governance of Bangladesh, shall be applied by the State in the making of laws, shall be a guide to the interpretation of the Constitution and of the other laws of Bangladesh, and shall form the basis of the work of the State and of its citizens'.[394] The Apex court of the country earlier reiterated that these principles are not judicially enforceable since these are mere principles and not laws, and their enforceability 'overnight' is not possible, given the socio-economic conditions and resource constraints of the state.[395]

554. It may be observed that some of these constitutional law landmark judgments were delivered at the beginning of the country's development process when

392. Article 7B, the Constitution of the People's Republic of Bangladesh, 1972.

393. Article 26, 44, 102 and 8(2) the Constitution of the People's Republic of Bangladesh, 1972.

394. Article 8(2), the Constitution of the People's Republic of Bangladesh, 1972.

395. *Sheikh Abdus Sabur v. Returning Officer, District Education Officer-in-charge, Gopalganj and others* (1989) 41 DLR (AD) 30; *Kudrat-E-Elahi Panir and Others v. Bangladesh* (1992) 44 DLR (AD) 319.

parliamentary democracy was reinstated in the 1990s, two decades after the country's independence. With the recent socio-economic progresses of the country, judges have also started to interpret these provisions more liberally. Besides, after the 15th amendment of the Constitution, 2011, both the fundamental rights and FPSP started to enjoy some identical status as a new article, i.e., art. 7B has been inserted which provides that notwithstanding provisions in art. 142, the FPSP (subject to the provisions on emergency) is not amendable by way of insertion, substitution, repeal, or by any other means. Nevertheless, the provisions on the enforceability of the FPSP will understandably remain the same; i.e., these are not judicially enforceable.

555. Interestingly, art. 47(1) of the Constitution, 1972 gives FPSP primacy over fundamental rights in certain situations. There shall be no judicial invalidation of policies or laws which are made to give the effect of FPSP even if such measures are inconsistent with, or take away, or abridging of any rights guaranteed by the fundamental rights part (Part II) of the Constitution.[396] It means that if initiatives are taken to give effect to introduce some of the FPSP, the judiciary should not intervene even if such measures are inconsistent with the fundamental rights part (Part II) of the Constitution. However, to enjoy this exception, the legislature must expressly declare that such provisions in question are made to give effect to FPSP as set out in Part II of the Constitution of Bangladesh.[397]

556. The right to seek justice is constitutionally guaranteed in Bangladesh, and any individual aggrieved can utilize various available forums, e.g., different types of courts and tribunals established within the domestic legal regime to bring actions against any kind of grievance, including environmental damages, etc., as the Preamble to the Constitution, 1972 provides that: '[t]his is one of the fundamental aims of the State is to realise through the democratic process a socialist society, free from exploitation a society in which the rule of law, fundamental human rights and freedom, equality, and justice, political, economic and social for all citizens'.[398] Thus, the Preamble to the Constitution, as the beacon light and pole star of the Constitution,[399] clearly stipulates that one of the fundamental aims of the state is to establish a socialist society, where the rule of law, fundamental human rights and political, economic and social justice can be realized.

557. Articles 31 & 32 of the Constitution of Bangladesh, 1972, while collectively incorporating the citizen's 'fundamental right to life', provide that: it is the inalienable right of every citizen 'to enjoy the protection of the law, and to be treated in accordance with law, and only in accordance with law', wherever he may be. This same right is extended to 'every other person for the time being within Bangladesh,

396. Article 47(1), the Constitution of the People's Republic of Bangladesh, 1972.
397. *Ibid.*
398. Preamble, the Constitution of Bangladesh, 1972.
399. *Anwar Hossain Chowdhury v. Government of the People's Republic of Bangladesh & others*, 1989 BLD Special Issue 1=1989, 41 DLR (AD) 165.

and in particular no action detrimental to the life, liberty, body, reputation or property of any person shall be taken except in accordance with law'. Thus, understandably, the illegal action of any person will not be protected.[400] The SC has interpreted these constitutional provisions time to time in different contexts.

558. The phrase 'in accordance with law', as used several times in articles 31 & 32 of the Constitution of Bangladesh, 1972 as shared above, deserves special attention and especially in the context of citizen's right to a healthy environment as the Supreme Court has already recognized this in several occasions that the right to the healthy environment comes within the ambit of citizen's right to life, though some legal provisions may be introduced to deprive the right to life of a group of people.[401] In the case of *Bangladesh Air Service (Pvt) Ltd. v. British Airways PLC.*, 1997, 26 CLC (AD) [568] = 49 DLR (AD) (1997) 187, Justice Mustafa Kamal attempted to explain the phrase, taking references from different dictionaries such as *Black's Law Dictionary (Abridged 5th Edn.), Stroud's Judicial Dictionary* 4th Edn, Vol. 3, *Biswas on Encyclopedic Law Dictionary,* 2nd Edn., and *Mitra in Legal and Commercial Dictionary*, 4th Edn. Accordingly, the word 'accordance' means 'agreement, harmony, concord, conformity', whereas 'in accordance' means 'in conformity' or 'as provided for', and 'in accordance with' means, *inter alia*, 'in substantial compliance with', 'not repugnant to', 'not in conflict with' or 'not inconsistent with'. Therefore, apparently any measures in the name of development, having consequences on citizen's right to life, can only be taken if these are in substantial compliance with the law.

559. Article 32 of the Constitution, 1972 provides that 'no person shall be deprived of life or personal liberty save in accordance with law'. The use of the word 'deprived' before 'life' in this provision might indicate that this provision was intended for the application of criminal law principles, particularly in relation to the death penalty,[402] but the heading of art. 32 makes it clear that the provision is dealing with the 'right to life', that is, all aspects of life. Thus, the extent of this provision is obviously wider than criminal law aspect and therefore, it may be worth considering the philosophy behind drafting the article in this manner. Since life is bestowed by the divine authority, the state cannot take it except in grave circumstances and perhaps, that is why it is stated that no one can be deprived of the right to life, not that 'everyone has the right to life'. Thus, it may be concluded that the right to life has been included in the Constitution as a fundamental right of great significance because this right can be enforced judicially under Articles 44 and 102 of the Constitution, 1972.

560. The HCD has observed, for example, that the expression 'life does not mean merely an elementary life or sub-human life but connotes in this expression

400. *Gias Uddin v. Dhaka Municipal Corporation and others*, 17 BLD (HCD) 577.
401. Md. Ershadul Karim et al. 'Noise Pollution in Dhaka and the Constitutional Right to Life (29 Jun. 2021)'. *Australian Journal of Asian Law* 21, no. 2 (2021): Article 5: 67–84, available at SSRN: https://ssrn.com/abstract=3875921.
402. The right to life has been frequently discussed in death penalty cases. *See*, for example, *BLAST and Another v. Bangladesh* (2010) 30 BLD (HCD) 194.

the life of the greatest creation of the Lord who has at least a right to a decent and healthy way of life in a hygienic condition'.[403] It also means a qualitative life, *inter alia*, free from environmental hazards.[404] The HCD further confirmed that: '[C]onstitutional remedy under Art. 102 will be available if this basic human right is threatened due to the violation of any of the provisions of the relevant laws enacted for such purpose or due to recklessness or negligence on the part of any person or authority which tends to upset the guarantees under Art. 31 and Art. 32 of the Constitution.'[405]

561. The HCD has also included the right to health, environment, and shelter within the broader meaning of the right to life. In the case of *Dr Mohiuddin Farooque v. Bangladesh & others* [Writ Petition No 300 of 1995 (Vehicular Pollution Case)], the petitioner, Dr Farooque, raised several issues, including the emission of hazardous smoke from motor vehicles and the use of audible signalling devices, which emit unduly harsh, shrill, loud or alarming noises. The petitioner submitted that, although it has not been explicitly included as a fundamental right in art 32 of the Constitution, the right to a safe and healthy environment is inherent and integrated into the 'right to life', and art 31 prohibits the taking of any action detrimental to life, body and property. Therefore, the right to a sound environment should be considered a fundamental right under art 32. The HCD was found to be convinced with such submission and interpretation.[406]

562. In another instance, the HCD also stated that: '[n]o one has any right to endanger the life of the people which includes their health and normal longevity of an ordinary healthy person by producing noise which is injurious to human health'. Moreover, it held that 'the right to life under Articles 31 and 32 of the Constitution not only means protection of life and limbs necessary for full enjoyment of life but also includes, amongst others, protection of health and normal longevity of an ordinary human being'.[407]

563. Human health, including mental health, is an important aspect of the right to life and a healthy environment is the prerequisite to ensure sound human health. Pollution of various environmental components harms both physical and mental health. The Bangladesh Constitution, 1972, and other municipal laws have recognized the importance of health, and the Apex court has also recognized this. For example, in the case of *Chairman, National Board of Revenue (NBR) v. Advocate Zulhas Uddin Ahmed and others*,[408] the AD declared that imposition of value-added tax in the health sector is illegal since it may hamper the right to life of the citizens. Under art. 18(1) of Bangladesh Constitution, 1972, improvement of public health is one of the primary duties of the state and art. 18A imposes obligations on the state

403. *Dr Mohiuddin Farooque v. Bangladesh and others* (2003) 55 DLR 69.
404. *Ibid.*
405. *Ibid.*
406. Writ Petition No 300 of 1995 (Vehicular Pollution Case).
407. *Dr Mohiuddin Farooque v. Bangladesh and others* (1996) 48 DLR 438, 441.
408. (2010)15 MLR (AD) 457.

to endeavour to protect and improve the environment. Thus, the state has constitutional obligations to make and apply the law as per the FPSP, and it is the responsibility of the state to take measures to ensure a healthy and pollution-free environment for the citizens. Therefore, it is evident that although the basic provision of health and environment is covered by the Constitution as FPSP which are not judicially enforceable theoretically, the Supreme Court has, from time to time, expanded the scope of these provisions by way of liberal interpretation and has included the right to health and environment within the meaning of the right to life.[409]

564. Very recently, the AD, in relation to the law on smoking and tobacco product control, summed up the overall position on this right in the context of Bangladesh in the following style:

> '[the r]ight to life is not only limited to protection of life and limbs but also extends to the protection of health, enjoyment of pollution-free water and air, bare necessaries of life, facilities for education, maternity benefit, maintenance and improvement of public health by creating and sustaining conditions congenial to good health and ensuring quality of life consistent to human dignity.'[410]

565. The court also emphasized that:

> [n]o one has any right to endanger the life of the people which includes their health and normal longevity of an ordinary healthy person. Articles 31 and 32 of the Constitution not only means protection of life and limbs necessary for full enjoyment of life but also includes amongst others protection of health and normal longevity of an ordinary human being. . . [the] State is bound to protect the health and longevity of the people living in the country as the right to life guaranteed under Articles 31 and 32 of the Constitution includes protection of health and longevity of a man free from threats of man-made hazards. Right to life . . . being [a] fundamental right it can be enforced by this Court to remove any unjustified threat to health and longevity of the people as the same are included in the right to life.[411]

§2. Environmental Protection and Criminal Law of the Land

566. Even though an individual or a group of people are affected, it is believed that all types of crimes are committed against the state. Therefore, in criminal matters, the state needs to take initiative, and generally, the state becomes a party to a suit. Of all the general laws relating to the protection of environmental components,

409. *Ibid.*
410. *Government of Bangladesh and others v. Professor Nurul Islam & another* (2017) 9 SCOB (AD) 46.
411. *Ibid.*

the Penal Code, 1860 (XLV of 1860), being the main substantive criminal law of the country, has included several provisions relating to the protection of environmental components. Chapter XIV of the Penal Code (sections 268–294B) contains various provisions relating to offences affecting, *inter alia*, public health and safety. For example, section 268 while dealing with public nuisance provides that a person can be guilty of a public nuisance by doing any act or illegal omission which may cause any common injury, danger or annoyance to the public. Besides, a common nuisance may not be excused though it causes some convenience or advantage.

567. Under the Penal Code, 1869, various activities, e.g., negligent and malignant act of spreading infection of diseases dangerous to life (sections 269- 270), sale of adulterated or noxious food or drink (sections 272–273), fouling water or public spring or reservoir (section 277), making atmosphere noxious to health (section 278), danger or obstruction in public way or line of navigation (section 283), negligent conduct with respect to poisonous substance (section. 284), negligent conduct with respect to fire or combustible matter (section 285), negligent conduct with respect to explosive substance (section 286), negligent conduct with respect to machinery (section 287), negligent conduct with respect to pulling down or repairing buildings (section 288), and negligent conduct with respect to animal (section 289), etc., are also recognized as offences for which the law provides for punishments.

568. Being one of the oldest laws in force in the country enacted after the Mutiny of 1857 during the British colonial time, there are some obvious limitations of the Penal Code, 1860. Though after the independence of Bangladesh in 1971, the law was amended a few times, which were mostly cosmetic, the law still maintains the terms of punishment, which might be reasonable at the time of enactment, but are not acceptable in the present context. Yet, it is so unfortunate that these provisions containing very lenient punishments are not properly implemented for various reasons; as a result, though the provisions of this law are still used in case of major offences such as murder, hurt and grievous hurt, defamation, etc., many other provisions are not used at all as not a single case has ever been contested in the Supreme Court and reported in law reports. Already some provisions on criminal offences relating to environmental components are discussed in various chapters of this monograph. The following sections will discuss some additional issues.

§3. Negligence

569. Many environmental disasters and accident can happen due to negligence on the part of an individual, a group of people, a government agency, including a government employee. Therefore, understanding of the legal aspects of 'negligence' within the national legal framework deserves special attention. In a predominantly English common law country, the law of tort is not developed satisfactorily and has not taken a mature shape in Bangladesh yet even after fifty years of independence; albeit, there are some isolated instances where the court of law considered various tort issues.[412] The Penal Code, 1860 (XLV of 1860), contains provisions on negligence relating to criminal activities.[413] The justice seekers, however, hardly exploit these provisions since one has to follow a troublesome and complex procedure. Besides, there are general beliefs among the people that they do not get enough cooperation from the members of the law enforcement agencies in these matters. Moreover, the punishments stipulated under these provisions are very nominal as the law was enacted long ago, and civil remedies under negligence cases are not very common.

570. Immediately, after the Independence of the country, in *Abdul Awal and ors v. Mofasiluddin Ahmed and others,* 1975, 4 CLC (HCD) [9518] = 27 DLR (HCD) (1975) 628, in a matter involving the issue of damages and compensation due to certain injuries resulting from the falling of materials from a corridor under construction, D.C. Bhattacharya J. shed light on the definition of negligence and elements of negligence. To him: '[n]egligence as a tort is the breach of a legal duty to take care which results in damage to the plaintiff. So, it involves three elements *viz.* (1) existence of a legal duty on the part of the defendants to the plaintiff (2) breach of that duty and (3) consequential damage to the plaintiff'.

571. The court of laws attempted to deal with the issue of negligence in different circumstances in recent times. In *Children's Charity Bangladesh Foundation (CCB Foundation) v. Bangladesh & ors.* 10 SOCB [2018] HCD 117, the HCD of the Bangladesh Supreme Court while dealing with the death of a 4-year old boy by falling into a 16 inches uncovered abandoned shaft discussed the various aspects of negligence in the following manner:

> 49. The word 'negligence' is defined as the breach of a duty caused by the omission to do something which a reasonable man would do or doing something which a prudent and reasonable man would not do. In other words, negligence may arise from non-feasance or from misfeasance.

---

412. For example, in *British American Tobacco Bangladesh Company Ltd. v. Begum Shamsun Nahar*, 2010, 39 CLC (AD) [8698] = 66 DLR (AD) (2014) 80, in a case for damages for sexual harassment of an employee by another employee, the AD of Bangladesh Supreme Court held that: 'A person can be liable for tort as well and damages may be claimed against him for such wrong doing as well as against an organization or establishment if it fails to ensure the prevention of sexual harassment and bullying to a woman, where she can work with honour and dignity and without being harassed or disturbed by her male boss or other male colleagues.'

413. *See*, for example, public servant negligently suffering such prisoner to escape (s. 129), deserter concealed on board merchant vessel through negligence of master (s. 137), escape from confinement or custody negligently suffered by public servant (s. 223), negligent act likely to spread infection of disease dangerous to life (s. 269), rash driving or riding on a public way (s. 279), rash navigation of vessel (280), negligent conduct with respect to poisonous substance (s. 284), negligent conduct with respect to fire or combustible matter (s. 285), negligent conduct with respect to explosive substance (s. 286), negligent conduct with respect to machinery (s. 287), negligent conduct with respect to pulling down or repairing buildings (s. 288), negligent conduct with respect to animal (s. 289), causing death by negligence (s. 304a), causing death by rash driving or riding on a public way (s. 304b), act endangering life or personal safety to others (s. 336), etc.

50. An action for negligence proceeds upon the idea of an obligation or duty on the part of the person concern to use care, a breach whereof results in the injury of the aggrieved person.
51. However, the standard or degree of care which a man is required to use in a particular situation varies with the obviousness of the risk. If the danger of doing injury to the person or property of another in pursuance of a certain line of conduct is great, great care is necessary. If the danger is slight, only a slight amount of care is required. The care that will be required of them will be the care that an ordinary prudent man is bound to exercise. But, persons who profess to have a special skill, or who have voluntarily undertaken a higher degree of duty, are bound to exercise more care than an ordinary prudent man.
52. In order to succeed in an action for negligence, the aggrieved person must prove the followings -1. that the other party was under a legal duty to exercise due care and skill; 2. That the duty was towards aggrieved person; 3. that in the circumstances of the case, the other party failed to perform that duty; 4. that the breach of such duty was the *causa causans* i.e., the direct and proximate cause, of the damage complained of; and 5. that the injury is caused on account of this breach of duty.
53. As a general rule, the onus of proving negligence is on the aggrieved person. He must not merely establish the facts of the other parties' negligence and of his own injury but must show that the one was the effect of the other.
54. However, in an action of negligence, the affected person must affirmatively prove negligence but may find hardship in cases where the aggrieved person can prove the accident, but cannot show how it happened, the fact being solely outside his knowledge and within the knowledge of the other party who causes it. In such cases, it is sufficient for the aggrieved person to prove the accident and nothing more, for, there is a presumption of negligence according to the maxim '*res ipsa loquitur*' (the thing speaks for itself). Such presumption arises when the cause of the mischief was apparently under the control of the other person or his servants. The accident itself constitutes reasonable evidence of negligence in the particular circumstances.
55. Thus, the following are the essential requirements for the application of the said maxim:
(i) The thing causing the damage must be under the control of the other party or his servants; (ii) the accident must be such as would not, in the ordinary course of things, have happened without negligence and (iii) there must be no evidence of the actual cause of the accident.

572. It is a general understanding that any act done in good faith by the government officials will get an exemption and cannot be sued in the court of law as this has been incorporated in various laws including the BECA, 1995. The provisions of relevant laws provide that the government shall not be responsible for any loss or damage which may occur in consequence of any officer failing in his duty, and no such officer shall be responsible for any such loss or damage unless he causes the same negligently, maliciously or fraudulently.[414] Similarly, the BECA, 1995 has also extended indemnity to the government, DG, or officer or employee of the DoE for any act done under this law in good faith.[415]

573. Even though there are such provisions, in some isolated instances, the courts of law awarded compensations in negligence cases where a public servant was found responsible. For example, in *Md. Shahanewas v. Government of Bangladesh,* 18 BLD (HCD) 337, the HCD of Bangladesh Supreme Court awarded 'compensatory' costs of Tk. 20,000/=, against a delinquent police officer for negligently arresting a poor fisherman in place of a convicted criminal merely based on their identical names by observing that the poor victim should be 'well compensated' for his 'immense sufferings' and loss of livelihood for six months due to sheer negligence of the public servant in discharging his public duty. Similarly, in recent times, the Supreme Court of Bangladesh has awarded compensation to the victims in negligence cases.

§4. Nuisance

574. Various types of nuisance create environmental hazards. 'Nuisance' is generally understood as a common law 'tort', i.e., a civil wrong. As a result, the term 'nuisance' has not been given any specific definition in the statutes of Bangladesh with an exception to section 2 (xxii) of the Cantonments Act, 1924 (Act No. II of 1924) which contained some provisions on nuisance. This law of 1924 was recently repealed and replaced by the Cantonments Act, 2018 (Act No. 27 of 2018). Section 2 (3) of this Act of 2018 provides that 'nuisance' includes any act, omission, place or thing which causes or is likely to cause injury, danger, annoyance or offence to the sense of sight, smell or hearing, or which is or may be dangerous to life or injurious to health or property. Apart from defining 'nuisance', this law like the previous law of 1924 has included various provisions on nuisance. Even though section 1(2) of the Law provides that the provisions of the law shall extend to the whole of Bangladesh, the law seems to be a special law as the law was enacted to provide for the administration of the cantonments.

575. Although a statutory definition of 'nuisance', other than the one available in the Cantonments Act, 2018 (Act No. 27 of 2018), is difficult to find out, there are references of the term 'nuisance' in several domestic statutes.[416] The HCD, on several occasions, has also interpreted the provisions on different aspects of nuisance. In *Wahid Mia alias Abdul Wahid Bhuiyan v. Dr. Rafiqul Islam and others,* 16 BLD (HCD) 255, Justice Syed Amirul Islam was of the opinion that: '[i]n the case of torts, there being no statutory Law of our own, our courts have always adopted the

414. For example, Section 9, the Telegraph Act, 1885 (Act No. XIII of 1885); Section 95, the Bangladesh Telecommunication Regulation Act, 2001 (Act No. 18 of 2001).
415. Section 18, the Bangladesh Environment Conservation Act, 1995 (Act No. 1 of 1995).
416. For example, ss 10, 11, the Ports Act, 1908 (Act No. XV of 1908); s. 9, the Sarais Act, 1867 (Act No. XXII of 1867); ss 15 & 16, the Bangladesh Hotels and Restaurants Ordinance, 2014 (Act No. XV of 2014).

English Common Law as being consonant to justice, equity and goods conscience. The concept of nuisance is a concept of Law. Nuisance is incapable of exact definition, but for the purpose of the Law of tort it may be described as unlawful interference with a person's use or enjoyment of land or of some right over it or in connection with it'.[417] Justice Islam rightly exposed that '[n]uisance is a mixed concept, partly subjective and partly objective. What is a nuisance to one may not be a nuisance to another and what again, may appear to be a repugnance to one class, may not be so to another. In short, it is a relative term depending entirely upon the environment, taste, habit and the standard of living of residents'.

576. Nuisances can be of two types: public and private. The Penal Code, 1860 (XLV of 1860) has contained some provisions on public nuisance. Section 268 while dealing with public nuisance provides that a person can be guilty of a public nuisance by doing any act or illegal omission which may cause any common injury, danger or annoyance to the public. Besides, a common nuisance may not be excused though it causes some convenience or advantage. However, under the Penal Code, 1860 (XLV of 1860), the annoyance of a few residents of a single house is not sufficient to constitute a public nuisance under section 290. It is not sufficient proof under the section to say that the complainant and a few of his tenants represent the people in general who occupy property in the vicinity, there being other dwellings within unpleasant range. Before an act is found to be a nuisance, enquiry by the Commissioner is mandatory.[418]

577. In *Wahid Mia alias Abdul Wahid Bhuiyan v. Dr. Rafiqul Islam and others,* 16 BLD (HCD) 255, it was revealed that though nuisances are divided into public and private, it is quite possible that the same conduct will amount to both. It was held that: '[a] public or common nuisance is one which affects the public and is an annoyance to the citizens generally; a private nuisance is one which injures a private person exclusively or else in some way which the Law regards as in excess of the annoyance suffered by the public at large'. Besides, '[i]n Order to give rise to an action in nuisance there must be interference with the use or enjoyment of land or of some rights over or in connection with it, causing damage to the plaintiff. The forms of interference are innumerable. Noise, smells, pollution of air or water, are the most usual instances, but there are many others'. It was also held that: '[w]here the interference is with personal comfort, it is not necessary. . . to establish a nuisance that any injury to health should be shown. . .it is enough that there is a material interference with the physical comfort of human existence reckoned, not merely according to elegant or dainty modes and habits of living, but according to plain, sober and simple notions among the common people'. Finally, Justice Syed Amirul Islam, sharing a 1869 judgment of Calcutta High Court, stated that: '[u]nder the English Common Law a public nuisance is an indictable misdemeanor; criminal proceedings are also sanctioned by particular statutes in particular cases. It is however a settled principle of the English Law, which has come down from very ancient times that a private individual has no right of action in respect of a public nuisance

417. *Wahid Mia alias Abdul Wahid Bhuiyan v. Dr. Rafiqul Islam and others,* 16 BLD (HCD) 255.
418. *A. Kader v. Chairman, Dacca Municipality* (1958) 10 DLR 205.

unless he can show that he has sustained some special damages over and above that inflicted upon the public at large; the objection being to avoid multiplicity of litigations'.[419]

578. In the same Judgment, Justice Syed Amirul Islam also discussed private nuisance. According to him, a private nuisance is an 'injury to the right of a person to the comfortable occupation of his own property' and is some unauthorized use of one's own property resulting in damage to the property of another in enjoyment of his property. To 'constitute private nuisance there must be interference with the use of enjoyment of land, or of some right over or in connection with it. A nuisance will be either a wrongly disturbance of an easement or servitude such as obstruction to light, air or right of support, or a wrongful escape of deleterious substances into another's property such as smokes, smell, noise, gas, fumes, water, heat, etc.' Justice Islam went on saying that: '[n]o one has a right to use his own land in such a way as to be a nuisance to his neighbor. For example, if A chooses to put filth in his own land he must take care not to let it escape, on to his neighbor's land. The two main beads under which nuisance may be ground are injury to property and interference with personal comfort, where interference with personal comfort it is not necessary with a view to establish a nuisance that an injury to health should be shown. It is enough that there is a material interference with the physical comfort of human existence reckoned not merely according to elegant or dainty modes and habits of living, but according to plain, sober and simple notions among the society concerned. In some cases, a private and public nuisance may occur simultaneously. For instance, a trade may cause offending noises or small injurious to the neighbors as well as to the general public'.

579. In *Star Alkaid Jute Mills Ltd. v. EPIWTA and Others* (1972) 24 DLR (HCD) 1, it was found that the construction of a wall on the river bank within the jurisdiction of the Port by a person other than the Port Authority is a nuisance under section 10 of the Ports Act, 1908 (Act No. XV of 1908) as it affects the lawful use of the bank by the Port Authority. Section 13 of the Canals Act, 1864 (Act No. V of 1864), which was enacted to amend and consolidate the law relating to the collection of tolls on canals and other lines of navigation, and for the construction and improvement of lines of navigation in Bangladesh, empowers the government to appoint any person as the supervisor to prevent or remove any other nuisance or obstruction to navigation.

580. There are two aspects of nuisance: civil and criminal, and therefore, relevant provisions can be found in civil and criminal laws. For nuisances under the criminal laws, an accused may be responsible for paying fine.[420] Chapter X of the Code of Criminal Procedure, 1898 (Act V of 1898) provides for prevention of public nuisance, Chapter XI of the said part IV (Temporary orders in urgent cases of

419. *Wahid Mia alias Abdul Wahid Bhuiyan v. Dr. Rafiqul Islam and others,* 16 BLD (HCD) 255.
420. For example, s. 290 of the Penal Code, 1860 (XLV of 1860) provides that if anyone commits a public nuisance in any case not otherwise punishable by this Code, he shall be punished with fine which may extend to BDK 200.

nuisances or apprehended danger). Section 23 of the Police Act, 1861 provides that it 'shall be the duty of every police-officer promptly to prevent the commission of offences and public nuisances', and relevant metropolitan police laws have also included similar provisions; i.e., it shall be the duty of every police officer to the best of his ability to prevent the commission of public nuisance.[421]

581. In case of public nuisance, if a member of the public wants to initiate a civil proceeding to get civil remedies, it is incumbent upon him to obtain sanction under section 91(1) of the Code of Civil Procedure, 1908 (Act No. V of 1908) from the Attorney General in the absence of any special damage to him. But if the plaintiff wants to bring an action against the defendant for his unlawful act on his land or building causing a private nuisance, the provision of Section 91(1) of the Code does not apply. In the case of a private nuisance, no special damage is required to be proved. It is enough if the plaintiff can prove that by the unlawful user of the land/building by the defendant some annoyance or discomfort has been caused to him.[422]

421. *See*, for example, s. 15, the Dhaka Metropolitan Police Ordinance, 1976 (Ordinance No. III of 1976); s. 15, the Chittagong Metropolitan Police Ordinance, 1978 (Ordinance No. XLVIII of 1978); s. 15, the Rajshahi Metropolitan Police Act, 1992 (Act No. 23 of 1992).

422. *Wahid Mia alias Abdul Wahid Bhuiyan v. Dr. Rafiqul Islam and others,* 16 BLD (HCD) 255.

Part V. Juridical Actions of Individuals

582. Similar to the types of laws, i.e., civil and criminal, general and special, different avenues and forums are also functioning in the country, and using these forums anyone aggrieved can get remedies, and this is also the same in the case of environmental matters. While there are generally civil and criminal courts, established under the general law, e.g., the Civil Courts Act, 1887; the Code of Criminal Procedure, 1898; and the Mobile Court Act, 2009, there are special laws also to deal with the environmental matter. Before the discussion on these forums, a general discussion on the court structures, at least briefly, especially of criminal courts, their formations and powers are necessary as most of the environment-related laws empower the criminal justice administration to take cognizance of environmental offences.

583. The Code of Criminal Procedure, 1898 (Act V of 1898), the principal criminal procedure law of the land, contains provisions relating to the Constitution of criminal courts and offices (Part II, Chapter II). Besides the Supreme Court, depending on the nature of crime and jurisdiction specified by the laws, there are generally two types of criminal courts in Bangladesh: (a) Courts of Sessions; and (b) Courts of Magistrates. Sessions courts are established in all the sixty-four districts of the country, and five Metropolitan Sessions courts are established in Dhaka, Chittagong, Rajshahi, Khulna, and Sylhet divisions.[423] There are two classes of Magistrate, i.e.: (a) Judicial Magistrate; and (b) Executive Magistrate, and there can be four classes of judicial Magistrate, namely: (i) Chief Metropolitan Magistrate (CMM) [including Additional Chief Metropolitan Magistrate (ACMM)] in Metropolitan Area and Chief Judicial Magistrate [CJM] [including Additional Judicial Magistrate (AJM)] to other areas; (ii) Magistrate of the first class, who shall in Metropolitan Area be known as Metropolitan Magistrate (MM); (iii) Magistrate of the second class; and (iv) Magistrate of the third class.[424]

584. The Cr.P.C. also stipulates provisions on the powers of these courts (Chapter III), and these criminal courts try offences included in the Penal Code, 1860, and other laws such as BECA, 1995.[425] As a general rule, the CMM, ACMM, CJM, and ACJM enjoy powers to try all offences except those punishable with death, and the

423. For an updated list of subordinate courts, *see*, Subordinate Courts, http://www.judiciary.org.bd/en/subordinate-courts.
424. Section 6, the Code of Criminal Procedure, 1898 (Act V of 1898).
425. Sections 28 & 29, the Code of Criminal Procedure, 1898 (Act V of 1898).

MM and any Magistrate of the first class are empowered to try all offences not punishable with death or with transportation or with imprisonment for a term exceeding ten years.[426] Simultaneously, the Cr.P.C. also provides for the sentences which may be passed by the courts of various classes (sections 31–35A), ordinary and additional powers (sections 36–38), and conferment, continuance, and cancellation of powers (sections 39–41).

585. The civil courts, on the other hand, are established under section 3 of Civil Courts Act, 1887 (Act No. XII of 1887). However, these civil courts will generally not have jurisdiction to entertain suits under special law such as the BECA, 1995. It is important to remember that where a right is created by a special law and a method of enforcing the right is pointed out by the law creating such right, the general civil remedy by way of suit under the Code of Civil Procedure, 1908 will be impliedly barred. In such a case, the method provided by the special law must be followed.[427]

586. The discussion on the mobile courts established under the Mobile Court Act, 2009 (Act No. 59 of 2009), a special law enacted for the public interest, protection of law and order, and prevention of offences, is also important as this law empowers the executive magistrates to try many offences, including offences relating to the protection of environmental components, even though relevant laws empower civil or criminal courts to try an issue. For example, even though environmental courts established under the Environment Court Act, 2000 (Act No. 11 of 2000) have the authority to try offences under the Brick Manufacturing and Brick Kiln Establishment (Control) Act, 2013 (Act No. 59 of 2013), it is also provided that the mobile courts shall also have the jurisdiction to try offences under the law of 2013 to ensure the speedy enforcement of the law.[428]

587. The Mobile Court Act, 2009 provides for the operational procedure, and limits penalty that can be imposed by the mobile courts and such courts are empowered to try offences under almost a hundred laws, including laws that are covered and relevant for the purpose of this monograph such as, *inter alia*, the Forest Act, 1927 (Act No. XVI of 1927); the Protection and Conservation of Fish Act, 1950 (East Bengal Act No. XVIII of 1950); the Building Construction Act, 1952 (East Bengal Act No. II of 1952); the Agricultural Produce Markets Regulation Act, 1964 (East Pakistan Act No. IX of 1964); the Pesticides Ordinance, 1971 (Ordinance No. II of 1971); the BECA, 1995; the Water Supply and Sanitation Authority Act, 1996; the Conservation of Playground, Open Space, Park and Natural Water Reservoir in the Metropolitan, Division and District Towns Act, 2000 (Act No. 36 of 2000); the Balumohal and Soil Management Act, 2010 (Act No. 62 of 2010), etc.

---

426. Section 29C, the Code of Criminal Procedure, 1898 (Act V of 1898).
427. *Jalaluddin Ahmed v. Matiur Rahman and others*, 9 BLD (HCD) 446.
428. Section 21, the Brick Manufacturing and Brick Kiln Establishment (Control) Act, 2013 (Act No. 59 of 2013).

588. The mobile courts have been playing an important supporting role in establishing environmental rule of law, though there are some concerns regarding the application of their powers. For example, it was found that though the Mobile Court Act, 2009 empowers the Magistrate to take cognizance of an alleged offence instantly at the spot when the same has been committed or unfolded in his presence and convict an accused and award the prescribed sentence; in one instance, the Magistrate convicted a person under the Law of 2009 who was already arrested by the Police. If something like this is done, then this will be treated as *mala fide* having no legality in the eye of law. Justice M Enayetur Rahim of the HCD held: 'It is true that Mobile Court Ain, 2009 provides for appeal against the judgment and order of conviction before the District Magistrate. But if *mala fide* is found on the face of the record in a Mobile Court proceeding and the conviction is 'non-est' in the eye of law, then this Court has every jurisdiction to interfere with the matter exercising power under Article 102 of the Constitution. It is by now well settled that *mala fide* vitiates everything.'[429]

589. There were also concerns if the executive magistrates, who often do not have a legal background with a law degree, possess the necessary qualifications to 'judge' an incident instantly, which is one of the important features of such a court's proceeding. Recently, one HCD divisional bench, consisting of Justice Moyeenul Islam Chowdhury and Justice Asish Ranjan Das, declared such mobile courts run by the executive magistrates as illegal as it is 'a frontal attack on the independence of the judiciary and is violative of the theory of separation of power'.[430] While delivering the judgment, the HCD was convinced that the mobile court as a fast-track court is necessary though this should be run by judicial or metropolitan magistrates. It was, however, reported that this decision of the HCD was stayed by the AD.

590. Since environment-related offences are special types of offence, in order to try these offences, back in 2000, the government first enacted the Environment Court Act, 2000 (Act No. 11 of 2000), which was subsequently updated, repealed, and replaced by the Environment Court Act, 2010 (Act No. 56 of 2010). The Environment Court Act, 2010 is a special law, and therefore, the provisions of this Law shall prevail over the provisions of other laws.[431] Following some specific procedures, the environment courts are generally empowered to try 'environmental law' offences, i.e., offences listed in the BECA, 1995 and any other law, e.g., the Brick Manufacturing and Brick Kiln Establishment (Control) Act, 2013, selected by the government through the government notification.[432] The Law provides for the establishment of one or more environmental courts in the headquarter of every district headed by a joint district judge, and a similar court can be established by a special

429. *The State v. UNO of Sakhipur, Tangail & another*, 2017 (1) LNJ 239.
430. *Kamruzzaman Khan and others v. Bangladesh* (Writ Petition No. 8437 of 2011, with Writ Petition No. 10482 of 2011 and Writ Petition No. 4879 of 2012).
431. Section 3, the Environment Court Act, 2000 (Act No. 11 of 2000).
432. Sections 2(c) and 7, the Environment Court Act, 2000 (Act No. 11 of 2000).

magistrate court headed by a MM or a first class Judicial Magistrate, if needed (sections 4 & 5). The Environment Court Act, 2010 also provides for the jurisdictions of these courts, i.e., the jurisdiction of Special Magistrate (section 6) and jurisdiction of environmental court (section 7).

591. Section 6(1) of the Environment Court Act, 2010 (Act No. 56 of 2010) provides that notwithstanding anything contained in any other law, the Director General or a person empowered by him may file a case directly in the Special Magistrate's Court for the trial of all offences specified in the BECA, 1995 or may file a complaint to the police station in accordance with the provisions of the Criminal Procedure Code. Thus, none can file a case relating to environmental offence other than the DG or anyone authorized by him.

592. The Special Magistrate Court may impose the penalty prescribed for the offences specified in the BECA, 1995, including offences under section 9 of this Act, and order to confiscate or dispose of the equipment or parts or vehicle used in the commission of the offence, and may issue a decree for compensation in appropriate cases; and additionally, the court may, in view of the circumstances of the offence or incident, make all or any of the following orders in the same judgment, viz.: (a) instructing the person convicted or any other person concerned not to repeat or continue the act for which the offence has been committed; (b) instructing the convicted person or any other person concerned to take appropriate preventive or corrective action at the discretion of the court in respect of the damage caused to the environment by such offence or incident; (c) to set a time limit giving directions for taking any action under clause (b) and to direct the Director General or any other appropriate authority to submit a report on the implementation of such instructions. Provided, however, that the person so directed may apply to reconsider the directions given under clauses (b) or (c) within not more than fifteen days from the date of delivery of the judgment, and the court after giving the Director General the opportunity to hear shall settle the issue within thirty days.

593. In *Sirajul Islam @ Siraj and another v. State*, 2003, 32 CLC (HCD) [4232] = 56 DLR (2004) 62, when a report was submitted by a Sub-Inspector of Police (SI) containing information that the petitioners by way of storing and selling banned polythene shopping bags violated the provisions of section 6 Ka of the BECA, 1995 as amended by Act No. 9 of 2002, the petitioner moved to the HCD with a question, i.e., whether a SI is an 'Inspector' within the meaning of the Environment Courts Act, as the said SI had not mentioned anything to indicate that he was authorized by the DG, DoE to submit such report. Justice Zinat Ara, by sharing the provisions of sections 5 Ga and 7 of the Environment Courts Act, which provide for the process as to how a Special Magistrate and an Inspector can deal with an offence and how the investigation of environmental offences can be initiated and investigation report can be submitted by an Inspector, and by sharing another circular issued by the DG, DoE, held that an SI of Police is very much an 'inspector' within the meaning of section 2 (Kha) of the Environment Courts Act, 2000 as the definition of the word 'inspector' clearly indicates that any person, e.g., in case of offences relating to polythene shopping bags, an SI of Police can be authorized to exercise the powers of an 'inspector' and an SI is competent as an 'inspector' to submit a report to the Special Magistrate in respect of the polythene shopping bag offences.

594. Though no special magistrate court shall take up any case for trial without the written report of the inspector, on the basis of any application if the Special Magistrate Court is, however, satisfied to the effect that, in spite of the request of the concerned inspector to accept the complaint of any offence, he has not taken necessary action within the next sixty days on the basis of it or there is reason to accept the complaint, then after giving the concerned inspector or the Director General to hear, the complaint may be accepted and tried or, the inspector may be directed to investigate the allegations, if deemed appropriate.[433]

595. Under section 7 of the Environment Court Act, 2010 (Act No. 56 of 2000), the Environment Court has some similar power in terms of instructing the person convicted or any other person concerned not to repeat or continue the act for which the offence has been committed; to take appropriate preventive or corrective action at the discretion of the court in respect of the damage caused to the environment by such offence or incident; to set a time limit giving directions for taking such action and to direct the Director General or any other appropriate authority to submit a report on the implementation of such instructions. The person so directed may apply to reconsider the directions given within not more than fifteen days from the date of delivery of the judgment, and the court, after giving the Director General the opportunity to hear shall settle the issue within thirty days. It is, however, provided that notwithstanding anything contained in any other law, the cases received from the Special Magistrate for trial of offences under the Environmental Act shall be tried and disposed of by the Environmental Court in accordance with the provisions of this Act. Besides, in order to obtain compensation under the Environment Act, a case shall be filed directly in the Environmental Court in accordance with the provisions of this Act and it shall be tried and disposed of in that court, by taking necessary action for trial.

Class Action or Public Interest Environmental Litigation

596. An individual's right to get the protection of law through civil and criminal courts, as has already been discussed, is constitutionally guaranteed. As the Constitution of Bangladesh, 1972 has granted the citizens some fundamental rights, and judicial enforcement of these fundamental rights is also a fundamental right as recognized by article 44 of the Constitution, 1972, an individual or an organization representing the individual can go to the HCD for judicial review in the form of a writ under article 102 of the Constitution of Bangladesh if any of his fundamental rights is violated by any of the government apparatus. Before granting any remedies under article 102 of the Constitution of Bangladesh, the petitioner needs to convince the HCD whether he or she can be considered as 'any person aggrieved' under the said constitutional provision, i.e., whether the petitioner has the *locus standi*.

433. Section 6(3), the Environment Court Act, 2010 (Act No. 56 of 2000).

597. In the common law legal systems, it is not very difficult to establish the *locus standi* or the right to sue arising out of the cause of action involving a small number of people. This issue of *locus standi*, one of the fundamental issues to be settled before getting justice for the violation of fundamental rights, is often difficult to establish directly in relation to the protection of environmental components as the issues are inherently complex and affect a larger number of people, both directly and indirectly, involving various legal concerns. Therefore, in most such cases, when any organization represents a group of people suffering from any environmental problems collectively, this matter of *locus standi* becomes the first issue for the HCD to decide.

598. The matter of *locus standi* in disputes not involving an individual only rather than in the name of public interest has been discussed in various judgments in Bangladesh. Public interest litigation (PIL) means the legal action initiated in a court of law for the enforcement of rights and interests of the citizens in general or a section thereof.[434] In the landmark judgment, *Dr. Mohiuddin Farooque v. Bangladesh*, 1997, 26 CLC (AD) [505]=49 DLR (AD) (1997) 1, Justice Mustafa Kamal stated the historical background of PIL in the USA in the following manner:

> . . .what is now known as 'public interest law' assumed wide currency in the United States in the 1960s. These words convey and sum up the activities of lawyers representing clients and interest still unrepresented or under represented in the American legal system. With the financial assistance from the Office of Economic Opportunity (OEO) of the Federal Government of the United States, a group of lawyers mobilised law students and social action groups to articulate in the legal arena the diffused interest of several million unorganised people in the lower socio- economic strata to force a change in the system of priorities, procedures and policies for the benefit of those who were till then kept outside of it. The result today in the United States is an astounding enlargement of the frontiers of *locus standi* and the development of wide-ranging 'public interest litigation' embracing the rights and plights of minorities, race and gender relations, ethnic groups, governmental lawlessness environmental pollution, public health, product safety, consumer protection, social exploitation, etc.

599. While Justice Mustafa Kamal attempted to draw the historical development of PIL in the USA context, Mr Justice Muhammad Khurshid Alam Sarkar in *Mohd. Emrul Kayes & others v. Syed Ejaz Kabir & others*, 3 LNJ (2014) 269 eloquently portrayed the history and development of PIL in the Indo-Pak subcontinent. It is shared that the concept of 'public interest litigation' was first introduced in India by Mr Justice VR Krishna Iyer in the case of *Mumbai Kamgar Sabha, Bombay v. Ms Abdul Bhai*, AIR 1976 (SC) 1466, and the jurisprudential basis of PIL was laid down by Justice Bhagwati in the case of *SP Gupta v. President of India*, AIR 1982 (SC) 149 in the following manner:

---

434. *Engineer Mahmudul Islam and others vs. Government of the People's Republic of Bangladesh and others*, 2002, 31 CLC (HCD) [8145] = 55 DLR (2003) 171.

> Where a legal wrong or a legal injury is caused to a person or to a determinate class of persons by reason of violation of any constitutional or legal right or any burden is imposed in contravention of any constitutional or legal provision or without authority of law or any such legal wrong or legal injury or illegal burden is threatened and such person or determinate class of persons is, by reason of poverty, helplessness or disability or socially or economically disadvantaged position, unable to approach the Court for relief, any member of the public maintains an application....... seeking judicial redress for the legal wrong or injury caused to such person or determinate class of persons.

600. Due to the complexities of issues involved in environmental matters, as this is difficult for an individual to establish *locus standi* and continue the case for long, some of the environmental NGOs of Bangladesh, most prominently Bangladesh Environment Lawyers' Association (BELA), Bangladesh Poribesh Andolon (BAPA), Poribesh Andalon Bangladesh (POBA), and other human rights NGOs, e.g., Bangladesh Legal Aid and Services Trust (BLAST), Human Rights and Peace for Bangladesh (HRPB) have been playing an instrumental role and thus, contributing marvellously in the development of environmental law jurisprudence, very often through PIL, in the country. The continuous and relentless efforts of these organizations help shape the general PIL framework domestically as well.

601. Back in 1974, the first attempt of PIL in Bangladesh was made in *Kazi Mukhlesur Rahman v. Bangladesh*, 1974, 26 DLR (SC) 44 (popularly known as the '*Berubari case*') when the appellant, who was neither a resident nor directly affected, challenged the Delhi treaty signed by the Prime Minister of Bangladesh and India regarding the ownership of enclaves on the ground that the agreement involved cession of Bangladesh territory and the said treaty was entered into by the executive head of the government without lawful authority. The HCD summarily dismissed the petition on the ground that the appellant had no *locus standi*.[435] The appellant moved to the AD and *locus standi* was granted to the appellant even though he was not affected. The AD granted the *locus standi* considering the fact that the appellant raised a constitutional issue of grave importance involving an international treaty affecting the territory of Bangladesh. The AD established several general principles in this regard and these, *inter alia*, are, i.e.: (1) the HCD will grant *locus standi* to a person who agitates a question affecting a constitutional issue of grave importance, posing a threat to his fundamental rights which pervade and extend to the entire territory of Bangladesh; (2) if a fundamental right is involved, the impugned matter need not affect a purely personal right of the applicant touching him alone, and it is enough if he shares that right in common with others; (3)

435. For the historical development of public interest litigation in Bangladesh, *see*, Naim Ahmed. Litigating in the Name of the People: Stresses and Strains of the Development of Public Interest Litigation in Bangladesh', PhD Thesis, Department of Law, School of Oriental and African Studies, University of London, 1998; for Public Interest Environmental Litigation in India, Pakistan, and Bangladesh, *see also*, Jona Razzaque, *Public Interest Environmental Litigation in India, Pakistan, and Bangladesh*. Vol. 7 (Kluwer Law International BV, 2004).

the HCD can exercise discretion in treating whether any person is aggrieved or not; (4) the HCD will exercise that jurisdiction upon due consideration of the facts and circumstances of each case.

602. One of the most important elements that a plaintiff needs to establish *locus standi* in PILs is that the petitioner needs to be affected directly, and the petitioner must have 'sufficient interest'.[436] In *Bangladesh Sangbadpatra Parishad v. Bangladesh,* 43 DLR (AD) (1991)126= 1991, 20 CLC (AD) [1454], the petitioner Bangladesh Sangbadpatra Parishad, an association of newspaper-owners, challenged various provisions of the Newspaper Employees (Conditions of Service) Act, 1974 (Act No. XXX of 1974), and the Constitution and decision of the Fourth Wage Board and the interim award dated 30.12.90 given by the Fourth Wage Board in so far as payment of dearness allowance, gratuity and income-tax were concerned as unconstitutional. Justice Mustafa Kamal, while sharing the position of India and England and mentioning the nature of the case, i.e., this is not a PIL, held that the owners and the employees of newspapers who were affected by the award could challenge it when the award was made since they were associated with the award-making process and since they did not do that they cannot be considered as an 'aggrieved person'. Therefore, the Bangladesh Sangbadpatra Parishad had no *locus standi* to challenge the award of the Wage Board.

603. Finally, in the landmark decision of *Dr. Mohiuddin Farooque v. Bangladesh*, 1997, 26 CLC (AD) [505] = 49 DLR (AD) (1997) 1, 17 BLD (AD) 1997, 1; 1 BLC (AD) (1996) 189, Justice Mustafa Kamal of the AD set the foundation and formal beginning of PIL in Bangladesh by clearly interpreting the phrase 'any person aggrieved'. According to him:

> when a public injury or public wrong or infraction of a fundamental right affecting an indeterminate number of people is involved it is not necessary, in the scheme of our Constitution, that the multitude of individuals who has been collectively wronged or injured or whose collective fundamental rights have been invaded are to invoke the jurisdiction under Article 102 in a multitude of individual writ petitions, each representing his own portion of concern. Insofar as it concerns public wrong or public injury or invasion of fundamental rights of an indeterminate number of people, any member of the public, being a citizen, suffering the common injury or common invasion in common with others or any citizen or an indigenous association, as distinguished from a local component of a foreign organisation, espousing that particular cause is a person aggrieved and has the right to invoke the jurisdiction under Article 102.

604. In *Ms. Syeda Rizwana Hasan v. Bangladesh and others*, 2010, 39 CLC (AD) [8508] = 9 ADC (2012) 816, 18 BLC (AD) (2013) 54, Justice Surendra Kumar Sinha of the AD stipulated that in considering a petition as PIL:

436. *SN Goswami v. Bangladesh*, 55 DLR 332.

> [i]t is to be seen that where there is undoubtedly public injury by the act or omission of the functionary of the State or a local authority or public authority or executive excess causes a legal injury to a specific class or group of individuals or a public injury or public wrong or infraction of fundamental rights affecting a number of people is involved, the exercise of jurisdiction by Court is justiciable. If grievances of those people are unredressed due to poverty, lack of education, helplessness, social disability, only then the Court would entertain a petition if a public spirited person or organisation comes to Court on their behalf. In other words, more clearly the underprivileged or the poor who are unable to come to Court due to illiteracy or monetary helplessness, a petition on their behalf will be welcomed. The litigation must have been initiated for the benefit of the poor or any number of people who have been suffering the common injury but their grievances cannot be redressed as they are not able to reach the Court.

605. Justice Sinha further stated that:

> However, if the said class or group who are injured by the action do not wish to claim a right or relief against such invasion and accept such act or omission without protest, no member of the public or organisation making the relief has suffered a secondary public injury can maintain any petition against such act or omission, or when an act or omission is of such a nature which shocks the judicial conscience, the Court should extend its jurisdiction. . . We want to make it clear that every wrong or curiosity is not and cannot be the subject matter of PIL. In the name of public interest frivolous applications should be avoided.

606. Earlier, in one instance, BLAST moved to the HCD on behalf of the ordinary people of the country to ask for directions to ensure adequate iodine content in the edible salt as it was noticed that the authorities responsible in this regard and the salt manufacturers were not performing their respective functions under the Iodine Deficiency Diseases Prevention Act, 1989 and the Iodine Deficiency Diseases Prevention Rules, 1994. The court, considering and understanding that the supply of iodine in the proportionate ratio in the human body and the interest of the health of the people of Bangladesh and to ensure the marketing of iodized salt, granted the rule.[437]

607. Similarly, in *Omar Sadat v. Bangladesh & Ors.* 9 BLT(HCD) 124, the petitioner, a lawyer of the Supreme Court, alleged that making unauthorized constructions and setting up illegal markets by the unauthorized users for their commercial purposes were creating obstructions to the footpaths in the Dhaka city, pavements goers and passers-by, and thereby making the city virtually unfit for habitation as the people cannot pass through the footpaths, pavements and the streets practically. According to the petitioner, the respondents are not taking any care; rather, they

437. *Bangladesh Legal Aid and Services Trust and another v. Bangladesh and others*, 2004, 33 CLC (HCD) [7685] = 25 BLD (HCD) (2005) 83.

were sleeping and neglecting to protect the same and keeping these free for use by the regular passers-by. Besides, Dhaka city was once a beautiful city in the east. But now it has been turned into a gloomy and ghost city because of blocking the foot-paths and pavements in the aforesaid unauthorized and illegal manner. This is why the petitioner being aggrieved has made this application by himself. The environment also has become very unhygienic, and it is also adding to the pollution of the air. The HCD was convinced and granted the rule and held that the government should protect the right of the people to move freely through the roads, streets, foot-paths and pavements of Dhaka and other cities in Bangladesh, and terms of the law should be implemented to protect the right of the petitioner as well as of every pedestrian and the city dwellers should be allowed to enjoy their right as given by law.[438]

608. Various organizations were subsequently found to exploit PIL though the HCD has not entertained many such attempts. In *Bangladesh Legal Aid and Services Trust v. Bangladesh and others*, 2007, 36 CLC (HCD) [5646] = 64 DLR (HCD) (2012) 203, the renowned NGO, BLAST and some other allottees of Gulshan Model Town moved to the HCD with a writ petition in the form of a PIL challenging the decision of RAJUK that, revising the existing lay out plan, took an initiative to convert a car park area into commercial plots, and according to the petitioner, the decision would 'cause environmental hazard by creating more traffic concentration'. The court did not find grounds on this contention of BLAST, rather held that BLAST does not have 'sufficient interest' in the issue and the allottees who joined BLAST 'are affluent residents of Gulshan and have enough money to seek their own redress'. Thus, a PIL cannot be entertained. According to the court, 'the petitioners have failed to show any breach of public duty resulting in violation of collective rights of public at large or that there is any public wrong or public injury or even violation of law by RAJUK by inviting auction to lease out the land in question for construction of commercial building. Since the petitioner no.1 [BLAST] has approached the Court for redress of private injury couched with public injury and having failed to show that the impugned action of RAJUK is causing environmental hazard in the said locality hence, it has no *locus standi* to move the High Court Division under Article 102 of the Constitution of Bangladesh'.

609. Similarly, in *BRAC and others v. Professor Mozaffar Ahmed and others*, 2002, 31 CLC (AD) [1331] = 54 DLR (AD) (2002) 36, a PIL was filed questioning the validity of a no objection certificate of Bangladesh Bank for the incorporation of BRAC Bank Limited by Bangladesh Rural Advancement Committee, briefly known as BRAC. The appellant pointed out that the writ petition in the form of 'PIL' is not maintainable as neither the fundamental right of the petitioner nor the right of any vulnerable and socially disadvantaged class of person was infringed. Chief Justice Mahmudul Amin Choudhury found that the petitioners are well-to-do

438. *Omar Sadat v. Bangladesh & Ors.* 9 BLT(HCD) 124.

people of the country who were capable of establishing banking companies or financial undertakings and were not less fortunate people in the society. Therefore, they were not entertained to move to the HCD under Article 102 of the Constitution as an aggrieved person.

610. An interesting situation arose in *City Sugar Industries Ltd. and others v. Human Rights and Peace for Bangladesh*, 2010, 39 CLC (AD) [3965] = 15 MLR (AD) (2010) 389, when the petitioner Human Rights and Peace for Bangladesh, a human rights NGO, moved to the HCD to stop the illegal encroachment, earth filling and temporary and permanent structures building on the River Buriganga, Turag at Dhaka and on the River Shitalakkha at Narayangonj, which were built violating the provisions of the BECA, 1995 (amended in 2000 and 2002), and the Conservation of Playgrounds, Open Spaces, Parks and Natural Reservoirs in all Metropolitan, Divisional Cities and District Towns including Municipal Areas of the Country Act, 2000 (Act XXXVI of 2000)[439] and to remove temporary & permanent structures built inside as such activities obstructed the normal movement of the water of the rivers as well as seriously affected the environment.

611. It was stated that: 'millions of people residing in Dhaka and Narayangonj city are depending on the source of water from Buriganga, Shitalakkha and Turag River. Main water supply comes from the above mentioned rivers. Not only that, some 'river transports' based on the above mentioned river are playing a great role in the transport sector. Due to continuous encroachment, earth filling and structure buildings in the above mentioned rivers, day by day it is losing its flow affecting the life of the citizen. All the rivers are also playing an effective role in protecting the environment. But due to illegal acts of the law violators the above mentioned rivers could not play effective role in environment'. The HCD was convinced with the grounds shared by the petitioners and was pleased to pass an order directing the responsible authorities to start removing all the structures/encroachments within the territories of rivers Buriganga, Turag, Balu and Shitalakkya within one month from the date of receipt of this order.

612. When the responsible authorities went to implement the order of the HCD, some of the commercial entities duly registered with the government entities that were running businesses legally by obtaining necessary permissions also moved to the HCD challenging the legality of the previous decision of the HCD. The AD, after evaluating the facts and evidence, and sharing the non-obstante clause as included in section 12(2) of the Act XXXVI of 2000 which provides that notwithstanding any provision in any other law for the time being in force, the provisions of Act XXXVI of 2000 shall prevail, refused to entertain the prayers of the commercial entities. The AD, referring to the issue from the public interest point of view, mentioned that: 'since rivers are "*joladhar*" . . . within the meaning of the *Ain* [Act], the law relating to Act XXXVI of 2000 must prevail over all other laws. We

439. It may be relevant to share here that in *Bangladesh Paribesh Andolan and another v. Bangladesh, represented by the Secretary, Ministry of Works and others*, 2004, 33 CLC (HCD) [4810] = 58 DLR (2006) 441, this law was referred to as 'the Wetland Conservation Act, 2000' for convenience.

also find that the public interest lies in protecting the rivers from encroachments and pollution by all means. The maxim *'Salus Papuli Suprema lex'* should be put in the imperative i.e. *'Salus Papuli Suprema lex esto'* i.e. let the safety of the people be the Supreme law'. Thus, the AD upholds the public interest over the private and commercial interest of some entities.

613. In some PIL, the HCD had to evaluate the balance between environmental protection and development. In *Ain-O-Salish Kendro (ASK) and other v. Bangladesh* (Writ Petition No. 8098 of 2013), seven NGOs, i.e., Ain-o-Salish Kendra, Association for Land Reforms and Development, BELA, Bangladesh Paribesh Andolon, Institute of Architects Bangladesh, Poribesh Bachao Andolon, and Nijera Kori – and in another PIL, *Mohammad Kamrul Ahsan (Sumon) and other vs. Bangladesh* (Writ Petition No. 1166 of 2012) – the petitioners moved to the HCD for directions to protect the vast tract of forest cover of the Barakau and Parabartha mauza under Kaliganj Thana in the district of Gazipur from being developed into residential plots of Purbachal New Town Project as this would impair environmental balance and destroy the unique ecosystem and biodiversity of the area. Both the petitions shared concerns for the protection of forests, biodiversity, and environmental balance and involved common questions of law and facts and, thus, were considered together.

614. It can be revealed from the fact of the cases that respondent No. 4, the RAJUK, acquisitioned 1,600 acres of land of the Barakau and Parabartha mauza for developing the 'Purbachal New Town Project,' the largest planned township in the country in 2002 (the actual process was started in 1994) intending to make a human habitat in an environment-friendly and sustainable atmosphere. The compensation money was duly paid, 500 plots were allotted for the affected people, and the necessary certificates were collected from the Department of Environment. An environmental study report, an environmental impact assessment (EIA), and a layout plan keeping the core forest unaffected and maintaining adequate spaces for greenery, an eco-park, golf course, park, urban green, lake, and so on were also prepared. In total, 251 acres of land were reserved as forest and greenery free from allotment to anyone. The project was then approved by the Executive Committee of National Economic Council, and 60 percent of the work was completed.

615. The petitioners had no intention of undoing or foiling the project. However, their main concern was to save a considerable amount of these two mauzas, which are covered by dense shaal forest, locally known as Gazarigarh, orchard, medicinal plants, and water bodies. This rare topographical feature of the area, apart from its ecosystem attributes, directly contributes to the environmental balance. Thus, they alleged that a threatened public injury was posed by the statutory public authority by way of the acquisition and impending transformation of a vast tract of forested land, orchards, water bodies, and so on into an urban habitat to the utter detriment of the environmental balance affecting the health and safety of millions of people. It will be relevant to share here that two writ petitions, i.e., Writ Petition No. 3941 of 2002 and Writ Petition No. 1460 of 2006, were already decided by the

HCD on the issue of deforestation and environmental degradation. The Bench of Justice M. Moazzam Husain and Justice Md. Badruzzaman observed that:

> Man as natural being sustain and grow depending on the natural environment around him. There can, therefore, be no doubt that deforestation and destruction of ecosystem tend to bring an impact to bear upon human life and lives of other living creatures. It is also equally true that human struggle for survival and better life is deeply embedded in human nature which gave rise to the concept of development in the modern day sense.
> But development, in absolute sense, is again impossible without causing some damage to nature. This nature-development paradox practically furnished the background of the contemporary theory of sustainable development which seeks to integrate nature with development. . . Sustainable development is yet not a comprehensive theory or an all weather remedy. It is an evolving concept subject to continual debate among experts.
> Except for its underlying concern for retarding environmental degradations there is no flat application of the theory to all conditions of human development in every corner of the globe. With the variations in development level in different countries priorities on the development agenda vis-à-vis its environmental components is bound to differ. In a developing country like Bangladesh where there is no significant industrialization, urbanization or other massive development projects up to affecting global climate and where governments are still striving to provide millions of low and mid-income families with shelter and accommodations in a more or less healthy environment, asserting as much exactitude and precision in development projects, in terms of their environmental integration as is possible in developed countries is impracticable.

616. The court, though appreciated the relentless efforts of the environmentalists such as the petitioner, did not find any additional concern, sufficient and reliable environmental degradation from the documents submitted by the petitioners than that which had already been settled in the previous judgments. Thus, the court observed that:

> [A]n ill-timed and casual move in the name of environment not founded on minimal homework, study or survey [is not] enough to satisfy judicial minds and [is] totally unconcerned with the socio-economic reality and basic needs and priorities of a particular population [that] can be judicially accommodated. No judicial arm can be extended unless it could be shown, that too in appropriate time and on a tangible basis, that there is reckless deforestation and destruction of ecosystem and the proposed project is going to be implemented beyond the carrying capacity of nature and ecological support system and the loss from such destruction is irreconcilable and far exceeds the gain derived from the destruction.

617. From the content of the judgment, it is apparent that both of the petitions were disposed of on procedural grounds that the petitions were not founded on proper study and survey. In both of the petitions, the principle of res judicata was an issue, and in the second petition, the court found that it lacked the characteristics of *pro bono publico* since the petitioners were not public-spirited persons to protect the environment. Nevertheless, the court directed the respondents 'not to efface, subtract, vary, modify, or otherwise change the forest (core), forest, lake/canals, urban green, parks, playgrounds/playlots, green-belt as well as similar other environment-oriented spaces of the project as demonstrated in the documents . . . to the derogation of their basic purposes without permission to be taken from this Court'. It was further held that '[s]ince the nature of direction demands pendency of at least one of the two writ petitions . . . The Writ Petition No. 8098 of 2013 shall remain pending and the direction given shall sustain as continuing mandamus as long as this court will not dispose of the same by an express order. The Registrar is directed to ensure safety and orderly maintenance of the records of Writ Petition No.8098 of 2013 including the EIA Report submitted by RAJUK'. Therefore, it is obvious that even if the court did not entertain the petitioners directly, it has actually admitted the concerns of the petitioners and, thus, directed the RAJUK to follow the project documents in a proper manner. As the petitioners were not successful, they moved to the AD with appeals, but these were dismissed there.

618. It is, therefore, evident that the HCD, as the interpreter of the Constitution of Bangladesh, 1972, has been leading from the front in the development of PIL in Bangladesh. At some point in time, unfortunately, it was revealed that some people use to utilize this for personal gain, name, fame, and publicity. In *National Board of Revenue v. Abu Saeed Khan and others,* 18 BLC (AD) 116 (2013), the court observed that:

> Now-a-days, it is noticeable that a group of lawyers have developed a tendency of filing PIL petitions on behalf of persons or organizations challenging the propriety of the Government in taking decision relating to policy matter, its development works, orders of promotion and transfer of public servants, imposition of taxes and fixation of tariff value by the authority for achieving dubious goal for generating publicity for themselves or to create public sensation. The High Court Division has been taking cognizance of those petitions without looking at whether or not such petitions are at all maintainable in the light of the principles settled by this Division . . . It is also noticeable that after seeking an order from the High Court Division by filing a PIL, the lawyers are appearing before the electronic and print media propagating that the Court has made such and such directions, which suggest that those petitions have not been made for the cause of the needy or underprivileged or less fortunate people, who could not seek redress for a wrong done by the Government or a local authority, rather it were moved for achieving dubious goal for generating personal publicity.

619. As a result, the AD had to intervene and lay down the parameters within which the High Court Division should extend its discretionary jurisdiction in entertaining a PIL:

1. Before entertaining a petition, the court will have to decide the extent of sufficiency of interest and the fitness of the person invoking the discretionary jurisdiction.
2. The court which considers the question of bona fide in a particular case will have to decide as to why the affected party has not come before it, and if it finds no satisfactory reason for non-appearance of such affected party, it may refuse to entertain the petition.
3. If a petition is filed to represent opulent members who were directly affected by the decision of the government or Public Authority, such petition would not be entertained.
4. The expression 'person aggrieved' used in Article 102(1) means not any person who is personally aggrieved but one whose heart bleeds for the less fortunate fellow beings for a wrong done by any person or authority in connection with the affairs of the Republic or a statutory public authority.
5. If the person making the application on enquiry is found to be an interloper who interferes with the action of any person or authority as above which does not concern him is not entitled to make such petition.
6. The court is under an obligation to guard that the filing of a PIL does not convert into a publicity interest litigation or private interest litigation.
7. Only a public-spirited person or organization can invoke the discretionary jurisdiction of the court on behalf of such disadvantaged and helpless persons.
8. The court should also guard that its processes are not abused by any person.
9. The court should also guard that the petition is initiated for the benefit of the poor or for any number of people who have been suffering from common injury, but their grievances cannot be redressed as they are not able to reach the court.
10. It must also be guarded that every wrong or curiosity is not and cannot be the subject matter of PIL.
11. No petitions will be entertained challenging the policy matters of the government, development works being implemented by the government, order of promotion or transfer of public servants, imposition of taxes by the competent authority.
12. The court has no power to entertain a petition which trespasses into the areas which are reserved to the executive and legislative by the Constitution.
13. A petition will be entertained if it is moved to protect the basic human rights of the disadvantaged citizens who are unable to reach the court due to illiteracy or monetary helplessness.
14. Apart from the above, the following are some categories of cases which will be entertained;
    a) For protection of the neglected children.
    b) Non-payment of minimum wages to workers and exploitation of casual workers complaints of violation of labour laws (except in individual case).

c) Petitions complaining death in jail or police custody; or caused by law; enforcing agencies.
d) Petitions against law enforcing agencies for refusing to register a case despite there are existing allegations of commission of cognizable offences.
e) Petitions against atrocities on women such as bride burning, rape, murder for dowry, kidnapping.
f) Petitions complaining about harassment or torture of citizens by police or other law enforcing agencies.
g) Petitions pertaining to environmental pollution, disturbance of ecological balance, drugs, food adulteration, maintenance of heritage and culture, antiques, forest and wildlife.
h) Petitions from riot victims.

Chapter 1. Administrative Remedies

620. The enactment and adaption of hundreds of laws, general, sectoral and special, primary and subsidiary, policy initiatives and institutional arrangements by the successive governments of Bangladesh in the last five decades after the independence clearly demonstrate their commitments towards the protection of environmental components and sustainable developments. These laws provide for substantive environmental rights and the forums for the implementation of these rights though there are concerns about their proper implementations due to various challenges, e.g., political, economic, social, procedural, and institutional. As a result, it can be noticed that the government is more interested in settling environment-related matters through administrative manners.

621. For the effective and proper implementation of the BECA, 1995 (Act No. 1 of 1995), the main single environmental legislation, the law provides for the appointment of a DG as the head of the DoE. The DG, subject to the provisions of this Act, is responsible for taking such measures which he considers necessary and expedient for the conservation of the environment, and improvement of environmental standards, and for the control and mitigation of environmental pollution, and he may issue necessary directions in writing to any person for the discharge of his duties under this Act.[440] Besides, the DG can take all or any of the following measures:

(a) coordination with the activities of any authority or agency having relevance to the objectives of this Act;
(b) undertake safety measures aiming at the prevention of possible accidents which may cause environmental degradation and pollution, take safety measures, determine remedial measures for such accidents and issue relevant directions;
(c) advise or, as the case may be, issue directions to the concerned person regarding the environmentally sound use, storage, transportation, import and export of any hazardous substance or its components.
(d) conduct enquiries and undertake research activities on conservation, improvement and pollution of the environment, and assist any other authority or organization on these matters;
(e) inspect any place and premise, examine any plant, equipment, production or other processes, ingredients, or substance for the purpose of improvement of the environment, control and mitigation of pollution; and issue direction or order to the appropriate authority or person for the prevention, control and mitigation of environmental pollution;
(f) collection, publication and dissemination of information about environmental pollution;
(g) advise the government to avoid such manufacturing processes, commodities and substances as are likely to cause environmental pollution;

440. Section 4(1), the Bangladesh Environment Conservation Act, 1995 (Act No. 1 of 1995).

(h) carry out programmes for observation of the quality of drinking water and prepare reports, and advise or, as the case may be, issue direction to the concerned persons to follow standards for drinking water.[441]

622. Besides, the DG can, on behalf of any individual, group, public affected due to non-adherence to the provisions of the BECA, 1995, or any Rule framed thereunder, file a case against the person liable.[442] Any direction issued by the DG may include matters relating to closure, prohibition, or regulation of any industry, undertakings, or processes, and these are bound to comply with. However, before any such direction of closure or prohibition of an industry, undertaking or process, the DG has to send a written notice to the owner or occupier so that he gets reasonable opportunity to make that industry, undertaking or process environmentally sound within a time specified. Nevertheless, in the case of particular environmental pollution due to which the public life is likely to be in danger, and if urgent action is needed, the DG may immediately issue necessary directions.[443] It will be pertinent to mention here that in serious cases, the action taken by the DG without the issuance of notice may not be challenged even though some people suffer some financial loss as '[c]oncern should be more for the betterment of the whole nation than the financial loss which may be sustained by an individual or individuals'.[444]

623. Besides, the law empowers the DG or a person authorized by him to request any law enforcing agency or any other Government or statutory authority to seek necessary assistance to exercise any power or perform any function under this Act. For example, if the DG issues a direction for closure, prohibition, or regulation of an industry, undertaking or process under section 4(3) of the BECA, 1995, and the owner or occupier thereof does not comply with the direction, the DG may direct the provider of electricity, gas, telephone or water or all such services or any other service provided to the industry, undertaking or process to disconnect the service, and the concerned person or institution shall be bound to take the necessary action as specified in the direction.[445]

624. It is prohibited to run any vehicle that emits smoke or gas, which is harmful to the environment or human health and means any gas which is emitted beyond the acceptable limit as prescribed by the Environment Conservation Rules, 1997. Such vehicles can be run only for examination purpose aiming to stop the emission of such smoke or gas. The law authorizes the DG or any person authorized by him to detain any vehicle, examine the papers and seize them to examine any vehicle in this regard. The driver or the owner of the vehicle has to cooperate with the DG or any person authorized as the non-cooperation will be considered as a violation of

---

441. Section 4(2), the Bangladesh Environment Conservation Act, 1995 (Act No. 1 of 1995).
442. Section 17, the Bangladesh Environment Conservation Act, 1995 (Act No. 1 of 1995).
443. Sections 4(2) & 4(3), the Bangladesh Environment Conservation Act, 1995 (Act No. 1 of 1995).
444. *K M Asadul Bari v. Bangladesh and others*, 22 BLD (HCD) 129.
445. Section 4A, the Bangladesh Environment Conservation Act, 1995 (Act No. 1 of 1995).

the provision of the law.[446] It may be noted that successive governments have taken various initiatives, irregular though, in this regard.

625. Under section 8 of the BECA, 1995, any person already affected or having the chance to get affected due to environmental pollution or degradation may inform the DG through an application following the procedure mentioned in the Environment Conservation Rules, 1997. The DG can take any measure to settle the issue including the arrangement of a public hearing. It is the responsibility of the person-in-charge to prevent and control the emission of pollutants, in excess of the limit set by the Rules, discharged as a result of any act, incident or accident.[447]

626. Section 7 of the BECA, 1995 has included the provision of polluter pay principle as it provides that if it appears to the DG that the actions or inactions of any person or group have been or have caused direct or indirect harm to the eco-system, then the DG, after calculating the amount of harm, can ask the polluter to pay for the loss, and in appropriate cases, instruct him to take corrective measures in this regard or both. The DG may file a criminal case against a defaulter for the collection of the fine and failure to comply with his order in a criminal court having the jurisdiction. Moreover, the DG may, on behalf of any affected individual, group, public, file another case for compensation against the defaulter who failed to comply with his instruction which caused the losses for those people affected.[448]

627. The issue of 'act done in good faith' is a concern. Under section 18 of the BECA, 1995, it is provided that no civil or criminal case or any other legal action shall be taken against the government, the Director General, any officer or employee of the Department or any person if any person is harmed or is likely to be harmed as a result of any act done in good faith under this Act or rules. Being the guardian of the Constitution of Bangladesh, 1972, the HCD is under an obligation to correct and remedy anything done or caused to be done by abuse or misuse of official power or process of law or violation of the provision of the Constitution, once it comes to the court in any proceeding, no matter how and who brings the same. Legal wrong done in performing public duty is an act of culpable negligence and dishonesty of law. A public authority is duty bound to act with fairness and consistency as per practised standard and norm in its dealing with state properties, and if such public authority makes inconsistent decisions unfairly or unjustly, it misuses its power and authority, and consequently, such decision becomes void and without lawful authority.[449]

628. The issue 'good faith' is difficult to establish as this is very much subjective and needs to settle case by case considering the surrounding circumstances. The Latin term 'bona fide' is frequently used in the legal texts in Bangladesh as an

---

446. The Bangladesh Environment Conservation Act, 1995 (Act No. 1 of 1995).
447. Section 9, the Bangladesh Environment Conservation Act, 1995 (Act No. 1 of 1995).
448. Section 15A, the Bangladesh Environment Conservation Act, 1995 (Act No. 1 of 1995).
449. *Engineer Mahmudul Islam and others v. Government of the People's Republic of Bangladesh and others*, 2002, 31 CLC (HCD) [8145] = 55 DLR (2003) 171.

equivalent of 'good faith'. Section 52 of the Penal Code, 1860 provides that: '[n]othing is said to be done or believed in "good faith" which is done or believed without due care and attention'. In the case of *Dr. Moosa Bin Shamsher v. Ayub Ali and another*, 2 LNJ (2013) 17, honourable judge, Justice Sharif Uddin Chaklader, in relation to a case on a monthly rent of a premise, referred the definition of 'bonafide' from different sources. It was stipulated that:

> Bonafide means, according to *Tomlin's Law Dictionary* 'in good faith, without fraud or deception, honestly, openly, sincerely. In the case of *Porkrn Kulty -Vs.- Attaucheri Velappil Manwared* AIR 1954 Mad 381, bonafide requirement given the meaning reasonably requires. The landlord must have a genuine present need of the building for his occupation. In the case of *Sohan Lal -Vs- Poonam Chand*, AIR 1961 Raj 32 bonafide has been given the meaning that 'Nothing is bonafide which is not done with due care and attention'. In Black's law Dictionary bonafide has been defined as in good faith, made in good faith, without fraud or deceit, sincere, genuine. In the case of *Sri Naresh -Vs- Kanailal*, AIR 1952 cal 1952, bonafide requirement defined as 'there must be a short of "must have" element in the need of land lord and also that his want or need of the house must be honestly felt by him.' In the case of *Giriza Deri Vs. R.C. & E. Office*, AIR 1965 All 366 the definition of bonafide requirement is the land lord has a genuine need to occupy the accommodation, that is, he must have necessary to occupy it and the necessity must be bonafide or genuine one.

629. As opposed to good faith, there is bad faith or '*mala fide*'. In the case of *Shah Abdul Hannan and others v. Bangladesh*, 2010, 39 CLC (HCD) [4694] = 16 BLC (HCD) (2011) 386, the HCD, while considering, *inter alia*, the issue of the legality of making a government policy, discussed the broader meaning of 'mala fide' sharing the reference of Indian Supreme Court Judgment *Jaichand v. West Bengal*, AIR 1967 SC 483 where it was held that the import of the concept 'mala fide' 'is not confined to moral turpitude, but also extends to a situation where power is exercised for purposes alien to those the law intended'.

630. Apart from the various offences as listed in the BECA, 1995, other environmental crimes, specially relating to those with wildlife and forest life, are transnational and organized in nature, and thus, this is listed in the United Nations Convention against Transnational Organised Crime. As a result, Bangladesh has been suffering from some common challenges with most other countries, and these have political, economic, institutional, and social elements and therefore, the researchers proposed to deal with the issue from green criminology perspectives and develop a green policing model.[450] Besides, the penal provisions as included in the relevant laws are lenient and there is a lack of social awareness about the protection

450. Sherajul Mustajib Sharif & Md Kamal Uddin. 'Environmental Crimes and Green Criminology in Bangladesh.' Criminology & Criminal Justice, November (2021): 17488958211057696.

of wildlife.[451] Right now, Bangladesh Customs, Bangladesh Border Guards, Wildlife Crime Control Unit, Bangladesh Forest Department, Bangladesh Police and DoE play crucial roles in this regard.

631. There are some significant legal developments recently. It is reported that in the fiscal year 2014–2015, 834 industries have installed Effluent Treatment Plant (ETP).[452] In the budget for the fiscal year 2014–2015, the government proposed the imposition of 1% Environment Protection Surcharge on an ad valorem basis through the Environment Safety Surcharge Collection Rules, 2014, which came into effect on 1 July 2014. It is provided that the polluting industries have to pay '1% surcharge' or 'green tax' on the prices of their manufactured goods, and the total amount would be considered as non-tax revenue which the government will spend for the protection of the environment.

632. Under this Environment Safety Surcharge Collection Rules, 2014, the 'polluting industries' are very broadly defined to include the industries that pollute the air; heat, taste, odour, density or any other characteristics of the water or soil, including the pollution of air, water and soil or change in their chemical or biological features, or any activities through which any liquid, gaseous, solid, radioactive substances are discharged and dangerous or destructive consequences are caused to the soil, water, air, domestic animals, wild animals, birds, fish, trees or any other living species including trade, industry, agriculture, recreation and other use.

633. So far, a total of 760 industries in Dhaka, Chittagong and Khulna were shortlisted from 2,500 industries selected earlier for imposing with green tax for polluting the environment. The National Board of Revenue has also formulated a policy that specifies that the tax shall be collected using a *chalan*. Though this initiative has been highly applauded by different corners, the actual implementation of the law is yet to take place.

634. In 2002, through the amendment in the BECA, 1995, a new section, i.e., section 6A, was inserted prohibiting, except for export or to be used in exported goods, to produce, import, market, sell, display for sales, stockpiling, distribution, transportation or use for commercial purposes of transportation or commercial purposes, the use of any type of polythene shopping bags, or polyethylene or polypropylene as these are harmful to the environment. This newly inserted section has also included a definition of 'plastic shopping bag' and provides that it means any bag or any other container that is made up of polyethylene, polypropylene, or any of its compound or a mixture which is used for goods sale and purchase or to keep or carry something. Accordingly, the Ministry of Environment issued a notification in 2002 and banned the use of all types of polythene shopping bags. Nevertheless, it has been regularly reported that various forms of polyethylene or polypropylene are

451. Sarker Faroque & Nigel South. 'Law-Enforcement Challenges, Responses and Collaborations Concerning Environmental Crimes and Harms in Bangladesh.' International *Journal of Offender Therapy and Comparative Criminology* (2020): 0306624X20969938.

452. Budget Speech 2014–2015, 5 Jun. 2014, p. 109.

rampantly used as a shopping bags, and therefore, a special law, i.e., the Compulsory Use of Jute based Packet in Products, 2010 (Act No. 53 of 2010) has also been enacted containing detail provision.

635. Hill cutting had been a regular incident especially in the southern hill tract areas in the country, and many people had to sacrifice lives from landslides caused due to rain or other natural calamities. In 2010, a new provision was inserted in the BECA, 1995 prohibiting the cutting and/or razing of any types of hills, be it owned by any government, semi-government or autonomous organization, except with the permission of the Department of Environment for essential and unavoidable national interest.[453] Under the BECA, 1995 'hills and hillocks', in simple terms, means the high places consisting of soils or rocks or rocks and soil, or any other solid material above the naturally formed surrounding flat surface, and referred to those lands as listed as hills or mounds in official records.[454]

453. Section 6B, the Bangladesh Environment Conservation Act, 1995 (Act No. 1 of 1995).
454. Section 2, the Bangladesh Environment Conservation Act, 1995 (Act No. 1 of 1995).

Chapter 2. Judicial Remedies

636. Despite the BECA, 1995 has given the DG and the Magistrates extensive powers to implement the relevant legal provisions administratively on the grounds, *inter alia*, that judicial processes are often time-consuming and the implementation of this sectoral law is financially beneficial from the government point of view; under the domestic legal framework, both general and special, there are options for the judicial forums using which an aggrieved person can ask for remedies if any of his statutory rights are violated.

637. The inspiring and encouraging role of the higher judiciary of the country in the protection and preservation of environmental components, often in the form of PIL, has already been shared in several sections of this monograph. It can be noticed that since the insertion of Article 18A in the Constitution of Bangladesh, 1972, and the country's commitment towards UN SDGs, the judges of the Apex court have also started to include the issue of sustainable development. In *Ms. Syeda Rizwana Hasan v. Bangladesh and others*, 2010, 39 CLC (AD) [8508] = 9 ADC (2012) 816, 18 BLC (AD) (2013) 54, it was held that: '[e]nvironmental protection encompasses not only pollution but also sustainable development and conservation of natural resources and the eco-system'.

638. Even before the insertion of Article 18A in the Constitution, 1971, in *Dr. Mohiuddin Farooque and other v. Bangladesh and others* (Writ Petition No 891 of 1994), citing constitutional provisions, i.e., article 18, which stipulates the improvement of public health as among the primary duties of the state and article 21, which provides for the duties of the citizens and of public servants, Justice A.B.M. Khairul Haque found that in spite of constitutional provisions and the BECA, 1995 and the Rules framed thereunder '. . ., the hiatus remained as before between the letters of law and the implementation thereof in the field of environmental pollution due to unresponsiveness of the apathetic concerned officials . . .,'.

639. Justice Haque further stated that: 'The oath of office of the Judges of the Supreme Court requires that they will preserve, protect and defend the Constitution and the laws of Bangladesh. These are not mere ornamental empty words. These glorifying words of oath eulogizes the supremacy of judiciary. It is by now well settled that if the Government or its functionaries fails to act and perform its duties cast upon them by the laws of this Republic, the High Court Division of the Supreme Court, shall not remain a silent spectator to the inertness on the part of the Government or its officials, rather, in order to vindicate its oath of office can issue, in its discretion, necessary orders and directions, under Article 102 of the Constitution to carry out the intents and purposes of any law to its letter, in the interest of the people of Bangladesh because all powers in the Republic belong to the people, and their exercise on behalf of the people shall be effected only under, and by the authority of the Constitution.'

640. An aggrieved person can move to the HCD and can file a writ petition under article 102 of the Constitution of Bangladesh, 1972 linking the environmental concerns of public importance with the constitutional right to life, and the HCD can give necessary directions. From the Annual Report of the DoE, it is seen that up to 2019, 1,332 writ petitions were filed, 212 were disposed and the highest number of writs, i.e., 198 writs, were disposed of in 2019. Between 2002 and 2011, 385 writ petitions were filed, and not a single petition was disposed of. Between 2012 and 2018, 796 writ petitions were filed and only 14 were disposed of.[455] The following sections highlight some of these writ petitions.

641. In the case of *Dr Mohiuddin Farooque and another v. Government of Bangladesh and others 55 DLR 613,* the HCD gave ad interim directions for taking urgent preventive measures to halt sagging environment pollution and degradation of Dhaka city, one of the worsts in the world, due to audible vehicular sounds and emission of hazardous black smoke from faulty and arrogant motor vehicles. Similarly, in *Bangladesh Legal Aid & Service Trust & Ors. v. Govt. of Bangladesh & Ors.* 10 BLT (HCD) 297, ad interim directions were found necessary as 'the environment and ecology of Bangladesh are being continuously endangered and threatened by various activities originating from private and public sources'.

642. It is prohibited to fill or to change the class of any wetland, notwithstanding anything contained in any law as in force for the time being, though this provision may be relaxed subject to the permission of the DoE for essential and unavoidable national interest.[456] The AD evaluated the issue of environment and human rights, protection and preservation of environment in the case of *Metro Makers and Developers Limited and others v. Bangladesh Environmental Lawyers' Association Limited (BELA) and others*, 2012, 41 CLC (AD) [8366] = 65 DLR (AD) (2013) 181. In this case, the issue of the continuously degrading environment of Dhaka due to various unplanned and illegal activities of the public and private bodies causing irreparable harm to human beings was raised, and the legality of a development project, i.e., Modhumati Model Town (MMT) started without the permission and authorization of RAJUK by MMDL violating the DMDP was challenged. For the MMDL, the argument was that their project is in an area which was not within the operative area of RAJUK and thus, they do not need to follow the original DMDP, though that areas were subsequently included by a separate master plan, i.e., Savar Master Plan which was formulated when their project was already started. Interestingly, it was, however, found that the MMT project was started converting the agricultural land which, without the permission of the government, was prohibited under section 5 of the Conservation of Playground, Open Space, Park and Natural Water Reservoir in the Metropolitan, Division, and District Towns Act, 2000 (Act No. 36 of 2000), which prohibits the change of nature of any land which is earmarked as natural reservoir including flood ones and under section 7 of the BECA, 1995, which imposed restriction of land use in derogation to conservation of environment. The HCD was partly convinced and permitted to continue MMT

455. Department of Environment, Annual Report, 2018–2019, pp. 107, 108.
456. Section 6E, the Bangladesh Environment Conservation Act, 1995 (Act No. 1 of 1995).

procuring necessary approval from RAJUK as the continuation of the project contrary to Master Plan would be illegal under section 75 of the Town Improvements Act, 1953. As the MMT was nearly completed, the HCD also considered the issue of bona fide purchasers and recognized that the management of MMT arranged money from the financial institutions.

643. Being dissatisfied with this decision, BELA moved to the AD where Justice SK Sinha and Justice Syed Mahmud Hossain found the observation of the HCD self-contradictory and also found inconsistency in the submission of the learned counsel of MMDL regarding the collection of permission from RAJUK as it was revealed that MMDL created a forged permission of RAJUK.

644. Justice SK Sinha shared that the 'environmental protection encompasses not only pollution but also sustainable developed and conservation of natural resources and the ecosystem' and 'environmental degradation can be either localized such as the depletion of the nation's wetland, forest resources, open spaces or global, such as destruction of the ozone layer. There are various laws and rules for protection and preservation of environment, but the protection and preservation of the environment is still a passing issue of the day despite such laws. The main cause for environmental degradation is lack of effective enforcement of the various laws'.

645. Justice Sinha, sharing the relationship of environmental rights as human rights and providing the references from the international instruments, e.g., the Additional Protocol to the Inter-American Convention of Human Rights, 1994; the Convention of the Rights of the Child, 1989; the African Charter on Human and People's Rights, 1981; the Stockholm Declaration on the Human Environment, 1972; the United Nations General Assembly, resolution No. 45/94, stated that:

> 55. The environmental problems of the day damage our natural environment and life on earth. Protection and preservation of the environment has been integral to the culture and religious ethos of most human communities. The international community has increased its awareness on the relationship between environmental degradation and human rights abuses. The international community has assumed the commitment to observe the realization of human rights and protection of environment. Thus, there is no gainsaying that the protection of the environment and internationalized-human rights are presented as universal and protection of the environment appears as everyone's responsibility. Human rights and environmental law have traditionally been envisaged as two distinct independent spheres of rights. Now-a-days, the people's perception is aroused to the notion that the cause of protection of the environment can be promoted by setting it in the framework of human rights, which has by now been established as a matter of international law and practice.
> 56. To avail the benefits of environmental law and human rights one must give protection to environmental law that would help ensure the well-being of future generations as well as the survival of those who depend immediately upon natural resources for their livelihood. Secondly, the protection of human

rights is an effective means to achieving the ends of conservation and environmental protection. The focus is on the existing human rights. There exists a raging debate on whether one should recognize an actual and independent right to a satisfactory environment as a legally enforceable right. This would obviously shift the emphasis on to the environment and away from the human rights. Thirdly, in the Stockholm Conference in 1972, it was argued by the delegates that international environmental law has developed to such extents that even the domestic environments of states have been internationalized. Environmental law has in many parts of the world, be it at the international or domestic level, suffered from the problem of standing. Because of this barrier, it is often difficult for individuals or groups to challenge infringements of environmental law, treaties or directives, as the case may be.

646. Justice Sinha further stated that:

67. There is a commonly-recognized link between laws and social values, but to ecologists a balance between laws and values is not alone sufficient to ensure a stable relationship between humans and their environment. Laws and values must also contend with the constraints imposed by the outside environment. Unfortunately, current legal doctrine rarely accounts for such constraints, and thus environmental stability is threatened. Historically, we have changed the environment to fit our conceptions of property. We have fenced, filled and paved. The environment has proven malleable and to a large extent still is. But there is a limit to this malleability, and certain types of ecologically important resources – for example, wet lands and riparian forests – can no longer be destroyed without enormous long-term effects on environmental and, therefore, social stability. To ecologists, the need for preserving sensitive resources does not reflect value choices but rather is the necessary result of objective observations of the laws of nature.
68. Ecologists view the environmental sciences as providing us with certain laws of nature. These laws, just like our own laws, restrict our freedom of conduct and choice. Unlike our laws, the laws of nature cannot be changed by legislative fiat; they are imposed on us by the natural world. An understanding of the laws of nature must therefore inform all of our social institutions. The ancient Roman Empire developed a legal theory known as the 'Doctrine of the Public Trust'. It was founded on the ideas that certain common properties such as rivers, seashore, forests and the air were held by Government in trusteeship for the free and unimpeded use of the general public. Our contemporary concern about 'the environment' bear a very close conceptual relationship to this legal doctrine. Under the Roman law these resources were either owned by no one (res nullious) or by everyone in common (res communious).
69. The Public Trust Doctrine primarily rests on the principle that certain resources like air, sea, waters and the forests have such a great importance to the people as a whole that it would be wholly unjustified to make them a subject of private ownership. The said resources being a gift of nature, they should

be made freely available to everyone irrespective of the status in life. The doctrine enjoins upon the Government to protect the resources for the enjoyment of the general public rather than to permit their use for private ownership or commercial purposes.

647. Finally, Justice Sinha shared at least thirty-six observations and directions. This is a landmark judgment for many reasons. Justice Syed Mahmud Hossain, while writing the operative part of the judgment, declared the MMT unlawful and MMDL was directed to restore the wetlands of project area to their original state within six months from the date of availability of the certified copy of the judgment, and directed RAJUK to undertake the work of restoration of the wetlands and recover the cost of restoration from MMDL and their directors treating the cost as a public demand. He further held that 'though the third party purchasers may not be treated as *bonafide*, yet it is a fact that they have been roped in by Metro Makers by misrepresentation that permission for the development work had been obtained from *RAJUK* and justice demands that they should be compensated. Accordingly, Metro Makers are further directed to refund the purchasers double the amount of the money including the cost of registration of the deeds of sale received by them from the purchasers within six months from the date of availability of the certified copy of the judgment'.

648. The AD in the case of *President, Bangladesh Garments Manufacturers and Exporters Association (BGMEA) v. Bangladesh* (Civil Petition 1162/2013) has ordered to demolish the Bangladesh Garments Manufacturers and Exporters Association (BGMEA) Building. BGMEA has constructed a fifteen-storied commercial complex on the 'BegunBari Khal' and 'Hatir jheel lake' which are natural water-bodies. These water bodies are connected with the River Buriganga, through canals, which play a pivotal role, like many other water bodies in and around the historic Dhaka city, in keeping the capital safe from waterlogging and flood during heavy monsoon. According to section 8 (2) of the Waterbodies Act 2000, class or the nature and character of water bodies cannot be changed, and therefore, the court ordered BGMEA to demolish the building at once at its own cost. It will be pertinent to mention here that a Division Bench of the HCD issued a *Suo Moto* Rule on 03.10.2010 based on a news report published in an English Daily *the Daily New Age* on 02.10.2010. Even though the illegal and improper allocation of transfer and possession of the said land was the main issue in the case, the Apex court of the country has really considered once again the importance of preserving water bodies to keep the city safe from waterlogging and thus to protect the ecosystem and biodiversity.

649. The HCD ordered to protect the river Jadukanta (in the *mouza*s of Puranlaur, Chaliarghat, Lamashram, Purbodoil, and Ghagra under police station – Tahirpur, district – Sunamganj) from illegal extraction of sand from its bed and banks. The HCD did not order to stop the sand extraction, rather ordered to extract sand only from the Sand Quarry as per lease granted by the concerned authority and illegal extraction of sands from outside the designated area of the said quarry and from the bed and banks of the River should be stopped.[457]

650. In the case of *Dr. Mohiuddin Farooque v. Bangladesh, represented by the Secretary, Ministry of Commerce, Government of the People's Republic of Bangladesh, Bangladesh Secretariat and others,* 48 DLR 438, respondent No. 6 Danish Condensed Milk Bangladesh Limited imported 500 metric tons of skimmed milk powder from Holland. Upon clearance of the consignment, radiation test was made and found 133 Bq radiation per kilogram which was above the minimum approved radiation level of 95 Bq and was opined that the consignment in question should not be marketed. The Secretary General of BELA filed a writ petition in the public interest as consumption of imported food items containing radiation levels above the acceptable limit is injurious to public health. Moreover, it was prayed that the respondents be directed to take measures for sending back the said milk powder to the exporter. The High Court Division on the fact of the said case held as under:

> It is the primary obligation of the State to raise the level of nutrition and the improvement of public health by preventing use of contaminated food, drink, etc. Though that obligation under Article 18(1) of the Constitution cannot be enforced state is bound to protect the health and longevity of the people living in the country as right to life guaranteed under Articles 31 and 32 of the Constitution includes protection of health and normal longevity of a man free from threats of man-made hazards unless that threat is justified by law. Right to life under the aforesaid Articles of the Constitution being a fundamental right it can be enforced by this Court to remove any unjustified threat to the health and longevity of the people as the same are included in the right to life.

651. While PILs can only be filed in the HCD in some exceptional instances, section 4 of the Environment Court Act, 2010, provides for the establishment of one or more environment courts in every administrative district of the country, though special magistrates can also try some offences relating to the protection of environmental components. Out of a total of sixty-four administrative districts in the country, only three environment courts (in Dhaka, Chittagong, and Sylhet) and only one Environment Appellate Court (in Dhaka) have so far been established. One joint district judge, who is appointed by the government in consultation with the Supreme Court, has the jurisdiction to decide cases in these courts. However, because of the mandatory statutory prerequisite of submission of a statement from the DoE, both the courts remain almost inactive. In addition, there is another important concern – that is, the DoE has limited-scale adjudicatory power using which the DoE can adjudicate cases administratively, which is also responsible for such a situation. Section 18 of the Environment Court Act, 2010 also provides that notwithstanding anything contained in the Cr.P.C., certain offences under the BECA, 1995 (Act No. 1 of 1995), i.e., the offences relating to the powers of the DG under section 4 of the

457. *Bangladesh Environment Lawyers Association (BELA) v. Bangladesh*, 2010, 39 CLC (HCD) [7276] = 62 DLR (HCD) (2010) 463.

BECA, 1995 and powers relating to the declaration of ECA, subject to the satisfaction of the DG may be settled amicably, at any stage of the suit, following some conditions, e.g., giving an undertaking and payment of a minimum fine of BDT 50,000, etc.

652. A few environment courts in Dhaka, Chittagong and Sylhet, and an environmental appellate court have been established in Dhaka. However, there are some serious concerns about the effectiveness and performance of these courts. Recently, it was reported by the leading Bangla Newspaper *Prothom Alo* (13 March 2021) that even though there are numerous instances of violations of provisions on environment-related laws, the environment courts do not get sufficient cases to decide and as a result, due to the small number of cases, these courts have been dealing with other matters to reduce the pending cases. It is reported that a total of 7,002 cases are pending in these three environment courts of which 388 cases are under the provisions of the BECA, 1995, which is only 5% of the total pending cases. The Environment Court was established in Dhaka in 2003, and since then, only 117 cases were filed under the BECA, 1995, and 11 cases are now pending for trial. Only a small number of cases were sent to the environment court in Dhaka in 2016(4), 2017 (6), 2018 (19) and 2019 (3), respectively. Between July 2015 and August 2020, 8,756 cases were filed in the mobile court run by the DoE. During this time, BDT 530 million were fined, and BDT 460 million were recovered. It has been reported that the DoE is not interested to ensure strict penalties and punishment for the polluters. Moreover, the fine imposed by them is also waived after appeal. As a result, the situation has not been improving.

653. One of the main challenges in the implementation of the provisions of the environment-related matters, as shared above, is that the proceedings can only be brought if a report is submitted by an executive magistrate.[458] An individual cannot go to the court directly; rather, he/she needs to inform the DoE first and if the DoE fails to settle the issue only then someone can go to the court. Some factors such as procedural complexities, absence of accountability in the functioning of power of the executives, and awareness of the general people are responsible for the improper or inadequate implementation of the environment-related legal provisions. Moreover, since the three environment courts are situated only in three districts, people from other districts, considering the issue of management of evidence and witnesses, do not find sufficient interest to go there and this hinders the success of such initiative. Thus, apparently, the environment legal regime of Bangladesh provides for only 'controlled rights' or selected rights for the persons affected and a 'controlled jurisdictions' for the environmental courts.[459] Realizing some of these limitations and understanding that the economy of the country has been taking a shift,

458. Section 7(1), the Environment Court Act, 2010 (Act No. 56 of 2000).

459. Abul Hasanat, 'Environmental Courts in Enforcement: The Role of Law in Environmental Justice in Bangladesh', *Australian Journal of Asian Law*, 21, no. 2 (2021): Article 6: 85–98.

i.e., from agro-based to industries-based one which demands sustainable and inclusive development, it has been also reported that the government has taken the initiative to establish environmental courts in all districts and appellate courts in all divisions.

654. The environmental courts and the appellate court have been facing various challenges including a shortage of officials. The Joint District Judge is designated to look after environment-related cases in addition to his/her normal duties as a Civil Court Judge. Moreover, a court cannot take cognizance of any case without the sanctions of the inspector of the DoE. These reasons prevent the aggrieved persons from moving to the courts. As a result, one may find very few reported cases relating to environmental issues.

Selected Bibliography

Al Faruque, A. *Environmental Law*: Global and *Bangladesh* Context. Dhaka: New Warsi Book Corporation, 2017.

Islam, Md Tasbirul, et al. 'A Public Survey on Knowledge, Awareness, Attitude and Willingness to Pay for WEEE Management: Case Study in Bangladesh'. *Journal of Cleaner Production* 137 (2016): 728–740.

Karim, Md. Ershadul, et al. 'Noise Pollution in Dhaka and the Constitutional Right to Life'. *Australian Journal of Asian Law* 21(2) (2021): Article 5: 67–84.

Karim, Saiful Okechukwu Benjamin Vincents & Mia Mahmudur Rahim. 'Legal Activism for Ensuring Environmental Justice'. *Asian Journal of Comparative Law* 7 (2012): 1–44.

M.H. Masud, Akram, W., Ahmed, A. *et al.* Towards the effective E-waste management in Bangladesh: a review. *Environmental Science Pollution Research* 26 (2019): 1250–1276. https://doi.org/10.1007/s11356-018-3626-2.

Md Khalid Hasan, Abrar Shahriar, and Kudrat Ullah Jim. 'Water Pollution in Bangladesh and Its Impact on Public Health'. *Heliyon* 5, no. 8 (2019): e02145.

Rahman, S.M Mizanur, and Audrey L. Mayer. 'Policy Compliance Recommendations for International Shipbreaking Treaties for Bangladesh.' *Marine Policy* 73 (2016): 122–129.

Sarker, Subrata et al. 'From Science to Action: Exploring the Potentials of Blue Economy for enhancing Economic Sustainability in Bangladesh'. *Ocean & Coastal Management* 157 (2018): 180–192.

Shammi, M., Hasan, N., Rahman, M.M., Begum, K., Sikder, M.T., Bhuiyan, M.H. and Uddin, M.K. Sustainable pesticide governance in Bangladesh: socio-economic and legal status interlinking environment, occupational health and food safety. *Environment Systems and Decisions* 37, no. 3 (2017): 243–260.

Syeda, Sultana Razia. 'Framework for Sound Management of Chemicals: Toward a Sustainable Chemicals Industry in Bangladesh'. *ACS Chemical Health & Safety* 27, no. 5 (2020): 288–298.

Zaman, Rafia, and Thomas Brudermann. 'Energy Governance in the Context of Energy Service Security: A Qualitative Assessment of the Electricity System in Bangladesh.' *Applied Energy* 223 (2018): 443–456.

Birnie, Patricia, Alan E. Boyle & Catherine Redgwell. *International Law & the Environment.* 3rd edn. Oxford: Oxford University Press, 2009.

Md. Mokarrom Hossan. 'Evolution of Environmental Policies in Bangladesh (1972–2010)'. *Journal of the Asiatic Society of Bangladesh (Hum.)* 59(1) (2014): 39–63.

Selected Bibliography

Dey, Tapan Kumar &a Md. Golam Rabbi, *Guideline Book on Wildlife Law Enforcement in Bangladesh*. Dhaka: Bangladesh Forest Department, Ministry of Environment and Forests, 2015, Preface.

Index

The numbers here refer to page numbers

Index

Index

Index

www.ingramcontent.com/pod-product-compliance
Lightning Source LLC
Chambersburg PA
CBHW071434230926
51846CB00001B/222
* 9 7 8 9 4 0 3 5 1 5 4 6 5 *